Praise for *Snowflake: The Definitive Guide*

Joyce's book adds insights and hands-on knowledge that go beyond
other Snowflake books or public resources, unveiling new venues to understand
and explore the art of possibilities with Snowflake.

—*Constantin Stanca, Principal Solutions Engineer, Snowflake*

This truly is a definitive guide, I love every bit of it and learned something new on
almost every page. It truly is a SELECT * on Snowflake, and a must read for everyone.

—*Jeno Yamma, Analytics Engineer*
and Snowflake Data Superhero, Canva

The best way to learn and get better at something is by doing. This book
is a well-written and easy-to-follow guide to everything Snowflake. But what really
sets it apart are all of the practical code examples and knowledge checks. Joyce teaches
us theory, encourages us to practice, and then tests our knowledge. Whether you are just
starting to explore Snowflake or someone who has experience I guarantee that you will
learn something from this book.

—*Veronika Durgin, Data and Analytics Leader*

Your first stop into the Snowflake Data Cloud. Getting started with Snowflake? Let
Snowflake Data Superhero Joyce Kay Avila guide you into the Data Cloud.

—*Daan Bakboord, Data and Analytics Consultant*

Snowflake: The Definitive Guide

Architecting, Designing, and Deploying
on the Snowflake Data Cloud

Joyce Kay Avila

Beijing · Boston · Farnham · Sebastopol · Tokyo

Snowflake: The Definitive Guide

by Joyce Kay Avila

Published by O'Reilly Media, Inc., 1005 Gravenstein Highway North, Sebastopol, CA 95472.

O'Reilly books may be purchased for educational, business, or sales promotional use. Online editions are also available for most titles (*http://oreilly.com*). For more information, contact our corporate/institutional sales department: 800-998-9938 or *corporate@oreilly.com*.

Acquisitions Editor: Jessica Haberman	**Indexer:** Potomac Indexing, LLC
Development Editor: Michele Cronin	**Interior Designer:** David Futato
Production Editor: Clare Laylock	**Cover Designer:** Karen Montgomery
Copyeditor: Audrey Doyle	**Illustrator:** Kate Dullea
Proofreader: Justin Billing	

August 2022:   First Edition

Revision History for the First Edition

2022-08-10: First Release
2022-12-16: Second Release

See *http://oreilly.com/catalog/errata.csp?isbn=9781098103828* for release details.

978-1-098-10382-8

[LSI]

Table of Contents

Preface

Origin of the Book

Back in April 2020, I published a video series about Snowflake on YouTube to help people become Snowflake-certified. The response I received from the series confirmed that the need for such knowledge was much greater than a video series could meet. However, the Snowflake journey began well before this video series.

Snowflake burst onto the public scene in 2015 after three years of operating in stealth mode. Snowflake's customers span several different industries including the public sector, healthcare, retail, financial services, and more. In 2017, Capital One became Snowflake's first Virtual Private Snowflake (VPS) customer and also invested $5 million in Snowflake to help further Snowflake's ability to deliver innovative technology to the financial services industry. In 2018, Snowflake grew its customer base by 300%, with additions including several more financial services companies.

Around this time, in 2018, I was first introduced to Snowflake when employed by a financial services company. In my role as a Salesforce developer, I designed and implemented data models in Salesforce that were then built in Snowflake by other members of the team.

I've always had a passion for data, a knack for data modeling, and a love of learning—especially learning about exciting new technologies. So naturally, the more I learned about Snowflake, the more I wanted to know. Throughout 2018 and 2019, I expanded my knowledge of Snowflake while continuing to gain more Salesforce experience. In late 2019, my passion for Snowflake was in full swing, and I became determined to become certified in Snowflake.

At that time, there was no Snowflake study guide per se, and not enough resources existed to prepare for the certification exam. So I went through every training module in Snowflake University and read page after page of Snowflake documentation. To help me better prepare, I made a set of study notes that grouped the content into specific topics. These notes ultimately helped me become Snowflake certified in April

2020. It just made sense to create a series of videos using those notes so that others could benefit from them as well. I never dreamed that would be the start of an amazing Snowflake journey.

Creating the Snowflake YouTube video series in 2020 led to me becoming a Snowflake Data Superhero. From there, I was invited to speak at Snowflake events and became more involved in the Snowflake community. My knowledge of the platform continued to grow. At the same time, many people watching my YouTube videos reached out to let me know how much they appreciated the content.

When the opportunity presented itself in early 2021 to author *Snowflake: The Definitive Guide* for O'Reilly, I committed fully to the long journey of writing the book. I've been amazed at how much freedom O'Reilly gives its authors to shape the contents of the book. With that incredible privilege comes a lot of responsibility to choose the right topics and decide how deep to dive into any one particular area.

This book is intended to be a definitive guide, which means I needed to cover a lot of information when writing it. Throughout the time I spent writing and rewriting, I had to lean on others to fill in my knowledge gaps so that I could provide the best content possible. Those folks, along with many others, were an integral part of making this book a reality. My acknowledgments below speak for themselves; I would be remiss if I didn't use the opportunity to individually thank those who have really made a difference in how this book turned out.

Who Is This Book For?

This book is essential reading for technical practitioners working in the areas of data warehousing, data science, and data analysis, as well as for anyone who wants to set themselves apart as a Snowflake certified professional. There is also a lot of value in this book for data stakeholders such as IT team leads, technical managers, and directors of technical teams or those who want to keep current with modern data technologies and trends.

While it is not necessary to have knowledge about nonrelational databases and other data-related tools, you should at least be familiar with relational databases and SQL. You'll get the most out of this book if you have at least one-to-two years of experience in any of the following data-related roles:

- Data architect
- Data engineer
- Data analyst

- Data scientist
- Database administrator
- Technical manager

Goals of the Book

This book was written with plenty of hands-on examples to help you build a solid foundational knowledge of Snowflake.

By the end of this book, you will understand:

- How the unique Snowflake architecture efficiently captures, stores, and processes large amounts of data at an amazing speed
- How to rapidly ingest and transform real-time data feeds in both structured and semi-structured formats and deliver meaningful data insights within minutes
- How to use Time Travel and zero-copy cloning to produce a sensible data recovery strategy that balances the need for system resilience with ongoing storage costs
- How to securely share data and how to reduce or eliminate data integration costs by accessing fresh, ready-to-query data sets available within the Snowflake Data Marketplace

And you'll be able to:

- Deploy, size, and monitor virtual warehouses to maximize query performance and throughput while also controlling cost
- Implement a role-based access control system, use dynamic data masking, and take advantage of discretionary access control and secure views to protect and limit data access
- Enable Snowsight to support data analysts' ability to work even more efficiently in the new Snowflake web interface
- Follow Snowflake best practices and avoid common pitfalls to achieve world-class results

Navigating this Book

The order of the chapters intends to ensure that the earlier chapters provide the necessary foundational knowledge so that you can get the most value out of later chapters. That said, each chapter's examples stand alone. The chapters begin with any prep work needed for that chapter, then take you step-by-step through the hands-on examples. At the end of every chapter, there are clean-up instructions. You won't need to complete any examples from previous chapters before starting a new chapter.

The first seven chapters are the foundational chapters. The next two chapters take you through the details of managing Snowflake costs and improving performance. Chapter 10 is a deep dive into secure data sharing, one of Snowflake's key differentiators. Chapter 11 focuses on visualizing data in Snowsight. You'll notice that, with few exceptions, the examples in the book are completed in the new Snowsight web user interface, although all code can be run successfully in the classic console. Chapter 12 explains all the various Snowflake workloads, including the new Unistore workload.

At the end of every chapter is a knowledge check section. The answers to those questions can be found in Appendix A. Snowflake object naming best practices are included in Appendix B. Finally, you can locate instructions for setting up a Snowflake trial account in Appendix C.

Using Code Examples

Supplemental material (code examples, exercises, etc.) is available for download at *https://github.com/SnowflakeDefinitiveGuide*.

If you have a technical question or a problem using the code examples, please send an email to *bookquestions@oreilly.com*.

This book is here to help you get your job done. In general, if example code is offered with this book, you may use it in your programs and documentation. You do not need to contact us for permission unless you're reproducing a significant portion of the code. For example, writing a program that uses several chunks of code from this book does not require permission. Selling or distributing examples from O'Reilly books does require permission. Answering a question by citing this book and quoting example code does not require permission. Incorporating a significant amount of example code from this book into your product's documentation does require permission.

We appreciate, but generally do not require, attribution. An attribution usually includes the title, author, publisher, and ISBN. For example: "*Snowflake: The Definitive Guide* by Joyce Kay Avila (O'Reilly). Copyright 2022 Joyce Kay Avila, 978-1-098-10382-8."

If you feel your use of code examples falls outside fair use or the permission given above, feel free to contact us at *permissions@oreilly.com*.

Conventions Used in This Book

The following typographical conventions are used in this book:

Italic
>   Indicates new terms, URLs, email addresses, filenames, and file extensions.

`Constant width`
>   Used for program listings, as well as within paragraphs to refer to program elements such as variable or function names, databases, data types, environment variables, statements, and keywords.

`Constant width bold`
>   Shows commands or other text that should be typed literally by the user.

`Constant width italic`
>   Shows text that should be replaced with user-supplied values or by values determined by context.

 This element signifies a tip or suggestion.

 This element signifies a general note.

 This element indicates a warning or caution.

O'Reilly Online Learning

 For more than 40 years, *O'Reilly Media* has provided technology and business training, knowledge, and insight to help companies succeed.

Our unique network of experts and innovators share their knowledge and expertise through books, articles, and our online learning platform. O'Reilly's online learning platform gives you on-demand access to live training courses, in-depth learning paths, interactive coding environments, and a vast collection of text and video from O'Reilly and 200+ other publishers. For more information, visit *https://oreilly.com*.

How to Contact Us

Please address comments and questions concerning this book to the publisher:

O'Reilly Media, Inc.
1005 Gravenstein Highway North
Sebastopol, CA 95472
800-998-9938 (in the United States or Canada)
707-829-0515 (international or local)
707-829-0104 (fax)

We have a web page for this book, where we list errata, examples, and any additional information. You can access this page at *https://oreil.ly/snowflake-the-definitive-guide*.

Email *bookquestions@oreilly.com* to comment or ask technical questions about this book.

For news and information about our books and courses, visit *https://oreilly.com*.

Find us on LinkedIn: *https://linkedin.com/company/oreilly-media*

Follow us on Twitter: *https://twitter.com/oreillymedia*

Watch us on YouTube: *https://www.youtube.com/oreillymedia*

Acknowledgments

The journey of writing an O'Reilly book has been a most challenging yet rewarding experience in my life. Throughout this incredible journey, I've never been alone. I've been fortunate to have had a village of people who have each played an important role in delivering this book to the world.

I'll admit that in the beginning, I didn't have a lot of faith in how the ebb and flow of the process would work. It was uncomfortable to share those early versions of the manuscript, and I really didn't want to do it. My development editor, Michele Cronin, convinced me to trust the process. My most sincere gratitude and appreciation go to Michele for being so supportive and patient while gently pushing me forward at times, when needed. Michele was but one of an amazing group of folks associated with O'Reilly Media who helped make this book a reality.

I am grateful to Audrey Doyle, the copyeditor, and Justin Billing, the proofreader, for the countless hours spent reading through the many pages of the book more than once. I appreciate Kristen Brown for managing the early release process on the O'Reilly platform to make the content available to users as quickly as possible. I'm also thankful for the amazing cover design by Karen Montgomery, the interior design by David Futato, and the illustrations by Kate Dullea that really bring beauty and professionalism to the book.

The level of quality control that an O'Reilly book undergoes is second to none. The O'Reilly team spent countless hours combing through everything, even the smallest of details, to make the book perfect. As such, a special thank you to Clare Jensen for a level of effort that was nothing less than extraordinary.

Of course, my journey as an author would never have begun had it not been for Jess Haberman, who had faith that I could use my passion for Snowflake to stay motivated through the long days, nights, and weekends it has taken to bring this book to life. I'd also like to thank Andy Kwan for his support of O'Reilly opportunities that coincide with writing the book and Suzanne Huston for her efforts to help market and promote the book. Other folks from O'Reilly who have been a part of my journey include Cassandra Furtado, Charlotte Ames, Elizabeth Kelly, Joan Baker, and Shannon Cutt.

I've also had an amazing group of reviewers who went through those very early rough drafts. Their feedback at the early stages helped shape the content of the book. Early reviewers include Jacob Thomas and Randy Pitcher II. Special shoutout to reviewers Veronika Durgin and Daan Bakboord for providing detailed feedback and for taking time to actually run all the code and prevent some errors from making their way into the final version of the book. And in two separate rounds of reviews, I received invaluable feedback from Michael Rainey, a Snowflake Principal Solutions Architect.

I'm thankful to a number of Snowflake data superheroes, including Slim Baltagi, Maja Ferle, and Jeno Yamma; with only a short window of time, they looked through the full preview edition of the book and provided feedback. I'm honored to be a part of such an amazing Snowflake data superhero group and am incredibly thankful to every Snowflake data superhero who has lent their support. There is something truly magical about the Snowflake data hero community led by Elsa Mayer and Howard Lio. And it was amazing to finally meet so many people in person for the first time at the 2022 Snowflake Summit. Thank you, Jena Donlin, for your genuine heartfelt support. And Dash Desai, you know that I loved seeing you wear those shoes!

Anyone can see that the values of the Snowflake data hero community directly reflect the company's core values. "Be inclusive and collaborative, bringing people and ideas together" is an example of one of Snowflake's core values that has been demonstrated to me firsthand in all my interactions with Snowflake employees, not just from the perspective of a data superhero who is championing for Snowflake. As an author working with the Snowflake product teams to help fill in my knowledge, I've been introduced to a number of incredibly smart and talented people. For almost a year, Aleks Todorova worked tirelessly to connect me with many different people within the company who could help me expand my Snowflake knowledge so I could provide better content for the book. And as a Snowflake consulting partner working with Snowflake account executives to serve customers, I've also had the pleasure of getting to know many more Snowflake employees.

For their continued support, I'd like to thank several current Snowflake employees, in addition to Michael, Elsa, Howard, Jena, and Dash who I've already mentioned. The list is long! Included here, in alphabetical order by first name, are just some of the Snowflake employees I'd like to call out: Alex Gutow, Carl Perry, Cassie Ageno-Wallgren, Chris Keithley, Constantin "Cristi" Stanca, Daniel Myers, Danny Shea, Diane Elinski, Emily Dillon, Emily Lin, Eric Feng, Felicia Dorng, Felipe Hoffa, Francis Mao, Ganesh Subramanian, Ines Marjanovic, Julian Forero, Justin Langseth, Kate Beispel, Katie Ecklund, Kelly Huang, Leith Darawsheh, Lisa Luscap, Marilyn Tan, Mike Miller, Nick Akincilar, Omer Singer, Patrick Cuba, Phillip Coletti, Phillip Owen, Raanan Sayag, Ryan Aldridge, Sanjay Kattimani, Saurin Shah, Scott Teal, Seeling Cheung, Shiyi Gu, Shravan Narayen, Tom Meacham, Travis Kaufman, William Fuentes, and Xer Cha.

I'd also like to thank my employer, SpringML. With their support, I've been able to effectively balance working a demanding full-time job with my desire to write for the best publisher of technical books in the world. I'm very grateful for Robert Anderson, who recruited me to SpringML and is my biggest supporter. Helping to grow the Snowflake practice at SpringML has also afforded me the opportunity to spend time getting to know our CTO, Girish Reddy, who never seems to tire of expanding his knowledge of innovative technologies like Snowflake. Janeesh Jayaraj, Sriram Mandadapu, Tamera Fall, Vineesh Sriramoju, and Vishal Deo are just a few more of the amazing team members I have had the pleasure of collaborating with on Snowflake projects. There are so many members of the SpringML team who are both excited about Snowflake and incredibly supportive of my personal journey to become a published O'Reilly author. Thank you, SpringML team, for letting me share that journey with you. I appreciate you all.

As you can imagine, completing this book would have been impossible without the support of my family. For over fifteen months, they have picked up the slack by taking on more household tasks every day, and they have encouraged me to keep going when I didn't think I could. For more than a year, my journey was their journey.

To my incredible child Alanna, you are an angel. There would be no sunshine in my life without you. My heart is filled with hope and optimism because of your unwavering faith in me. You continually see the best in me and that makes me want to be a better person and a better mother. I hope you always think I'm the coolest Mom ever. I love you, Alanna Kay Avila.

To my husband Robert, our house is a home because of you. Thank you for reading every word of the book, often many times, and for taking on the lion's share of responsibilities at home so I could focus on writing. From the first draft to the first print of the book, you were always the first person to read each chapter. With every chapter, I trusted you to give me honest feedback and help me make it better before I shared it with others. We continue to make a great team in everything we do. You are my best friend, Robert, and I love you.

To our amazing dog Zelda, thank you for reminding me to take a pause. There were lots of times this past year when you wanted me to stop and play but I couldn't. I'm committed to making it up to you in the coming year.

To my beautiful mother, Carolyn Kay Hare, thank you for planting the seeds long ago to make me strong and fearless even when I'm sometimes afraid I'll fall short. You removed the word "can't" from the dictionary for me, and that made all the difference.

To the readers, thank you for choosing this book. Together, let's #MakeItSnow definitively!

CHAPTER 1

Getting Started

Cloud computing is characterized by on-demand availability of data storage and computing power. A primary benefit of cloud computing is that it doesn't require users to be directly or actively involved in the management of those computer system resources. Other benefits include access to unlimited storage capacity, automatic software updates, instant scalability, high speed, and cost reductions. As expected, the recent explosion of cloud computing led by AWS Redshift, Google BigQuery, and Microsoft Azure Data Warehouse resulted in the decline of on-premises data centers.

Many of the major data warehouse providers, such as Oracle and IBM, that were created as a traditionally hosted solution later adapted to the cloud environment. Unlike those traditional solutions, Snowflake was built natively for the cloud from the ground up. While Snowflake originated as a disruptive cloud data warehouse, it has evolved over time, and today it is far more than an innovative modern data warehouse.

Along the way, Snowflake earned some impressive recognition. Snowflake won first place at the 2015 Strata + Hadoop World startup competition and was named a "Cool Vendor" in Gartner's Magic Quadrant 2015 DBMS report. In 2019, Snowflake was listed as number 2 on *Forbes* magazine's Cloud 100 list and was ranked number 1 on LinkedIn's U.S. list of Top Startups. On September 16, 2020, Snowflake became the largest software initial public offering (IPO) in history.

Today the Snowflake Data Cloud Platform breaks down silos and enables many different workloads. In addition to the traditional data engineering and data warehouse workloads, Snowflake supports data lake, data collaboration, data analytics, data applications, data science, cybersecurity, and Unistore workloads. Snowflake's "Many Data Workloads, One Platform" approach gives organizations a way to quickly derive value from rapidly growing data sets in secure and governed ways that enable companies to meet compliance requirements. Since its inception 10 years ago, Snowflake has continued its rapid pace of innovation across the Data Cloud.

Snowflake's founders first gathered in 2012 with a vision of building a data warehouse for the cloud from the ground up that would unlock the true potential of limitless insights from enormous amounts of varying types of data. Their goal was to build this solution to be secure and powerful but cost-effective and simple to maintain. Just three years later, in 2015, Snowflake's cloud-built data warehouse became commercially available. Immediately, Snowflake disrupted the data warehousing market with its unique architecture and cloud-agnostic approach. The disruptive Snowflake platform also made data engineering more business oriented, less technical, and less time-consuming, which created more opportunities to democratize data analytics by allowing users at all levels within an organization to make data-driven decisions.

To gain an appreciation for Snowflake's unique qualities and approach, it's important to understand the underlying Snowflake architecture. Beginning in Chapter 2 and carrying on throughout the book, you'll discover the many ways that Snowflake offers near-zero management capability to eliminate much of the administrative and management overhead associated with traditional data warehouses. You'll get a firsthand look at how Snowflake works, because each chapter includes SQL examples you can try out yourself. There are also knowledge checks at the end of each chapter.

Some of the most innovative Snowflake workloads rely on Snowflake's Secure Data Sharing capabilities, which were introduced in 2018. Snowflake Secure Data Sharing enables virtually instantly secure governed data to be shared across your business ecosystem. It also opens up many possibilities for monetizing data assets. Chapter 10 is devoted entirely to this innovative Snowflake workload.

In 2021, Snowflake introduced the ability to manage multiple accounts with ease using Snowflake Organizations. Managing multiple accounts makes it possible to separately maintain different environments, such as development and production environments, and to adopt a multicloud strategy. It also means you can better manage costs since you can select which features you need for each separate account. We'll explore Snowflake Organization management in Chapter 5.

Snowflake also expanded the scope of what's possible in the Data Cloud with the introduction of Snowpark in June 2021. Across the industry, Snowpark is recognized as a game changer in the data engineering and machine learning spaces. Snowpark is a developer framework that brings new data programmability to the cloud and makes it possible for developers, data scientists, and data engineers to use Java, Scala, or Python to deploy code in a serverless manner.

The Security Data Lake, introduced by Snowflake in 2022, is an innovative workload that empowers cybersecurity and compliance teams to gain full visibility into security logs, at a massive scale, while reducing the costs of security information and event management (SIEM) systems. Interestingly, this cybersecurity workload can be enhanced with cybersecurity partners on the Snowflake Data Exchange who can deliver threat detection, threat hunting, anomaly detection, and more. We'll take a deep dive into Snowpark and the Security Data Lake workloads in Chapter 12. We'll also discuss the newest Snowflake workload, Unistore (a workload for transactional and analytical data), in Chapter 12.

This first chapter will introduce you to Snowflake and get you comfortable navigating in Snowsight, the new Snowflake web UI. In addition, the chapter includes information about the Snowflake community, certifications, and Snowflake events. There is also a section which describes caveats about code examples in the book. Taking time to get oriented in this chapter will set you up for success as you navigate the successive chapters.

Snowflake Web User Interfaces

Two different Snowflake web user interfaces are available: the Classic Console and *Snowsight*, the new Snowflake web UI. Snowsight was first introduced in 2021 and is now the default user interface in newly created Snowflake accounts. Snowsight is expected to become the default user interface for all accounts in early 2023, with the Classic Console being deprecated shortly thereafter. Unless otherwise stated, all our hands-on examples will be completed in Snowsight.

As with all other Snowflake features and functionality, Snowsight is continually being improved. As such, there may be times when the screenshots in the chapters deviate slightly from what is shown in the Snowsight web UI in which you are working.

To support rapid innovation, Snowflake deploys two scheduled releases each week and one behavior change release each month. You can find more information about Snowflake releases in the Snowflake documentation (*https://oreil.ly/wfPch*).

Prep Work

In the prep section of each chapter in the book, we'll create any folders, worksheets, and Snowflake objects that will be needed for that chapter's hands-on examples.

You'll need access to a Snowflake instance in order to follow along and complete the hands-on examples while going through the chapters. You can set up a free trial Snowflake account if you do not already have access to a Snowflake instance. If you need information on how to create a free trial Snowflake account, refer to Appendix C.

If you have access to a Snowflake org that defaults to the Classic Console, you can access Snowsight in one of two ways. In the Classic Console web interface, you can click the Snowsight button in the upper-right corner of the screen (as shown in Figure 1-1). Alternatively, you can log in to Snowsight directly (*https://oreil.ly/ 55CLH*).

| Partner Connect | Help | Notifications | Snowsight |

Figure 1-1. Classic Console web interface showing the Snowsight button

Once you are inside Snowsight, Worksheets is the default tab (as shown in Figure 1-2). You can also click some of the different tabs, including the Data tab and the Compute tab, to see some of the available menu options. As we will see later, the Databases subtab will display the databases available to you within your access rights.

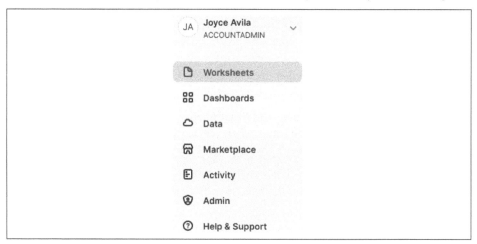

Figure 1-2. Snowsight UI tabs with the Worksheets tab as the default

If you have been working in the Classic Console web interface before now or if this is the first time you're logging in, you'll be presented the option to import your worksheets when you first enter Snowsight (as shown in Figure 1-3).

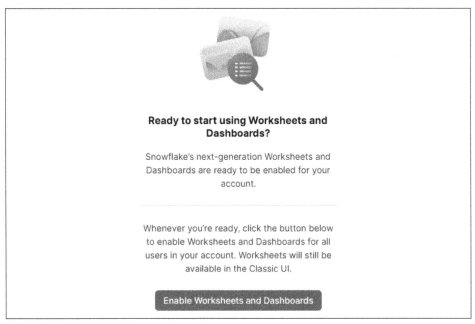

Figure 1-3. An option to import worksheets is presented to you the first time you use Snowsight

If you import a worksheet from the Classic Console UI, a new timestamped folder will be created (as shown in Figure 1-4).

Figure 1-4. The folder name defaults to the day and time when you import your worksheets

You can access Snowsight using one of the latest versions of Google Chrome, Mozilla Firefox, or Apple Safari for macOS. After you log in, a client session is maintained indefinitely with continued user activity. After four hours of inactivity, the current session is terminated and you must log in again. The default session timeout policy of four hours can be changed; the minimum configurable idle timeout value for a session policy is five minutes.

Snowsight Orientation

When logging in to Snowsight, you'll have access to your *User menu* and your *Main menu*. The User menu is where you can see your username and your current role. By default, you'll be assigned the SYSADMIN role when you first sign up for a trial account.

You'll also notice that the Main menu defaults to the Worksheets selection. The area to the right of the Main menu is where you have more options for your Main menu selection. In Figure 1-5, you can see the Worksheets menu to the right of the Main menu. Underneath the Worksheets menu are submenus specific to the Main menu selection.

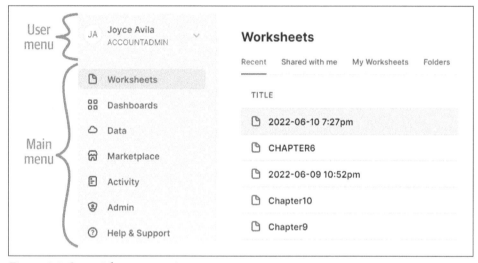

Figure 1-5. Snowsight menu options

Next, we will set our Snowsight preferences and spend a few minutes navigating the Snowsight Worksheets area.

Snowsight Preferences

To get your preferences set up, click directly on your name, or use the drop-down arrow beside your name to access the submenus (as shown in Figure 1-6). You'll notice that it is possible to switch roles here. Try switching your role to a different role and then switch it back to SYSADMIN. This will be important throughout the chapter exercises as we'll periodically need to switch between roles.

You'll also notice that Snowflake *Support* is available from within the User menu. Whenever you need to submit a case, just click Support. It's important to note that you won't be able to create a support case when using a free trial account.

Figure 1-6. User menu selections

Click the Profile option and the Profile submenu will be available to you (as shown in Figure 1-7). Among other things, you'll be able to change your preferred language and enroll in multifactor authentication (MFA) here. This is also where you would go if you wanted to change your password.

If you make changes to your profile, click the Save button. Otherwise, click the Close button.

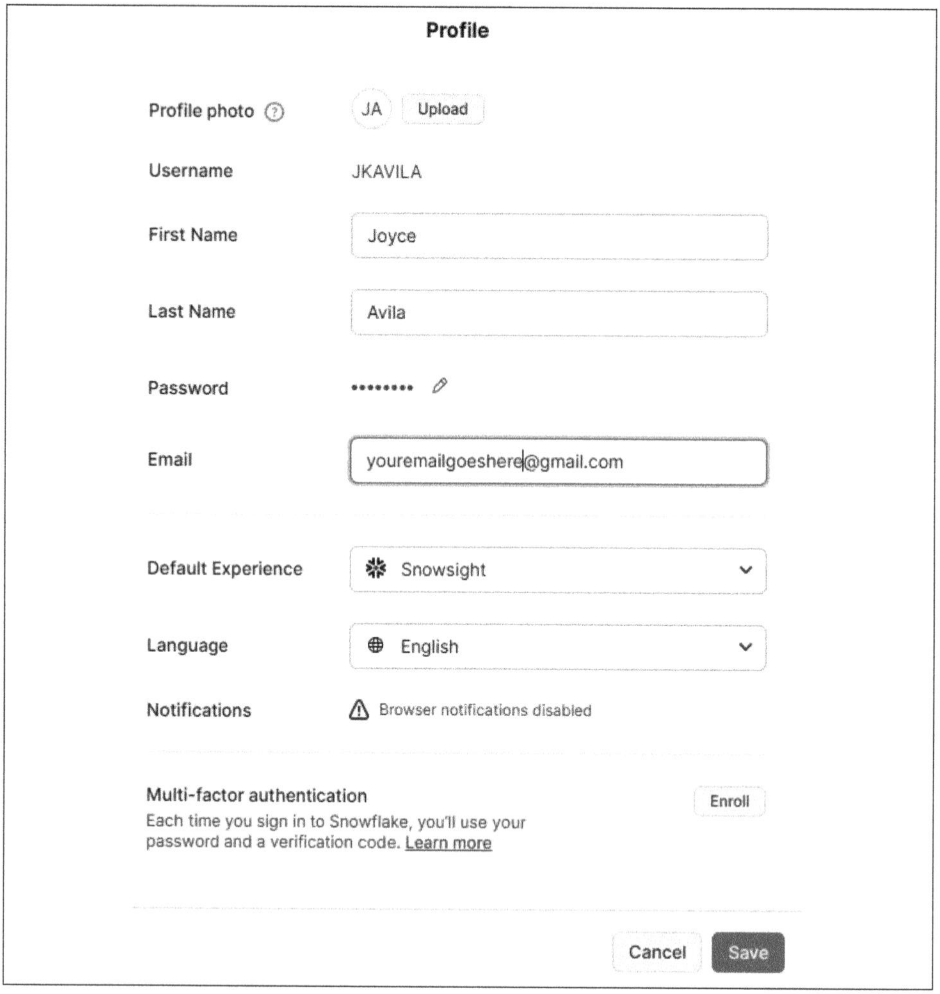

Figure 1-7. Profile submenu

Navigating Snowsight Worksheets

As you navigate Snowsight and do the exercises in the book, you will notice that auto-save is enabled in Snowsight. Along these lines, one of the great features in Snowsight is versioning history; you can revert back to a previous worksheet version if necessary.

Context Setting

Setting the context for queries is something we'll be doing throughout our examples. For context to be set, we need to select the virtual warehouse we'll be using as well as the role we want to use to execute the queries. We'll also need to select the database and schema we want to use for our queries.

Virtual warehouses, roles, and other Snowflake objects will be introduced in the coming chapters. For now, just know that your current role determines what data you can see and what actions you can take within Snowflake. The current virtual warehouse you're using is the compute power chosen to run your queries. Most, but not all, queries require a virtual warehouse to execute the query. If you are using a Snowflake trial org, your default role is SYSADMIN and your default virtual warehouse is COMPUTE_WH.

Before we set our context for upcoming queries, we'll find out what role and virtual warehouse we're currently using. To do this, we'll need to execute some SQL queries in a worksheet. Let's create a new folder and new worksheet where we can run our queries. In the upper-right corner, click the ellipsis and then click New Folder (as shown in Figure 1-8).

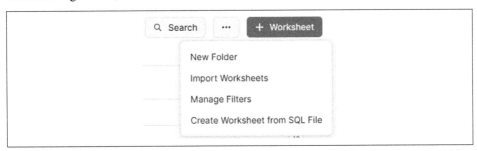

Figure 1-8. Clicking the ellipsis offers choices for the user, including creating a new folder

Name the new folder *Chapter1* and click the Create Folder button (as shown in Figure 1-9).

Figure 1-9. Menu to create a new folder

Click the + Worksheet button to create a new worksheet (as shown in Figure 1-10).

Figure 1-10. Creating a new worksheet within Snowsight by clicking the + Worksheet button

Once you click the + Worksheet button, a new worksheet is created in the *Chapter1* folder. You'll notice that the name of the worksheet defaults to the current date and time (as shown in Figure 1-11) and the cursor is in the worksheet awaiting your SQL statement. One other important thing to notice is that no database has been selected. We'll get around to setting the context for the database a little later.

Figure 1-11. A new worksheet created in the Chapter1 folder

Before executing any queries, though, let's change the name of the worksheet. Click the drop-down arrow beside the name of the worksheet and enter a new worksheet name of *Chapter1 Getting Started* (as shown in Figure 1-12).

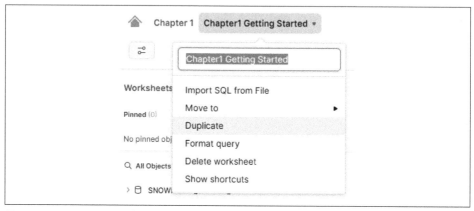

Figure 1-12. Renaming the worksheet

You are now ready to enter your first queries into the Snowsight worksheet. Enter the following statements:

```
SELECT CURRENT_ROLE();
SELECT CURRENT_WAREHOUSE();
```

Your worksheet should look like the one shown in Figure 1-13, where there are two statements on two separate lines and the cursor is sitting at the beginning of line 3. The SELECT statements simply return information; they do not change your current role or current virtual warehouse.

No Database selected ▾

```
1    SELECT CURRENT_ROLE();
2    SELECT CURRENT_WAREHOUSE();
3
4
```

Figure 1-13. Cursor on line 3 of the worksheet

In the upper-right corner of your screen is a button with a blue arrow in it (as shown in Figure 1-14). This button, which we'll refer to from now on as the Run button, is what you'll click to run the queries in a worksheet.

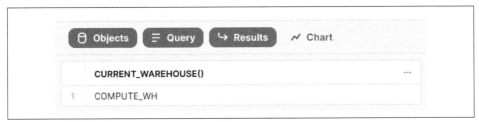

Figure 1-14. The blue arrow button, which is the Run button in Snowflake

Making sure your cursor is at the beginning of line 3, click the Run button. You should see the current virtual warehouse, as shown in Figure 1-15.

⊟ Objects   ≡ Query   ↳ Results   ∿ Chart

CURRENT_WAREHOUSE()	...
1 COMPUTE_WH	

Figure 1-15. Query results from the worksheet

Now let's see what happens if we put the cursor at the beginning of the worksheet, on line 1, and then click the Run button. You'll see the result shown in Figure 1-16.

Figure 1-16. Query result for showing the current role

What you'll notice is that only the first query was executed. Now let's try one more way to execute these queries. Highlight both statements as in Figure 1-17, and this time hit Ctrl + Enter rather than the Run button. Ctrl + Enter is a shortcut for the Run button. You'll notice that both statements were executed.

```
No Database selected  ▾

1 | SELECT CURRENT_ROLE();
2 | SELECT CURRENT_WAREHOUSE();
3
4
```

Figure 1-17. All the Snowflake statements are highlighted before executing the code

Next, let's find out what our current database is. Execute the following code:

```
SELECT CURRENT_DATABASE();
```

When we run the preceding statement to select the current database, a null value is returned. That is because we haven't yet set the context for our database. We can set the context for our database in one of two ways: by using the drop-down menu or by executing a query with the USE command. You can use the drop-down menu if you aren't sure which databases you can use. The drop-down menu will list for you all the databases your role can access. We'll use the query this time. When we start entering the statement, Snowflake uses its *Smart Autocomplete* feature to help us (as shown in Figure 1-18).

```
No Database selected  ▾

1    USE DATABASE SNOW
2              SNOWFLAKE_SAMPLE_DATA
3              database
4
5
```

Figure 1-18. Smart Autocomplete in action

Go ahead and execute the statement to use the Snowflake sample database:

```
USE DATABASE SNOWFLAKE_SAMPLE_DATA;
```

When you execute that query, the database context is changed. You can see the changed context directly on the worksheet now where the drop-down menu, when you click it, shows the current database (as shown in Figure 1-19). It also shows the schemas accessible within that database. None of the schemas are highlighted or have a checkmark beside them, which means no schema has been selected yet.

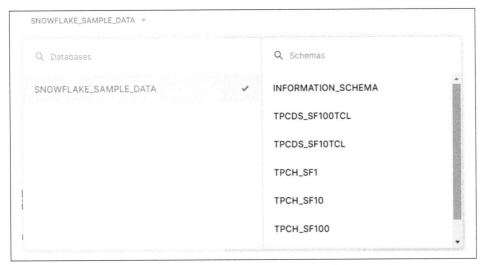

Figure 1-19. The current database selected is SNOWFLAKE_SAMPLE_DATA

This time, instead of executing a USE command to set the current schema, we'll select from the menu. Go ahead and select the schema TPCDS_SF100TCL (as shown in Figure 1-20).

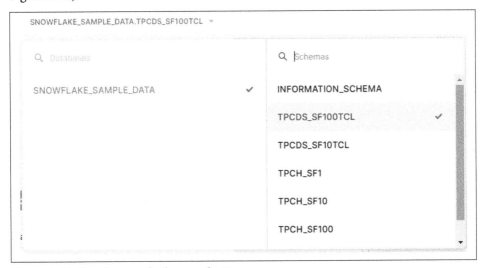

Figure 1-20. Database and schema selections

One of the things you'll notice about Snowsight is that there are four buttons below the query and just to the right of the object listings. Currently three of the buttons are highlighted in Figure 1-21. All four buttons can't be selected at the same time because Results can only be selected if Chart is deselected.

Figure 1-21. Four buttons in Snowsight, just below the query

Select the Objects button. Now deselect and then reselect each of the other three buttons one at a time to see what happens to your workspace area. The Objects button determines whether you see the objects to the left of your screen. You can deselect the Query button to get a full-screen view of the results, or you can deselect the Results button to get a full-screen view of the worksheet queries. If you select the Chart button, the Results button is deselected. Changing up the Snowsight viewing area allows you to customize the Snowflake UI.

In the next section, we'll take a look at new Snowsight features that improve user productivity. In Chapter 11 we'll look at Snowsight charts and dashboards as well as some new Snowsight collaboration features.

Improved Productivity

You'll appreciate the many improvements that come with Snowsight if you've been working in the Snowflake Classic Console web interface. Snowsight provides automatic contextual suggestions, script version history, worksheet folder structures, shortcuts, and much more. Let's dig into some of the features.

Using contextual suggestions from Smart Autocomplete

When we were writing our query to set the context for the database, the Snowflake Smart Autocomplete feature gave us contextual suggestions. Indeed, Snowflake showed us our choices before we could complete the name of the database (as shown in Figure 1-22). If you were to begin entering a function name, Snowflake would give you information about the parameters needed as well as link to the Snowflake docs.

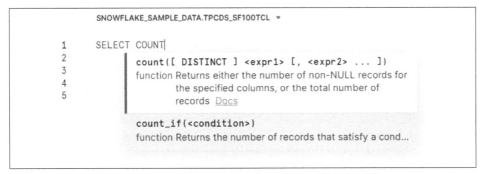

Figure 1-22. Snowsight contextual suggestions from Smart Autocomplete

Formatting SQL

Snowsight gives you the ability to neatly format your SQL code. Use the drop-down menu to select "Format query" to have your SQL query reformatted, as in Figure 1-23.

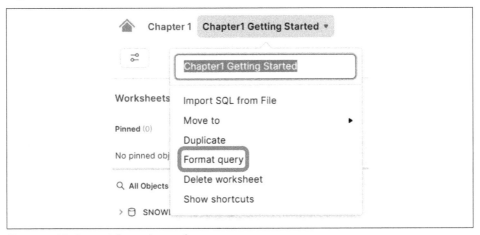

Figure 1-23. Snowsight option to format a query

It is no longer necessary to spend time formatting your messy code before sharing it with others or collaborating on your dashboards. The "Format query" option takes care of that for you. You can use the "Format query" option to clean up any messy formatting before you share your SQL code or collaborate on visualizations with others.

Using shortcuts

You'll find that there are a number of shortcut commands in Snowsight commands. Click the drop-down arrow beside the name of the worksheet and then click "Show shortcuts" to access those commands (as shown in Figure 1-24).

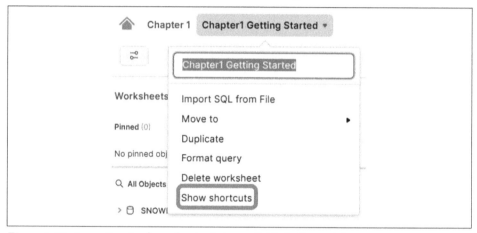

Figure 1-24. An option to show shortcuts is available in Snowsight

Accessing version history

The current worksheet is automatically saved each time a SQL statement is run in a Snowsight worksheet. If a statement or script is executed multiple times, the version history will be available. The various versions can be accessed by accessing the drop-down menu on the right side of the screen, which shows the last time the worksheet was updated (as shown in Figure 1-25).

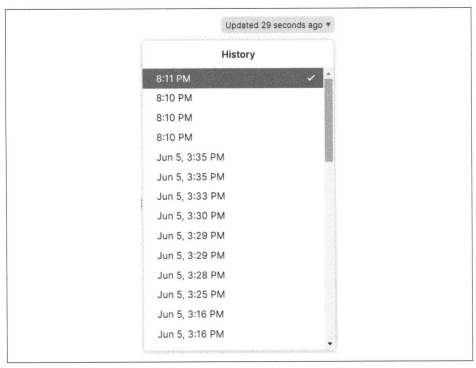

Figure 1-25. Query history showing recent updates

As we navigate Snowsight in the coming chapters, I will point out other Snowsight functionality. Once you're ready to return to the Main menu, just click the House icon in the upper-left corner of your screen (as shown in Figure 1-26).

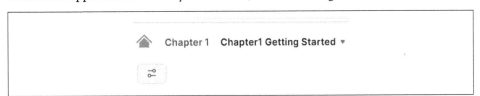

Figure 1-26. The House icon, which returns you to the Main menu

Snowflake Community

This book will teach you about the Snowflake architecture and how to use Snowflake. The information and lessons in the book are comprehensive; nevertheless, you may find that you have questions about a particular topic. For this reason, I encourage you to join and participate in the Snowflake community.

If you would like to connect with others who have a similar passion for Snowflake, there are user groups you may be interested in joining. Some user groups hold in-person events in North America, Europe, the Middle East, and the Asia Pacific region. You can find more information about Snowflake user groups on their website (*https://oreil.ly/0K3M7*). There are also virtual special interest groups (see Figure 1-27 for the list of them) in addition to regional user groups. I help manage the Data Collaboration special interest group.

Figure 1-27. Snowflake special interest groups (virtual)

Snowflake user groups are just one of the ways you can get involved in the Snowflake community. There are also community groups, a link to resources, and access to discussions available from the Snowflake community login page (*https://oreil.ly/YDOIZ*). To access these groups and resources, click Log In at the upper-right corner of the page and then click the "Not a member?" link to create your free Snowflake community member account.

Snowflake has a special Data Superhero program for Snowflake experts who are highly active in the community. Each person recognized as a Data Superhero receives a custom Data Superhero character created by Francis Mao, Snowflake's director of corporate events. Figure 1-28 shows a gathering of some of the Snowflake Data Superheroes, including me!

Figure 1-28. Snowflake Data Superheroes

Snowflake Certifications

As you progress through the chapters in the book, you'll find your Snowflake knowledge will grow quickly. At some point, you may want to consider earning a Snowflake certification to demonstrate that knowledge to the community.

All Snowflake certification paths begin with the SnowPro Core certification exam. Passing the SnowPro exam enables you to sit for any or all of the five role-based advanced certifications: Administrator, Architect, Data Analyst, Data Engineer, and Data Scientist. A Snowflake certificate is valid for two years, after which time a recertification exam must be passed. Passing any advanced Snowflake certification resets the clock on the SnowPro Core certification, so you have two more years before you'll need to recertify. More information about Snowflake certifications can be found on their website (*https://oreil.ly/26NEu*).

Snowday and Snowflake Summit Events

Snowflake hosts many events throughout the year, including its Data for Breakfast events. The two Snowflake main events for new-product release information are Snowday and Snowflake Summit. Snowday is a virtual event that happens each November. Snowflake Summit (*https://oreil.ly/nyHwC*) is an in-person event held each June. Snowflake Summit features keynotes, breakout sessions, hands-on labs, an exposition floor, and more.

Important Caveats About Code Examples in the Book

The code examples created for each chapter in the book were designed so that they can be completed independent of other chapters. This enables you to revisit the examples of any particular chapter as well as perform code cleanup at the end of each chapter.

Occasionally, I will point out how things look or function in a free trial account versus how they look or function in a paid account. We'll see very few differences, but it's important to realize that there are some ways in which the two differ.

The functionality demonstrated in the chapters assumes you have an Enterprise Edition Snowflake instance or higher. If you are currently working in a Snowflake Standard Edition org, you'll want to set up a free trial account and select Enterprise Edition. Otherwise, there will be some examples you won't be able to complete if you use a Standard Edition Snowflake org. More information about different Snowflake editions can be found in Appendix C.

Earlier in the chapter, you saw how to use Snowsight to format your SQL statements. The statements provided for you in this book will follow that formatting when possible, but the format may vary slightly at times due to space limitations. Also, in some chapters we'll be using the Snowflake sample database that is provided with your Snowflake account. Because the underlying data in that Snowflake sample data set sometimes changes, the result sets included in the chapter examples may be slightly different from your results. Alternative exercises will be made available at *https://github.com/SnowflakeDefinitiveGuide* for tables or schemas in the Snowflake sample database that later become unavailable.

In this chapter, we executed USE commands to set the context for our database. Throughout the upcoming chapter examples, we'll include the USE commands to set context. You have the option of executing the USE commands or selecting the context from the drop-down menus.

For coding examples throughout the book, we'll be following the naming standards best practices in Appendix B whenever we create our own Snowflake objects. Following best practices helps make code simpler, more readable, and easier to maintain. It also enables the creation of reusable code and makes it easier to detect errors. In this section, I'll call out a few of the most important best practices.

For object names, we'll be using all uppercase letters. We could achieve the same results by using all lowercase letters or mixed case, because Snowflake converts object names to uppercase. If you want to have an object name with mixed-case or all lowercase letters, for example, you'll need to enclose your object name in quotes. It is also important to keep this functionality in mind when you work with third-party tools that connect to Snowflake. Some third-party tools can't accept whitespace or special characters, so it's best to avoid both of those when naming Snowflake objects.

Another important best practice is to avoid using the same name being used by a different object. In later chapters you'll learn about the different table types, including temporary tables and permanent tables. You'll discover that temporary tables are session based; thus, they are not bound by uniqueness requirements. Even though you can create a temporary table with the same name as another table, it is not a good practice to do so. This will be discussed in more detail in Chapter 3.

Snowflake controls access through roles, and specific roles are responsible for creating certain types of objects. For example, the SYSADMIN role is used to create databases and virtual warehouses. We'll learn more about roles in Chapter 5, and whenever possible, we'll follow best practices in our examples. Sometimes we'll need to diverge from best practices to keep the example simple. When that happens, I'll mention that we're using a different role than the recommended role.

When creating a new object, you can use the CREATE statement alone or, optionally, you can add either the IF NOT EXISTS or the OR REPLACE syntax to the CREATE statement. For our examples, we'll use the CREATE OR REPLACE syntax so that you can always go back to the beginning of the chapter exercises to start over without having to drop objects first. In practice, though, be sure to use the CREATE IF NOT EXISTS syntax, especially in a production environment. If you do mistakenly use the OR REPLACE syntax in production, you have the option to use Snowflake Time Travel capabilities to return the object to its original state. Time Travel is demonstrated in Chapter 7.

The code examples in the book have been thoroughly tested; nevertheless, it is always possible to have errors. If you find an error in the code or in the text, please submit your errata to O'Reilly at *https://oreil.ly/snowflake-the-definitive-guide*.

Code Cleanup

We didn't create any new Snowflake objects in this chapter, so no cleanup is needed. It's OK to leave the folder and worksheets we created as they don't take up any storage or result in any compute charges.

Summary

There is a reason why Snowflake became the largest software IPO in history, and why Snowflake continues to innovate and enable industry disruption. The Snowflake Data Cloud is secure, scalable, and simple to manage; its ability to eliminate data silos and run workloads from a single platform creates opportunities to democratize data analytics. As you make your way through each chapter in the book, you'll see firsthand why Snowflake is a leader in the new data economy.

In this introductory chapter, you've been able to familiarize yourself with Snowsight, the Snowflake web user interface. You've also had an opportunity to learn about Snowflake community events as well as Snowflake certifications. Importantly, you learned about caveats for the code examples in this book. Most notably, with only a few exceptions, we'll be following the Snowflake best practices outlined in Appendix B.

The next chapter will compare traditional data platform architectures to Snowflake. We'll then take a deep dive into the three distinct Snowflake layers. It's an important foundational chapter to help you better understand some of the more technical aspects of Snowflake. You'll also get hands-on experience creating new clusters of compute resources called *virtual warehouses*.

Knowledge Check

The following questions are based on the information provided in this chapter:

1. The Snowflake free trial account allows you to use almost all the functionality of a paid account. What are a few of the differences, though, when using a Snowflake trial account?

2. What are your options if you are unable to create a support case within Snowflake?

3. Explain what it means to set the context for your Snowflake worksheet.

4. What does "Format query" do? Specifically, does "Format query" correct your spelling for commands or table names?

5. For how long are Snowflake certifications valid? What are two ways you can extend the date for Snowflake certifications?

6. What are two different ways you can execute a SQL query in a Snowflake worksheet?

7. From within a Snowflake worksheet, how do you return to the Main menu?

8. What is the reason we'll be using all uppercase letters when naming our Snowflake objects? Could we instead use mixed case? If so, explain how we would accomplish that.

9. We'll be using the CREATE OR REPLACE statement in future chapters to create new Snowflake objects. Why is it better not to do this in a production environment?

10. When you create a new Snowflake worksheet, what is the default name of the worksheet?

Answers to these questions are available in Appendix A.

CHAPTER 2

Creating and Managing the Snowflake Architecture

A decade ago, data platform architectures lacked the scalability necessary to make it easier for data-driven teams to share the same data simultaneously regardless of the size of the team or their proximity to the data. The need for scalability grew and demand increased for governed access to that data to generate actionable insights. To meet this demand, modifications were made to existing data platform architectures. However, this did not solve the problem given the sheer number and complexity of the platforms and the data-intensive nature of the applications until Snowflake burst onto the stage with a unique architecture.

Snowflake is an evolutionary modern data platform that solved the scalability problem. Compared to traditional cloud data platform architectures, Snowflake enables data storage and processing that is significantly faster, easier to use, and more affordable. Snowflake's Data Cloud provides users with a unique experience by combining a new SQL query engine with an innovative architecture designed and built, from the ground up, specifically for the cloud.

Prep Work

Create a new worksheet titled *Chapter2 Creating and Managing Snowflake Architecture*. Refer to "Navigating Snowsight Worksheets" on page 8 if you need help creating a new worksheet. To set the worksheet context, make sure you are using the SYSADMIN role and the COMPUTE_WH virtual warehouse.

Traditional Data Platform Architectures

In this section, we'll briefly review some traditional data platform architectures and how they were designed in an attempt to improve scalability. *Scalability* is the ability of a system to handle an increasing amount of work. We'll also discuss the limitations of these architectures, and we will discover what makes the Snowflake Data Cloud architecture so unique. Afterward, we will learn about each of the three different Snowflake architecture layers in detail: the cloud services layer, query processing (virtual warehouse) compute layer, and centralized (hybrid columnar) database storage layer.

Shared-Disk (Scalable) Architecture

The shared-disk architecture was an early scaling approach designed to keep data stored in a central storage location and accessible from multiple database cluster nodes (as shown in Figure 2-1). The data accessed by each cluster node is consistently available because all data modifications are written to the shared disk. This architecture is a traditional database design and is known for the simplicity of its data management. While the approach is simple in theory, it requires complex on-disk locking mechanisms to ensure data consistency which, in turn, causes bottlenecks. *Data concurrency*, allowing many users to affect multiple transactions within a database, is also a major problem, and adding more compute nodes only compounds the problem in a shared-disk architecture. Therefore, the true scalability of this architecture is limited.

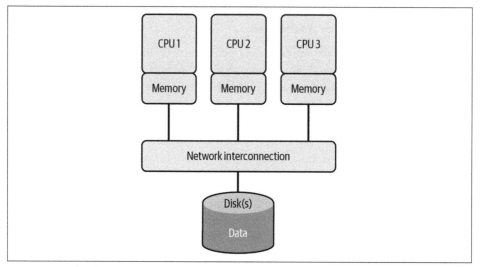

Figure 2-1. The shared-disk architecture, which is limited by the performance of the disk

Oracle RAC is an example of a shared-disk architecture.

Shared-Nothing (Scalable) Architecture

The shared-nothing architecture, in which storage and compute are scaled together (as shown in Figure 2-2), was designed in response to the bottleneck created by the shared-disk architecture. This evolution in architecture was made possible because storage had become relatively inexpensive. However, distributed cluster nodes along with the associated disk storage, CPU, and memory requires data to be shuffled between nodes, which adds overhead. The way the data is distributed across the nodes will determine the extent of the additional overhead. Striking the right balance between storage and compute is especially difficult. Even when it is possible to resize a cluster, it takes time to do so. Thus, organizations often overprovision shared-nothing resources, which results in unused, unneeded resources. Examples of a shared-nothing architecture include IBM DB2, Vertica, and Pivotal Greenplum.

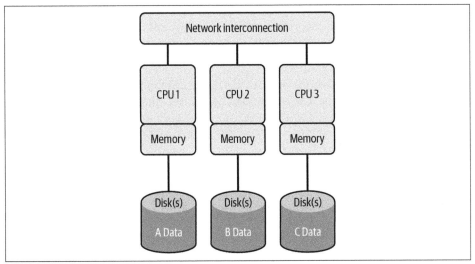

Figure 2-2. The shared-nothing architecture, which is limited by the need to distribute and query data across nodes

NoSQL Alternatives

Most NoSQL solutions rely on a shared-nothing architecture; thus, they have many of the same limitations. However, the benefit of NoSQL solutions is that they can store nonrelational data without first requiring transformation of the data. Additionally, most NoSQL systems don't require schemas. *NoSQL*, a term that implies "Not Only SQL" rather than "No to SQL," is a good choice for storing email, web links, social media posts and tweets, road maps, and spatial data.

There are four types of NoSQL databases: document stores, key-value (KV) stores, column family data stores or wide column data stores, and graph databases.

Document-based NoSQL databases such as MongoDB store data in JSON objects where each document has key-value pair–like structures. Key-value databases such as DynamoDB are especially useful for capturing customer behavior in a specific session. Cassandra is an example of a column-based database where large numbers of dynamic columns are logically grouped into column families. Graph-based databases, such as Neo4j and Amazon Neptune, work well for recommendation engines and social networks where they're able to help find patterns or relationships among data points.

A major limitation of NoSQL stores is that they perform poorly when doing calculations involving many records, such as aggregations, window functions, and arbitrary ordering. Thus, NoSQL stores can be great when you need to quickly create, read, update, and delete (CRUD) individual entries in a table, but they aren't recommended for ad hoc analysis. Additionally, NoSQL alternative solutions require specialized skill sets, and they aren't compatible with most SQL-based tools.

Note that the NoSQL solutions are not database warehouse replacements. While NoSQL alternatives can be useful for data scientists, they do not perform well for analytics.

The Snowflake Architecture

Even the improved traditional data platforms, especially those that were implemented on premises, couldn't adequately address modern data problems or solve the long-standing scalability issue. The Snowflake team made the decision to take a unique approach. Rather than trying to incrementally improve or transform existing software architectures, they built an entirely new, modern data platform, just for the cloud, that allows multiple users to concurrently share live data.

The unique Snowflake design physically separates but logically integrates storage and compute along with providing services such as security and management. As we explore the many unique Snowflake features throughout the upcoming chapters, you'll be able to see for yourself why the Snowflake architecture is the only architecture that can enable the Data Cloud.

The Snowflake hybrid-model architecture is composed of three layers, which are shown in Figure 2-3: the cloud services layer, the compute layer, and the data storage layer. Each layer, along with the three Snowflake caches, is discussed in more detail in the following sections.

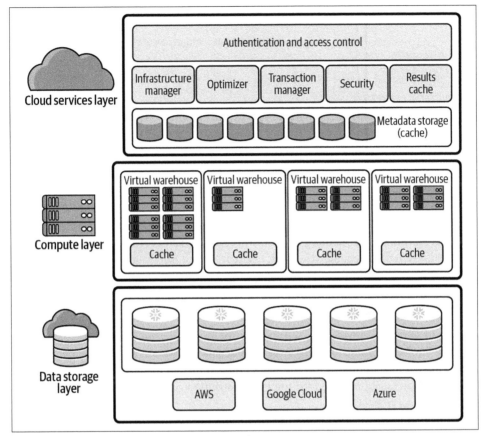

Figure 2-3. Snowflake's hybrid columnar architecture

Snowflake's processing engine is native SQL, and as we will see in later chapters, Snowflake is also able to handle semi-structured and unstructured data.

The Cloud Services Layer

All interactions with data in a Snowflake instance begin in the cloud services layer, also called the global services layer (as shown in Figure 2-4). The Snowflake cloud services layer is a collection of services that coordinate activities such as authentication, access control, and encryption. It also includes management functions for handling infrastructure and metadata, as well as performing query parsing and optimization, among other features. The cloud services layer is sometimes referred to as the Snowflake *brain* because all the various service layer components work together to handle user requests that begin from the time a user requests to log in.

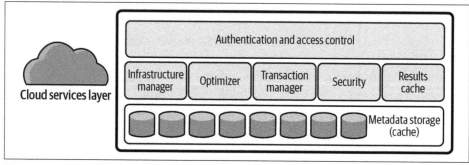

Figure 2-4. Snowflake's cloud services layer

Each time a user requests to log in, the request is handled by the cloud services layer. When a user submits a Snowflake query, the SQL query will be sent to the cloud services layer optimizer before being sent to the compute layer for processing. The cloud services layer is what enables the SQL client interface for Data Definition Language (DDL) and Data Manipulation Language (DML) operations on data.

Managing the Cloud Services Layer

The cloud services layer manages data security, including the security for data sharing. The Snowflake cloud services layer runs across multiple availability zones in each cloud provider region and holds the *result cache*, a cached copy of the executed query results. The metadata required for query optimization or data filtering are also stored in the cloud services layer.

 Just like the other Snowflake layers, the cloud services layer will scale independently of the other layers. Scaling of the cloud services layer is an automated process that doesn't need to be directly manipulated by the Snowflake end user.

Billing for the Cloud Services Layer

Most cloud services consumption is already incorporated into Snowflake pricing. However, when customers occasionally exceed 10% of their daily compute credit usage, they are billed for the overage. Note that daily compute credit usage is calculated in the UTC time zone.

All queries use a small number of cloud services resources. DDL operations are metadata operations, and as such, they use only cloud services. Keeping both facts in mind, we should evaluate some situations when we know the cost will be higher for cloud services to consider whether the benefits will be worth the increased costs.

Increased usage of the cloud services layer will likely occur when using several simple queries, especially queries accessing session information or using session variables. Increased usage also occurs when using large, complex queries with many joins. Single row inserts, rather than bulk or batch loading, will also result in higher cloud services consumption. Finally, you'll consume only cloud services resources if you use commands on the INFORMATION_SCHEMA tables or certain metadata-only commands such as the SHOW command. If you are experiencing higher than expected costs for cloud services, you may want to investigate these situations. Be sure to also investigate any partner tools, including those using the JDBC driver, as there could be opportunities for improvement from these third-party tools.

Even though the cloud services cost for a particular use case is high, sometimes it makes sense economically and/or strategically to incur the cost. For example, taking advantage of the result cache for queries, especially for large or complex queries, will mean zero compute cost for that query. Thoughtful choices about the right frequency and granularity for DDL commands, especially for use cases such as cloning, helps to better balance cloud services consumption costs and virtual warehouse costs to achieve an overall lower cost.

The Query Processing (Virtual Warehouse) Compute Layer

A Snowflake compute cluster, most often referred to simply as a *virtual warehouse*, is a dynamic cluster of compute resources consisting of CPU memory and temporary storage. Creating virtual warehouses in Snowflake makes use of the compute clusters—virtual machines in the cloud which are provisioned behind the scenes. Snowflake doesn't publish the exact server in use at any given time; it could change as the cloud providers modify their services. The Snowflake compute resources are created and deployed on demand to the Snowflake user, to whom the process is transparent.

A running virtual warehouse is required for most SQL queries and all DML operations, including loading and unloading data into tables, as well as updating rows in tables. Some SQL queries can be executed without requiring a virtual warehouse, and we'll soon see examples of that when we discuss the query result cache later in this chapter.

Snowflake's unique architecture allows for separation of storage and compute, which means any virtual warehouse can access the same data as another, without any contention or impact on performance of the other warehouses. This is because each Snowflake virtual warehouse operates independently and does not share compute resources with other virtual warehouses (as shown in Figure 2-5).

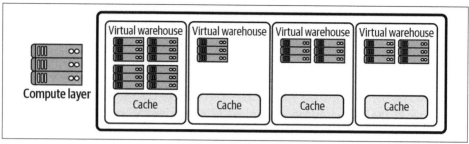

Figure 2-5. Snowflake's compute (virtual warehouse) layer

A virtual warehouse is always consuming credits when it is running in a session. However, Snowflake virtual warehouses can be started and stopped at any time, and can be resized at any time, even while running. Snowflake supports two different ways to scale warehouses. Virtual warehouses can be scaled up by resizing a warehouse and can be scaled out by adding clusters to a warehouse. It is possible to use one or both scaling methods at the same time.

Unlike the Snowflake cloud services layer and the data storage layer, the Snowflake virtual warehouse layer (as shown in Figure 2-5) is not a multitenant architecture. Snowflake predetermines the CPU, memory, and solid-state drive (SSD) configurations for each node in a virtual warehouse (see Table 2-1). While these definitions are subject to change, they are consistent in configuration across all three cloud providers.

Virtual Warehouse Size

A Snowflake compute cluster is defined by its size, with size corresponding to the number of servers in the virtual warehouse cluster. For each virtual warehouse size increase, the number of compute resources on average doubles in capacity (see Table 2-1). Beyond 4X-Large, a different approach is used to determine the number of servers per cluster. However, the credits per hour do still increase by a factor of 2 for these extremely large virtual warehouses.

Table 2-1. Snowflake virtual warehouse sizes and the associated number of servers per cluster

X-Small	Small	Medium	Large	X-Large	2X-Large	3X-Large	4X-Large
1	2	4	8	16	32	64	128

Virtual warehouse resizing to a larger size, also known as *scaling up*, is most often undertaken to improve query performance and handle large workloads. This will be discussed in more detail in the next section.

Because Snowflake utilizes per-second billing, it can often be cost-effective to run larger virtual warehouses because you are able to suspend virtual warehouses when they aren't being used. The exception is when you are running a lot of small or very basic queries on large virtual warehouse sizes. There won't likely be any benefit from adding the additional resources regardless of the number of concurrent queries.

Scaling Up a Virtual Warehouse to Process Large Data Volumes and Complex Queries

In a perfect world (i.e., simple workload, exact same per test), you'd pay the same total cost for using an X-Small virtual warehouse as using a 4X-Large virtual warehouse. The only difference would be a decrease in the time to completion. In reality, though, it isn't quite that simple. Many factors affect the performance of a virtual warehouse. The number of concurrent queries, the number of tables being queried, and the size and composition of the data are a few things that should be considered when sizing a Snowflake virtual warehouse.

Sizing appropriately matters. A lack of resources, due to the virtual warehouse being too small, could result in taking too long to complete the query. There could be a negative cost impact if the query is too small and the virtual warehouse is too large.

Resizing a Snowflake virtual warehouse is a manual process and can be done even while queries are running because a virtual warehouse does not have to be stopped or suspended to be resized. However, when a Snowflake virtual warehouse is resized, only subsequent queries will make use of the new size. Any queries already running will finish running while any queued queries will run on the newly sized virtual warehouse. Scaling a virtual warehouse *up* will increase the number of servers (as shown in Figure 2-6). An example would be from Medium to Large. Scaling a virtual warehouse *down* will decrease the number of servers.

It is recommended that you experiment with different types of queries and different virtual warehouse sizes to determine the best way to manage your virtual warehouses effectively and efficiently. The queries should be of a certain size and complexity that you would typically expect to complete within no more than 5 to 10 minutes. Additionally, it is recommended that you start small and increase in size as you experiment. It is easier to identify an undersized virtual warehouse than an underutilized one.

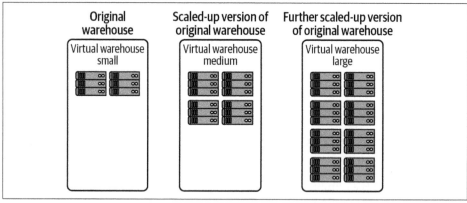

Figure 2-6. Scaling up a Snowflake virtual warehouse increases the size of the cluster

In Snowflake, we can create virtual warehouses through the user interface or with SQL. A little later we'll create some virtual warehouses using both methods. But first let's review a few things about virtual warehouses before we dive into some hands-on.

When we create a new virtual warehouse using the Snowsight user interface, as shown in Figure 2-7, we'll need to know the name of the virtual warehouse and the size we want the virtual warehouse to be. We'll also need to decide whether or not we want the virtual warehouse to be a multicluster virtual warehouse. A multicluster virtual warehouse allows Snowflake to scale in and out automatically. You'll learn more about multicluster virtual warehouses in the next section.

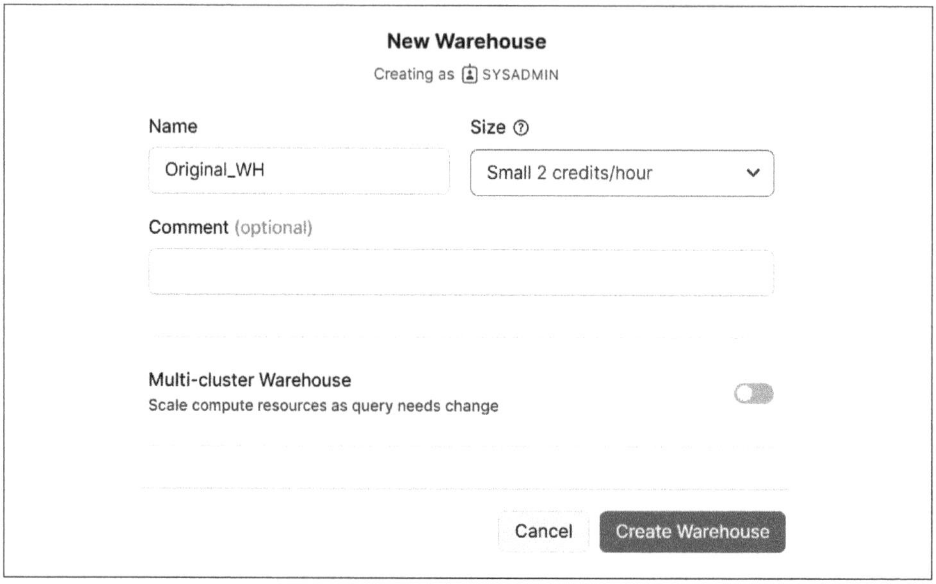

New Warehouse

Creating as 👤 SYSADMIN

Name

Original_WH

Size ⓘ

Small 2 credits/hour ⌄

Comment (optional)

Multi-cluster Warehouse

Scale compute resources as query needs change

Cancel | Create Warehouse

Figure 2-7. Creating a new virtual warehouse in the Snowflake web UI

Once we create the virtual warehouse, we can always go back and resize it. Resizing the virtual warehouse means we are scaling it up or down. Scaling up and down is done manually by editing the existing virtual warehouse.

A virtual warehouse can be resized, either up or down, at any time, including while it is running and processing statements. Resizing a virtual warehouse doesn't have any impact on statements that are currently being executed by the virtual warehouse. Resizing to a larger size makes the new, larger virtual warehouse available for any queries that are in the queue as well as for any future statements.

Scaling a virtual warehouse up or down can be achieved in the user interface or by using SQL statements in the worksheet. Another thing you'll notice is that you have the choice to use some advanced virtual warehouse options such as Auto Suspend and Auto Resume (as shown in Figure 2-8). Auto Suspend and Auto Resume are enabled by default. With Auto Suspend enabled, Snowflake will automatically suspend the virtual warehouse if it is inactive for a specified period of time. The Auto Suspend functionality ensures that you don't leave a virtual warehouse running when there are no incoming queries. This is important because you are only charged when a virtual warehouse is running, so you want to have the virtual warehouse suspended when it is not in use.

The value of the Auto Resume and Auto Suspend times should equal or exceed any regular gaps in your query workload. For example, if you have regular gaps of four minutes between queries, it wouldn't be advisable to set Auto Suspend for less than four minutes. If you did, your virtual warehouse would be continually suspending and resuming, which could potentially result in higher costs since the minimum credit usage billed is 60 seconds. Therefore, unless you have a good reason for changing the default Auto Suspend and Auto Resume times, it is recommended to leave the default at 10 minutes.

Figure 2-8. Increasing the cluster size to Medium in the Snowflake web UI (manually scaled up)

Larger virtual warehouses do not necessarily result in better performance for query processing or data loading. It is the query complexity, as part of query processing, that should be a consideration for choosing a virtual warehouse size because the time it takes for a server to execute a complex query will likely be greater than the time it takes to run a simple query. The amount of data to be loaded or unloaded can also greatly affect performance. Specifically, the number of files being loaded and the size of each file are important factors for data loading performance. As such, you'll want to carefully consider your use case before selecting any virtual warehouse that is greater in size than Large. One exception to that general rule would be if you are bulk-loading hundreds or thousands of files concurrently.

Scaling Out with Multicluster Virtual Warehouses to Maximize Concurrency

A multicluster virtual warehouse operates in much the same way as a single-cluster virtual warehouse. The goal is to optimize the Snowflake system performance in terms of size and number of clusters. In the previous section, we learned that when there was a queuing problem due to either very long-running SQL queries or a large data volume to be loaded or unloaded, scaling up could result in increased performance since the queries could run faster.

If a concurrency problem is due to many users, or connections, scaling up will not adequately address the problem. Instead, we'll need to scale out by adding clusters (as shown in Figure 2-9)—going from a Min Clusters value of 1 to a Max Clusters value of 3, for example. Multicluster virtual warehouses can be set to automatically scale if the number of users and/or queries tends to fluctuate.

Multicluster virtual warehouses are available on the Enterprise, Business Critical, and Virtual Private Snowflake editions.

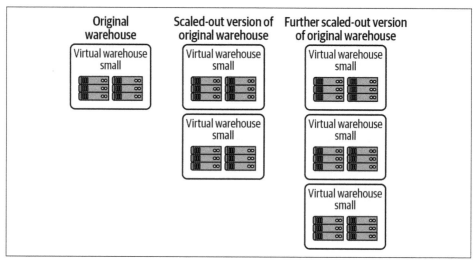

Figure 2-9. Scaling out a Snowflake virtual warehouse increases the number of Snowflake compute clusters

Just like single-cluster virtual warehouses, multicluster virtual warehouses can be created through the web interface or by using SQL for Snowflake instances. Unlike single-cluster virtual warehouses where sizing is a manual process, scaling in or out for multicluster virtual warehouses is an automated process. You'll just need to let Snowflake know how much you want the multicluster virtual warehouse to scale out. As an example, you can edit a Snowflake virtual warehouse to have a minimum of one small cluster and a maximum of three small clusters, as shown in Figure 2-10.

The two modes that can be selected for a multicluster virtual warehouse are Auto-scale and Maximized. The Snowflake scaling policy, designed to help control the usage credits in the Auto-scale mode, can be set to Standard or Economy.

Whenever a multicluster virtual warehouse is configured with the scaling policy set to Standard, the first virtual warehouse immediately starts when a query is queued, or if the Snowflake system detects that there is one more query than the currently running clusters can execute. Each successive virtual warehouse starts 20 seconds after the prior virtual warehouse has started.

If a multicluster virtual warehouse is configured with the scaling policy set to Economy, a virtual warehouse starts only if the Snowflake system estimates the query load can keep the virtual warehouse busy for at least six minutes. The goal of the Economy scaling policy is to conserve credits by keeping virtual warehouses fully loaded. As a result, queries may end up being queued and could take longer to complete.

Figure 2-10. A multicluster virtual warehouse in the Snowflake web UI (automatically scales in/out)

It is recommended to set the Max Clusters value as high as possible, while being aware of the associated costs. For example, if you set the Max Clusters at 10, keep in mind that you could experience a tenfold compute cost for the length of time all 10 clusters are running. A multicluster virtual warehouse is Maximized when the Min Clusters value is greater than 1 and both the Min Clusters and Max Clusters values are equal. We'll see an example of that in the next section.

Compute can be scaled up, down, in, or out. In all cases, there is no effect on storage used.

Creating and Using Virtual Warehouses

Commands for virtual warehouses can be executed in the web UI or within a worksheet by using SQL. We'll first take a look at creating and managing virtual warehouses with SQL. Then we'll look at the web UI functionality for virtual warehouses.

Auto Suspend and Auto Resume are two options available when creating a Snowflake virtual warehouse. Auto Suspend is the number of seconds that the virtual warehouse will wait if no queries need to be executed before going offline. Auto Resume will restart the virtual warehouse once there is an operation that requires compute resources.

The following SQL script will create a medium-sized virtual warehouse, with four clusters, that will automatically suspend after five minutes. One thing you'll notice is that when you create a virtual warehouse using SQL, you'll need to state the suspend time in total seconds. In the user interface, the time is entered in minutes. Navigate to your *Chapter2 Creating and Managing Snowflake Architecture* worksheet and execute the following SQL statement to create a new virtual warehouse:

```
USE ROLE SYSADMIN;
CREATE WAREHOUSE CH2_WH WITH WAREHOUSE_SIZE = MEDIUM
    AUTO_SUSPEND = 300 AUTO_RESUME = true INITIALLY_SUSPENDED = true;
```

It is a best practice to create a new virtual warehouse in a suspended state. Unless the Snowflake virtual warehouse is created initially in a suspended state, the initial creation of a Snowflake virtual warehouse could take time to provision compute resources.

Earlier we discussed how we can change the size of a virtual warehouse by scaling it up or down and that doing so is a manual process. In order to scale up or down, we'll use the ALTER command:

```
USE ROLE SYSADMIN;
ALTER WAREHOUSE CH2_WH
SET WAREHOUSE_SIZE = LARGE;
```

Any SQL statements executed in this workbook after creating this virtual warehouse will run on that virtual warehouse. If you prefer to use a certain virtual warehouse to execute a script instead, you can specify that warehouse in the worksheet:

```
USE WAREHOUSE CH2_WH;
```

Alternatively, you can update the virtual warehouse in the context menu located at the upper right of the web UI (as shown in Figure 2-11).

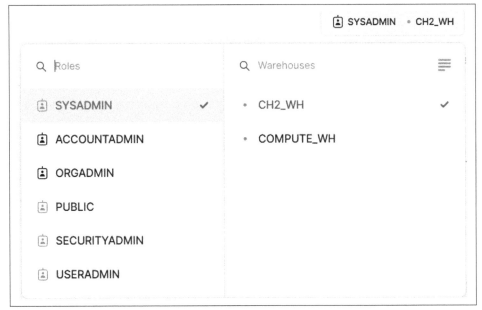

Figure 2-11. The Snowflake web UI virtual warehouses selection

We created our virtual warehouse using SQL commands, but we can also use the Snowsight web UI to create and/or edit Snowflake virtual warehouses. Let's navigate there now. Click the Home icon in the upper left and then select Admin → Warehouses. You'll see the virtual warehouse that we just created (see CH2_WH in Figure 2-12). If you don't see both virtual warehouses, try refreshing the page.

Figure 2-12. Virtual warehouses available for the current role

Look to the far right, click the ellipsis, and then select the Edit option (as shown in Figure 2-13). Notice that you could have chosen to create a new virtual warehouse by selecting the + Warehouse button, rather than selecting to edit an existing virtual warehouse.

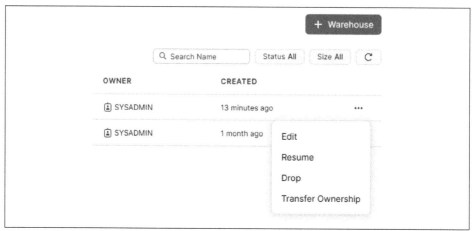

Figure 2-13. The Snowflake web UI Edit selection

Upon selecting the Edit option, you should now see the Edit Warehouse screen, as shown in Figure 2-14.

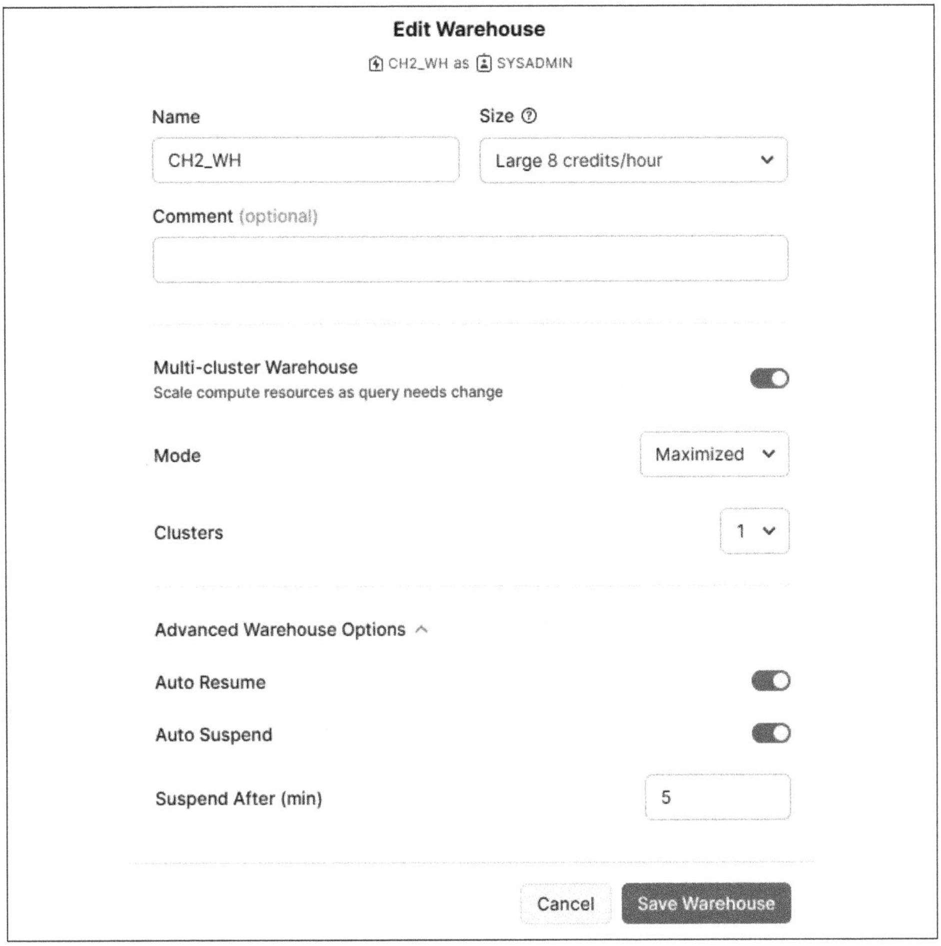

Figure 2-14. The Snowflake web UI Edit Warehouse screen

If you are working in a Snowflake Standard Edition org, you won't see the multicluster virtual warehouse option. For the Enterprise Edition, Business Critical Edition, and Virtual Private Snowflake Edition, multicluster virtual warehouses are enabled. Even though the multicluster virtual warehouse is toggled on when a cluster of one is selected, scaling out beyond a single cluster is not possible. To scale out, the number of clusters needs to be two or greater. When you increase the number of clusters to two or more, be sure to evaluate the mode. You'll most likely want to change the mode to Auto-scale from the default Maximized mode. In that way, your multicluster virtual warehouse will scale as needed.

To create a Snowflake multicluster virtual warehouse via SQL, you'll need to specify the scaling policy as well as the minimum and maximum number of clusters. As stated previously, the scaling policy, which applies only if the virtual warehouse is running in Auto-scale mode, can be either Economy or Standard.

 A multicluster virtual warehouse is said to be Maximized when the minimum number of clusters and maximum number of clusters are the same. Additionally, value(s) must be more than one. An example of a Maximized multicluster virtual warehouse is when MIN_CLUSTER_COUNT = 3 and MAX_CLUSTER_COUNT = 3.

Separation of Workloads and Workload Management

Query processing tends to slow down when the workload reaches full capacity on traditional database systems. In contrast, Snowflake estimates the resources needed for each query, and as the workload approaches 100%, each new query is suspended in a queue until there are sufficient resources to execute them. Several options exist to efficiently handle workloads of varying size. One way is to separate the workloads by assigning different virtual warehouses to different users or groups of users (as shown in Figure 2-15). The virtual warehouses depicted in Figure 2-15 are all the same size, but in practice, the virtual warehouses for different workloads will likely be of different sizes.

Different groups of users can be assigned to different Snowflake virtual warehouses of varying size. Thus, users who are querying the data will experience a consistent average query time. Marketing and sales teams can create and evaluate campaigns while also capturing sales activities. Accounting and finance teams can access their reports and delve into the details of the underlying data. Data scientists can run large, complex queries on vast amounts of data. And ETL processes can continuously load data.

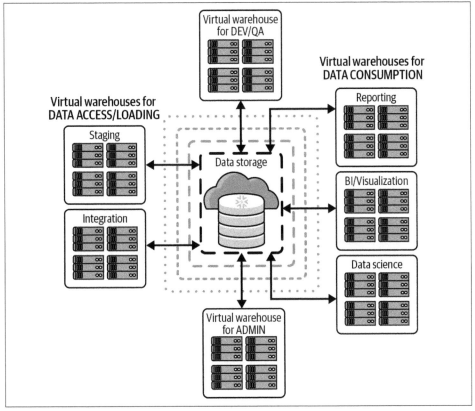

Figure 2-15. Separating Snowflake workloads by assigning different virtual warehouses to groups of users

We learned earlier in the chapter that multicluster virtual warehouses can be set to automatically scale to avoid concurrency problems. For an automatically scaling multicluster virtual warehouse, we will still need to define the virtual warehouse size and the minimum and maximum number of clusters. Previously, we saw how to create a new virtual warehouse through the Snowflake UI. Now let's use SQL to create a multicluster virtual warehouse for accounting and finance, then take a look at an example of how automatic scaling for that virtual warehouse might work. Navigate back to the *Chapter2 Creating and Managing Snowflake Architecture* worksheet:

```
USE ROLE SYSADMIN;
CREATE OR REPLACE WAREHOUSE ACCOUNTING_WH
    WITH Warehouse_Size = MEDIUM MIN_CLUSTER_COUNT = 1
    MAX_CLUSTER_COUNT = 6 SCALING_POLICY = 'STANDARD';
```

The scaling process occurs automatically once the multicluster virtual warehouse is configured. Figure 2-16 illustrates how automatic scaling works when the number of concurrent SQL statements increases.

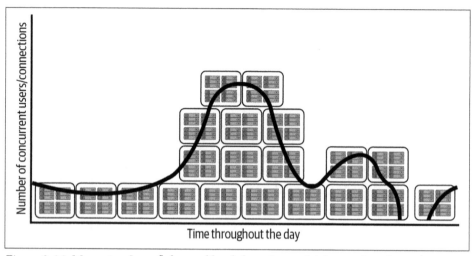

Figure 2-16. Managing Snowflake workloads by using multicluster virtual warehouses to scale in and out

You can see that on an hourly basis, the workload is heavier between core working hours for employees. We might also want to investigate to confirm that the daily workload is heavier overall at the beginning of the month for the consumption virtual warehouse for reporting, as the accounting department works to prepare and review the accounting statements for the prior month.

Billing for the Virtual Warehouse Layer

Consumption charges for Snowflake virtual warehouses are calculated based on the warehouse size, as determined by the number of servers per cluster, the number of clusters if there are multicluster virtual warehouses, and the amount of time each cluster server runs. Snowflake utilizes per-second billing with a 60-second minimum each time a virtual warehouse starts or is resized. When a virtual warehouse is scaled up, credits are billed for one minute of the additional resources that are provisioned. All billing, even though calculated in seconds, is reported in fractions of hours.

When using the ACCOUNTADMIN role, you can view the virtual warehouse credit usage for your account by clicking Account → Usage in the UI. You can also query the Account Usage view in the SNOWFLAKE shared database to obtain the information. It is recommended that you choose an X-Small virtual warehouse to do so because of the small size of the data set and simplicity of the query.

Centralized (Hybrid Columnar) Database Storage Layer

Snowflake's centralized database storage layer holds all data, including structured and semi-structured data. As data is loaded into Snowflake, it is optimally reorganized into a compressed, columnar format and stored and maintained in Snowflake databases. Each Snowflake database consists of one or more *schemas*, which are logical groupings of database objects such as tables and views. Chapter 3 is devoted to showing you how to create and manage databases and database objects. In Chapter 9, we will learn about Snowflake's physical data storage as we take a deep dive into micro-partitions to better understand data clustering.

Data stored in Snowflake databases is always compressed and encrypted. Snowflake takes care of managing every aspect of how the data is stored. Snowflake automatically organizes stored data into *micro-partitions*, an optimized, immutable, compressed columnar format which is encrypted using AES-256 encryption. Snowflake optimizes and compresses data to make metadata extraction and query processing easier and more efficient. We learned earlier in the chapter that whenever a user submits a Snowflake query, that query will be sent to the cloud services optimizer before being sent to the compute layer for processing.

Snowflake's data storage layer is sometimes referred to as the remote disk layer. The underlying file system is implemented on Amazon, Microsoft, or Google Cloud (as shown in Figure 2-17). The specific provider used for data storage is the one you selected when you created your Snowflake account. Snowflake doesn't place limits on the amount of data you can store or the number of databases or database objects you can create. Snowflake tables can easily store petabytes of data. There is no effect on virtual warehouse size as the storage increases or decreases in a Snowflake account. The two are scaled independently from each other and from the cloud services layer.

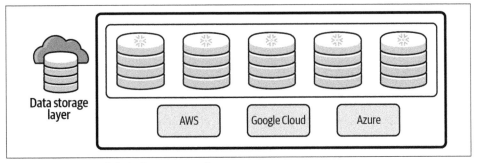

Figure 2-17. Snowflake's data storage layer

There are two unique features in the storage layer architecture: Time Travel and zero-copy cloning. Both of these very powerful Snowflake features will be introduced in this chapter and covered in more detail in later chapters. To prepare for those later chapters, you'll want to have a thorough understanding of these two features.

Introduction to Zero-Copy Cloning

Zero-copy cloning offers the user a way to *snapshot* a Snowflake database, schema, or table along with its associated data. There is no additional storage charge until changes are made to the cloned object, because zero-copy data cloning is a metadata-only operation. For example, if you clone a database and then add a new table or delete some rows from a cloned table, at that point storage charges would be assessed. There are many uses for zero-copy cloning other than creating a backup. Most often, zero-copy clones will be used to support development and test environments. We'll see examples of this in Chapter 8.

Introduction to Time Travel

Time Travel allows you to restore a previous version of a database, table, or schema. This is an incredibly helpful feature that gives you an opportunity to fix previous edits that were done incorrectly or restore items deleted in error. With Time Travel, you can also back up data from different points in the past by combining the Time Travel feature with the clone feature, or you can perform a simple query of a database object that no longer exists. How far back you can go into the past depends on a few different factors. Time Travel will be discussed in detail in Chapter 7. For the purposes of this chapter, it is important to note that data storage fees will be assessed for any data that has been deleted but is still available to restore.

Billing for the Storage Layer

Snowflake data storage costs are calculated based on the daily average size of compressed rather than uncompressed data. Storage costs include the cost of persistent data stored in permanent tables and files staged for bulk data loading and unloading. Fail-safe data and the data retained for data recovery using Time Travel are also considered in the calculation of data storage costs. Clones of tables referencing data that has been deleted are similarly considered.

Snowflake Caching

When you submit a query, Snowflake checks to see whether that query has been previously run and, if so, whether the results are still cached. Snowflake will use the cached result set if it is still available rather than executing the query you just submitted. In addition to retrieving the previous query results from a cache, Snowflake supports other caching techniques. There are three Snowflake caching types: the query result cache, the virtual warehouse cache, and the metadata cache.

Query Result Cache

The fastest way to retrieve data from Snowflake is by using the query result cache. The results of a Snowflake query are cached, or persisted, for 24 hours and then purged. This contrasts with how the virtual warehouse cache and metadata cache work. Neither of those two caches is purged based on a timeline. Even though the result cache only persists for 24 hours, the clock is reset each time the query is re-executed, up to a maximum of 31 days from the date and time when the query was first executed. After 31 days, or sooner if the underlying data changes, a new result is generated and cached when the query is submitted again.

The result cache is fully managed by the Snowflake global cloud services (GCS) layer, as shown in Figure 2-18, and is available across all virtual warehouses since virtual warehouses have access to all data. The process for retrieving cached results is managed by GCS. However, once the size of the results exceeds a certain threshold, the results are stored in and retrieved from cloud storage.

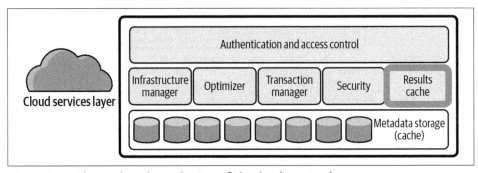

Figure 2-18. The result cache in the Snowflake cloud services layer

Query results returned to one user are also available to any user who has the necessary access privileges and who executes the same query. Therefore, any user can run a query against the result cache with no running virtual warehouse needed, assuming the query is cached and the underlying data has not changed.

Another unique feature of the query result cache is that it is the only cache that can be disabled by a parameter. Navigate to the *Chapter2* worksheet and execute the following SQL statement:

```
ALTER SESSION SET USE_CACHED_RESULT=FALSE;
```

Disabling the result cache is necessary before performing A/B testing, and it is important to enable query result caching once the testing is complete.

Metadata Cache

The metadata cache is fully managed in the global services layer (as shown in Figure 2-19) where the user does have some control over the metadata but no control over the cache. Snowflake collects and manages metadata about tables, micro-partitions, and even clustering. For tables, Snowflake stores row count, table size in bytes, file references, and table versions. Thus, a running virtual warehouse will not be needed, because the count statistics are kept in the metadata cache when running a SELECT COUNT(*) on a table.

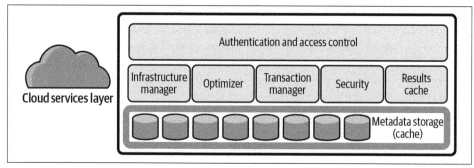

Figure 2-19. The metadata storage cache in the Snowflake cloud services layer

The Snowflake metadata repository includes table definitions and references to the micro-partition files for that table. The range of values in terms of MIN and MAX, the NULL count, and the number of distinct values are captured from micro-partitions and stored in Snowflake. As a result, some queries don't require a running virtual warehouse to return results. For example, the MIN of zip code, an integer data type column, wouldn't require virtual compute-only cloud services. Snowflake also stores the total number of micro-partitions and the depth of overlapping micro-partitions to provide information about clustering.

> The information stored in the metadata cache is used to build the query execution plan.

Virtual Warehouse Local Disk Cache

The traditional Snowflake data cache is specific to the virtual warehouse used to process the query. Running virtual warehouses use SSD storage to store the micro-partitions that are pulled from the centralized database storage layer when a query is processed. This is necessary to complete the query requested, whenever a query is executed. The size of the virtual warehouse's SSD cache is determined by the size of the virtual warehouse's compute resources (as shown in Figure 2-20).

 The virtual warehouse data cache is limited in size and uses the LRU (Least Recently Used) algorithm.

Whenever a virtual warehouse receives a query to execute, that warehouse will scan the SSD cache first before accessing the Snowflake remote disk storage. Reading from SSD is faster than from the database storage layer but still requires the use of a running virtual warehouse.

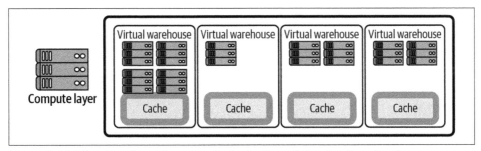

Figure 2-20. The virtual warehouse cache in the Snowflake cloud services layer

Although the virtual warehouse cache is implemented in the virtual warehouse layer where each virtual warehouse operates independently, the global services layer handles overall system data freshness. It does so via the query optimizer, which checks the freshness of each data segment of the assigned virtual warehouse and then builds a query plan to update any segment by replacing it with data from the remote disk storage.

Note that the virtual warehouse cache is sometimes referred to as the *raw data cache*, the *SSD cache*, or the *data cache*. This cache is dropped once the virtual warehouse is suspended, so you'll want to consider the trade-off between the credits that will be consumed by keeping a virtual warehouse running and the value from maintaining the cache of data from previous queries to improve performance. By default, Snowflake will automatically suspend a virtual warehouse after 10 minutes of idle time, but this can be changed.

Whenever possible, and where it makes sense, assign the same virtual warehouse to users who will be accessing the same data for their queries. This increases the likelihood that they will benefit from the virtual warehouse local disk cache.

Code Cleanup

In the *Chapter2* worksheet, make sure to set the cached results back to TRUE:

```
USE ROLE SYSADMIN;
ALTER SESSION SET USE_CACHED_RESULT=TRUE;
```

Go ahead and drop the virtual warehouses:

```
USE ROLE SYSADMIN;
DROP WAREHOUSE CH2_WH;
DROP WAREHOUSE ACCOUNTING_WH;
```

Summary

Hopefully these first two chapters have given you an understanding of the power of the Snowflake Data Cloud and its ease of use. We executed a few SQL statements in this chapter, but in the upcoming chapters we'll be demonstrating Snowflake's many capabilities by deep-diving into core concepts with hands-on learning examples. If you haven't already done so, now is a good time to sign up for a Snowflake free trial account so that you'll get the most out of the chapters. Refer to Appendix C for more details on getting set up in a trial account. Also, be sure to read the important caveats to code examples in Chapter 1 if you haven't already done so.

Knowledge Check

The following questions are based on the information provided in this chapter:

1. Name the three Snowflake architecture layers.

2. Which of the three Snowflake layers are multitenant?

3. In which of the three Snowflake architecture layers will you find the virtual warehouse cache? The result cache?

4. If you are experiencing higher than expected costs for Snowflake cloud services, what kinds of things might you want to investigate?

5. Explain the difference between scaling up and scaling out.

6. What effect does scaling up or scaling out have on storage used in Snowflake?

7. The shared-nothing architecture evolved from the shared-disk architecture. NoSQL alternatives have also been created. What one main problem have they all been trying to solve?

8. In a Snowflake multicluster environment, what scaling policies can be selected?

9. What components do you need to configure specifically for multicluster virtual warehouses?

10. What are two options to change the virtual warehouse that will be used to run a SQL command within a specific worksheet?

Answers to these questions are available in Appendix A.

CHAPTER 3

Creating and Managing Snowflake Securable Database Objects

Within Snowflake, all data is stored in database tables. Snowflake database tables are logically structured into collections of rows and columns. This chapter focuses on the logical structure of databases and database objects, such as tables and views. The physical structure of Snowflake data storage, including Snowflake micro-partitions, will be explained in Chapter 9.

In this chapter, we will cover topics in a specific order because the series of examples build upon each other. We'll start with creating databases and schemas, reviewing the INFORMATION_SCHEMA and ACCOUNT_USAGE views, and then creating tables and views. Next, we'll learn about stages, stored procedures, and user-defined functions (UDFs). We'll close out the chapter with pipes, sequences, streams, and tasks. All the objects discussed in this chapter are securable database objects (as shown in Figure 3-1).

A Snowflake securable object is an entity for which you grant access to specific roles. Roles, which have been granted access privileges, are assigned to users. A Snowflake user can be either an individual person or an application. Users and roles will be discussed in Chapter 5.

In the previous chapter, we completed hands-on exercises with Snowflake virtual warehouses. Snowflake resource monitors, used to help manage virtual warehouses, will be explained in detail in Chapter 8.

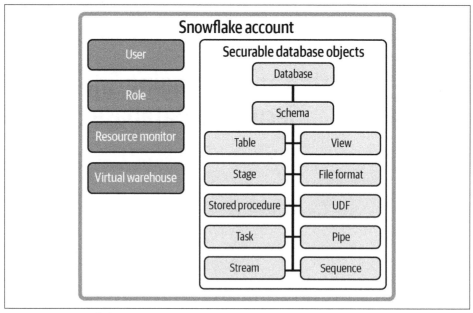

Figure 3-1. Snowflake account entities

Prep Work

Create a new worksheet titled *Chapter3 Creating Database Objects*. Refer to "Navigating Snowsight Worksheets" on page 8 if you need help creating a new worksheet. To set the worksheet context, make sure you are using the SYSADMIN role and the COMPUTE_WH virtual warehouse.

Creating and Managing Snowflake Databases

In a relational environment, database objects such as tables and views are maintained within databases. In Snowflake, the database logically groups the data while the schema organizes it. Together, the database and schema comprise the namespace. In the examples throughout this chapter, whenever we work with database objects we'll need to specify a namespace, unless the schema and database we want to use are the active context in the workspace. If the database or schema needs to be specified, we'll include the USE command. That way, it is clear to Snowflake the location where objects are to be created and which specific object is being referenced in the commands.

We can create two main types of databases: permanent (persistent) and transient. At the time we create a database, the default will be a permanent database, if we don't specify which of the two types we want to create.

Snowflake is designed so that your data is accessible and recoverable at every stage within the data lifecycle. This is achieved through Continuous Data Protection (CDP), Snowflake's comprehensive set of features that help protect data stored in Snowflake against human error, malicious acts, and software or hardware failure. The important Snowflake CDP features introduced in this chapter are Time Travel and fail-safe.

Transient databases have a maximum one-day data retention period, aka Time Travel period, and do not have a fail-safe period.

The Snowflake Time Travel period is the time during which table data within the database can be queried at a historical point in time. This also enables databases and database objects to be cloned or undropped and historical data to be restored. The default Time Travel period is one day but can be up to 90 days for permanent databases; or a user could set the Time Travel period to zero days if no Time Travel period is desired. Note that the Enterprise Edition or higher is necessary to take advantage of the 90-day Time Travel period.

Snowflake's fail-safe data recovery service provides a seven-day period during which data from permanent databases and database objects may be recoverable by Snowflake. The fail-safe data recovery period is the seven-day period *after* the data retention period ends. Unlike Time Travel data, which is accessible by Snowflake users, fail-safe data is recoverable *only* by Snowflake employees.

It is important to note that data storage costs are incurred for those seven days. That is one consideration when deciding what database type you want to create. Another consideration is the ability to recover data from other sources if the data stored in the database is lost after a single data Time Travel period is up.

These are the basic SQL commands for Snowflake databases that we will be covering in this section:

- CREATE DATABASE
- ALTER DATABASE
- DROP DATABASE
- SHOW DATABASES

CREATE DATABASE is the command used to create a new database, clone an existing database, create a database from a share provided by another Snowflake account, or create a replica of an existing primary database (i.e., a secondary database).

We can create databases from the UI or by using SQL code in the Snowflake work-sheet. We'll first demonstrate how to use the UI to create one database. The rest of the objects in this chapter will be created using SQL commands in the Snowflake worksheet.

For all exercises in this chapter, make sure you have your role set to SYSADMIN unless otherwise directed. As we'll learn in Chapter 5, it is a best practice to use the SYSADMIN role, rather than the ACCOUNTADMIN or SECURITYADMIN role, to create most Snowflake objects.

Let's go ahead and get started. We'll create one permanent database using the Snow-flake web UI and one transient database using SQL code in a worksheet. Navigate to the Data → Databases menu option, as shown in Figure 3-2. It is very important that you confirm your role is set to SYSADMIN.

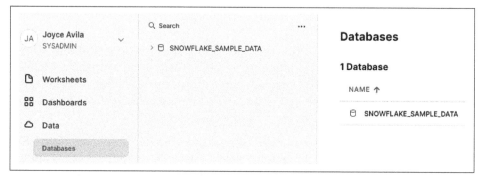

Figure 3-2. The Main menu showing the Data → Databases selection

In the upper-right corner of the screen, you should see a + Database button (as shown in Figure 3-3).

Figure 3-3. Use the + Database button to create new Snowflake databases

Click the + Database button, and when the New Database menu appears, enter the information to create a new DEMO3A_DB database (as shown in Figure 3-4). Then click the Create button.

Figure 3-4. *The Snowsight user interface New Database screen*

You'll now see that the new DEMO3A_DB database has been created and is one of the two databases accessible to the SYSADMIN role (as shown in Figure 3-5).

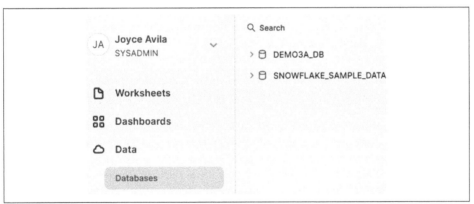

Figure 3-5. *A list of Snowflake databases available for the (current) SYSADMIN role*

Now we'll create another database, but this time we'll use a Snowflake worksheet to do so. Navigate to the Worksheets menu and then click the *Creating Database Objects* worksheet that you created previously in the Prep Work section (as shown in Figure 3-6).

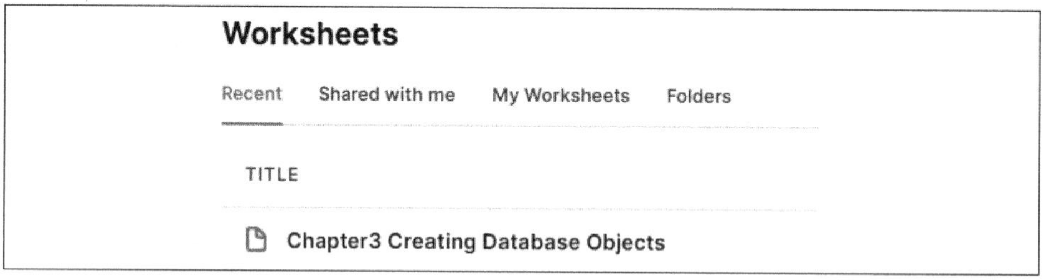

Worksheets

Recent   Shared with me   My Worksheets   Folders

TITLE

📄 Chapter3 Creating Database Objects

Figure 3-6. The Snowsight user interface showing current worksheets

Make sure your context is set for the SYSADMIN role and the COMPUTE_WH virtual warehouse. Execute the following statements to create a new transient database:

```
USE ROLE SYSADMIN;
USE WAREHOUSE COMPUTE_WH;
CREATE OR REPLACE TRANSIENT DATABASE DEMO3B_DB
Comment = 'Transient Database for Chapter 3 Exercises';
```

Notice in the preceding code that we used the optional keywords OR REPLACE in the command. That way, an error will not be returned if the database already exists, though the existing database would be completely overwritten.

Use the CREATE OR REPLACE statement sparingly in production so as not to overwrite an existing database. As an alternative, if you don't want to have an error but also don't want to overwrite an existing database, use the CREATE DATABASE DEMO3B_DB IF NOT EXISTS statement instead. The OR REPLACE and IF NOT EXISTS optional keywords cannot both be used in the same statement. As mentioned in Chapter 1, the choice was made to use the optional keywords OR REPLACE throughout the book so that you can easily go back anywhere in the chapter to rework a section or make a correction. However, this approach is not a best practice in your production environment. See Appendix B for more information about best practices.

Whenever you create a new database, that database is automatically set as the active database for the current session. It's the equivalent of using the USE DATABASE command. If we needed or wanted to use a database other than the one we just created, we'd have to include the USE DATABASE command in the worksheet to select the appropriate database. Alternatively, we could use the drop-down menu to select a different database.

If you navigate to the Databases UI, as shown in Figure 3-7, you will see that it shows the two databases we just created plus the Snowflake sample database that automatically comes with the Snowflake account.

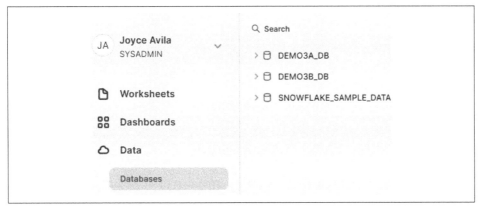

Figure 3-7. A list of available databases for the (current) SYSADMIN role

Navigate back to the *Creating Database Objects* worksheet and then change your role to ACCOUNTADMIN by using the drop-down menu in the upper-right corner. Open the drop-down menu for databases in the worksheet and you'll now see one more database, the SNOWFLAKE database, included as one of the databases you can select (as shown in Figure 3-8).

Figure 3-8. A list of available databases within the current Snowsight worksheet

While using the ACCOUNTADMIN role in the worksheet, execute the following command:

```
USE ROLE ACCOUNTADMIN;
SHOW DATABASES;
```

Notice in Figure 3-9 that all databases, including the ones we just created, have a one-day retention time. Data retention time (in days) is the same as the Time Travel number of days and specifies the number of days for which the underlying data is retained after deletion, and for which the CLONE and UNDROP commands can be performed on the database.

	name	is_default	is_current	origin	owner	comment	options	retention_time
1	DEMO3A_DB	N	N		SYSADMIN	Permanent		1
2	DEMO3B_DB	N	Y		SYSADMIN	Transient D	TRANSIENT	1
3	SNOWFLAKE	N	N	SNOWFLAK				1
4	SNOWFLAKE_SAMPLE_DATA	N	N	SFC_SAMPL	ACCOUNTAD	Provided by		1

Figure 3-9. Results of the SHOW DATABASES command

We can change the data retention time for a permanent database but not for a transient one. We can change the retention time to up to 90 days for permanent databases, assuming we have an Enterprise or higher Snowflake edition. We'll go ahead and change the retention time for our permanent database to 10 days by using the ALTER DATABASE command. Be sure to change your role back to SYSADMIN before issuing the following commands:

```
USE ROLE SYSADMIN;
ALTER DATABASE DEMO3A_DB
SET DATA_RETENTION_TIME_IN_DAYS=10;
```

We just changed the data retention time for the DEMO3A_DB database. Let's see what happens if we attempt to change the data retention time for a transient database:

```
USE ROLE SYSADMIN;
ALTER DATABASE DEMO3B_DB
SET DATA_RETENTION_TIME_IN_DAYS=10;
```

If you run the previous statements, you'll receive an error telling you that the value 10 is an invalid value for the DATA_RETENTION_TIME_IN_DAYS parameter. That is because a transient database can have a maximum data retention time of one day. You could change the retention time to zero days, but then you wouldn't be able to CLONE or UNDROP that database.

We'll be covering tables in more detail in a later section, but for now, it is important to mention a few things about tables as they relate to permanent versus transient databases.

Snowflake uses a mixed approach when it comes to permanent databases but not transient databases. Permanent databases are not limited to the different types of objects that can be stored within them. For example, you can store transient tables within a permanent database but you cannot store permanent tables within a transient database. As a reminder, transient tables are designed to hold transitory data that doesn't need the same level of protection and recovery as permanent tables but does need to be maintained beyond a session.

Here is an example of creating a table in our transient database:

```
USE ROLE SYSADMIN;
CREATE OR REPLACE TABLE DEMO3B_DB.PUBLIC.SUMMARY
   (CASH_AMT number,
    RECEIVABLES_AMT number,
    CUSTOMER_AMT number);
```

Notice that we didn't specify the type of table as either permanent or transient. By default, Snowflake creates a permanent table in a database unless you indicate otherwise when you are creating the table. The exception would be when you are creating a table within a transient database. In that case, the table would also have to be transient.

By default, all tables created in a transient schema are transient. We can see that is the case by using the SHOW TABLES command, which gives us the result shown in Figure 3-10 for the table we just created.

	name	database_name	schema_name	kind
1	SUMMARY	DEMO3B_DB	PUBLIC	TRANSIENT

Figure 3-10. Result of using the SHOW TABLES command

There is no limit to the number of database objects, schemas, and databases that can be created within a Snowflake account.

Each Snowflake account also comes with certain databases, schemas, and tables already included, as shown in Figure 3-11. The following two databases initially come with a Snowflake account:

- SNOWFLAKE database
- SNOWFLAKE_SAMPLE_DATA database

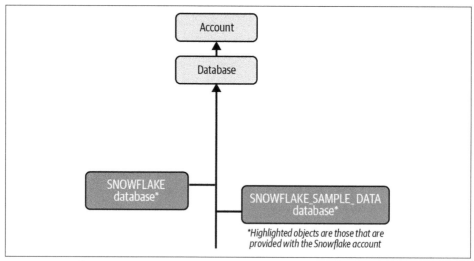

Figure 3-11. The objects hierarchy for a Snowflake database

The SNOWFLAKE database is owned by Snowflake Inc. and is a system-defined, read-only, shared database which provides object metadata and usage metrics about your account. Unlike the SNOWFLAKE_SAMPLE_DATA database imported into your account at the time of setup, the SNOWFLAKE database cannot be deleted from your account.

 While using the SYSADMIN role, we are not able to see the SNOWFLAKE database because, by default, the SNOWFLAKE database is shown only to those using the ACCOUNTADMIN role. However, that privilege can be granted to other roles.

If you signed up for your Snowflake trial account prior to 2022, your account may also have included the UTIL_DB database and DEMO_DB database, also imported into your account at the time of setup. These two databases can be dropped from your Snowflake account if you want.

Upon first look, the SNOWFLAKE_SAMPLE_DATA database appears to be something similar to what you might create in your Snowflake account. However, the sample database is actually one that has been shared from the Snowflake SFC_SAMPLES account and the database is read-only in your account, which means that no Data Definition Language (DDL) commands can be executed on that database. In other words, database objects cannot be added, dropped, or altered within the sample database. In addition, no Data Manipulation Language (DML) commands for actions such as cloning can be performed on the tables. You can, however, view the sample database and execute queries on the tables.

We'll be using the SNOWFLAKE_SAMPLE_DATA database in some of our examples in this chapter. In Chapter 10 we'll be learning about shared databases, but for now what is important to know is that while we don't incur any storage costs for the shared sample database, we do need a running virtual warehouse to run queries, so there will be an associated compute cost for running those queries on the Snowflake sample database.

Even though it may be obvious, one important consideration for how to architect your solution and whether to choose permanent or transient objects for storing data is that there is a monetary cost for storing data in Snowflake, as well as performance implications. We'll discuss both of those in more detail in later chapters.

> Neither of the databases that come automatically with a Snowflake account, including the SNOWFLAKE account, will result in data storage charges for you.

Creating and Managing Snowflake Schemas

When we created databases, we didn't have to specify the account, because we can only operate in one account at a time. But when we create a schema, we need to let Snowflake know which database we want to use. If we don't specify a particular database, Snowflake will use the one that is active.

There are different ways to create a schema that will achieve the same end result. Following are two examples that accomplish the same thing. In this example, the USE command lets Snowflake know for which database the schema will be created:

```
USE ROLE SYSADMIN; USE DATABASE DEMO3A_DB;
CREATE OR REPLACE SCHEMA BANKING;
```

In this example, we simply use the fully qualified schema name:

```
USE ROLE SYSADMIN;
CREATE OR REPLACE SCHEMA DEMO3A_DB.BANKING;
```

If we use the SHOW SCHEMAS command as demonstrated in Figure 3-12, we notice that the retention time of the new schema also has a retention time of 10 days, just like the database in which it was created, rather than the default one-day retention.

	created_on	name	is_default	is_current	database_name	owner	comment	options	retention_time
1	3.409 -0700	BANKING	N	Y	DEMO3A_DB	SYSADMIN			10
2	4.320 -0700	INFORMATION_SCHEMA	N	N	DEMO3A_DB		Views describing the contents of schemas in this database		10
3	4.799 -0700	PUBLIC	N	N	DEMO3A_DB	SYSADMIN			10

Figure 3-12. Results of the SHOW SCHEMAS command

However, we can always change the retention time to one day for the schema:

```
USE ROLE SYSADMIN;
ALTER SCHEMA DEMO3A_DB.BANKING
SET DATA_RETENTION_TIME_IN_DAYS=1;
```

Now run the SHOW SCHEMAS command again and you'll see the retention time has been changed for the BANKING schema.

In the previous section, we created a SUMMARY table in the DEMO3B_DB.PUBLIC schema. Let's assume we've now decided we want that table to exist in a different schema. How do we achieve that? First we'll create the new schema, if it doesn't exist, and then we'll rename the table with the newly created schema:

```
USE ROLE SYSADMIN;
CREATE OR REPLACE SCHEMA DEMO3B_DB.BANKING;
ALTER TABLE DEMO3B_DB.PUBLIC.SUMMARY
RENAME TO DEMO3B_DB.BANKING.SUMMARY;
```

 Just like databases, schemas can be either permanent or transient, with the default being permanent. And just like databases, the same SQL commands are available to us. However, for schemas we have something unique, called a *managed access schema*. In a managed access schema, the schema owner manages grants on the objects within a schema, such as tables and views, but doesn't have any of the USAGE, SELECT, or DROP privileges on the objects.

The following code demonstrates how to create a schema with managed access:

```
USE ROLE SYSADMIN; USE DATABASE DEMO3A_DB;
CREATE OR REPLACE SCHEMA MSCHEMA WITH MANAGED ACCESS;
```

Now when you run the SHOW SCHEMAS command, you'll notice that MANAGED ACCESS will be displayed under the options column for the schema named MSCHEMA (as shown in Figure 3-13).

	name ...	is_default	is_current	database_nam	owner	comment	options
1	BANKING	N	N	DEMO3A_DB	SYSADMIN		
2	INFORMATION_SCHEMA	N	N	DEMO3A_DB		Views desc	
3	MSCHEMA	N	Y	DEMO3A_DB	SYSADMIN		MANAGED ACCESS
4	PUBLIC	N	N	DEMO3A_DB	SYSADMIN		

Figure 3-13. Results of the SHOW SCHEMAS command on a schema with managed access

As we will see in Chapter 5, for regular schemas, the object owner role can grant object access to other roles and can also grant those roles the ability to manage grants for the object. However, in managed access schemas, object owners are unable to issue grant privileges. Instead, only the schema owner or a role with the MANAGE GRANTS privilege assigned to it can manage the grant privileges.

 The SECURITYADMIN and ACCOUNTADMIN roles inherently have the MANAGE GRANTS privilege. Thus, both roles can manage the grant privileges on all managed schemas.

Two database schemas, as shown in Figure 3-14, are included in every database that is created: INFORMATION_SCHEMA and PUBLIC. The PUBLIC schema is the default schema and can be used to create any other objects, whereas the INFORMATION_SCHEMA is a special schema for the system that contains views and table functions which provide access to the metadata for the database and account. The INFORMATION_SCHEMA will be discussed in the next section.

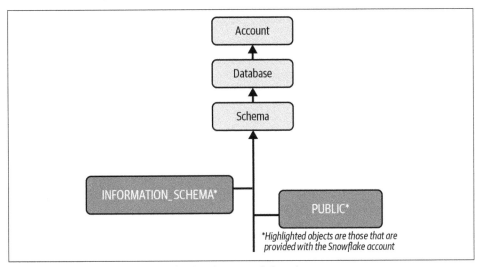

Figure 3-14. The objects hierarchy for the Snowflake schema

INFORMATION_SCHEMA

As we just learned, the Snowflake INFORMATION_SCHEMA is included within every database created in Snowflake. The INFORMATION_SCHEMA, also known as the Data Dictionary, includes metadata information about the objects within the database as well as account-level objects such as roles. In Chapter 8, we'll explore INFORMATION_SCHEMA table functions, which can be used to return historical information and account usage information. For now, we'll be exploring INFORMATION_SCHEMA database views in a little more detail.

More than 20 system-defined views are included in every INFORMA-TION_SCHEMA. These views can be divided into two categories: account views and database views.

INFORMATION_SCHEMA account views include the following:

APPLICABLE_ROLES
Displays one row for each role grant

DATABASES
Displays one row for each database defined in your account

ENABLED_ROLES
Displays one row for each currently enabled role in the session

INFORMATION_SCHEMA_CATALOG_NAME
Displays the name of the database in which the INFORMATION_SCHEMA resides

LOAD_HISTORY
Displays one row for each file loaded into tables using the COPY INTO <table> command, and returns history for all data loaded in the past 14 days *except* for data loaded using Snowpipe

REPLICATION_DATABASES
Displays one row for each primary and secondary database (i.e., a database for which replication has been enabled) in your organization

You may want to look at what is within each of these views. You'll notice that for some of them, all views in the account contain the same information. Try the following two SQL statements, one at a time:

```
SELECT * FROM SNOWFLAKE_SAMPLE_DATA.INFORMATION_SCHEMA.DATABASES;
SELECT * FROM DEMO3A_DB.INFORMATION_SCHEMA.DATABASES;
```

You'll notice the results are the same for each statement, as shown in Figure 3-15.

	DATABASE_NAME	DATABASE_OWNER	IS_TRANSIENT	COMMENT
1	DEMO3A_DB	SYSADMIN	NO	Permanent Database for Chapter 3 Exercises
2	DEMO3B_DB	SYSADMIN	YES	Transient Database for Chapter 3 Exercises
3	SNOWFLAKE_SAMPLE_DATA	ACCOUNTADMIN	NO	Provided by Snowflake during account provisioning

Figure 3-15. INFORMATION_SCHEMA account views return the same result regardless of the database selected

Now try the following two SQL statements, one at a time:

```
SELECT * FROM SNOWFLAKE_SAMPLE_DATA.INFORMATION_SCHEMA.APPLICABLE_ROLES;
SELECT * FROM DEMO3A_DB.INFORMATION_SCHEMA.APPLICABLE_ROLES;
```

Again you'll notice the results are the same for each statement. For all the INFOR-MATION_SCHEMA account views, you'll receive the same information no matter which database INFORMATION_SCHEMA you query.

Now let's take a look at the INFORMATION_SCHEMA database views. We'll see in the query results that the INFORMATION_SCHEMA database views will return results specific to a database.

INFORMATION_SCHEMA database views include the following views:

COLUMNS
Displays one row for each column in the tables defined in the specified (or current) database.

EXTERNAL_TABLES
Displays one row for each external table in the specified (or current) database.

FILE_FORMATS
Displays one row for each file format defined in the specified (or current) database.

FUNCTIONS
Displays one row for each UDF or external function defined in the specified (or current) database.

OBJECT_PRIVILEGES
Displays one row for each access privilege granted for all objects defined in your account.

PIPES
Displays one row for each pipe defined in the specified (or current) database.

PROCEDURES
Displays one row for each stored procedure defined for the specified (or current) database.

REFERENTIAL_CONSTRAINTS
Displays one row for each referential integrity constraint defined in the specified (or current) database.

SCHEMATA
Displays one row for each schema in the specified (or current) database.

SEQUENCES
Displays one row for each sequence defined in the specified (or current) database.

STAGES

Displays one row for each stage defined in the specified (or current) database.

TABLE_CONSTRAINTS

Displays one row for each referential integrity constraint defined for the tables in the specified (or current) database.

TABLE_PRIVILEGES

Displays one row for each table privilege that has been granted to each role in the specified (or current) database.

TABLE_STORAGE_METRICS

Displays table-level storage utilization information, includes table metadata, and displays the number of storage types billed for each table. Rows are maintained in this view until the corresponding tables are no longer billed for any storage, regardless of various states that the data in the tables may be in (i.e., active, Time Travel, fail-safe, or retained for clones).

TABLES

Displays one row for each table and view in the specified (or current) database.

USAGE_PRIVILEGES

Displays one row for each privilege defined for sequences in the specified (or current) database.

VIEWS

Displays one row for each view in the specified (or current) database.

There are different ways to look at database-specific metadata in Snowflake, some of which use the INFORMATION_SCHEMA database view. If you try each of the following two commands, you'll see that there are two different ways we can get the information about schemas within the Snowflake sample database:

```
SELECT *  FROM SNOWFLAKE_SAMPLE_DATA.INFORMATION_SCHEMA.SCHEMATA;
SHOW SCHEMAS IN DATABASE SNOWFLAKE_SAMPLE_DATA;
```

One thing you will notice is that the metadata contained with the INFORMATION_SCHEMA is much more complete, with several more columns of information, than when you simply use the `SHOW SCHEMAS` command.

Let's drill down further to look at the table privileges in the two databases we previously created. As a reminder, we created a table in the second database but have not yet created any tables in the first database. So, what happens if we try to get information about the tables in each database? Run each of the two statements separately to find out:

```
SELECT * FROM DEMO3A_DB.INFORMATION_SCHEMA.TABLE_PRIVILEGES;
SELECT * FROM DEMO3B_DB.INFORMATION_SCHEMA.TABLE_PRIVILEGES;
```

You will notice that one row was returned for the second query and no rows were returned for the first query. The reason is because there are no tables in the first database; thus, there will be no table privileges.

The INFORMATION_SCHEMA, one of the two schemas that are included with every Snowflake database, has a great many uses. Among other things, the INFOR-MATION_SCHEMA provides a great deal of information about an account's object metadata and usage metrics. There is also another place within Snowflake where object metadata and usage metrics are stored, which we'll cover in the next section.

ACCOUNT_USAGE Schema

The SNOWFLAKE database, viewable by the ACCOUNTADMIN by default, includes an ACCOUNT_USAGE schema that is very similar to the INFORMA-TION_SCHEMA, but with three differences:

- The SNOWFLAKE database ACCOUNT_USAGE schema includes records for dropped objects whereas the INFORMATION_SCHEMA does not.

- The ACCOUNT_USAGE schema has a longer retention time for historical usage data. Whereas the INFORMATION_SCHEMA has data available ranging from seven days to six months, the ACCOUNT_USAGE view retains historical data for one year.

- Most views in the INFORMATION_SCHEMA have no latency, but the latency time for ACCOUNT_USAGE could range from 45 minutes to three hours. Specifically, for the INFORMATION_SCHEMA, there may be a one- to two-hour delay in updating storage-related statistics for ACTIVE_BYTES, TIME_TRAVEL_BYTES, FAILSAFE_BYTES, and RETAINED_FOR_CLONE_BYTES.

One of the common uses for the ACCOUNT_USAGE schema is to keep track of credits used over time by each virtual warehouse in your account (month to date). Change your role to ACCOUNTADMIN and execute the following statements:

```
USE ROLE ACCOUNTADMIN;USE DATABASE SNOWFLAKE;USE SCHEMA ACCOUNT_USAGE;
USE WAREHOUSE COMPUTE_WH;
SELECT start_time::date AS USAGE_DATE, WAREHOUSE_NAME,
        SUM(credits_used) AS TOTAL_CREDITS_CONSUMED
FROM warehouse_metering_history
WHERE start_time >= date_trunc(Month, current_date)
GROUP BY 1,2
ORDER BY 2,1;
```

The SNOWFLAKE database, which includes the ACCOUNT_USAGE schema, is only available to the ACCOUNTADMIN role, unless the ACCOUNTADMIN grants imported privileges from the underlying share to another role. We'll explore the ACCOUNT_USAGE schema in more detail in future chapters, especially in

Chapter 8 and Chapter 9 when we learn more about improving performance and reducing costs. For now, though, the results of the code you just executed should look something like what is shown in Figure 3-16. You'll notice that there are credits consumed by the COMPUTE_WH virtual warehouse and by cloud services.

WAREHOUSE_NAME ···	TOTAL_CREDITS_CONSUMED
CLOUD_SERVICES_ONLY	0.105878667
COMPUTE_WH	0.278027222

Figure 3-16. Credits consumed by the COMPUTE_WH virtual warehouse and cloud services

Be sure to change your role back to SYSADMIN before continuing on to the next section.

Schema Object Hierarchy

Thus far, we've learned about the schema object and explored the two schemas that come with each Snowflake database. A look back at Figure 3-14 shows us the schema object hierarchy that exists above the schema object and includes the database object and the account. Next, we'll want to explore the Snowflake objects below the schema in the hierarchy.

Many objects exist within a Snowflake schema object, including tables, views, stages, policies, stored procedures, UDFs, and more. In the next sections, we'll take a closer look at several of these Snowflake objects. While we will explore some of these Snowflake objects in detail, the explanations in this chapter are meant to be foundational; we'll dive deeper into these objects throughout many of the subsequent chapters.

Introduction to Snowflake Tables

As previously mentioned, all Snowflake data is stored in tables. In addition to permanent and transient tables, it is also possible to create hybrid, temporary, and external tables, as shown in Figure 3-17. Snowflake hybrid tables support the new Unistore workload and are described in more detail in Chapter 12. Snowflake temporary tables only exist within the session in which they were created and are frequently used for storing transitory data such as ETL data. Snowflake external tables give you the ability to directly process or query your data that exists elsewhere without ingesting it into Snowflake, including data that lives in a data lake.

One new way you can work with your external data is by integrating Apache Hive metastores with Snowflake. You can use the new Hive Metastore connector to connect to your Hadoop environments. The Snowflake support is also available if you are using newer technologies, such as Delta Lake or Apache Iceberg.

Delta Lake is a table format on a data lake Spark-based platform. A Snowflake external table can be created which will reference your Delta Lake cloud storage locations.

Apache Iceberg tables have addressed many of the challenges associated with object stores, which has made this a popular choice as a data lake. Whereas Hive keeps track of data at the folder level, Iceberg keeps track of a complete list of all files within a table using a persistent tree structure. Keeping track of the data at the folder level can lead to performance problems, and there is the potential for data to appear as if it were missing when file list operations are performed at the folder level. The Apache Iceberg table format is used by many leading technology companies, including Apple, AWS, Expedia, LinkedIn, and Netflix.

In June 2022, Snowflake announced a new table type, dynamic tables (previously referred to as materialized tables). Dynamic tables allow users to declaratively specify the pipelines where transformations can occur. Snowflake then handles the incremental refresh to materialize the data. In this way, Snowflake dynamic tables automatically refresh as new data streams in. Dynamic tables have some of the characteristics of materialized views and tasks and can be thought of as the logical progression of streams. This new dynamic table type gives Snowflake users the ability to dramatically improve their incremental materialization experience.

Like databases and schemas, we can use the CREATE, ALTER, DROP, and SHOW TABLES commands. In addition, we'll need to use INSERT INTO or COPY INTO to place data into a table. For Snowflake tables we create, we can also use the TRUNCATE or DELETE command to remove data from a table but not remove the table object itself.

> TRUNCATE and DELETE are different in that TRUNCATE also clears table load history metadata while DELETE retains the metadata.

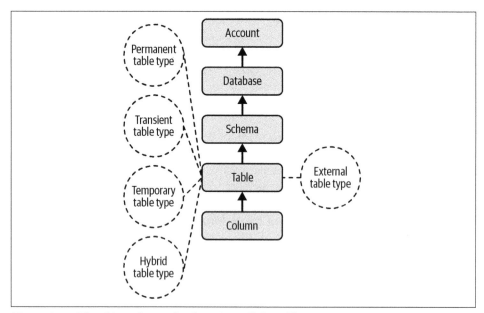

Figure 3-17. The objects hierarchy for a Snowflake table

As we saw in "Creating and Managing Snowflake Databases" on page 54, Snowflake assumes it should create a permanent table if the table type is not specified, unless the table is created within a transient database.

Transient tables are unique to Snowflake and have characteristics of both permanent and temporary tables. Transient tables are designed for transitory data that needs to be maintained beyond a session but doesn't need the same level of data recovery as permanent tables. As a result, the data storage costs for a transient table would be less than for a permanent table. One of the biggest differences between transient tables and permanent tables is that the fail-safe service is not provided for transient tables.

It isn't possible to change a permanent table to a transient table by using the ALTER command, because the TRANSIENT property is set at table creation time. Likewise, a transient table cannot be converted to a permanent table. If you would like to make a change to a transient or permanent table type, you'll need to create a new table, use the COPY GRANTS clause, and then copy the data. Using the COPY GRANTS clause will ensure that the table will inherit any explicit access privileges.

It was mentioned that the default for creating tables is that a permanent table would be created unless otherwise specified. If it makes sense to have new tables automatically created as a transient type by default, you can first create a transient database or schema. As we saw in "Creating and Managing Snowflake Databases" on page 54, all tables created afterward will be transient rather than permanent.

Transient tables can be accessed by other users who have the necessary permissions. However, temporary tables exist only within the session in which they are created. This means they are not available to other users and cannot be cloned. Temporary tables have many uses, including being used for ETL data and for session-specific data needs.

A temporary table, as well as the data within it, is no longer accessible once the session ends. During the time a temporary table exists, it does count toward storage costs; therefore, it is a good practice to drop a temporary table once you no longer need it.

Table 3-1 summarizes some characteristics of the different Snowflake tables.

Table 3-1. Snowflake table characteristics

Characteristics	Permanent table	Transient table	Temporary table	External table
Persistence	Until explicitly dropped	Until explicitly dropped	Remainder of session	Until explicitly dropped
Time Travel retention (days)	0–90 [a]	0 or 1	0 or 1	0
Fail-safe period (days)	7	0	0	0
Cloning possible?	Yes	Yes	Yes	No
Create views possible?	Yes	Yes	Yes	Yes

[a] In Enterprise Edition and above, 0–90 days. In Standard Edition, 0 or 1 day.

Interestingly, you can create a temporary table that has the same name as an existing table in the same schema since the temporary table is session based. No errors or warnings will be given. Thus, it is a best practice to give temporary tables unique names to avoid unexpected problems given that the temporary table takes precedence.

We will now create some tables that we'll use later in the chapter. Make sure you are using the SYSADMIN role to create the tables:

```
USE ROLE SYSADMIN; USE DATABASE DEMO3A_DB;
CREATE OR REPLACE SCHEMA BANKING;
CREATE OR REPLACE TABLE CUSTOMER_ACCT
    (Customer_Account int, Amount int, transaction_ts timestamp);
CREATE OR REPLACE TABLE CASH
    (Customer_Account int, Amount int, transaction_ts timestamp);
CREATE OR REPLACE TABLE RECEIVABLES
    (Customer_Account int, Amount int, transaction_ts timestamp);
```

After creating this table, the active role is the SYSADMIN role, the active database is DEMO3A_DB, and the active schema is BANKING. We specified the database with the USE command. We then created the BANKING schema, which made DEMO3A_DB.BANKING the default schema. Thus, a newly created table will be located within the BANKING schema if you create a new table without specifically using a different namespace. Let's try that now:

```
USE ROLE SYSADMIN;
CREATE OR REPLACE TABLE NEWTABLE
    (Customer_Account int,
    Amount int,
    transaction_ts timestamp);
```

Now navigate back by clicking the Home icon in the upper-left corner, then select Data → Databases from the menu. Use the drop-down menu on the right to expand the BANKING schema and the Tables option to see a list of all the tables in the BANKING schema in the DEMO3A_DB database. In Figure 3-18, we can see that NEWTABLE was created in the active namespace.

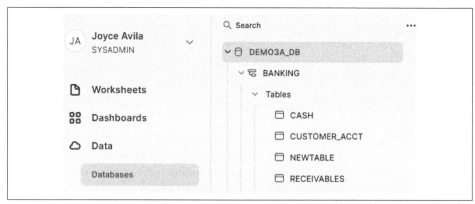

Figure 3-18. A list of the tables in the BANKING schema of the DEMO3A_DB database

Let's now drop the new table we just created by using the fully qualified table name. Navigate back to the *Chapter3 Creating Database Objects* worksheet. Make sure the SYSADMIN role is the current role. In the upper-left corner, you'll see that you are currently on the Worksheets tab. Click the Databases tab (which is circled in Figure 3-19).

Figure 3-19. The Databases tab within the Chapter3 Creating Objects worksheet

After clicking the Databases tab, you can expand the objects until you are able to see the NEWTABLE table in the BANKING schema for the DEMO3A_DB database (as shown in Figure 3-20).

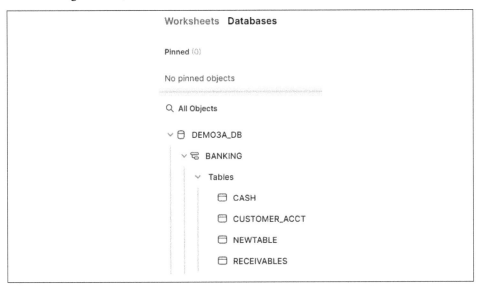

Figure 3-20. The NEWTABLE table within the BANKING schema of the DEMO3A_DB database

In the worksheet, enter **DROP TABLE** with a space after it. Then click the NEWTABLE table on the left and select the "Place name in SQL" option. You'll notice that the fully qualified name of the table is added to the SQL statement (as shown in Figure 3-21). Put a semicolon at the end, if you want, and then execute the statement.

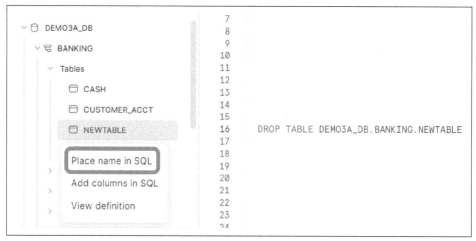

Figure 3-21. Selecting the fully qualified table name

We weren't required to use the fully qualified table name, because we were in the active space where we wanted to drop the table. We could have just used the command DROP TABLE NEWTABLE; instead of using the fully qualified name. However, it is a best practice to use a table's fully qualified name or to include the USE command, which achieves the same goal.

Creating and Managing Views

Along with tables, Snowflake views are the primary objects maintained in database schemas, as shown in Figure 3-22. Views are of two types: materialized and nonmaterialized. Whenever the term *view* is mentioned and the type is not specified, it is understood that it is a nonmaterialized view.

 I've mentioned the importance of using fully qualified names for tables. Using a fully qualified name for the table is even more important when creating views, because the connected reference will be invalid if the namespace of the base table is not used and this table or the view is moved to a different schema or database later.

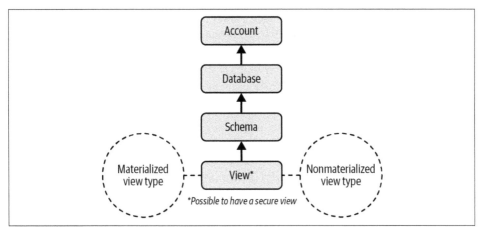

Figure 3-22. The objects hierarchy for the Snowflake view

A view is considered to be a virtual table created by a query expression; something like a window into a database. Let's create a new view by selecting one column from the Snowflake sample data:

```
USE ROLE SYSADMIN;
CREATE OR REPLACE VIEW DEMO3B_DB.PUBLIC.NEWVIEW AS
SELECT CC_NAME
FROM (SELECT * FROM SNOWFLAKE_SAMPLE_DATA.TPCDS_SF100TCL.CALL_CENTER);
```

One purpose of views is to display selected rows and columns from one or more tables. This is a way to provide some security by only exposing certain data to specific users. Views can provide even more security by creating a specific *secure view* of either a nonmaterialized or materialized view. We'll dive deeper into secure views when we discuss implementing account security and protections in Chapter 7. We'll also learn more about secure views in Chapter 10.

It's important to remember that creating materialized views requires Snowflake Enterprise Edition. Let's create a materialized view using the same query as before:

```
USE ROLE SYSADMIN;
CREATE OR REPLACE MATERIALIZED VIEW DEMO3B_DB.PUBLIC.NEWVIEW_MVW AS
SELECT CC_NAME
FROM (SELECT * FROM SNOWFLAKE_SAMPLE_DATA.TPCDS_SF100TCL.CALL_CENTER);
```

You can run a SHOW VIEWS command and both views will be returned in the results. If you run a SHOW MATERIALIZED VIEWS command, only the materialized view result will be returned. You'll need to make sure the correct schema is selected from the drop-down menu or include the USE command in the statement:

```
USE SCHEMA DEMO3B_DB.PUBLIC;
SHOW VIEWS;
```

If you run a SELECT * command for each view, you'll notice that the results are identical. That is because we haven't really used a materialized view for its intended purpose. Unlike a regular view, a materialized view object gets periodically refreshed with the data from the base table. Thus, it is illogical to consider using a materialized view for the Snowflake sample database because the Snowflake sample database cannot be updated with new data.

Also, the query to retrieve a single column is not one typically used for materialized views. Materialized views are generally used to aggregate as well as filter data so that the results of resource-intensive operations can be stored in a materialized view for improved data performance. The performance improvement is especially good when that same query is used frequently.

Snowflake uses a background service to automatically update materialized views. As a result, data accessed through materialized views is always current, regardless of the amount of DML that has been performed on the base table. Snowflake will update the materialized view or use the up-to-date portions of the materialized view and retrieve newer data from the base table if a query is run before the materialized view is up to date.

To see this in action, we're going to create a materialized view. We will revisit the materialized view later in the chapter to see for ourselves that it contains up-to-date information:

```
CREATE OR REPLACE MATERIALIZED VIEW DEMO3B_DB.BANKING.SUMMARY_MVW AS
SELECT * FROM (SELECT * FROM DEMO3B_DB.BANKING.SUMMARY);
```

Let's also create a nonmaterialized view, for comparison:

```
CREATE OR REPLACE VIEW DEMO3B_DB.BANKING.SUMMARY_VW AS
SELECT * FROM (SELECT * FROM DEMO3B_DB.BANKING.SUMMARY);
```

As you would expect, views are read-only. Thus, it isn't possible to use the INSERT, UPDATE, or DELETE command on views. Further, Snowflake doesn't allow users to truncate views. While it is not possible to execute DML commands on a view, you can use a subquery within a DML statement to update the underlying base table. An example might be something like this:

```
DELETE FROM <Base_Table> WHERE <Column_Name> >
    (SELECT AVG <Column> FROM <View_Name>);
```

Another thing to be aware of is that a view definition cannot be updated with the ALTER VIEW command. However, the ALTER MATERIALIZED VIEW command can be used to rename a materialized view, to add or replace comments, to modify the view to be a secure view, and much more. The SHOW and DESCRIBE commands are also available for views.

If you wanted to change something structural about the view, you would have to re-create it with a new definition.

 Changes to a source table's structure do not automatically propagate to views. For example, dropping a table column won't drop the column in the view.

There are many considerations when deciding between a regular view and a materialized view. One consideration beyond whether to create a regular view or a materialized view is whether to use ETL to materialize the data set in a table.

As a general rule, it is best to use a nonmaterialized view when the results of the view change frequently and the query isn't so complex and expensive to rerun. Regular views do incur compute costs but not storage costs. The compute cost to refresh the view and the storage cost will need to be weighed against the benefits of a materialized view when the results of a view change often.

 Generally, it is beneficial to use a materialized view when the query consumes a lot of resources, as well as when the results of the view are used often and the underlying table doesn't change frequently. Also, if a table needs to be clustered in multiple ways, a materialized view can be used with a cluster key that is different from the cluster key of the base table.

There are some limitations for materialized views. For example, a materialized view can query only a single table, and joins are not supported. It is recommended that you consult the Snowflake documentation for more detail on materialized view limitations.

 One thing to remember is that we are using the SYSADMIN role currently and we're creating the views using that role. Someone who doesn't have the SYSDAMIN role will need to have assigned to them the privileges on the schema, the database objects in the underlying table(s), and the view itself if they are to work with the materialized view.

Introduction to Snowflake Stages: File Format Included

There are two types of Snowflake stages: internal and external. *Stages* are Snowflake objects that point to a storage location, either internal to Snowflake or on external cloud storage. Internal stage objects can be either *named* stages or a *user* or *table* stage. The `temporary` keyword can be used to create a session-based named stage object.

In most cases, the storage is permanent while the stage object, a pointer to the storage location, may be temporary or dropped at any time. Snowflake stages are often used as an intermediate step to load files to Snowflake tables or to unload data from Snowflake tables into files.

Snowflake permanent and internal temporary stages are used to store data files internally, on cloud storage managed by Snowflake, whereas external stages reference data files that are stored in a location outside of Snowflake. Outside locations, whether private/protected or public, like Amazon S3 buckets, Google Cloud Storage buckets, and Microsoft Azure containers, are supported by Snowflake and can be used in external stages.

Each Snowflake user has a stage for storing files which is accessible only by that user. The User stage can be referenced by @~. Likewise, each Snowflake table has a stage allocated for storing files, and each table stage can be referenced by using @%*<name of table>*.

 Table stages are useful if multiple users need to access the files and those files only need to be copied into a single table, whereas a user stage is best when the files only need to be accessed by one user but will need to be copied into multiple tables.

User and table stages cannot be altered or dropped, and neither of these stages supports setting the file format. But you can specify the format and copy options at the time the `COPY INTO` command is issued. Additionally, table stages do not support transforming the data while loading it. A table stage is tied to the table itself and is not a separate database object. To perform actions on the table stage, you must have been granted the table ownership role.

The command to list a user stage is `ls@~;` or `LIST @~;`. We'll dive into stages in more depth when we discuss data loading and unloading in Chapter 6.

User stages and table stages, both of which are types of internal stages, are automatically provided for each Snowflake account. In addition to user and table stages, internal named stages can also be created (see Figure 3-23). Internal named stages are database objects, which means they can be used not just by one user but by any user who has been granted a role with the appropriate privileges.

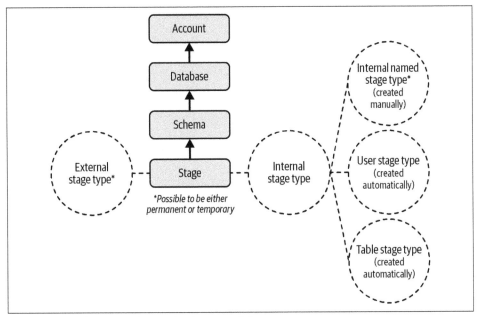

Figure 3-23. The objects hierarchy for Snowflake stages

Internal named stages and external stages can be created as either a permanent or a temporary stage. When a temporary external stage is dropped, no data files are removed, because those files are stored external to Snowflake. Only the stage object is dropped. For a temporary internal stage, however, the data and stage are both dropped and the files are not recoverable. It is important to note that the behavior just described is not limited to temporary stage objects. Both temporary and permanent stages, internal or external, have the same characteristics described.

When using stages, we can use file formats to store all the format information we need for loading data from files to tables. The default file format is CSV. However, you can create file formats for other formats such as JSON, Avro, ORC, Parquet, and XML. There are also optional parameters that can be included when you create a file format. Here we are creating a very basic file format, without any optional parameters, for loading JSON data into a stage:

```
USE ROLE SYSADMIN; USE DATABASE DEMO3B_DB;
CREATE OR REPLACE FILE FORMAT FF_JSON TYPE = JSON;
```

Once we create the file format, we can make use of it when creating an internal named stage:

```
USE DATABASE DEMO3B_DB; USE SCHEMA BANKING;
CREATE OR REPLACE TEMPORARY STAGE BANKING_STG FILE_FORMAT = FF_JSON;
```

We introduced file formats briefly here by creating a file format using SQL in a Snowflake worksheet. We'll explore file formats much more in Chapter 6, including using the Snowsight web UI to create file formats.

Table 3-2 summarizes some characteristics of the different Snowflake stages.

Table 3-2. Snowflake stage characteristics

Characteristics	Named stage[a]	User stage[a]	Table stage[a]	External stage
Stage is a database object?	Yes	No	No	Yes
Default type	Permanent	Permanent	Permanent	Permanent
Temporary type possible?	Yes	No	No	Yes
Creation method	User-created	Automatic	Automatic	User-created
How to reference	@<stage_name>	@~	@%<table_name>	<stage_name>
Drop/alter stage possible?	Yes	No	No	Yes
Data actually stored in stage?	Yes	No	No	No
Supports setting file formats?	Yes	No	No	Yes
Directory tables possible?	Yes	No	No	Yes

[a] Internal stage

> The data is always in an encrypted state, whether it is in flight to an internal named stage or at rest while stored in a Snowflake database table.

Extending SQL with Stored Procedures and UDFs

To extend SQL capabilities in Snowflake, you can create stored procedures and UDFs to achieve functionalities not possible with Snowflake's built-in functions. Both stored procedures and UDFs encapsulate and return a single value (scalar). User-defined table functions (UDTFs) can return multiple values (tabular) whereas stored procedures can return only a single value. You can create Snowflake stored procedures natively using JavaScript or with Snowflake scripting. Additionally, by using Snowpark, you can create Snowflake stored procedures using Java, Python, or Scala. UDFs can be created natively by using SQL, JavaScript, Python, and Java languages. It is possible to create secure UDFs (see Figure 3-24).

The return value for stored procedures is scalar, but procedures can return multiple values if the return type is a variant.

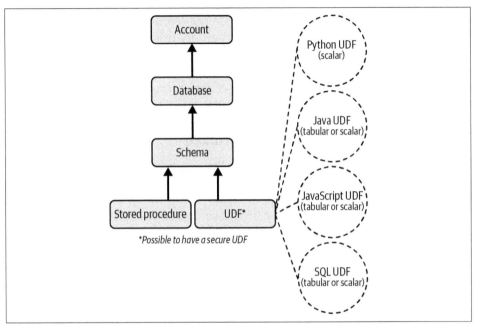

Figure 3-24. The objects hierarchy for Snowflake stored procedures and UDFs

Both stored procedures and UDFs extend SQL capabilities, but there are many differences between the two. One of the most important differences is how they are used.

If you need to perform a database operation such as SELECT, DELETE, or CREATE, you'll need to use a stored procedure. If you want to use a function as part of the SQL statement or expression, or if your output needs to include a value for every input row, you'll want to use a UDF.

A UDF is called as part of the SQL statement, but a stored procedure cannot be called within a SQL statement. Instead, a stored procedure is called as an independent statement using the CALL statement. The CALL statement can call only one stored procedure per statement.

A UDF is required to return a value, and you can use the UDF return value inside your SQL statements. Although not required, a stored procedure is allowed to return a value, but the CALL command doesn't provide a place to store the returned value. The stored procedure also doesn't provide a way to pass it to another operation.

The next two sections provide a total of five examples. The first example is a simple JavaScript UDF that returns a scalar value and the second example is a secure SQL UDF that returns tabular results. Following those are three stored procedures examples: the first example is where an argument is directly passed in; the next example is lengthier and demonstrates the basics of an accounting information system where each banking transaction has a debit and credit entry; the last example is more advanced and combines a stored procedure with a task.

User-Defined Function (UDF): Task Included

UDFs allow you to perform some operations that are not available through the built-in, system-defined functions provided by Snowflake. Snowflake supports four languages for UDFs. Python UDFs are limited to returning scalar results. SQL, JavaScript, and Java UDFs can return either scalar or tabular results.

A SQL UDF evaluates SQL statements and can refer to other UDFs, although a SQL UDF cannot refer to itself either directly or indirectly.

A JavaScript UDF is useful for manipulating variant and JSON data. A JavaScript UDF expression can refer to itself recursively, although it cannot refer to other UDFs. JavaScript UDFs also have size and depth limitations that don't apply to SQL UDFs. We'll see that demonstrated in one of our examples.

JavaScript UDFs have access to the basic standard JavaScript library needed to create arrays, variables, and simple objects. You cannot use math functions or use error handling, because Snowflake does not let you import external libraries. The properties that are available for both JavaScript UDFs and JavaScript procedures can be found by using the following commands:

```
USE ROLE SYSADMIN;
CREATE OR REPLACE DATABASE DEMO3C_DB;
CREATE OR REPLACE FUNCTION JS_PROPERTIES()
RETURNS string LANGUAGE JAVASCRIPT AS
    $$ return Object.getOwnPropertyNames(this); $$;
```

Now let's use the SELECT command to see what is included in the JavaScript UDF properties:

```
SELECT JS_PROPERTIES();
```

Figure 3-25 displays the results of the previous command.

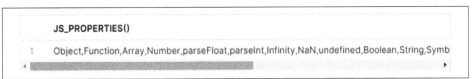

JS_PROPERTIES()
1   Object,Function,Array,Number,parseFloat,parseInt,Infinity,NaN,undefined,Boolean,String,Symb

Figure 3-25. Results of using the SELECT command on the JS_PROPERTIES user-defined function

For our first UDF example, we are going to create a simple JavaScript UDF which returns a scalar result. We mentioned that JavaScript UDFs have size and depth limitations, and we'll be able to demonstrate that in this example:

```
USE ROLE SYSADMIN; USE DATABASE DEMO3C_DB;
CREATE OR REPLACE FUNCTION FACTORIAL(n variant)
RETURNS variant LANGUAGE JAVASCRIPT AS
    'var f=n;
    for (i=n-1; i>0; i--) {
        f=f*i}
    return f';
```

You would expect the result of 120 to be returned when the number 5 is used for the factorial function. Try it now and see:

```
SELECT FACTORIAL(5);
```

 If you use a number greater than 33, you'll receive an error message.

Try finding the result of FACTORIAL(50) and see what happens. If you use the number 50 in the factorial function, you'll receive an error message telling you that the numeric value is out of range (as shown in Figure 3-26).

Numeric value is out of range, error: 50 is too large for factorial function.

Figure 3-26. An error message is received because the number 50 is greater than what can be used with the FACTORIAL function

One thing you'll notice is that when we created the JS_PROPERTIES and FACTORIAL functions we didn't specify a schema to be used. What schema do you think Snowflake used to create the functions? By default, the PUBLIC schema will be used if you don't specify a schema. You can expand the PUBLIC schema of the DEMO3C_DB database to confirm (as shown in Figure 3-27).

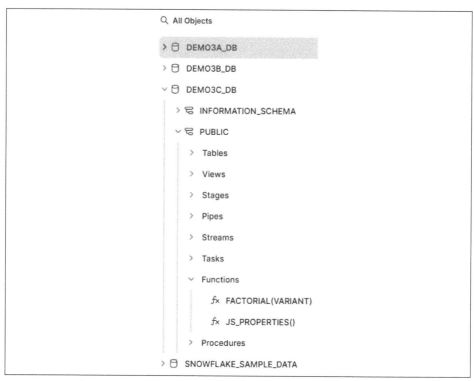

Figure 3-27. The PUBLIC schema was the default schema used when DEMO3C_DB was created

We previously mentioned that it is possible to create secure UDFs. Secure UDFs are the same as nonsecure UDFs, except that they hide the DDL from the consumer of the UDF. Secure UDFs do have limitations on performance functionality due to some optimizations being bypassed. Thus, data privacy versus performance is the consideration because only secure UDFs can be shared. Secure SQL UDFs and secure JavaScript UDFs are both shareable but operate differently and are generally used for different purposes. Secure JavaScript UDFs are often used for data cleansing, address matching, or other data manipulation operations.

Unlike secure JavaScript UDFs, a secure SQL UDF can run queries. For a secure shared UDF, the queries can only be run against the provider's data. When a provider shares a secure UDF with a customer, the cost of data storage for any tables being accessed by the function is paid by the provider and the compute cost is paid by the consumer. There may be shared functions that don't incur storage costs.

In the example created for you, no data storage cost will be incurred because we are using the Snowflake sample data set.

Secure SQL UDTF That Returns Tabular Value (Market Basket Analysis Example)

Market basket analysis is a common use of secure SQL user-defined table functions (UDTFs), and that is what we'll be demonstrating. In our example, the output is aggregated data in which a consumer would like to see how many times other items were sold with their particular item. We wouldn't want the consumer account to have access to our raw sales data, so we'll wrap the SQL statement in a secure UDF and create an input parameter. When the secure UDF is used with an input parameter, the consumer still gets the same results as running the SQL statement directly on the underlying raw data.

We want to use data that is already provided for us in the Snowflake sample database, but there are more records than we need for this demonstration. Let's create a new table and select 100,000 rows from the sample database, which will be more than enough:

```
USE ROLE SYSADMIN;
CREATE OR REPLACE DATABASE DEMO3D_DB;
CREATE OR REPLACE TABLE DEMO3D_DB.PUBLIC.SALES AS
    (SELECT * FROM SNOWFLAKE_SAMPLE_DATA.TPCDS_SF100TCL.WEB_SALES)
LIMIT 100000;
```

Next, we'll run our query directly on the new table. In this instance, we are interested in the product with an SK of 1. We want to know the different items that were sold with this product in the same transaction. We can use this query to find that information:

```
SELECT 1 AS INPUT_ITEM, WS_WEB_SITE_SK AS BASKET_ITEM,
    COUNT (DISTINCT WS_ORDER_NUMBER) BASKETS
FROM DEMO3D_DB.PUBLIC.SALES
WHERE WS_ORDER_NUMBER IN
    (SELECT WS_ORDER_NUMBER
     FROM DEMO3D_DB.PUBLIC.SALES
     WHERE WS_WEB_SITE_SK = 1)
GROUP BY WS_WEB_SITE_SK
ORDER BY 3 DESC, 2;
```

 The results of your query will probably vary slightly from what is shown here, for a few different reasons. First, the underlying sample data set could change. And second, because we've limited the previous results to 10,000 records, your limited data set could be different even if the underlying data set is still the same.

The result of this query shows us the product with an SK of 1 was sold in 5,050 unique transactions within our records. The item with an SK of 31 was sold in the same transaction as the item with an SK of 1 a total of four times. The items with an

SK of 16, 19, 40, 58, 70, and 80 were each sold in the same transaction as the items with an SK of 1 a total of two times each (as shown in Figure 3-28). That isn't a log, though. If, instead, there had been an SK that was sold in high numbers alongside the SK of 1, this could be valuable information for the manufacturers of the product.

	INPUT_ITEM	BASKET_ITEM	BASKETS
1	1	1	5,050
2	1	31	4
3	1	16	2
4	1	19	2
5	1	40	2
6	1	58	2
7	1	70	2
8	1	80	2

Figure 3-28. Results showing how many times an item with an SK of 1 was used in baskets

We might be willing to share those kinds of related sales details with the manufacturers, but we wouldn't want to allow access to the underlying sales data. We can achieve our objectives by creating a secure SQL UDF function:

```
USE ROLE SYSADMIN;
CREATE OR REPLACE SECURE FUNCTION
    DEMO3D_DB.PUBLIC.GET_MKTBASKET(INPUT_WEB_SITE_SK number(38))
RETURNS TABLE (INPUT_ITEM NUMBER(38, 0), BASKET_ITEM NUMBER(38, 0),
            BASKETS NUMBER(38, 0)) AS
'SELECT input_web_site_sk, WS_WEB_SITE_SK as BASKET_ITEM,
        COUNT(DISTINCT WS_ORDER_NUMBER) BASKETS
    FROM DEMO3D_DB.PUBLIC.SALES
    WHERE WS_ORDER_NUMBER IN
        (SELECT WS_ORDER_NUMBER
                FROM DEMO3D_DB.PUBLIC.SALES
                WHERE WS_WEB_SITE_SK = input_web_site_sk)
        GROUP BY ws_web_site_sk
    ORDER BY 3 DESC, 2';
```

If we were to share with another user this secure UDF through a Snowflake consumer account, that user could run the secure UDF without seeing any of the underlying data, table structures, or SQL code. This is the command the owner of the consumer account would use to obtain the results. You can try this command with the number 1 that we used earlier when we queried the table directly, and you'll get the same exact result with the UDF function. You can also try other product SKs:

```
SELECT * FROM TABLE(DEMO3D_DB.PUBLIC.GET_MKTBASKET(1));
```

 Secure UDFs should be used for instances in which data privacy is of concern and you want to limit access to sensitive data. It is important to consider the purpose and necessity of creating a secure UDF and weigh that against the decreased query performance that is likely to result from using a secure UDF.

Stored Procedures

Stored procedures are similar to functions in that they are created once and can be executed many times. Stored procedures allow you to extend Snowflake SQL by combining it with JavaScript in order to include branching and looping, as well as error handling. Stored procedures, which must be written in JavaScript, can be used to automate tasks that require multiple SQL statements performed frequently. Although stored procedures can only be written in JavaScript at this time, SQL stored procedures are now in private preview.

While you can use SELECT statements inside a stored procedure, the results must be used within the stored procedure. If not, only a single value result can be returned. Stored procedures are great for batch actions because a stored procedure runs by itself and, similar to a trigger, can be conditionally tied to database events.

In the first stored procedures example, we are going to pass in an argument to the stored procedure:

```
USE ROLE SYSADMIN;
CREATE OR REPLACE DATABASE DEMO3E_DB;
CREATE OR REPLACE PROCEDURE STOREDPROC1(ARGUMENT1 VARCHAR)
RETURNS string not null
language javascript AS
$$
var INPUT_ARGUMENT1 = ARGUMENT1;
var result = `${INPUT_ARGUMENT1}`
return result;
$$;
```

Now let's call the stored procedure:

```
CALL STOREDPROC1('I really love Snowflake ❄');
```

JavaScript is case sensitive, so make sure you pay close attention when creating the stored procedure.

Figure 3-29 shows the result of passing an argument to the stored procedure.

STOREDPROC1
1 I really love Snowflake ✳

Figure 3-29. Result of passing an argument to the STOREDPROC1 stored procedure

You can use the INFORMATION_SCHEMA to take a look at the information for Snowflake procedures in the database:

```
SELECT * FROM DEMO3E_DB.INFORMATION_SCHEMA.PROCEDURES;
```

In the next stored procedure example, we are demonstrating the very basics of an accounting information system in which tabular results are returned for banking transactions that record debits and credits. If you remember, earlier in the chapter we created the tables needed for this example, so we can just dive right into creating the stored procedure.

We are recording the accounting transactions for a bank that deals with customers giving cash to the bank and getting cash from the bank. We'll keep the accounting portion of the example limited to three types of transactions: deposits, withdrawals, and loan payments.

First we'll want to create a stored procedure for a deposit transaction in which the bank's cash account is debited and the customer account on the bank's balance sheet is credited whenever a customer gives the bank cash to add to their account:

```
USE ROLE SYSADMIN; USE DATABASE DEMO3A_DB; USE SCHEMA BANKING;
CREATE OR REPLACE PROCEDURE deposit(PARAM_ACCT FLOAT, PARAM_AMT FLOAT)
returns STRING LANGUAGE javascript AS
    $$
    var ret_val = ""; var cmd_debit = ""; var cmd_credit = "";
    // INSERT data into tables
    cmd_debit = "INSERT INTO DEMO3A_DB.BANKING.CASH VALUES ("
        + PARAM_ACCT + "," + PARAM_AMT + ",current_timestamp());";
    cmd_credit = "INSERT INTO DEMO3A_DB.BANKING.CUSTOMER_ACCT VALUES ("
        + PARAM_ACCT + "," + PARAM_AMT + ",current_timestamp());";
    // BEGIN transaction
    snowflake.execute ({sqlText: cmd_debit});
    snowflake.execute ({sqlText: cmd_credit});
        ret_val = "Deposit Transaction Succeeded";
    return ret_val;
    $$;
```

Next, we'll create the transaction for a withdrawal. In this case, it is just the reverse of what happens for a deposit:

```
USE ROLE SYSADMIN;USE DATABASE DEMO3A_DB; USE SCHEMA BANKING;
CREATE OR REPLACE PROCEDURE withdrawal(PARAM_ACCT FLOAT, PARAM_AMT FLOAT)
returns STRING LANGUAGE javascript AS
    $$
    var ret_val = "";  var cmd_debit = "";  var cmd_credit = "";
    // INSERT data into tables
    cmd_debit = "INSERT INTO DEMO3A_DB.BANKING.CUSTOMER_ACCT VALUES ("
            + PARAM_ACCT + "," + (-PARAM_AMT) + ",current_timestamp());";
    cmd_credit = "INSERT INTO DEMO3A_DB.BANKING.CASH VALUES ("
            + PARAM_ACCT + "," + (-PARAM_AMT) + ",current_timestamp());";
    // BEGIN transaction
    snowflake.execute ({sqlText: cmd_debit});
    snowflake.execute ({sqlText: cmd_credit});
        ret_val = "Withdrawal Transaction Succeeded";
    return ret_val;
    $$;
```

Finally, the transaction for the loan payment is one in which the bank's cash account is debited and the receivables account is credited:

```
USE ROLE SYSADMIN;USE DATABASE DEMO3A_DB; USE SCHEMA BANKING;
CREATE OR REPLACE PROCEDURE loan_payment(PARAM_ACCT FLOAT, PARAM_AMT FLOAT)
returns STRING LANGUAGE javascript AS
    $$
    var ret_val = "";  var cmd_debit = "";  var cmd_credit = "";
    // INSERT data into the tables
    cmd_debit = "INSERT INTO DEMO3A_DB.BANKING.CASH VALUES ("
            + PARAM_ACCT + "," + PARAM_AMT + ",current_timestamp());";
    cmd_credit = "INSERT INTO DEMO3A_DB.BANKING.RECEIVABLES VALUES ("
            + PARAM_ACCT + "," +(-PARAM_AMT) + ",current_timestamp());";
    //BEGIN transaction
    snowflake.execute ({sqlText: cmd_debit});
    snowflake.execute ({sqlText: cmd_credit});
            ret_val = "Loan Payment Transaction Succeeded";
    return ret_val;
    $$;
```

Now let's run a few quick tests to see if the procedures are working. Run each CALL statement separately:

```
CALL withdrawal(21, 100);
CALL loan_payment(21, 100);
CALL deposit(21, 100);
```

We can review the details of what happened when we called the procedures by executing the SELECT command:

```
SELECT CUSTOMER_ACCOUNT, AMOUNT FROM DEMO3A_DB.BANKING.CASH;
```

After using the CALL command followed by the SELECT command to test a few transactions, we feel confident that the procedure is working as intended.

So, now we can truncate the tables, leaving the tables intact but removing the data:

```
USE ROLE SYSADMIN; USE DATABASE DEMO3A_DB; USE SCHEMA BANKING;
TRUNCATE TABLE DEMO3A_DB.BANKING.CUSTOMER_ACCT;
TRUNCATE TABLE DEMO3A_DB.BANKING.CASH;
TRUNCATE TABLE DEMO3A_DB.BANKING.RECEIVABLES;
```

Note that if we rerun the previous SELECT statements now, we'll see that there is no data in the tables. We are ready to input some transactions by calling the procedures and supplying the inputs:

```
USE ROLE SYSADMIN;
CALL deposit(21, 10000);
CALL deposit(21, 400);
CALL loan_payment(14, 1000);
CALL withdrawal(21, 500);
CALL deposit(72, 4000);
CALL withdrawal(21, 250);
```

We'd like to see a transaction summary, so we'll create one final stored procedure:

```
USE ROLE SYSADMIN; USE DATABASE DEMO3B_DB; USE SCHEMA BANKING;
CREATE OR REPLACE PROCEDURE Transactions_Summary()
returns STRING LANGUAGE javascript AS
    $$
    var cmd_truncate = `TRUNCATE TABLE IF EXISTS DEMO3B_DB.BANKING.SUMMARY;`
    var sql = snowflake.createStatement({sqlText: cmd_truncate});
    //Summarize Cash Amount
    var cmd_cash = `Insert into DEMO3B_DB.BANKING.SUMMARY (CASH_AMT)
    select sum(AMOUNT) from DEMO3A_DB.BANKING.CASH;`
    var sql = snowflake.createStatement({sqlText: cmd_cash});
    //Summarize Receivables Amount
    var cmd_receivables = `Insert into DEMO3B_DB.BANKING.SUMMARY
    (RECEIVABLES_AMT) select sum(AMOUNT) from DEMO3A_DB.BANKING.RECEIVABLES;`
    var sql = snowflake.createStatement({sqlText: cmd_receivables});
    //Summarize Customer Account Amount
    var cmd_customer = `Insert into DEMO3B_DB.BANKING.SUMMARY (CUSTOMER_AMT)
    select sum(AMOUNT) from DEMO3A_DB.BANKING.CUSTOMER_ACCT;`
    var sql = snowflake.createStatement({sqlText: cmd_customer});
    //BEGIN transaction
    snowflake.execute ({sqlText: cmd_truncate});
    snowflake.execute ({sqlText: cmd_cash});
    snowflake.execute ({sqlText: cmd_receivables});
    snowflake.execute ({sqlText: cmd_customer});
    ret_val = "Transactions Successfully Summarized";
    return ret_val;
    $$;
```

Now we can see the transaction summary. We'll call the stored procedure so that all the debit and credit transactions are summarized and then we'll take a look at the table:

```
CALL Transactions_Summary();
```

```
SELECT * FROM DEMO3B_DB.BANKING.SUMMARY;
```

Let's also take a look at the materialized view we created earlier:

```
USE ROLE SYSADMIN; USE DATABASE DEMO3B_DB;USE SCHEMA BANKING;
SELECT * FROM DEMO3B_DB.BANKING.SUMMARY_MVW;
```

Interestingly, the materialized view has been kept updated with the information from the SUMMARY base table (as shown in Figure 3-30).

	CASH_AMT	RECEIVABLES_AMT	CUSTOMER_AMT
1	14,650	null	null
2	null	-1,000	null
3	null	null	13,650

Figure 3-30. Results of the materialized view

For comparison, let's look at the nonmaterialized view as well:

```
USE ROLE SYSADMIN; USE DATABASE DEMO3B_DB;USE SCHEMA BANKING;
SELECT * FROM DEMO3B_DB.BANKING.SUMMARY_VW;
```

Now we have our final stored procedure example. It's an advanced example because we are going to add a task to execute this stored procedure.

As a quick side note, tasks are incredibly powerful and an important topic. We'll cover tasks in more detail later in this chapter when we'll see how tasks can be combined with table streams. For now, it's enough to understand that a task can call a stored procedure, as we are going to see in this example, or it can execute a single SQL statement.

We will be creating a stored procedure that will delete a database. Thus, it's important that we create the stored procedure in a different database than the one we'll want to delete using the stored procedure:

```
USE ROLE SYSADMIN; USE DATABASE DEMO3E_DB;
CREATE OR REPLACE PROCEDURE drop_db()
RETURNS STRING NOT NULL LANGUAGE javascript AS
    $$
    var cmd = `DROP DATABASE DEMO3A_DB;`
    var sql = snowflake.createStatement({sqlText: cmd});
    var result = sql.execute();
```

```
    return 'Database has been successfully dropped';
    $$;
```

Now we can call the stored procedure and the database will be dropped. This is part of our cleanup for this chapter:

```
CALL drop_db();
```

Refresh the worksheet and you'll see that the DEMO3A_DB database has been dropped. Now that you've seen how this stored procedure works, we'll modify it so that it will drop a different database, and we'll add a task so that the database will be dropped 15 minutes later. That way, you can see how a task works.

Let's go ahead and change our drop_db procedure so that we'll be dropping the DEMO3B_DB database. Note that we will need to replace the drop_db procedure because it is not possible to alter the contents of the stored procedure. However, it is possible to use the ALTER command to rename the procedure, set and unset the comments, or change whether the procedure is executed with the rights of the owner or the caller:

```
USE ROLE SYSADMIN;
CREATE OR REPLACE PROCEDURE drop_db() RETURNS STRING NOT NULL
    LANGUAGE javascript AS
    $$
    var cmd = `DROP DATABASE "DEMO3B_DB";`
    var sql = snowflake.createStatement({sqlText: cmd});
    var result = sql.execute();
    return 'Database has been successfully dropped';
    $$;
```

Next, we'll want to create the task that will delay the stored procedure by 15 minutes:

```
USE ROLE SYSADMIN; USE DATABASE DEMO3E_DB;
CREATE OR REPLACE TASK tsk_wait_15
WAREHOUSE = COMPUTE_WH SCHEDULE = '15 MINUTE'
AS CALL drop_db();
```

The SYSADMIN role is going to need some privileges to execute the task, so be sure to use the ACCOUNTADMIN role for this command. Even though the SYSADMIN role is the task owner, an elevated account-level privilege to execute tasks is required. Make sure you set the role to ACCOUNTADMIN:

```
USE ROLE ACCOUNTADMIN;
GRANT EXECUTE TASK ON ACCOUNT TO ROLE SYSADMIN;
```

You can now set the role to SYSADMIN. Because tasks are always created in a suspended state, they'll need to be resumed:

```
USE ROLE SYSADMIN;
ALTER TASK IF EXISTS tsk_wait_15 RESUME;
```

Now our task is in a scheduled state. We'll be able to see that by using this query against the `INFORMATION_SCHEMA.TASK_HISTORY` table function:

```
SELECT * FROM table(information_schema.task_history
    (task_name => 'tsk_wait_15',
    scheduled_time_range_start =>
    dateadd('hour', -1, current_timestamp())));
```

Figure 3-31 shows the results of the query.

	SCHEDULED_TIME	QUERY_START_TIME	⋯	NEXT_SCHEDULED_TIME
1	2022-05-30 17:07:16.846 -0700	null		2022-05-30 17:22:16.846 -0700

Figure 3-31. Results showing the task is in a scheduled state

You can use the next 15 minutes to answer the questions at the end of the chapter to test your knowledge, and then come back. Once you see that the task has been completed and the database has been dropped (you can refresh your screen, or you can run the query again to see the state of the task), you can suspend the task:

```
USE ROLE SYSADMIN;
ALTER TASK IF EXISTS tsk_15 SUSPEND;
```

After you suspend the task, you can run the query one last time, and you'll see that the task succeeded and that there are no tasks scheduled.

Introduction to Pipes, Streams, and Sequences

Pipes, streams, and sequences are Snowflake objects we've not yet covered. *Pipes* are objects that contain a `COPY` command that is used by Snowpipe. Snowpipe is used for continuous, serverless loading of data into a Snowflake target table. Snowflake *streams*, also known as change data capture (CDC), keep track of certain changes made to a table including inserts, updates, and deletes. Snowflake streams have many useful purposes, including recording changes made in a staging table which are used to update another table.

A *sequence* object is used to generate unique numbers. Often, sequences are used as surrogate keys for primary key values. Here is how you can generate a sequence that begins with the number 1 and increments by one:

```
USE ROLE SYSADMIN; USE DATABASE DEMO3E_DB;
CREATE OR REPLACE SEQUENCE SEQ_01 START = 1 INCREMENT = 1;
CREATE OR REPLACE TABLE SEQUENCE_TEST(i integer);
```

You can use the `SELECT` command three or four times to see how the `NEXTVAL` increments. Each time you execute the statement, you'll notice the `NEXTVAL` increases by one:

```
SELECT SEQ_01.NEXTVAL;
```

Now let's create a new sequence with a different increment:

```
USE ROLE SYSADMIN;USE DATABASE DEMO3E_DB;
CREATE OR REPLACE SEQUENCE SEQ_02 START = 1 INCREMENT = 2;
CREATE OR REPLACE TABLE SEQUENCE_TEST(i integer);
```

Take a look at what happens when you try this:

```
SELECT SEQ_02.NEXTVAL a, SEQ_02.NEXTVAL b,SEQ_02.NEXTVAL c,SEQ_02.NEXTVAL d;
```

You should see that the value of A is 1, the value of B is 3, the value of C is 5, and the value of D is 7.

Some important things to remember are that the first value in a sequence cannot be changed after the sequence is created, and sequence values, although unique, are not necessarily free of gaps. This is because sequences are user-defined database objects; thus, the sequence value can be shared by multiple tables because sequences are not tied to any specific table. An alternative to creating a sequence is to use identity columns in which you would generate auto-incrementing numbers, often used as a primary key, in one specific table.

 A consideration when using sequences is that they may not be appropriate for situations such as a secure UDF case. In some instances, a consumer may be able to use the difference between sequence numbers to infer information about the number of records. In that case, you can exclude the sequence column from the consumer results or use a unique string ID instead of a sequence.

We'll explore Snowpipe in Chapter 6. Streams will be discussed in depth in the next section, where we'll discover how to use them for CDC. We'll also see how to combine the power of streams and tasks.

Snowflake Streams (Deep Dive)

A Snowflake stream works like a pointer that keeps track of the status of a DML operation on a defined table. A Snowflake table stream creates a change table that shows what has changed, at a row level, between two transactional points in time. Streams are like processing queues and can be queried just like a table. Table streams make it easy to grab the new data in a table so that one can have more efficient processing. Streams do that by taking a snapshot of all the rows in a table at a point in time and only storing an offset for the source table. In that way, a stream can return the CDC records by leveraging the versioning history.

To get an in-depth understanding of Snowflake streams, let's go through an example. We'll be creating a table for a bank branch that stores the branch ID, city, and associated dollar amount of deposits for a particular day.

To prepare for the example, we'll create a new database, schema, and table. We'll insert some values to get us started. We are going to use the INSERT command in our example, but typically you wouldn't be using insert statements to load data into your Snowflake instance. Instead, you'd probably use something like Snowpipe. To keep things simple, we'll be inserting only a few records at a time, so we'll use the INSERT command. Here are the statements to set things up for our Snowflake stream example:

```
USE ROLE SYSADMIN;
CREATE OR REPLACE DATABASE DEMO3F_DB;
CREATE OR REPLACE SCHEMA BANKING;
CREATE OR REPLACE TABLE BRANCH (ID varchar, City varchar, Amount number (20,2));
INSERT INTO BRANCH (ID, City, Amount)
values
    (12001, 'Abilene', 5387.97),
    (12002, 'Barstow', 34478.10),
    (12003, 'Cadbury', 8994.63);
```

Before moving on, you can pause and view the records in the table by using the following statement:

```
SELECT * FROM BRANCH;
```

We'll create two streams and then use the SHOW STREAMS command to see the created streams:

```
CREATE OR REPLACE STREAM STREAM_A ON TABLE BRANCH;
CREATE OR REPLACE STREAM STREAM_B ON TABLE BRANCH;
SHOW STREAMS;
```

If you run SELECT * statements on these streams, you will see that both are empty. What happens if we insert some new records into the table? We expect that the streams would then have records:

```
INSERT INTO BRANCH (ID, City, Amount)
values
    (12004, 'Denton', 41242.93),
    (12005, 'Everett', 6175.22),
    (12006, 'Fargo', 443689.75);
```

Now execute each SELECT * statement, one at a time, for the BRANCH table and two streams:

```
SELECT * FROM BRANCH;
SELECT * FROM STREAM_A;
SELECT * FROM STREAM_B;
```

You should see that there are now six records in the BRANCH table and three records each in the streams. If we add another stream, STREAM_C, we will expect that there will be no records in that stream:

```
CREATE OR REPLACE STREAM STREAM_C ON TABLE BRANCH;
```

Now let's go ahead and insert some records a third time:

```
INSERT INTO BRANCH (ID, City, Amount)
values
    (12007, 'Galveston', 351247.79),
    (12008, 'Houston', 917011.27);
```

If you run SELECT * statements on the table and the three streams, you'll see that the table has eight records, STREAM_A and STREAM_B each have five records, and STREAM_C has two records.

Let's do one more thing. Let's re-create STREAM_B to see what happens in the next section:

```
CREATE OR REPLACE STREAM STREAM_B ON TABLE BRANCH;
```

At this point, STREAM_B will have zero records.

To see the impact of deleting records, let's go ahead and delete the first record from each of the previous inserts:

```
DELETE FROM BRANCH WHERE ID = 12001;
DELETE FROM BRANCH WHERE ID = 12004;
DELETE FROM BRANCH WHERE ID = 12007;
```

If we run SELECT * on the table and then on all three streams, we should see five records in the BRANCH table (as shown in Figure 3-32), four records in STREAM_A, three records in STREAM_B, and three records in STREAM_C.

	ID	CITY	AMOUNT
1	12002	Barstow	34,478.1
2	12003	Cadbury	8,994.63
3	12005	Everett	6,175.22
4	12006	Fargo	443,689.75
5	12008	Houston	917,011.27

*Figure 3-32. Results of the SELECT * query on the BRANCH table*

After STREAM_A was created, three records were entered: 12004, 12005, and 12006. Then two more records were entered: 12007 and 12008. When records 12004 and 12007 were deleted, they were removed from STREAM_A. When record 12001 was deleted, this showed up as a new entry in STREAM_A because record 12001 didn't previously exist. In total there should now be four records in STREAM_A (as shown in Figure 3-33).

	ID	CITY	AMOUNT	METADATA$ACTION	METADATA$ISUPDATE
1	12005	Everett	6,175.22	INSERT	FALSE
2	12006	Fargo	443,689.75	INSERT	FALSE
3	12008	Houston	917,011.27	INSERT	FALSE
4	12001	Abilene	5,387.97	DELETE	FALSE

*Figure 3-33. Results of the SELECT * query on STREAM_A*

As a reminder, STREAM_B was re-created. From the time STREAM_B was re-created, no new records were inserted. When records 12001, 12004, and 12007 were deleted, they all appeared in STREAM_B because they had not appeared there previously. Thus, there should now be three records in STREAM_B (as shown in Figure 3-34).

	ID	CITY	AMOUNT	METADATA$ACTION	METADATA$ISUPDATE
1	12004	Denton	41,242.93	DELETE	FALSE
2	12007	Galveston	351,247.79	DELETE	FALSE
3	12001	Abilene	5,387.97	DELETE	FALSE

*Figure 3-34. Results of the SELECT * query on STREAM_B*

After STREAM_C was created, two records were entered: 12007 and 12008. When record 12007 was deleted, it was removed from STREAM_C. When records 12001 and 12004 were deleted, they showed up as new entries in STREAM_C because those records didn't previously exist. In total, there should now be three records in STREAM_C (as shown in Figure 3-35).

	ID	CITY	AMOUNT	METADATA$ACTION	METADATA$ISUPDATE
1	12008	Houston	917,011.27	INSERT	FALSE
2	12004	Denton	41,242.93	DELETE	FALSE
3	12001	Abilene	5,387.97	DELETE	FALSE

*Figure 3-35. Results of the SELECT * query on STREAM_C*

Our examples demonstrate the impact of inserting and deleting records, and we can see the results in the METADATA$ACTION columns. But what happens when we update a record? Let's update the city to Fayetteville where the BRANCH ID equals 12006:

```
UPDATE BRANCH
SET City = 'Fayetteville' WHERE ID = 12006;
SELECT * FROM BRANCH;
```

As expected, the BRANCH table shows the updated city (as shown in Figure 3-36).

	ID	CITY	AMOUNT
1	12002	Barstow	34,478.1
2	12003	Cadbury	8,994.63
3	12005	Everett	6,175.22
4	12006	Fayetteville	443,689.75
5	12008	Houston	917,011.27

*Figure 3-36. Results of the SELECT * query on the BRANCH table with the city set to Fayetteville*

Record 12006 already existed in STREAM_A and, thus, no new entry was needed. The value was simply updated in the stream (as shown in Figure 3-37).

	ID	...	CITY	AMOUNT	METADATA$ACTION	METADATA$ISUPDATE
1	12005		Everett	6,175.22	INSERT	FALSE
2	12006		Fayetteville	443,689.75	INSERT	FALSE
3	12008		Houston	917,011.27	INSERT	FALSE
4	12001		Abilene	5,387.97	DELETE	FALSE

*Figure 3-37. Results of the SELECT * query on STREAM_A*

Record 12006 did not previously exist in STREAM_B. Therefore, we see that there is an entry for the deletion of record 12006 with the city of Fargo and then an entry for the insertion of the new 12006 record with the value of Fayetteville. You can see that those two new entries show as having a value of TRUE in the METADATA$ISUPDATE column. With the addition of those two new entries, STREAM_B now has five records (as shown in Figure 3-38).

	ID	CITY	AMOUNT	METADATA$ACTION	METADATA$ISUPDATE
1	12006	Fayetteville	443,689.75	INSERT	TRUE
2	12006	Fargo	443,689.75	DELETE	TRUE
3	12004	Denton	41,242.93	DELETE	FALSE
4	12007	Galveston	351,247.79	DELETE	FALSE
5	12001	Abilene	5,387.97	DELETE	FALSE

*Figure 3-38. Results of the SELECT * query on STREAM_B*

Record 12006 did not previously exist in STREAM_C. Therefore, we see that there is an entry for the deletion of record 12006 with the city of Fargo and then an entry for the insertion of the new 12006 record with the value of Fayetteville. You can see that those two entries show as having a value of TRUE in the METADATA$ISUPDATE column. With the addition of those two new entries, STREAM_C now has five records (as shown in Figure 3-39). Interestingly, you'll notice that STREAM_B and STREAM_C both have five records at this point, but they don't have the same five entries.

	ID	CITY	AMOUNT	METADATA$ACTION	METADATA$ISUPDATE
1	12006	Fayetteville	443,689.75	INSERT	TRUE
2	12008	Houston	917,011.27	INSERT	FALSE
3	12006	Fargo	443,689.75	DELETE	TRUE
4	12004	Denton	41,242.93	DELETE	FALSE
5	12001	Abilene	5,387.97	DELETE	FALSE

*Figure 3-39. Results of the SELECT * query on STREAM_C*

To summarize the metadata, let's review the stream metadata columns. The META-DATA$ACTION column tells us whether the row was inserted or deleted. If the row is updated, the METADATA$ISUPDATE column will be TRUE. And lastly, there is a unique hash key for the METADATA$ROW_ID column.

As you can see in the examples presented, Snowflake streams are a powerful way to handle changing data sets. In Snowflake, one of the most important reasons for using table streams is to keep the staging table and production table in sync. Using a staging table, along with streams, helps to protect undesired changes from being made to the production table. Snowflake table streams are also often used in conjunction with other features, such as Snowflake pipelines or Snowflake tasks.

Snowflake Tasks (Deep Dive)

Snowflake tasks are frequently used with Snowflake streams, as our next examples will show. They can also be useful in scenarios that don't call for the use of streams. As you may recall, Snowflake tasks were introduced earlier in the chapter, when we created a task that called a stored procedure to delete a database as part of our cleanup efforts.

In this section, we're going to demonstrate how Snowflake tasks can be used with streams. Before we tackle some hands-on examples, let's first review some important details about Snowflake tasks.

One way Snowflake tasks can be completed is by using compute resources that are managed by users. We used this method earlier, where we designated a virtual warehouse for the task to use. Alternatively, the completion of tasks can be managed by Snowflake via a serverless compute model. In a serverless compute model, the compute resources are automatically resized and scaled up or down by Snowflake as the workload requirements change.

The option to enable the serverless compute model must be specified when the task is created.

Tasks run on a schedule which is defined at the time a task is created. Alternatively, you can establish task dependencies whereby a task can be triggered by a predecessor task. There is no event source that can trigger a task; a task that is not triggered by a predecessor task must be run on a schedule.

You can see in Figure 3-40, which includes the CREATE statements for each task type, that tasks can be either scheduled or triggered by a predecessor task. You'll notice that we elected to include a small virtual warehouse as the initial warehouse size for all the tasks, but we could have selected different sizes for different tasks.

Whenever there are task dependencies, there is a root task which is run on a schedule. Each task that completes then triggers associated child tasks. Each child task is triggered by one predecessor task. Each individual task is limited to a single predecessor task but can have up to 100 child tasks. A task tree is limited to 1,000 tasks in total, including the root task.

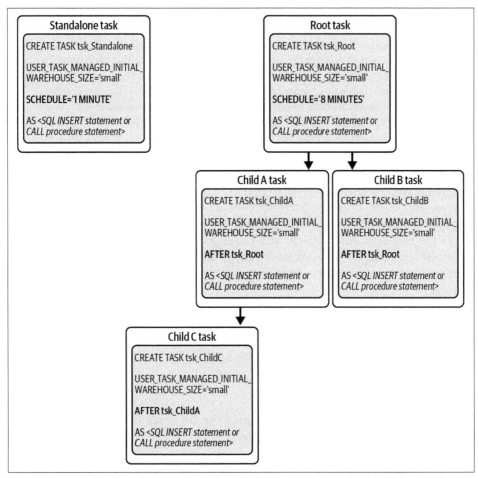

Figure 3-40. Task examples for creating standalone, root, and child tasks

 You can use the cron expression in a task definition, rather than defining the number of minutes, to support specifying a time zone when scheduling tasks. To avoid unexpected task executions due to daylight saving time, consider scheduling tasks at a time other than 1 a.m. to 3 a.m. daily or on days of the week that include Sundays.

The `EXECUTE TASK` command manually triggers a single run of a scheduled task that is either a standalone task or the root task in a task tree. If it is necessary to recursively resume all dependent tasks tied to a root task, be sure to use the `SYSTEM$TASK_DEPENDENTS_ENABLE` function, rather than resuming each task individually by using the `ALTER TASK RESUME` command.

By default, Snowflake ensures that only one instance of a particular tree of tasks is allowed to run at one time. As a result, at least one run of the task tree will be skipped if the cumulative time required to run all tasks in the tree exceeds the explicit scheduled time set in the definition of the root task. When read/write SQL operations executed by overlapping runs of a task tree don't produce incorrect or duplicate data, overlapping runs may not be problematic. In this situation, if it makes sense to do so, the default behavior can be changed by setting the ALLOW_OVERLAPPING_EXECUTION parameter in the root task to TRUE.

If it would be problematic to have overlapping runs of a task tree, you have several options. You could choose a more appropriate warehouse size or use Snowflake-managed compute resources so that the task tree will finish before the next scheduled run of the root task. Alternatively, you could analyze the SQL statements or stored procedures executed by each task to determine whether the code could be optimized. Another option is that you could increase the scheduling time between runs of the root task.

Three Snowflake task functions can be used to retrieve information about tasks:

SYSTEM$CURRENT_USER_TASK_NAME
> This function returns the name of the task currently executing when invoked from the statement or stored procedure defined by the task.

TASK_HISTORY
> This function returns task activity within the last seven days or the next scheduled execution within the next eight days.

TASK_DEPENDENTS
> This is a table function that returns the list of child tasks for a given root task.

Because many access control privileges are needed to create and manage tasks, it is recommended that a custom TASKADMIN role be created so that a role can alter its own tasks. Having a custom TASKADMIN role also allows for a SECURITYADMIN role, or any role with MANAGE GRANTS privileges, to manage the TASKADMIN role. Otherwise, only an ACCOUNTADMIN can revoke any task privileges assigned to the task owner.

The following example demonstrates how you would create a TASKADMIN role:

```
USE ROLE SECURITYADMIN;
CREATE ROLE TASKADMIN;

USE ROLE ACCOUNTADMIN;
GRANT EXECUTE TASK, EXECUTE MANAGED TASK ON ACCOUNT TO ROLE TASKADMIN;
```

```
USE ROLE SECURITYADMIN;
GRANT ROLE TASKADMIN TO ROLE <USER_ROLE>;
GRANT ROLE TASKADMIN TO ROLE SYSADMIN;
```

In practice, you'd need to make sure the USER_ROLE to which the TASKADMIN role is assigned has all the necessary access to the database, schema, and tables. We won't be executing all those statements in this chapter. Please refer to Chapter 5 for more information about creating roles, granting access to objects, and best practices for specific roles like SECURITYADMIN and ACCOUNTADMIN. For this task's hands-on examples, we'll use the ACCOUNTADMIN role instead of the TASKADMIN role:

```
USE ROLE ACCOUNTADMIN;
USE WAREHOUSE COMPUTE_WH;
USE DATABASE DEMO3F_DB;
CREATE OR REPLACE SCHEMA TASKSDEMO;
```

We will want to create a product table which lists the product ID and description, the category and segment, and the manufacturer ID and name:

```
CREATE OR REPLACE TABLE DEMO3F_DB.TASKSDEMO.PRODUCT
    (Prod_ID int,
    Prod_Desc varchar(),
    Category varchar(30),
    Segment varchar(20),
    Mfg_ID int,
    Mfg_Name varchar(50));
```

Let's insert some values into the product table:

```
INSERT INTO DEMO3F_DB.TASKSDEMO.PRODUCT values
(1201, 'Product 1201', 'Category 1201', 'Segment 1201', '1201', 'Mfg 1201');
INSERT INTO DEMO3F_DB.TASKSDEMO.PRODUCT values
(1202, 'Product 1202', 'Category 1202', 'Segment 1202', '1202', 'Mfg 1202');
INSERT INTO DEMO3F_DB.TASKSDEMO.PRODUCT values
(1203, 'Product 1203', 'Category 1203', 'Segment 1203', '1203', 'Mfg 1203');
INSERT INTO DEMO3F_DB.TASKSDEMO.PRODUCT values
(1204, 'Product 1204', 'Category 1204', 'Segment 1204', '1204', 'Mfg 1204');
INSERT INTO DEMO3F_DB.TASKSDEMO.PRODUCT values
(1205, 'Product 1205', 'Category 1205', 'Segment 1205', '1205', 'Mfg 1205');
INSERT INTO DEMO3F_DB.TASKSDEMO.PRODUCT values
(1206, 'Product 1206', 'Category 1206', 'Segment 1206', '1206', 'Mfg 1206');
```

Next, we'll create a sales table and then a stream on the sales table:

```
CREATE OR REPLACE TABLE DEMO3F_DB.TASKSDEMO.SALES
    (Prod_ID int,
    Customer varchar(),
    Zip varchar(),
    Qty int,
    Revenue decimal(10,2));
```

We'll want our table stream to record insert-only values on the sales table:

```
CREATE OR REPLACE STREAM DEMO3F_DB.TASKSDEMO.SALES_STREAM
ON TABLE DEMO3F_DB.TASKSDEMO.SALES
APPEND_ONLY = TRUE;
```

Before we create a task, we want to make sure our stream and other statements work properly. Let's go ahead and insert some values into the sales table:

```
INSERT INTO DEMO3F_DB.TASKSDEMO.SALES VALUES
(1201, 'Amy Johnson', 45466, 45, 2345.67);
INSERT INTO DEMO3F_DB.TASKSDEMO.SALES VALUES
(1201, 'Harold Robinson', 89701, 45, 2345.67);
INSERT INTO DEMO3F_DB.TASKSDEMO.SALES VALUES
(1203, 'Chad Norton', 33236, 45, 2345.67);
INSERT INTO DEMO3F_DB.TASKSDEMO.SALES VALUES
(1206, 'Horatio Simon', 75148, 45, 2345.67);
INSERT INTO DEMO3F_DB.TASKSDEMO.SALES VALUES
(1205, 'Misty Crawford', 10001, 45, 2345.67);
```

When we run a SELECT * command, we'll be able to see that the values we entered into the sales table were then captured in the SALES_STREAM:

```
SELECT * FROM DEMO3F_DB.TASKSDEMO.SALES_STREAM;
```

Now it's time to create our sales transaction table which combines the SALES_STREAM with the product table and adds a timestamp so that we can know when the sales data was recorded:

```
CREATE OR REPLACE TABLE DEMO3F_DB.TASKSDEMO.SALES_TRANSACT
    (Prod_ID int,
    Prod_Desc varchar(),
    Category varchar(30),
    Segment varchar(20),
    Mfg_ID int,
    Mfg_Name varchar(50),
    Customer varchar(),
    Zip varchar(),
    Qty int,
    Revenue decimal (10, 2),
    TS timestamp);
```

We'll eventually want to automate the creation of the sales transaction table, but first we need to see what happens when we manually insert data. If things work as expected, we'll proceed to creating a task for the insertion:

```
INSERT INTO
    DEMO3F_DB.TASKSDEMO.SALES_TRANSACT
        (Prod_ID,Prod_Desc,Category,Segment,Mfg_Id,
        Mfg_Name,Customer,Zip,Qty,Revenue,TS)
SELECT
    s.Prod_ID,p.Prod_Desc,p.Category,p.Segment,p.Mfg_ID,
    p.Mfg_Name,s.Customer,s.Zip,s.Qty,s.Revenue,current_timestamp
```

```
FROM
    DEMO3F_DB.TASKSDEMO.SALES_STREAM s
    JOIN DEMO3F_DB.TASKSDEMO.PRODUCT p ON s.Prod_ID = p.Prod_ID;
```

If we use a SELECT * statement, we'll confirm that the records were in fact inserted into the transaction table:

```
SELECT * FROM DEMO3F_DB.TASKSDEMO.SALES_TRANSACT;
```

Success! We've demonstrated that the INSERT statement works. Now it's time to automate the insertion by creating a task:

```
CREATE OR REPLACE TASK DEMO3F_DB.TASKSDEMO.SALES_TASK
WAREHOUSE = compute_wh
SCHEDULE  = '1 minute'
WHEN system$stream_has_data('DEMO3F_DB.TASKSDEMO.SALES_STREAM')
AS
INSERT INTO
    DEMO3F_DB.TASKSDEMO.SALES_TRANSACT
        (Prod_ID,Prod_Desc,Category,Segment,Mfg_Id,
        Mfg_Name,Customer,Zip,Qty,Revenue,TS)
SELECT
    s.Prod_ID,p.Prod_Desc,p.Category,p.Segment,p.Mfg_ID,
    p.Mfg_Name,s.Customer,s.Zip,s.Qty,s.Revenue,current_timestamp
FROM
    DEMO3F_DB.TASKSDEMO.SALES_STREAM s
    JOIN DEMO3F_DB.TASKSDEMO.PRODUCT p ON s.Prod_ID = p.Prod_ID;
ALTER TASK DEMO3F_DB.TASKSDEMO.SALES_TASK RESUME;
```

> Created tasks are suspended by default. Therefore, you'll need to execute the ALTER TASK…RESUME statement to allow the task to run.

Alternatively, for nonroot tree tasks, use the SYSTEM$TASK_DEPENDENTS_ENABLE function.

Note that it is possible for the root task to execute something on a stream event. However, there is a limitation that it can be scheduled at the lowest granulation to one minute. The previous example was used to demonstrate how you would use SYSTEM $STREAM_HAS_DATA to accomplish this.

Now let's see what happens when we insert values into the sales table. Once we insert values into the sales table, the SALES_STREAM should reflect the newly inserted records. Then the task should insert the new sales records after joining with the product table and generating a timestamp. Let's see what happens:

```
INSERT INTO DEMO3F_DB.TASKSDEMO.SALES VALUES
(1201, 'Edward Jameson', 45466, 45, 2345.67);
INSERT INTO DEMO3F_DB.TASKSDEMO.SALES VALUES
```

```
(1201, 'Margaret Volt', 89701, 45, 2345.67);
INSERT INTO DEMO3F_DB.TASKSDEMO.SALES VALUES
(1203, 'Antoine Lancaster', 33236, 45, 2345.67);
INSERT INTO DEMO3F_DB.TASKSDEMO.SALES VALUES
(1204, 'Esther Baker', 75148, 45, 2345.67);
INSERT INTO DEMO3F_DB.TASKSDEMO.SALES VALUES
(1206, 'Quintin Anderson', 10001, 45, 2345.67);
```

We can confirm that the values were captured by the SALES_STREAM:

```
SELECT * FROM DEMO3F_DB.TASKSDEMO.SALES_STREAM;
```

We'll need to wait a minute to give the task time to execute. If your next query produces no results, wait just a little longer and then try again. We only have to wait a minute because that is the time we set for the task. We could have increased the time if we had wanted:

```
SELECT * FROM DEMO3F_DB.TASKSDEMO.SALES_TRANSACT;
```

We've confirmed that our task works! We'll do cleanup at the end of the chapter, but let's go ahead and suspend the task now. We don't need the sales task to be checking every minute for new records in the SALES_STREAM:

```
ALTER TASK DEMO3F_DB.TASKSDEMO.SALES_TASK SUSPEND;
```

The costs associated with using tasks depend on whether you choose the virtual warehouse dedicated to the task or whether you opt to use the USER_TASK_MANAGED_INI TIAL_WAREHOUSE_SIZE command. The latter is a serverless feature. You can refer to Chapter 8 for a deep dive into Snowflake billing and ways to monitor virtual warehouse usage and reduce costs. Importantly, billing for Snowflake is based on usage so that you end up paying only for resources that you use.

Code Cleanup

Let's perform code cleanup to remove the objects in your Snowflake account in preparation for working on another chapter example.

Note that there is no need to drop objects in the hierarchy below the database before dropping the databases. If you've been following along, you dropped two databases already. Let's drop the remaining databases now:

```
DROP DATABASE DEMO3C_DB; DROP DATABASE DEMO3D_DB;
DROP DATABASE DEMO3E_DB; DROP DATABASE DEMO3F_DB;
```

Summary

This chapter provided several hands-on examples of creating and managing Snowflake objects such as databases, schemas, tables, views, stages, stored procedures, and UDFs. In addition, the INFORMATION_SCHEMA and ACCOUNT_USAGE views

---

were reviewed. To build on our foundational knowledge of Snowflake architecture and objects, we'll explore the different Snowflake data types and learn how to use more SQL commands and functions in the next chapter.

Knowledge Check

The following questions are based on the information provided in this chapter:

1. What are the different types of databases, schemas, and tables that can be created? If a particular type is not specifically stated at the time of creation, what is the default type for each?
2. What is the difference between scalar and tabular UDFs?
3. What kinds of things can you do with a stored procedure that you cannot do with a UDF?
4. What would happen if we used the CREATE DATABASE command and the database we want to create already exists? What if we used the CREATE OR REPLACE DATABASE command?
5. What is the default retention time for a database? Can the database retention time be changed? Can the default retention time be changed?
6. Why might you choose to use the TRUNCATE TABLE command rather than the DROP TABLE command?
7. Are there any storage or compute costs associated with views?
8. What is the difference between a *fully* qualified object name and a *partially* qualified object name?
9. When using stages, what is the default file format? What other file formats does Snowflake support?
10. What is unique about the SNOWFLAKE database that comes with every Snowflake account?
11. In what ways can Snowflake tasks be triggered?
12. Describe the METADATA$ACTION, METADATA$ISUPDATE, and METADATA$ROW_ID columns in a Snowflake stream.
13. Give examples of use cases or reasons why you might want to use Snowflake streams.

Answers to these questions are available in Appendix A.

Exploring Snowflake SQL Commands, Data Types, and Functions

As we learned in previous chapters, Snowflake was built to store data in an optimized, compressed, columnar format within a relational database. Snowflake's data end users need to access the stored data and be able to give instructions to perform tasks, call functions, and execute queries on the data. The way that can be accomplished is with the standard programming language for relational databases, Structured Query Language (SQL). Snowflake supports SQL:ANSI, the most common standardized version of SQL. In addition to SQL support for structured data, Snowflake offers native support for semi-structured data formats such as JSON and XML. Snowflake also supports unstructured data.

The main focus of this chapter is on learning the fundamentals of using Snowflake worksheets to execute a variety of SQL commands using different data types and functions. Other than using worksheets in the Snowflake web UI, it is possible to use a Snowflake-native command-line client, known as SnowSQL, to create and execute SQL commands. More detail about SnowSQL will be provided in Chapter 6.

Besides connecting to Snowflake via the web UI or SnowSQL, you can use ODBC and JDBC drivers to access Snowflake data through external applications such as Tableau and Looker. We'll explore connections to Tableau and Looker in Chapter 12. Native connectors such as Python and Spark can also be used to develop applications for connecting to Snowflake.

To help you prepare for mastering advanced topics in upcoming chapters, we'll want to focus first on learning the basics of Snowflake SQL commands, data types, and Snowflake functions.

Prep Work

Create a new worksheet titled *Chapter4 Syntax Examples, Data Types, and Functions*. Refer to "Navigating Snowsight Worksheets" on page 8 if you need help creating a new worksheet. To set the worksheet context, make sure you are in the *Syntax Examples* worksheet and using the SYSADMIN role and the COMPUTE_WH virtual warehouse.

Working with SQL Commands in Snowflake

SQL can be divided into five different language command types. To create Snowflake objects, you need to use Data Definition Language (DDL) commands. Giving access to those objects requires the Data Control Language (DCL). Next, you'll use Data Manipulation Language (DML) commands to manipulate the data into and out of Snowflake. Transaction Control Language (TCL) commands enable you to manage transaction blocks. Data Query Language (DQL) statements are then used to actually query the data. Following is a list of common SQL commands, organized by type:

DDL commands:
- CREATE
- ALTER
- TRUNCATE
- RENAME
- DROP
- DESCRIBE
- SHOW
- USE
- SET/UNSET
- COMMENT

DCL commands:
- GRANT
- REVOKE

DML commands:
- INSERT
- MERGE
- UPDATE
- DELETE

- COPY INTO
- PUT
- GET
- LIST
- VALIDATE
- REMOVE

TCL commands:
- BEGIN
- COMMIT
- ROLLBACK
- CREATE

DQL command:
- SELECT

Each of these five different command language types, and their associated commands, will be discussed briefly in the following sections. A comprehensive list of all Snowflake SQL commands can be found in the Snowflake online documentation (*https://oreil.ly/tlQJJ*).

DDL Commands

DDL commands are the SQL commands used to define the database schema. The commands create, modify, and delete database structures. In addition, DDL commands can be used to perform account-level session operations, such as setting parameters, as we'll see later in the chapter when we discuss the SET and UNSET commands. DDL commands include CREATE, ALTER, TRUNCATE, RENAME, DROP, DESCRIBE, SHOW, USE, and COMMENT. With the exception of the COMMENT command, each DDL command takes an object type and identifier.

Snowflake DDL commands manipulate objects such as databases, virtual warehouses, schemas, tables, and views; however, they do not manipulate data. Refer back to Chapter 3, which is devoted to demonstrating Snowflake DDL commands, for in-depth explanations and many hands-on examples.

DCL Commands

DCL commands are the SQL commands used to enable access control. Examples of DCL commands include GRANT and REVOKE. Chapter 5 will take you through a complete and detailed series of examples using DCL commands to show you how to secure Snowflake objects.

DML Commands

DML commands are the SQL commands used to manipulate the data. The traditional DML commands such as INSERT, MERGE, UPDATE, and DELETE exist to be used for general data manipulation. For data loading and unloading, Snowflake provides COPY INTO *<table>* and COPY INTO *<location>* commands. Additionally, Snowflake's DML commands include some commands that do not perform any actual data manipulation but are used to stage and manage files stored in Snowflake locations. Some examples include VALIDATE, PUT, GET, LIST, and REMOVE. Chapter 6 will explore many of Snowflake's DML commands.

TCL Commands

TCL commands are the SQL commands used to manage transaction blocks within Snowflake. Commands such as BEGIN, COMMIT, and ROLLBACK can be used for multi-statement transactions in a session. A Snowflake transaction is a set of read and write SQL statements that are processed together as one unit. By default, and upon query success, a DML statement that is run separately will be committed individually or will be rolled back at the end of the statement, if the query fails.

DQL Command

The DQL command is the SQL command used as either a statement or a clause to retrieve data that meets the criteria specified in the SELECT command. Note that the SELECT command is the only DQL command; it is used to retrieve data and does so by specifying the location and then using the WHERE statement to include attributes necessary for data selection inclusion.

The Snowflake SELECT command works on external tables and can be used to query historical data. In certain situations, using the SELECT statement will not require a running virtual warehouse to return results; this is because of Snowflake caching, as described in Chapter 2. Examples of the SELECT statement, the most common SQL statement, can be found throughout most of the chapters in this book. The following section provides details on how to make the most of the SELECT command.

SQL Query Development, Syntax, and Operators in Snowflake

Within Snowflake, SQL development can be undertaken natively, using Snowflake UI worksheets or SnowSQL, as well as via the many third-party SQL tools available.

Query syntax is how Snowflake SQL queries are structured or built. Often there are many different ways to write a SQL query that will yield the desired result. It is important to consider how to optimize the query for the best database performance and lowest cost. Chapter 9 includes a section devoted to discussing the topic of analyzing query performance and optimization techniques.

Query operators include terms reserved to specify conditions in a SQL query statement and are most often used in the WHERE clause. They can also be used as conjunctions for multiple conditions in a statement. We'll explore query operators later in this section.

SQL Development and Management

There are two native Snowflake options for developing and querying data. It is easy to get started with Snowflake SQL development using the Worksheets browser-based SQL editor within the Snowflake interface. Using Snowflake Worksheets requires no installation or configuration. Thus far, we've used only the Snowflake Worksheets for creating objects and querying data.

An alternative to Worksheets is SnowSQL, a Python-based client that can be downloaded from the Snowflake client repository and used to perform Snowflake tasks such as querying or executing DDL and DML commands. SnowSQL is frequently used for loading and unloading data. We'll get some hands-on experience with SnowSQL in Chapter 6.

Snowflake provides SnowSQL versions for Linux, macOS, and Microsoft Windows. Executable SnowSQL can be run as an interactive shell or in batch mode. Snowflake provides complete instructions (*https://oreil.ly/wVCHF*) on how to download and install SnowSQL for all supported platforms.

You can view the recently used client versions, including the SnowSQL version, in your Snowflake account by querying Snowflake's query history. To view that information, click Activity → Query History if you are using the new Snowsight web interface. Should you not see the client driver information right away, click the Columns button and select Client Driver (as shown in Figure 4-1).

Figure 4-1. Available columns for reviewing query history activity in Snowsight

Alternatively, click the History tab in the Classic Console web interface. From there, you can view the Client Info column by clicking the Column button at the upper right and selecting Client Driver. Interestingly, the Client Info column in the Classic Console web interface includes an icon to indicate whether the client version is support, unsupported, or nearing the end of support. We've been using the Snowsight web UI, so we'll see that the Go client driver has been used and it is supported, as indicated by a checkmark (as shown in Figure 4-2).

Figure 4-2. The Client Info column from the History tab (Classic Console web interface)

In addition to native Snowflake tools, a wide variety of third-party SQL tools are available for modeling, developing, and deploying SQL code in Snowflake applications. Some of these third-party tools, such as DataOps.live and SqlDBM, are available for a free trial by using Snowflake Partner Connect. You can visit the Snowflake online documentation (*https://oreil.ly/EVyOF*) for a more comprehensive list of third-party SQL tools available for use with Snowflake.

 For drivers and connectors that support sending a SQL statement for preparation before execution, Snowflake will prepare DML commands, and will execute SELECT and SHOW *<objects>* SQL statements received from those drivers and connectors. Other types of SQL statements received from drivers and connectors will be executed by Snowflake without preparation.

Query Syntax

Snowflake SQL queries begin with either the WITH clause or the SELECT command. The WITH clause, an optional clause that precedes the SELECT statement, is used to define common table expressions (CTEs) which are referenced in the FROM clause. Most queries, however, begin with the SELECT command and other syntax which appears afterward. The other syntax, described in Table 4-1, is evaluated in the following order:

- FROM
- WHERE
- GROUP BY
- HAVING
- WINDOW
- QUALIFY
- ORDER BY
- LIMIT

Table 4-1. Snowflake query syntax

Query syntax	Query clause	Comments
WITH		Optional clause that precedes the body of the SELECT statement
TOP<n>		Contains the maximum number of rows returned, recommended to include ORDER BY
FROM	AT | BEFORE, CHANGES, CONNECT BY, JOIN, MATCH_RECOGNIZE, PIVOT or UNPIVOT, SAMPLE or TABLESAMPLE_VALUE	Specifies the tables, views, or table functions to use in a SELECT statement

Query syntax	Query clause	Comments
WHERE		Specifies a condition that matches a subset of rows; can filter the result of the FROM clause; can specify which rows to operate on in an UPDATE, MERGE, or DELETE
GROUP BY	GROUP BY CUBE, GROUP BY GROUPING SETS, GROUP BY ROLLUP, HAVING	Groups rows with the same group-by-item expressions and computes aggregate functions for resultant group; can be a column name, a number referencing a position in the SELECT list, or a general expression
QUALIFY		Filters the results of window functions
ORDER BY		Specifies an ordering of the rows of the result table from a SELECT list
LIMIT/ FETCH		Constrains the maximum number of rows returned; recommended to include ORDER BY

Note that QUALIFY is evaluated after a window function; QUALIFY works with window functions in much the same way as HAVING does with the aggregate functions and GROUP BY clauses. More information on window functions can be found later in this chapter.

Subqueries, derived columns, and CTEs

A subquery is a query within another query and can be used to compute values that are returned in a SELECT list, grouped in a GROUP BY clause, or compared with other expressions in the WHERE or HAVING clause.

A Snowflake subquery is a nested SELECT statement supported as a block in one or more of the following Snowflake SQL statements:

- CREATE TABLE AS
- SELECT
- INSERT
- INSERT INTO
- UPDATE
- DELETE

To prepare for our hands-on exercises for subqueries and derived columns, we need to create a few simple tables and insert some values into those tables. We'll create one database for this chapter. We'll also create a schema and table for our subqueries and derived column examples. Navigate to the *Chapter4* worksheet in Snowsight to execute the following statements:

```
USE ROLE SYSADMIN;
USE WAREHOUSE COMPUTE_WH;
CREATE OR REPLACE DATABASE DEMO4_DB;
CREATE OR REPLACE SCHEMA SUBQUERIES;
CREATE OR REPLACE TABLE DEMO4_DB.SUBQUERIES.DERIVED
    (ID integer, AMT integer, Total integer);
INSERT INTO DERIVED (ID, AMT, Total)
VALUES (1,1000,4000),(2,2000,3500),(3,3000, 9900),(4,4000,3000),
    (5,5000,3700),(6,6000,2222);
SELECT * FROM DEMO4_DB.SUBQUERIES.DERIVED;
```

Your results should match what is shown in Figure 4-3.

	ID	AMT	TOTAL
1	1	1,000	4,000
2	2	2,000	3,500
3	3	3,000	9,900
4	4	4,000	3,000
5	5	5,000	3,700
6	6	6,000	2,222

Figure 4-3. Results of inserting values into a new Snowflake DERIVED table

We'll need a second table in the SUBQUERIES schema; after adding the table, we'll see the results shown in Figure 4-4:

```
CREATE OR REPLACE TABLE DEMO4_DB.SUBQUERIES.TABLE2
    (ID integer, AMT integer, Total integer);
INSERT INTO TABLE2 (ID, AMT, Total)
VALUES (1,1000,8300),(2,1001,1900),(3,3000,4400),(4,1010,3535),
    (5,1200,3232),(6,1000,2222);
SELECT * FROM DEMO4_DB.SUBQUERIES.TABLE2;
```

	ID	AMT	TOTAL
1	1	1,000	8,300
2	2	1,001	1,900
3	3	3,000	4,400
4	4	1,010	3,535
5	5	1,200	3,232
6	6	1,000	2,222

Figure 4-4. Results of inserting values into a new Snowflake TABLE2 table

Having now created both tables, we can write an uncorrelated subquery:

```
SELECT ID, AMT
FROM DEMO4_DB.SUBQUERIES.DERIVED
WHERE AMT = (SELECT MAX(AMT)
    FROM DEMO4_DB.SUBQUERIES.TABLE2);
```

You'll notice that an uncorrelated subquery is an independent query, one in which the value returned doesn't depend on any columns of the outer query. An uncorrelated subquery returns a single result that is used by the outer query only once. On the other hand, a correlated subquery references one or more external columns. A correlated subquery is evaluated on each row of the outer query table and returns one result per row that is evaluated.

Let's try executing a correlated subquery now:

```
SELECT ID, AMT
FROM DEMO4_DB.SUBQUERIES.DERIVED
WHERE AMT = (SELECT AMT
    FROM DEMO4_DB.SUBQUERIES.TABLE2
    WHERE ID = ID);
```

We receive an error message telling us that a single-row subquery returns more than one row (as shown in Figure 4-5). This probably isn't what you expected.

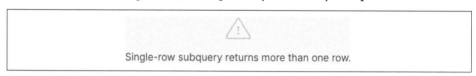

Figure 4-5. The error message received when executing a correlated subquery without an aggregate

Logically, we know there is only one row per ID; so, the subquery won't be returning more than one row in the result set. However, the server can't know that. We must use a MIN, MAX, or AVG function so that the server can know for certain that only one row will be returned each time the subquery is executed.

Let's go ahead and add MAX to the statement to see for ourselves how this works:

```
SELECT ID, AMT
FROM DEMO4_DB.SUBQUERIES.DERIVED
WHERE AMT = (SELECT MAX(AMT)
    FROM DEMO4_DB.SUBQUERIES.TABLE2
    WHERE ID = ID);
```

Success! We get a result set of one row with the ID equal to the value of 3. Let's see what happens if we change the equals sign to a greater-than sign:

```
SELECT ID, AMT
FROM DEMO4_DB.SUBQUERIES.DERIVED
WHERE AMT > (SELECT MAX(AMT)
```

```
FROM DEMO4_DB.SUBQUERIES.TABLE2
WHERE ID = ID);
```

Now we get a result set with three values (as shown in Figure 4-6).

	ID	AMT
1	4	4,000
2	5	5,000
3	6	6,000

Figure 4-6. A correlated query result set with three values

Let's see what happens if we change MAX to AVG:

```
SELECT ID, AMT
FROM DEMO4_DB.SUBQUERIES.DERIVED
WHERE AMT > (SELECT AVG(AMT)
    FROM DEMO4_DB.SUBQUERIES.TABLE2
    WHERE ID = ID);
```

There are five records in the result set. You may want to try different operators in the WHERE clause and different aggregators in the SELECT clause to see for yourself how correlated subqueries actually work.

Correlated subqueries are used infrequently because they result in one query per row, which is probably not the best scalable approach for most use cases.

Subqueries can be used for multiple purposes, one of which is to calculate or derive values that are then used in a variety of different ways. Derived columns can also be used in Snowflake to calculate another derived column, can be consumed by the outer SELECT query, or can be used as part of the WITH clause. These derived column values, sometimes called *computed column values* or *virtual column values*, are not physically stored in a table but are instead recalculated each time they are referenced in a query.

Our next example demonstrates how a derived column can be used in Snowflake to calculate another derived column. We'll also discover how we can use derived columns in one query, in subqueries, and with CTEs.

Let's create a derived column, AMT1, from the AMT column and then directly use the first derived column to create the second derived column, AMT2:

```
SELECT ID, AMT, AMT * 10 as AMT1, AMT1 + 20 as AMT2
FROM DEMO4_DB.SUBQUERIES.DERIVED;
```

The results of running that query can be seen in Figure 4-7.

	ID	AMT	AMT1	AMT2
1	1	1,000	10,000	10,020
2	2	2,000	20,000	20,020
3	3	3,000	30,000	30,020
4	4	4,000	40,000	40,020
5	5	5,000	50,000	50,020
6	6	6,000	60,000	60,020

Figure 4-7. Results of running the query with two derived columns

We can achieve the same results by creating a derived column, AMT1, which can then be consumed by an outer SELECT query. The subquery in our example is a Snowflake uncorrelated scalar subquery. As a reminder, the subquery is considered to be an uncorrelated subquery because the value returned doesn't depend on any outer query column:

```
SELECT sub.ID, sub.AMT, sub.AMT1 + 20 as AMT2
FROM (SELECT ID, AMT, AMT * 10 as AMT1
    FROM DEMO4_DB.SUBQUERIES.DERIVED) AS sub;
```

Lastly, we get the same results by using a derived column as part of the WITH clause. You'll notice that we've included a CTE subquery which could help increase modularity and simplify maintenance. The CTE defines a temporary view name, which is CTE1 in our example. Included in the CTE are the column names and a query expression, the result of which is basically a table:

```
WITH CTE1 AS (SELECT ID, AMT, AMT * 10 as AMT2
    FROM DEMO4_DB.SUBQUERIES.DERIVED)
SELECT a.ID, b.AMT, b.AMT2 + 20 as AMT2
FROM DEMO4_DB.SUBQUERIES.DERIVED a
    JOIN CTE1 b ON(a.ID = b.ID);
```

A major benefit of using a CTE is that it can make your code more readable. With a CTE, you can define a temporary table once and refer to it whenever you need it instead of having to declare the same subquery every place you need it. While not demonstrated here, a CTE can also be recursive. A recursive CTE can join a table to itself many times to process hierarchical data.

 Whenever the same names exist for a CTE and a table or view, the CTE will take precedence. Therefore, it is recommended to always choose a unique name for your CTEs.

Caution about multirow inserts

Now is a good time for a brief pause to learn a little more about multirow inserts. One or more rows of data can be inserted using a select query, or can be inserted as explicitly stated values in a comma-separated list. To keep things simple, we've been inserting values in comma-separated lists in this chapter.

There is one important thing to be aware of regarding multirow inserts. When inserting multiple rows of data into a VARCHAR data type, each data type being inserted into VARCHAR columns must be the same or else the insert will fail. A VARCHAR data type can accept data values such as the word *one* or the number 1, but never both types of values in the same INSERT statement. We can best see this with some examples.

We'll first create a new schema and table to do some multirow insert testing. In the first example, we'll insert the value *one* into the VARCHAR DEPT column:

```
USE ROLE SYSADMIN;
CREATE OR REPLACE SCHEMA DEMO4_DB.TEST;
CREATE OR REPLACE TABLE DEMO4_DB.TEST.TEST1 (ID integer, DEPT Varchar);
INSERT INTO TEST1 (ID, DEPT)
VALUES (1,'one');
SELECT * FROM DEMO4_DB.TEST.TEST1;
```

As expected, the value was entered successfully. Let's see what happens if we instead insert a numerical value into the VARCHAR column:

```
USE ROLE SYSADMIN;
CREATE OR REPLACE SCHEMA DEMO4_DB.TEST;
CREATE OR REPLACE TABLE DEMO4_DB.TEST.TEST1 (ID integer, DEPT Varchar);
INSERT INTO TEST1 (ID, DEPT)
VALUES (1,1);
SELECT * FROM DEMO4_DB.TEST.TEST1;
```

Again, the value was entered successfully. Now let's try inserting both types into the column within the same INSERT statement:

```
USE ROLE SYSADMIN;
CREATE OR REPLACE SCHEMA DEMO4_DB.TEST;
CREATE OR REPLACE TABLE DEMO4_DB.TEST.TEST1 (ID integer, DEPT Varchar);
INSERT INTO TEST1 (ID, DEPT)
VALUES (1,'one'), (2,2);
SELECT * FROM DEMO4_DB.TEST.TEST1;
```

When we try to insert two different data types into the VARCHAR column at the same time, we experience an error, as shown in Figure 4-8.

Numeric value 'one' is not recognized

Figure 4-8. The error message that is received when attempting to insert two different data types into a VARCHAR column in one multirow INSERT statement

Let's try again, but this time we'll insert two values with the same data type:

```
USE ROLE SYSADMIN;
CREATE OR REPLACE SCHEMA DEMO4_DB.TEST;
CREATE OR REPLACE TABLE DEMO4_DB.TEST.TEST1 (ID integer, DEPT Varchar);
INSERT INTO TEST1 (ID, DEPT)
VALUES (1,'one'), (2,'two');
SELECT * FROM DEMO4_DB.TEST.TEST1;
```

We're also successful if we insert two numerical values into the VARCHAR column:

```
USE ROLE SYSADMIN;
CREATE OR REPLACE SCHEMA DEMO4_DB.TEST;
CREATE OR REPLACE TABLE DEMO4_DB.TEST.TEST1 (ID integer, DEPT Varchar);
INSERT INTO TEST1 (ID, DEPT)
VALUES (1,1), (2,2);
SELECT * FROM DEMO4_DB.TEST.TEST1;
```

You'll notice that we are able to successfully load two different data types into the VARCHAR column, but not at the same time. And once we have two different data types in the VARCHAR column, we can still add additional values:

```
INSERT INTO TEST1 (ID, DEPT)
VALUES (5, 'five');
SELECT * FROM DEMO4_DB.TEST.TEST1;
```

Multirow inserts are one way of getting data into Snowflake. Chapter 6 is devoted to data loading and unloading, and includes an in-depth discussion of bulk data loading options and continuous data loading options.

Query Operators

There are several different types of query operators, including arithmetic, comparison, logical, subquery, and set operators.

Arithmetic operators, including +, -, *, /, and %, produce a numeric output from one or more inputs. The scale and precision of the output depends on the scale and precision of the input(s). Note that subtraction is the only arithmetic operation allowed on DATE expressions.

Comparison operators, typically appearing in a WHERE clause, are used to test the equality of two inputs. Comparison operators include the following:

- Equal (=)
- Not equal (!= or <>)
- Less than (<)
- Less than or equal (<=)
- Greater than (>)
- Greater than or equal (>=)

 Remember that TIMESTAMP_TZ values are compared based on their times in UTC, which does not account for daylight saving time. This is important because, at the moment of creation, TIMESTAMP_TZ stores the offset of a given time zone, not the actual time zone.

Logical operators can only be used in the WHERE clause. The order of precedence of these operators is NOT then AND then OR. *Subquery operators* include [NOT] EXISTS, ANY or ALL, and [NOT] IN. Queries can be combined when using *set operators* such as INTERSECT, MINUS or EXCEPT, UNION, and UNION ALL.

The default set operator order of preference is INTERSECT as the highest precedence, followed by EXCEPT, MINUS, and UNION, and finally UNION ALL as the lowest precedence. Of course, you can always use parentheses to override the default. Note that the UNION set operation is costly because it needs to sort the records to eliminate duplicate rows.

 When using set operators, make sure each query selects the same number of columns and the data type of each column is consistent, although an explicit type cast can be used if the data types are inconsistent.

Long-Running Queries, and Query Performance and Optimization

The Snowflake system will cancel long-running queries. The default duration for long-running queries is two days, but the STATEMENT_TIMEOUT_IN_SECONDS duration value can always be set at an account, session, object, or virtual warehouse level.

During the Snowflake SQL query process, one of the things that happens is the optimization engines find the most efficient execution plan for a specific query. In Chapter 9, we'll learn more about analyzing query performance and optimization techniques as well as how to use Snowflake's query profiler.

Snowflake Query Limits

SQL statements submitted through Snowflake clients have a query text size limit of 1 MB. Included in that limit are literals, including both string and binary literals. The query text size limit applies to the compressed size of the query. However, because the compression ratio for data varies widely, it is recommended to keep the uncompressed query text size below 1 MB.

Additionally, Snowflake limits the number of expressions allowed in a query to 16,384. There are ways to resolve this type of error depending on what are you trying to do with your SQL query statement. If you're attempting to insert data when you receive the error, try breaking up the statement into smaller queries. However, an even better choice would probably be to use the COPY INTO command instead of the INSERT command.

Another type of query limit error occurs when using a SELECT statement with an IN clause that has more than 16,384 values. Here is an example of what that code might look like:

```
SELECT  <column_1> FROM  <table_1>
WHERE <column_2> IN  (1, 2, 3, 4, 5,...);
```

One solution would be to use a JOIN or UNION command after placing those values in a second table. The SQL code could look like this:

```
SELECT <column_1>
FROM  <table_1> a
    JOIN  <table_2> b ON a.<column_2>  = b.<column_2>;
```

Introduction to Data Types Supported by Snowflake

Snowflake supports the basic SQL data types including geospatial data types, and a Boolean logical data type which provides for ternary logic. Snowflake's BOOLEAN data type can have an *unknown* value, or a TRUE or FALSE value. If the Boolean is used in an expression, such as a SELECT statement, an unknown value returns a NULL. If the Boolean is used as a predicate, such as in a WHERE clause, the unknown results will evaluate to FALSE. There are a few data types not supported by Snowflake, such as Large Object (LOB), including BLOB and CLOB, as well as ENUM and user-defined data types.

Snowflake offers native support for geospatial features such as points, lines, and polygons on the earth's surface. The Snowflake GEOGRAPHY data type follows the WGS standard. Points on the earth are represented as degrees of longitude and latitude. Altitude is not currently supported.

If you have geospatial data such as longitude and latitude, WKT, WKB, or GeoJSON, it is recommended that you convert and store this data in GEOGRAPHY columns rather than keeping the data in their original formats in VARCHAR, VARIANT, or NUMBER columns. This could significantly improve the performance of queries that use geospatial functionality.

In this section, we'll take a deeper dive into several Snowflake data types including numeric, string and binary, date and time, semi-structured, and unstructured.

Numeric Data Types

Snowflake's numeric data types include fixed-point numbers and floating-point numbers, as detailed in Table 4-2. Included in the table is information about each numeric data type's precision and scale. *Precision*, the total number of digits, impacts storage, whereas *scale*, the number of digits following the decimal point, does not. However, processing numeric data values with a larger scale could cause slower processing.

Table 4-2. Snowflake numeric data types

Fixed-point number data types	Precision	Comments
NUMBER	Optional (38, 0)	Numbers up to 38 digits; maximum scale is 37
DECIMAL, NUMERIC	Optional (38,0)	Synonymous with NUMBER
INT, INTEGER, BIGINT, SMALLINT, TINYINT, BYTEINT	Cannot be specified; always (38,0)	Possible values: -99999999999999999999999999999999999999 to +99999999999999999999999999999999999999 (inclusive)
Floating-point number data types		Comments
FLOAT, FLOAT4, FLOAT8	Approximately 15 digits	Values range from approximately 10-308 to 10+308
DOUBLE, DOUBLE PRECISION, REAL	Approximately 15 digits	Synonymous with FLOAT

It is a known issue that DOUBLE, DOUBLE PRECISION, and REAL columns are stored as DOUBLE but displayed as FLOAT.

Fixed-point numbers are exact numeric values and, as such, are often used for natural numbers and exact decimal values such as monetary amounts. In contrast, floating-point data types are used most often for mathematics and science.

You can see how fixed-point numbers vary based on the data type. Be sure to navigate to the *Chapter4* worksheet and then try the following example:

```
USE ROLE SYSADMIN;
CREATE OR REPLACE SCHEMA DEMO4_DB.DATATYPES;
CREATE OR REPLACE TABLE NUMFIXED (
    NUM NUMBER,
    NUM12 NUMBER(12, 0),
    DECIMAL DECIMAL (10, 2),
    INT INT,
    INTEGER INTEGER
);
```

To see what was created, you can run the DESC TABLE NUMFIXED statement to get the results shown in Figure 4-9.

	name	type	kind	null?
1	NUM	NUMBER(38,0)	COLUMN	Y
2	NUM12	NUMBER(12,0)	COLUMN	Y
3	DECIMAL	NUMBER(10,2)	COLUMN	Y
4	INT	NUMBER(38,0)	COLUMN	Y
5	INTEGER	NUMBER(38,0)	COLUMN	Y

Figure 4-9. Results showing the Snowflake fixed-point number data type

Now you can compare fixed-point numbers to floating-point numbers by using this next example:

```
USE ROLE SYSADMIN; USE SCHEMA DEMO4_DB.DATATYPES;
CREATE OR REPLACE TABLE NUMFLOAT (
    FLOAT FLOAT,
    DOUBLE DOUBLE,
    DP DOUBLE PRECISION,
    REAL REAL
);
```

Once again, use the Desc command to see the results, as shown in Figure 4-10:

```
DESC TABLE NUMFLOAT;
```

	name	type	kind	null?
1	FLOAT	FLOAT	COLUMN	Y
2	DOUBLE	FLOAT	COLUMN	Y
3	DP	FLOAT	COLUMN	Y
4	REAL	FLOAT	COLUMN	Y

Figure 4-10. Results showing the Snowflake floating-point number data type

In traditional computing, float data types are known to be faster for computation. But is that still an accurate statement about float data types in modern data platforms such as Snowflake? Not necessarily. It is important to consider that integer values can be stored in a compressed format in Snowflake, whereas float data types cannot. This results in less storage space and less cost for integers. Querying rows for an integer table type also takes significantly less time.

 Because of the inexact nature of floating-point data types, floating-point operations could have small rounding errors and those errors can accumulate, especially when using aggregate functions to process a large number of rows.

Snowflake's numeric data types are supported by numeric constants. Constants, also referred to as *literals*, represent fixed data values. Numeric digits 0 through 9 can be prefaced by a positive or negative sign. Exponents, indicated by e or E, are also supported in Snowflake numeric constants.

String and Binary Data Types

Snowflake supports both text and binary string data types, the details of which can be seen in Table 4-3.

Table 4-3. Snowflake text and binary string data types

Text string data types	Parameters	Comments
VARCHAR	Optional parameter (N), max number of characters	Holds Unicode characters; no performance difference between using full-length VARCHAR (16,777,216) or a smaller length
CHAR, CHARACTERS		Synonymous with VARCHAR; length is CHAR(1) if not specified
STRING, TEXT		Synonymous with VARCHAR
Binary string data types		**Comments**
BINARY		Has no notion of Unicode characters, so length is always measured in bytes; if length is not specified, the default is 8 MB (the maximum length)
VARBINARY		Synonymous with BINARY

You can see how the text string data types vary by attempting the following example, which creates the text string fields and then describes the table:

```
USE ROLE SYSADMIN; USE SCHEMA DEMO4_DB.DATATYPES;
CREATE OR REPLACE TABLE TEXTSTRING(
    VARCHAR VARCHAR,
    V100 VARCHAR(100),
    CHAR CHAR,
    C100 CHAR(100),
    STRING STRING,
    S100 STRING(100),
```

```
    TEXT TEXT,
    T100 TEXT(100)
);

DESC TABLE TEXTSTRING;
```

If you followed along with the example, you should see the output shown in Figure 4-11.

	name	type	kind	null?
1	VARCHAR	VARCHAR(16777216)	COLUMN	Y
2	V100	VARCHAR(100)	COLUMN	Y
3	CHAR	VARCHAR(1)	COLUMN	Y
4	C100	VARCHAR(100)	COLUMN	Y
5	STRING	VARCHAR(16777216)	COLUMN	Y
6	S100	VARCHAR(100)	COLUMN	Y
7	TEXT	VARCHAR(16777216)	COLUMN	Y
8	T100	VARCHAR(100)	COLUMN	Y

Figure 4-11. Results of creating a TEXTSTRING table

Snowflake's string data types are supported by string constants, which are always enclosed between delimiters, either single quotes or dollar signs. Using dollar sign symbols as delimiters is especially useful when the string contains many quote characters.

Date and Time Input/Output Data Types

Snowflake uses the Gregorian calendar, rather than the Julian calendar, for all dates and timestamps. The Snowflake date and time data types are summarized in Table 4-4.

Table 4-4. Snowflake date and time data types

Date and time data types	Default mapping	Comments
DATE		Single DATE type; most common date forms are accepted; all accepted timestamps are valid inputs with TIME truncated; the associated time is assumed to be midnight
DATETIME		Alias for TIMESTAMP_NTZ
TIME		Single TIME type in the form HH:MI:SS, internally stored as wall clock time; time zones not taken into consideration
TIMESTAMP	Default is TIMESTAMP_NTZ	User-specified alias of one of the three TIMESTAMP_ variations

Date and time data types	Default mapping	Comments
TIMESTAMP_LTZ		Internally UTC time with a specified precision; TIMESTAMP with local time zone
TIMESTAMP_NTZ		Internally wall clock time; TIMESTAMP without time zone
TIMESTAMP_TZ		Internally UTC time with a time zone offset; TIMESTAMP with time zone

Snowflake's data and time data types are supported by interval constants as well as date and time constants. Interval constants can be used to add or subtract a specific period of time to or from a date, time, or timestamp. The interval is not a data type; it can be used only in date, time, or timestamp arithmetic and will represent seconds if the date or time portion is not specified.

 The order of interval increments is important because increments are added or subtracted in the order in which they are listed. This could be important for calculations affected by leap years.

Semi-Structured Data Types

Structured data, known as quantitative data, can be easily stored in a database table as rows and columns whereas semi-structured data, such as XML data, is not schema dependent, which makes it more difficult to store in a database. In some situations, however, semi-structured data can be stored in a relational database.

Snowflake supports data types for importing and operating on semi-structured data such as JSON, Avro, ORC, Parquet, and XML data. Snowflake does so through its universal data type VARIANT, a special column type which allows you to store semi-structured data. Table 4-5 provides more information about Snowflake semi-structured data types. Note that it is possible for a VARIANT value to be missing, which is considered to be different from a true null value.

Table 4-5. Snowflake semi-structured data types

Semi-structured data types	Characteristics	Comments
VARIANT	Can store OBJECT and ARRAY	Stores values of any other type, up to a maximum of 16 MB uncompressed; internally stored in compressed columnar binary representation
OBJECT		Represents collections of key-value pairs with the key as a nonempty string and the value of VARIANT type
ARRAY		Represents arrays of arbitrary size whose index is a non-negative integer and values have VARIANT type

When loaded into a VARIANT column, non-native values such as dates and timestamps are stored as strings. Storing values in this way will likely cause operations to be slower and to consume more space as compared to storing date and timestamp values in a relational column with the corresponding data type.

The hands-on exercises for semi-structured data will use the Snowflake sample weather data, which is stored in native JSON format. We'll spend some time getting a feel for the data that exists and then we'll learn how to use the FLATTEN function to produce a lateral view of the semi-structured data.

At the time of this writing, the weather dataset was available in the Snowflake free trial accounts. However, Snowflake may be deprecating this dataset over time. Please see *https://github.com/ SnowflakeDefinitiveGuide* for further information.

Let's first just take a quick look at a few rows of data:

```
USE ROLE SYSADMIN;
USE SCHEMA SNOWFLAKE_SAMPLE_DATA.WEATHER;
SELECT * FROM DAILY_16_TOTAL
LIMIT 5;
```

You should see that there are two columns: one VARIANT column (V) and one TIMESTAMP column (T), as shown in Figure 4-12.

	V	...	T
1	{ "city": { "coord": { "lat": 47.616669, "lon": 9.78333 }, "country": "DE", "id": 2906110, "name": "Hergensweiler" }, "data": [{		2016-09-07 00:38:01.000
2	{ "city": { "coord": { "lat": 50.166672, "lon": 8.56667 }, "country": "DE", "id": 2828737, "name": "Steinbach am Taunus" }, "data":		2016-09-07 00:38:01.000
3	{ "city": { "coord": { "lat": 52.316669, "lon": 7.58333 }, "country": "DE", "id": 2898603, "name": "Horstel" }, "data": [{ "clou		2016-09-07 00:38:01.000
4	{ "city": { "coord": { "lat": 50.816669, "lon": 8.96667 }, "country": "DE", "id": 2890504, "name": "Kirchhain" }, "data": [{ "cl		2016-09-07 00:38:02.000
5	{ "city": { "coord": { "lat": 51.799999, "lon": 10.33333 }, "country": "DE", "id": 2939995, "name": "Clausthal-Zellerfeld" }, "data":		2016-09-07 00:38:02.000

Figure 4-12. Two columns in the Snowflake weather sample data table

Let's focus on the data in the VARIANT column:

```
SELECT v:city
FROM SNOWFLAKE_SAMPLE_DATA.WEATHER.DAILY_16_TOTAL
LIMIT 10;
```

Once the results are returned, click V:CITY at the top of the column. This will highlight the column and give you the details you need to see that there are four distinct object keys in this column (as shown in Figure 4-13). In order, the object keys relating to V:CITY are coordinates, country, ID, and name.

	V:CITY
1	{ "coord": { "lat": 51.050121, "lon": -112.685173 }, "country": "CA", "id": 5978906, "name": "Hussar" }
2	{ "coord": { "lat": 52.716709, "lon": -103.65097 }, "country": "CA", "id": 5902121, "name": "Bjorkdale" }
3	{ "coord": { "lat": 46.683449, "lon": -64.165443 }, "country": "CA", "id": 5925150, "name": "Coleman" }
4	{ "coord": { "lat": 44.750111, "lon": -79.699654 }, "country": "CA", "id": 6177107, "name": "Waubaushene" }
5	{ "coord": { "lat": 52.250111, "lon": -107.501289 }, "country": "CA", "id": 5886799, "name": "Arelee" }
6	{ "coord": { "lat": 45.55011, "lon": -78.58287 }, "country": "CA", "id": 5883647, "name": "Algonquin Park" }
7	{ "coord": { "lat": 45.96677, "lon": -71.815804 }, "country": "CA", "id": 5921064, "name": "Chesterville" }
8	{ "coord": { "lat": 52.500061, "lon": -105.734421 }, "country": "CA", "id": 5933765, "name": "Cudworth" }
9	{ "coord": { "lat": 47.533249, "lon": -55.931641 }, "country": "CA", "id": 5974193, "name": "Hermitage" }
10	{ "coord": { "lat": 49.340729, "lon": -55.083961 }, "country": "CA", "id": 6055114, "name": "Little Burnt Bay" }

Figure 4-13. Four distinct object keys for CITY data in the VARIANT column

Let's now manually break out some of the CITY data and list them in a more logical order (as shown in Figure 4-14):

```
SELECT v:city:id, v:city:name, v:city:country, v:city:coord
FROM SNOWFLAKE_SAMPLE_DATA.WEATHER.DAILY_16_TOTAL
LIMIT 10;
```

	V:CITY:ID	V:CITY:NAME	V:CITY:COUNTRY	V:CITY:COORD
1	5978906	"Hussar"	"CA"	{ "lat": 51.050121, "lon": -112.685173 }
2	5902121	"Bjorkdale"	"CA"	{ "lat": 52.716709, "lon": -103.65097 }
3	5925150	"Coleman"	"CA"	{ "lat": 46.683449, "lon": -64.165443 }
4	6177107	"Waubaushene"	"CA"	{ "lat": 44.750111, "lon": -79.699654 }
5	5886799	"Arelee"	"CA"	{ "lat": 52.250111, "lon": -107.501289 }
6	5883647	"Algonquin Park"	"CA"	{ "lat": 45.55011, "lon": -78.58287 }
7	5921064	"Chesterville"	"CA"	{ "lat": 45.96677, "lon": -71.815804 }
8	5933765	"Cudworth"	"CA"	{ "lat": 52.500061, "lon": -105.734421 }
9	5974193	"Hermitage"	"CA"	{ "lat": 47.533249, "lon": -55.931641 }
10	6055114	"Little Burnt Bay"	"CA"	{ "lat": 49.340729, "lon": -55.083961 }

Figure 4-14. Detail of the CITY data in the VARIANT column

The latitude and longitude details are nested in the coordinate information. Let's separate those out and give the columns some appropriate names:

```
SELECT v:city:id AS ID, v:city:name AS CITY,
    v:city:country AS COUNTRY, v:city:coord:lat AS LATITUDE,
    v:city:coord:lon AS LONGITUDE
FROM SNOWFLAKE_SAMPLE_DATA.WEATHER.DAILY_16_TOTAL
LIMIT 10;
```

We can convert a variant data type to another data type. In the next example, we'll cast the city and country VARIANT data to a VARCHAR data type, and we'll assign meaningful labels to the columns:

```
SELECT v:city:id AS ID, v:city:name::varchar AS city,
    v:city.country::varchar AS country, v:city:coord:lon
    AS longitude, v:city:coord:lat AS latitude
FROM SNOWFLAKE_SAMPLE_DATA.WEATHER.DAILY_16_TOTAL
LIMIT 10;
```

The results are shown in Figure 4-15.

	ID	CITY	COUNTRY	LONGITUDE	LATITUDE
1	2806746	Wolfsbehringen	DE	10.48333	51
2	2840860	Schaderode	DE	10.91667	51.01667
3	2807471	Wischuer	DE	11.7	54.099998
4	6549273	Giersleben	DE	11.5667	51.766701
5	2920582	Giersleben	DE	11.56667	51.76667
6	2820258	Ullrichsberg	DE	13.15	51.083328
7	2857048	Orsberg	DE	7.25	50.599998
8	2863104	Niedermörsbach	DE	7.78333	50.716671
9	6551468	Krukow	DE	10.4833	53.416698
10	2883432	Krukow	DE	10.48333	53.416672

Figure 4-15. Casting of the city and country VARIANT data to a VARCHAR data type

We can confirm that we successfully cast the two columns by asking Snowflake to describe the results of our last query:

```
DESC RESULT LAST_QUERY_ID();
```

Next, let's look at more data in the VARIANT column:

```
SELECT v:data
FROM SNOWFLAKE_SAMPLE_DATA.WEATHER.DAILY_16_TOTAL
LIMIT 10;
```

Once the results are returned, click V:DATA at the top of the column. This will highlight the column and give you column details that you'll see on the right side (as shown in Figure 4-16). You'll notice that there is one array in this column relating to the DATA information.

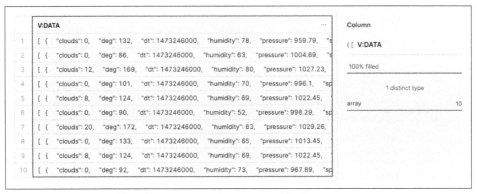

V:DATA					···	Column
1	[{ "clouds": 0,	"deg": 132,	"dt": 1473246000,	"humidity": 78,	"pressure": 959.79, "s	{[**V:DATA**
2	[{ "clouds": 0,	"deg": 86,	"dt": 1473246000,	"humidity": 63,	"pressure": 1004.69, "s	
3	[{ "clouds": 12,	"deg": 169,	"dt": 1473246000,	"humidity": 80,	"pressure": 1027.23,	100% filled
4	[{ "clouds": 0,	"deg": 101,	"dt": 1473246000,	"humidity": 70,	"pressure": 996.1, "sp	
5	[{ "clouds": 8,	"deg": 124,	"dt": 1473246000,	"humidity": 69,	"pressure": 1022.45,	1 distinct type
6	[{ "clouds": 0,	"deg": 90,	"dt": 1473246000,	"humidity": 52,	"pressure": 998.29, "s	array 10
7	[{ "clouds": 20,	"deg": 172,	"dt": 1473246000,	"humidity": 63,	"pressure": 1029.26,	
8	[{ "clouds": 0,	"deg": 133,	"dt": 1473246000,	"humidity": 65,	"pressure": 1013.45,	
9	[{ "clouds": 8,	"deg": 124,	"dt": 1473246000,	"humidity": 69,	"pressure": 1022.45,	
10	[{ "clouds": 0,	"deg": 92,	"dt": 1473246000,	"humidity": 73,	"pressure": 967.89, "sp	

Figure 4-16. The weather data array in the VARIANT column

Because the DATA information is stored as an array, we can look at a particular element in the array. Be sure to click each result row to see that only one element was selected for each row:

```
SELECT v:data[5]
FROM SNOWFLAKE_SAMPLE_DATA.WEATHER.DAILY_16_TOTAL
LIMIT 10;
```

We can further limit the information returned by taking a look at the humidity value for a particular day for a specific city and country:

```
SELECT v:city:name AS city, v:city:country AS country,
    v:data[0]:humidity AS HUMIDITY
FROM SNOWFLAKE_SAMPLE_DATA.WEATHER.DAILY_16_TOTAL
LIMIT 10;
```

Now let's do a quick review. When we look at the DATA array, `v:data AS DATA` in the following statement, we notice that each row contains a complete data array. Within each data array there are 16 elements for each distinct piece of data (as shown in Figure 4-17). In our SQL query, we'll include the first two data elements for the humidity and the day temperature:

```
SELECT v:data[0]:dt::timestamp AS TIME,
v:data[0]:humidity AS HUMIDITY0, v:data[0]:temp:day AS DAY_TEMP0,
v:data[1]:humidity AS HUMIDITY1, v:data[1]:temp:day AS DAY_TEMP1,
v:data AS DATA
FROM SNOWFLAKE_SAMPLE_DATA.WEATHER.DAILY_16_TOTAL
LIMIT 100;
```

	TIME	HUMIDITY0	DAY_TEMP0	HUMIDITY1	DAY_TEMP1	DATA	|{ DATA
1	I-07 11:00:00.000	78	295.03	65	297.5	[{ "clouds": 0, "deg": 132, "dt": 1473246000, "humidity": 78, "pressu	[
2	I-07 11:00:00.000	83	301.31	55	299.75	[{ "clouds": 0, "deg": 86, "dt": 1473246000, "humidity": 63, "pressu	"clouds": 0,
3	I-07 11:00:00.000	80	300.4	75	298.65	[{ "clouds": 12, "deg": 169, "dt": 1473246000, "humidity": 80, "pressu	"deg": 132,
4	I-07 11:00:00.000	70	299.19	66	297.85	[{ "clouds": 0, "deg": 101, "dt": 1473246000, "humidity": 70, "pressu	"dt": 1473246000,
5	I-07 11:00:00.000	69	298.6	62	299.8	[{ "clouds": 8, "deg": 124, "dt": 1473246000, "humidity": 69, "pressu	"humidity": 78,
6	I-07 11:00:00.000	52	298.82	39	301.1	[{ "clouds": 0, "deg": 90, "dt": 1473246000, "humidity": 52, "pressure	"pressure": 969.79,
7	I-07 11:00:00.000	83	300.34	64	299.7	[{ "clouds": 20, "deg": 172, "dt": 1473246000, "humidity": 63, "pressi	"temp": {
8	I-07 11:00:00.000	65	298.9	65	299.35	[{ "clouds": 0, "deg": 133, "dt": 1473246000, "humidity": 65, "pressu	"day": 295.03,
9	I-07 11:00:00.000	69	298.6	62	299.8	[{ "clouds": 8, "deg": 124, "dt": 1473246000, "humidity": 69, "pressu	"eve": 290.67,
10	I-07 11:00:00.000	73	297.54	66	297.45	[{ "clouds": 0, "deg": 92, "dt": 1473246000, "humidity": 73, "pressu	"max": 295.94,
11	I-07 11:00:00.000	78	297.46	71	298.45	[{ "clouds": 0, "deg": 90, "dt": 1473246000, "humidity": 78, "pressu	"min": 283.11,
12	I-07 11:00:00.000	78	299.78	69	298.7	[{ "clouds": 8, "deg": 145, "dt": 1473246000, "humidity": 78, "pressu	"morn": 287.37,
13	I-07 11:00:00.000	54	299.83	56	300.15	[{ "clouds": 12, "deg": 194, "dt": 1473246000, "humidity": 54, "pressi	"night": 283.11
							},
							"uvi": 0,
							"weather": [
							{
							"description":

Figure 4-17. One DATA array element (path) per row

Let's see how we can leverage the FLATTEN table function. The FLATTEN function produces a lateral view of a VARIANT, OBJECT, or ARRAY column. We'll demonstrate how FLATTEN works on the DATA array in the sample weather data table:

```sql
SELECT d.value:dt::timestamp AS TIME,
    v:city:name AS CITY, v:city:country AS COUNTRY,
    d.path AS PATH, d.value:humidity AS HUMIDITY,
        d.value:temp:day AS DAY_TEMP,v:data AS DATA
FROM SNOWFLAKE_SAMPLE_DATA.WEATHER.DAILY_16_TOTAL,
LATERAL FLATTEN(input => daily_16_total.v:data) d
LIMIT 100;
```

You'll notice that the same DATA array appears for each of the 16 *flattened* rows, but the HUMIDITY and DAY_TEMP reported in each row are associated with the specific PATH of the array (as shown in Figure 4-18).

	TIME	CITY	COUNTRY	PATH	HUMIDITY	DAY_TEMP	DATA	|{ DATA
1	:00:00.000	"Socuellamos"	"ES"	[0]	83	280.78	[{ "clouds": 0, "deg": 292, "dt": 1516536000, "humidity": 83, "pressu	[
2	:00:00.000	"Socuellamos"	"ES"	[1]	100	282.38	[{ "clouds": 0, "deg": 292, "dt": 1516536000, "humidity": 83, "pressu	{
3	:00:00.000	"Socuellamos"	"ES"	[2]	100	282.19	[{ "clouds": 0, "deg": 292, "dt": 1516536000, "humidity": 83, "pressu	"clouds": 0,
4	:00:00.000	"Socuellamos"	"ES"	[3]	90	286.53	[{ "clouds": 0, "deg": 292, "dt": 1516536000, "humidity": 83, "pressu	"deg": 292,
5	:00:00.000	"Socuellamos"	"ES"	[4]	0	282.15	[{ "clouds": 0, "deg": 292, "dt": 1516536000, "humidity": 83, "pressu	"dt": 1516536000,
6	:00:00.000	"Socuellamos"	"ES"	[5]	0	281.01	[{ "clouds": 0, "deg": 292, "dt": 1516536000, "humidity": 83, "pressu	"humidity": 83,
7	:00:00.000	"Socuellamos"	"ES"	[6]	0	282.27	[{ "clouds": 0, "deg": 292, "dt": 1516536000, "humidity": 83, "pressu	"pressure": 949.59,
8	:00:00.000	"Socuellamos"	"ES"	[7]	0	282.99	[{ "clouds": 0, "deg": 292, "dt": 1516536000, "humidity": 83, "pressu	"speed": 2.85,
9	:00:00.000	"Socuellamos"	"ES"	[8]	0	283.92	[{ "clouds": 0, "deg": 292, "dt": 1516536000, "humidity": 83, "pressu	"temp": {
10	:00:00.000	"Socuellamos"	"ES"	[9]	0	283.65	[{ "clouds": 0, "deg": 292, "dt": 1516536000, "humidity": 83, "pressu	"day": 280.78,
11	:00:00.000	"Socuellamos"	"ES"	[10]	0	283.35	[{ "clouds": 0, "deg": 292, "dt": 1516536000, "humidity": 83, "pressu	"eve": 276.33,
12	:00:00.000	"Socuellamos"	"ES"	[11]	0	284.82	[{ "clouds": 0, "deg": 292, "dt": 1516536000, "humidity": 83, "pressu	"max": 280.78,
13	:00:00.000	"Socuellamos"	"ES"	[12]	0	284.08	[{ "clouds": 0, "deg": 292, "dt": 1516536000, "humidity": 83, "pressu	"min": 271.91,
								"morn": 280.78,
								"night": 271.91
								},
								"uvi": 1.673,
								"weather": [
								{
								"description":

Figure 4-18. The flattened DATA array

The temperature information in the DATA array has six nested values: day, eve, max, min, morn, and night. We can use a *nested* FLATTEN to further flatten the DATA array. When we do this, each DATA row appears 96 times, six times for each of the 16 PATH values (as shown in Figure 4-19):

```
SELECT d.value:dt::timestamp AS TIME,
t.key,
v:city:name AS CITY, v:city:country AS COUNTRY,
d.path AS PATH,
d.value:humidity AS HUMIDITY,
d.value:temp:day AS DAY_TEMP,
d.value:temp:night AS NIGHT_TEMP,
v:data AS data
FROM SNOWFLAKE_SAMPLE_DATA.WEATHER.DAILY_16_TOTAL,
LATERAL FLATTEN(input => daily_16_total.v:data) d,
LATERAL FLATTEN(input => d.value:temp) t
WHERE v:city:id = 1274693
LIMIT 100;
```

	TIME	KEY	CITY	COUNTRY	PATH	HUMIDITY	DAY_TEMP	NIGHT_TEMP	DATA		DATA
1	0.000	day	"Chandrapur"	"IN"	[0]	44	308.46	288.08	[{ "clouds": 0, "deg": 127, "dt": 1516600800,		[
2	0.000	eve	"Chandrapur"	"IN"	[0]	44	308.46	288.08	[{ "clouds": 0, "deg": 127, "dt": 1516600800,		{
3	0.000	max	"Chandrapur"	"IN"	[0]	44	308.46	288.08	[{ "clouds": 0, "deg": 127, "dt": 1516600800,		"clouds": 0,
4	0.000	min	"Chandrapur"	"IN"	[0]	44	308.46	288.08	[{ "clouds": 0, "deg": 127, "dt": 1516600800,		"deg": 127,
5	0.000	morn	"Chandrapur"	"IN"	[0]	44	308.46	288.08	[{ "clouds": 0, "deg": 127, "dt": 1516600800,		"dt": 1516600800,
6	0.000	night	"Chandrapur"	"IN"	[0]	44	308.46	288.08	[{ "clouds": 0, "deg": 127, "dt": 1516600800,		"humidity": 44,
7	0.000	day	"Chandrapur"	"IN"	[1]	51	300.83	293.7	[{ "clouds": 0, "deg": 127, "dt": 1516600800,		"pressure": 998.73,
											"speed": 2.78,
8	0.000	eve	"Chandrapur"	"IN"	[1]	51	300.83	293.7	[{ "clouds": 0, "deg": 127, "dt": 1516600800,		"temp": {
9	0.000	max	"Chandrapur"	"IN"	[1]	51	300.83	293.7	[{ "clouds": 0, "deg": 127, "dt": 1516600800,		"day": 308.46,
											"eve": 303.73,
10	0.000	min	"Chandrapur"	"IN"	[1]	51	300.83	293.7	[{ "clouds": 0, "deg": 127, "dt": 1516600800,		"max": 308.46,
											"min": 288.08,
11	0.000	morn	"Chandrapur"	"IN"	[1]	51	300.83	293.7	[{ "clouds": 0, "deg": 127, "dt": 1516600800,		"morn": 300.42,
12	0.000	night	"Chandrapur"	"IN"	[1]	51	300.83	293.7	[{ "clouds": 0, "deg": 127, "dt": 1516600800,		"night": 288.08
											},
13	0.000	day	"Chandrapur"	"IN"	[2]	48	298.71	288.55	[{ "clouds": 0, "deg": 127, "dt": 1516600800,		"uvi": 7.574,
											"weather": [
											{
											"description":

Figure 4-19. The flattened, nested DATA array

As we've just seen, the Snowflake FLATTEN function is used to convert semi-structured data to a relational representation.

> It is possible to combine a LATERAL JOIN with a FLATTEN function to separate events into individual JSON objects while preserving the global data.

Unstructured Data Types

There are many advantages to using unstructured data to gain insight. Unstructured data is often qualitative, but it can also be quantitative data lacking rows, columns, or delimiters, as would be the case with a PDF file that contains quantitative data. Media logs, medical images, audio files of call center recordings, document images, and many other types of unstructured data can be used for analytical purposes and for the purpose of sentiment analysis. Storing and governing unstructured data is not easy. Unstructured data is not organized in a predefined manner, which means it is not well suited for relational databases. Typically, unstructured data has been stored in blob storage locations, which has several inherent disadvantages, making it difficult and time-consuming to search for files.

To improve searchability of unstructured data, Snowflake recently launched built-in directory tables. Using a tabular file catalog for searches of unstructured data is now as simple as using a SELECT * command on the directory table. Users can also build a table stream on top of a directory table, which makes it possible to create pipelines for processing unstructured data. Additionally, Snowflake users can create secure views on directory tables and, thus, are also able to share those secure views with others.

How Snowflake Supports Unstructured Data Use

Unstructured data represents an increasingly larger percentage of data being generated today. Examples of unstructured data types include video, audio, or image files, logfiles, sensor data, and social media posts. Unstructured data, which can be human generated or machine generated, has an internal structure but not one that is storable in a structured database format.

There are many reasons why you'd want to make use of all this unstructured data. Such use cases could include deriving insights like sentiment analysis from call center recordings; extracting text for analytics by using optical character recognition processes on insurance cards or prescription pills; using machine learning on DICOM medical images; or extracting key-value pairs from stored PDF documents.

It's no secret that unstructured data is complex; hence, there are many challenges to storing, searching, and analyzing it. Traditional data warehouses and data lakes have been unable to adequately support the workload demands of today's data formats, especially unstructured data. However, Snowflake is not your traditional data warehouse or data lake. Instead, it is a data platform built from the ground up for the cloud; therefore, it has removed much of the difficulty associated with storing, searching, and analyzing or processing unstructured data.

The first consideration in using unstructured data is how and where to store the unstructured files. When using Snowflake, there are two ways to do this: internal stages and external stages. We'd use an internal stage if we wanted to store data internally on Snowflake; especially if we were looking for a simple, easy-to-manage solution. That is because Snowflake automatically manages the scalability, encryption, data compression, and other aspects of storage. We'd alternatively use an external stage, known as *bring your own storage*, if we have legacy data stored elsewhere across the cloud as there is no need to move all your data into Snowflake.

While it is possible to store unstructured data internally in a Snowflake table using the VARIANT column type, it is usually not recommended because there is a file storage limitation of 16 MB. If we instead use a stage, there are no size limitations other than those imposed by the major cloud providers upon which your Snowflake instance is built: 5 TB of data for AWS and GCP or 256 GB of data for Azure.

Whether you use internal or external Snowflake stages, control access to data is easily achieved through role-based access controls. By using GRANT and REVOKE statements, privileges can be given to Snowflake resources like stages by granting permissions to roles which are then granted to individuals. It's easy to understand and learn how to give fine-grain access to data in an internal or external stage, or to a subset of the data stored in views which are Snowflake objects created on top of stages. For a refresher about Snowflake access controls, refer to Chapter 5.

Using Snowflake, storing and granting access to unstructured data can be done in three different ways: stage file URLs, scoped URLs, or presigned URLs.

Stage file URL access

A stage file URL is used to create a permanent URL to a file on a Snowflake stage and is used most frequently for custom applications. Access to a file URL is through a GET request to the REST API endpoint along with the authorization token. Note that the user must have read privileges on the stage. Stage file URLs have a unique feature in that they can be listed in a Snowflake directory table.

The ability to create a directory table, like a file catalog, which you can easily search to retrieve file URLs to access the staged files as well as other metadata, is a unique feature that Snowflake provides for unstructured data. Snowflake roles that have been granted privileges can query a directory table to retrieve URLs to access staged files.

Whether you want to, for example, sort by file size or by last modified date, or only take the top 100 files or the largest files, it is possible to do so with Snowflake directory tables. You can also use Snowflake streams and tasks with directory tables for a powerful combination. Using table streams, for example, you can easily find all the new files that were recently added. Because a directory table is a table, you can perform fine-grain select and search operations. Search operations in regular blob stores are extremely difficult because they don't have the catalog information in a tabular format.

A Snowflake directory table is a built-in read-only table. As such, you cannot add more columns or modify the columns in a directory table. What you can do is use Snowflake streams and tasks to calculate values and put them into a new table with a column containing the results of the calculation. You'll then be able to join that table with the directory table by creating a view. You can also add tags, if desired.

Scoped URL access

A scoped URL is frequently used for custom applications; especially in situations where access to the data will be given to other accounts using the data share functionality or when ad hoc analysis is performed internally using Snowsight. Sharing unstructured data securely in the cloud is easy with Snowflake. No privileges are required on the stage. Instead, you'd create a secure view, and using the scoped URL, you would share the contents of the secure view. The scoped URL is encoded, so it is not possible to determine the account, database, schema, or other storage details from the URL.

Access to files in a stage using scoped URL access is achieved in one of two ways. One way is for a Snowflake user to click a scoped URL in the results table in Snowsight. The other way is to send the scoped URL in a request which results in Snowflake authenticating the user, verifying the scoped URL has not expired, and then redirecting the user to the staged file in the cloud storage service. Remember, the location of the staged file in the cloud storage is encoded, so the user is unable to determine the location. The scoped URL in the output from the API call is valid for 24 hours, the current length of time the result cache exists.

 For security reasons, it is impossible to share a scoped URL that has been shared with you. If you were to share the link with someone else who does not have similar access granted to them, the message *access denied* would appear.

Presigned URL access

A presigned URL is most often used for business intelligence applications or reporting tools that need to display unstructured file contents for open files. Because the presigned URLs are already authenticated, a user or application can directly access or download files without the need to pass an authorization token.

The GET_PRESIGNED_URL function generates the presigned URL to a stage file using the stage name and relative file path as inputs. Access to files in a stage using a presigned URL can be accomplished in three different ways: use the presigned URL in a web browser to directly navigate to the file, click a presigned URL in the results table in Snowsight, or send the presigned URL in a REST API call request.

Processing unstructured data with Java functions and external functions

The ability to run processes on the unstructured data inside files is one of the most exciting features offered by Snowflake. Currently, there are two ways to process unstructured data using Snowflake: Java functions and external functions. In the future, Snowflake plans to add the ability to process unstructured data using Python functions.

If you already have Java code that you've written for use on unstructured data, it makes sense to use a Java user-defined function (UDF). Note that Java UDFs are executed directly in Snowflake, using a Snowflake virtual warehouse. As such, Java UDFs do not make any API calls outside the boundaries of Snowflake. Everything is tightly secured and managed within the Snowflake environment.

If there are external API services such as machine learning models, geocoders, or other custom code that you want to utilize, external functions can be used. External functions make it possible to use existing machine learning services to extract text from images, or to process PDF files to extract key-value pairs. In an external function, you can use any of the AWS, Azure, or GCP functionalities, including AWS Rekognition or Azure Cognitive Services. External functions executed on unstructured data, whether stored within internal or external stages, can be used to eliminate the need to export and reimport data.

Snowflake SQL Functions and Session Variables

Snowflake offers users the ability to create UDFs and to use external functions, as well as to access many different built-in functions. Session variables also extend Snowflake SQL capabilities.

Using System-Defined (Built-In) Functions

Examples of Snowflake built-in functions include scalar, aggregate, window, table, and system functions.

Scalar functions accept a single row or value as an input and then return one value as a result, whereas *aggregate functions* also return a single value but accept multiple rows or values as inputs.

Scalar functions

Some scalar functions operate on a string or binary input value. Examples include CONCAT, LEN, SPLIT, TRIM, UPPER and LOWER case conversion, and REPLACE. Other scalar file functions, such as GET_STAGE_LOCATION, enable you to access files staged in Snowflake cloud storage.

Additionally, you can do many things in Snowflake with date and time data types. Some examples of scalar date and time functions and data generation functions include the following:

- Construct/deconstruct (extract) using month, day, and year components.
- Truncate or "round up" dates to a higher level.
- Parse and format dates using strings.
- Add/subtract to find and use date differences.
- Generate system dates or a table of dates.

Aggregate functions

A Snowflake aggregate function will always return one row even when the input contains no rows. The returned row from an aggregate function where the input contains zero rows could be a zero, an empty string, or some other value. Aggregate functions can be of a general nature, such as MIN, MAX, MEDIAN, MODE, and SUM. Aggregate functions also include linear regression, statistics and probability, frequency estimation, percentile estimation, and much more.

Snowflake *window functions* are a special type of aggregate function that can operate on a subset of rows. This subset of related rows is called a *window*. Unlike aggregate functions which return a single value for a group of rows, a window function will return an output row for each input row. The output depends not only on the individual row passed to the function but also on the values of the other rows in the window passed to the function.

Window functions are commonly used for finding a year-over-year percentage change, a moving average, and a running or cumulative total, as well as for ranking rows by groupings or custom criteria.

Let's compare an aggregate function with a window function. In this first example, we'll create an aggregate function by using the vowels in the alphabet and their corresponding locations:

```
SELECT LETTER, SUM(LOCATION) as AGGREGATE
FROM (SELECT 'A' as LETTER, 1 as LOCATION
        UNION ALL (SELECT 'A' as LETTER,1 as LOCATION)
        UNION ALL (SELECT 'E' as LETTER,5 as LOCATION)
     ) as AGG_TABLE
GROUP BY LETTER;
```

The results of this query are shown in Figure 4-20.

	LETTER	AGGREGATE
1	A	2
2	E	5

Figure 4-20. Results of an aggregate function query

Next, we'll create a window function using the same logic:

```
SELECT LETTER, SUM(LOCATION) OVER (PARTITION BY LETTER) as WINDOW_FUNCTION
FROM (SELECT 'A' as LETTER, 1 as LOCATION
        UNION ALL (SELECT 'A' as LETTER, 1 as LOCATION)
        UNION ALL (SELECT 'E' as LETTER, 5 as LOCATION)
     ) as WINDOW_TABLE;
```

Notice, in Figure 4-21, how the letter A has the same sum value in the window function as in the aggregate function, but repeats in the results because the input has two separate A listings.

	LETTER	WINDOW_FUNCTION
1	A	2
2	A	2
3	E	5

Figure 4-21. Results of a window function

Table functions

Table functions, often called *tabular functions*, return results in a tabular format with one or more columns and none, one, or many rows. Most Snowflake table functions are 1-to-*N* functions where each input row generates *N* output rows, but there exist some *M*-to-*N* table functions where a group of *M* input rows produces a group of *N* output rows. Table functions can be system defined or user defined. Some examples of system-defined table functions include VALIDATE, GENERATOR, FLATTEN, RESULT_SCAN, LOGIN_HISTORY, and TASK_HISTORY.

System functions

Built-in *system functions* return system-level information or query information, or perform control operations.

One oft-used system information function is SYSTEM$CLUSTERING_INFORMATION, which returns clustering information, including the average clustering depth, about one or more columns in a table.

System control functions allow you to execute actions in the system. One example of a control function is SYSTEM$CANCEL_ALL_QUERIES and requires the session ID. You can obtain the session ID by logging in as the ACCOUNTADMIN. From the Main menu in Snowsight, go to Activity → Query History and then use the Column button to select the session ID so that it will be displayed. Alternatively, go to Account → Sessions in the Classic Console interface:

```
SELECT SYSTEM$CANCEL_ALL_QUERIES(<session_id>);
```

If you need to cancel queries for a specific virtual warehouse or user rather than the session, you'll want to use the ALTER command along with ABORT ALL QUERIES instead of a system control function.

Creating SQL and JavaScript UDFs and Using Session Variables

SQL functionality can be extended by SQL UDFs, Java UDFs, Python UDFs, and session variables. We took a deep dive into both SQL and JavaScript UDFs in Chapter 3, so we'll focus on learning more about session variables in this section.

Snowflake supports SQL variables declared by the user, using the SET command. These session variables exist while a Snowflake session is active. Variables are distinguished in a Snowflake SQL statement by a $ prefix and can also contain identifier names when used with objects. You must wrap a variable inside the identifier, such as *IDENTIFIER($Variable)*, to use a variable as an identifier. Alternatively, you can wrap the variable inside an object in the context of a FROM clause.

To see all the variables defined in the current session, use the SHOW VARIABLES command.

Some examples of session variable functions include the following:

- SYS_CONTEXT and SET_SYS_CONTEXT
- SESSION_CONTEXT and SET_SESSION_CONTEXT
- GETVARIABLE and SETVARIABLE

All variables created during a session are dropped when a Snowflake session is closed. If you want to destroy a variable during a session, you can use the UNSET command.

External Functions

An *external function* is a type of UDF that calls code which is stored and executed outside of Snowflake. Snowflake supports scalar external functions, which means the remote service must return exactly one row for each row received. Within Snowflake, the external function is stored as a database object that Snowflake uses to call the remote service.

It is important to note that rather than calling a remote service directly, Snowflake most often calls a proxy service to relay the data to the remote service. The Amazon API Gateway and Microsoft Azure API management service are two examples of proxy services that can be used. A remote service can be implemented as an AWS Lambda function, a Microsoft Azure function, or an HTTPS server (e.g., Node.js) running on an EC2 instance.

Any charges by providers of remote services will be billed separately. Snowflake charges normal costs associated with data transfer and virtual warehouse usage when using external functions.

There are many advantages of using external functions. External functions can be created to be called from other software programs in addition to being called from within Snowflake. Also, the code for the remote services can be written in languages such as Go or C#—languages that cannot be used within other UDFs supported by Snowflake. One of the biggest advantages is that the remote services for Snowflake external functions can be interfaced with commercially available third-party libraries, such as machine learning scoring libraries.

Code Cleanup

Code cleanup for this chapter is simple. You can use the following command to drop the database we created earlier:

```
DROP DATABASE DEMO4_DB;
```

Notice that we don't have to remove all the tables first, because dropping the database will automatically drop the associated tables.

Summary

In this chapter, we created and executed all our Snowflake queries using the SYSADMIN role. This was done intentionally so that we could focus on learning the basics of Snowflake SQL commands, functions, statements, and data types without adding the complexity of needing to navigate Snowflake access controls. Now it's time to build on this foundational knowledge, along with what we learned in Chapter 3 about creating and managing architecture objects.

In the next chapter, we'll take a deep dive into leveraging Snowflake access controls. If you expect to be assigned administrator responsibilities for one of the core admin roles, the next chapter will likely be one of the most important chapters for you in your Snowflake journey of learning. Even if you never expect to perform administrator duties, you'll still need to know how to leverage the full functionality of Snowflake within the permissions you are assigned. Also, even if you are not assigned a Snowflake admin role, it's still likely that you will be given access to perform some functions once reserved only for administrators.

Snowflake has taken great care to design and build access controls that address some of the weaknesses of other platforms. One example of this is that Snowflake has purposely designed an access control system that removes the concept of a *super user*, a major risk of many platforms. That said, it is important to recognize that there is still much you can learn about Snowflake's unique access controls even if you have experience with access controls built for other platforms.

Knowledge Check

The following questions are based on the information contained in this chapter:

1. What can you use to ensure that a line of text is a comment rather than having it be treated as code?

2. Snowflake's string data types are supported by string constants. What delimiters can be used to enclose strings?

3. What are some advantages of using external functions?

4. What is the default duration Snowflake uses to determine when to cancel long-running queries? Can you change that duration and, if so, how would you do that?

5. What are the risks of using floating-point number data types?

6. How does a window function differ from an aggregate function?

7. Does Snowflake support unstructured data types?

8. What semi-structured data types does Snowflake support?

9. Does Snowflake's TIMESTAMP data type support local time zones and daylight saving time? Explain.

10. What are derived columns and how can they be used in Snowflake?

11. What are the three ways you can gain access to unstructured data files in Snowflake?

12. List some examples of unstructured data.

13. What type of table is a directory table?

Answers to these questions are available in Appendix A.

Leveraging Snowflake Access Controls

An organization's data repositories may be filled with valuable, confidential information. Thus, securing and protecting this data is essential and is often a regulatory or statutory requirement. Though critical, the need for data security must be reasonably balanced against business needs for efficient data access. In other words, data access should not be so restrictive as to hobble a business's ability to operate effectively and efficiently for the sake of security. Rather, the necessary data must be made available to just the right users at just the right time without sacrificing security. To achieve that balance, developing a good security model must encompass planning and involvement with the right stakeholders. Snowflake makes achieving this balance easy.

Creating multiple layers of security that take advantage of Snowflake's built-in security options is among the best practices for managing security. The outer security layer (the outermost concentric square in Figure 5-1) relies on network policies, key pair authentication, multifactor authentication (MFA), and secure private networks as options to ensure that only authenticated users gain access to a Snowflake account. Snowflake provides data security protection through data encryption. Both of these outer layers of security are discussed in more detail in Chapter 7.

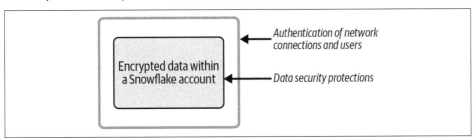

Figure 5-1. All data within a Snowflake account is encrypted and is protected by authentication

In this chapter, we'll learn about the next layer, user management and object security. This security type uses role-based access control and discretionary access control to open access to certain data for users (see Figure 5-2). Beyond that, data privacy access restrictions, also covered in Chapter 7, are those things that restrict access, such as dynamic data masking, row-level security, and use of secure views and secure user-defined functions (UDFs), to provide limited access to sensitive and private data.

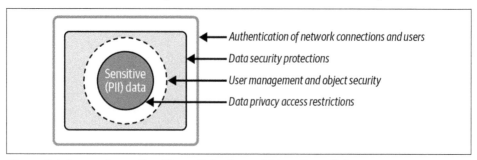

Figure 5-2. Layered security of Snowflake data within a Snowflake account

In this chapter, you will learn how access control is used to secure Snowflake objects by going through a series of examples which build upon each other. Here are the steps you will work through:

- Learn about Snowflake's access control model
- Create securable objects
- Create custom roles
- Assign role hierarchies
- Grant privileges to roles
- Assign roles to users
- Test and validate the work
- Perform user management
- Code cleanup
- Knowledge check

Prep Work

Create a new worksheet titled *Chapter5 Snowflake Access Controls*. Refer to "Navigating Snowsight Worksheets" on page 8 if you need help creating a new worksheet. To set the worksheet context, make sure you are using the SYSADMIN role and the COMPUTE_WH virtual warehouse.

Snowflake's hybrid access control provides for access at a granular level. A combination of discretionary access control and role-based access control approaches determines who can access what object and perform operations on those objects, as well as who can create or alter the access control policies themselves. *Discretionary access control* (DAC) is a security model in which each object has an owner who has control over that object. *Role-based access control* (RBAC) is an approach in which access privileges are assigned to roles and roles are then assigned to one or more users.

In the Snowflake hybrid approach, all securable objects are owned by a role rather than a user. Further, each securable object is owned by only one role, which is usually the role used to create the object. Note that because a role can be assigned to more than one user, every user granted the same role also has inherent privileges in a shared, controlled fashion. Object ownership can be transferred from one role to another. The Snowflake access control key concepts are described by the following definitions and Figure 5-3:

Securable object
  Entity such as a database or table. Access to a securable object is denied unless specifically granted.

Role
  Receives privileges to access and perform operations on an object or to create or alter the access control policies themselves. Roles are assigned to users. Roles can also be assigned to other roles, creating a role hierarchy.

Privileges
  Inherent, assigned, or inherited access to an object.

User
  A person, service account, or program that Snowflake recognizes.

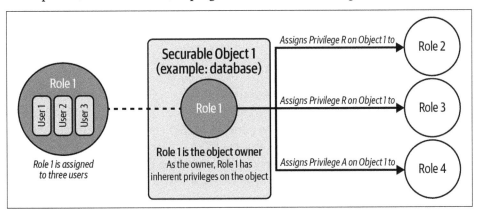

Figure 5-3. Access control key concepts

As explained in Chapter 3, every securable database object resides in a logical container within a hierarchy that includes a schema and a database, with the account as the top container for all securable objects. Figure 5-4 illustrates Snowflake objects along with the system-defined role that inherently owns each type of securable object.

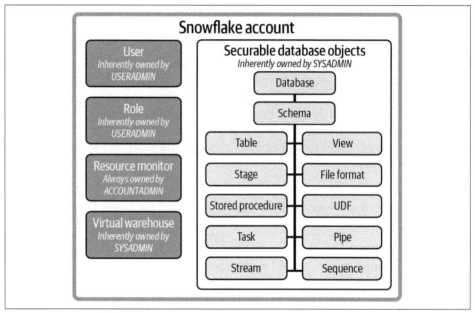

Figure 5-4. Snowflake account objects

 Resource monitors are *always* owned by the ACCOUNTADMIN role. Only the ACCOUNTADMIN can create or drop this object. The ACCOUNTADMIN cannot grant this privilege to any other role, but can grant another role the ability to modify a resource monitor already created.

Creating Snowflake Objects

To illustrate how Snowflake access controls work, it is necessary to have Snowflake objects in your Snowflake account on which to practice. Let's start by creating a few virtual warehouses, which are needed to perform SELECT statements and Data Manipulation Language (DML) operations. First, the SYSADMIN role is used to create new virtual warehouses. The SHOW command, as demonstrated by Figure 5-5, can then be used to confirm that the virtual warehouses were created:

```
USE ROLE SYSADMIN;
USE WAREHOUSE COMPUTE_WH;
CREATE OR REPLACE WAREHOUSE VW1_WH WITH WAREHOUSE_SIZE='X-SMALL'
INITIALLY_SUSPENDED=true;
```

```
CREATE OR REPLACE WAREHOUSE VW2_WH WITH WAREHOUSE_SIZE='X-SMALL'
INITIALLY_SUSPENDED=true;
CREATE OR REPLACE WAREHOUSE VW3_WH WITH WAREHOUSE_SIZE='X-SMALL'
INITIALLY_SUSPENDED=true;
SHOW WAREHOUSES;
```

	name	state	type	size	min_cluster_count	max_cluster_count	started_clusters	running	queued	is_default	is_current	auto_suspend
1	COMPUTE_WH	SUSPENDED	STANDARD	X-Small	1	1	0	0	0	Y	N	600
2	VW1_WH	SUSPENDED	STANDARD	X-Small	1	1	0	0	0	N	N	600
3	VW2_WH	SUSPENDED	STANDARD	X-Small	1	1	0	0	0	N	N	600
4	VW3_WH	SUSPENDED	STANDARD	X-Small	1	1	0	0	0	N	Y	600

Figure 5-5. Newly created virtual warehouses

Next, the SYSADMIN role is used again to create two databases and three schemas. Before creating these objects, see how the SHOW DATABASES command returns different results depending on the role that is used to issue the command. The difference occurs because the results are meant to return only the databases to which the role has access.

Three databases are included and made available to every role, including the PUBLIC role, at the time when a Snowflake account is created. Therefore, using role SYSADMIN or role PUBLIC to view the list of databases will return the same results, as seen in Figure 5-6:

```
USE ROLE SYSADMIN;
SHOW DATABASES;
```

Now try using the PUBLIC role:

```
USE ROLE PUBLIC;
SHOW DATABASES;
```

	name	...	is_default	is_current	origin	owner
1	SNOWFLAKE_SAMPLE_DATA		N	N	SFC_SAMPLES.SAMPLE_DATA	ACCOUNTADMIN

Figure 5-6. Existing Snowflake databases available to the PUBLIC role

However, a user assigned the ACCOUNTADMIN role will observe a fourth database listed, shown in Figure 5-7. The additional database is a system-defined and read-only shared database provided by Snowflake:

```
USE ROLE ACCOUNTADMIN;
SHOW DATABASES;
```

	name	...	is_default	is_current	origin	owner
1	SNOWFLAKE		N	N	SNOWFLAKE.ACCOUNT_USAGE	
2	SNOWFLAKE_SAMPLE_DATA		N	N	SFC_SAMPLES.SAMPLE_DATA	ACCOUNTADMIN

Figure 5-7. Existing Snowflake databases available to the ACCOUNTADMIN role

Let's use the SYSADMIN role to create the databases and schemas.

 The order in which the SQL commands are written to create databases and schemas is important. You'll need to create schemas immediately after creating the database or else use the fully qualified object names for creating the schema.

For DB1 we'll create the schema at the end using the fully qualified object name, and for DB2 we'll create the schemas right after creating the database:

```
USE ROLE SYSADMIN;
CREATE OR REPLACE DATABASE DB1;
CREATE OR REPLACE DATABASE DB2;
CREATE OR REPLACE SCHEMA DB2_SCHEMA1;
CREATE OR REPLACE SCHEMA DB2_SCHEMA2;
CREATE OR REPLACE SCHEMA DB1.DB1_SCHEMA1;
SHOW DATABASES;
```

The results are shown in Figure 5-8.

	name	is_default	is_current	origin	owner	...
1	DB1	N	Y		SYSADMIN	
2	DB2	N	N		SYSADMIN	
3	SNOWFLAKE_SAMPLE_DATA	N	N	SFC_SAMPLES.SAMPLE_DATA	ACCOUNTADMIN	

Figure 5-8. Existing Snowflake databases available to the SYSADMIN role

Resource monitors will be described in more detail in Chapter 8. Only an account administrator can create a resource monitor. The following code is used to create a resource monitor:

```
USE ROLE ACCOUNTADMIN;
CREATE OR REPLACE RESOURCE MONITOR MONITOR1_RM WITH CREDIT_QUOTA=10000
TRIGGERS ON 75 PERCENT DO NOTIFY
    ON 98 PERCENT DO SUSPEND
    ON 105 PERCENT DO SUSPEND_IMMEDIATE;
SHOW RESOURCE MONITORS;
```

The result of the preceding code is shown in Figure 5-9.

	name	credit_quota	used_credits	remaining_credits	level	frequency
1	MONITOR1_RM	10000.00	0.00	10000.00	null	MONTHLY

Figure 5-9. A resource monitor created by the ACCOUNTADMIN role

Later in this chapter we'll explore Snowflake user management in detail. For now, let's create a few users with minimal information:

```
USE ROLE USERADMIN;
CREATE OR REPLACE USER USER1 LOGIN_NAME=ARNOLD;
CREATE OR REPLACE USER USER2 LOGIN_NAME=BEATRICE;
CREATE OR REPLACE USER USER3 LOGIN_NAME=COLLIN;
CREATE OR REPLACE USER USER4 LOGIN_NAME=DIEDRE;
```

We were able to successfully create the users. Let's see what happens when we attempt to use the USERADMIN role to show a list of users:

```
USE ROLE USERADMIN;
SHOW USERS;
```

Figure 5-10 shows the result.

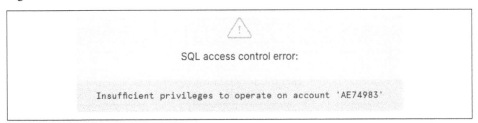

SQL access control error:

Insufficient privileges to operate on account 'AE74983'

Figure 5-10. An error was displayed because USERADMIN has insufficient privileges

The listing of all users can be viewed by using the role in the hierarchy just above the USERADMIN role, as shown in Figure 5-11:

```
USE ROLE SECURITYADMIN;
SHOW USERS;
```

	name	created_on	login_name	display_name
1	JKA2022	.945 -0700	JKA2022	JKA2022
2	SNOWFLAKE	.959 -0700	SNOWFLAKE	SNOWFLAKE
3	USER1	.974 -0700	ARNOLD	USER1
4	USER2	.295 -0700	BEATRICE	USER2
5	USER3	.596 -0700	COLLIN	USER3
6	USER4	.917 -0700	DIEDRE	USER4

Figure 5-11. A listing of Snowflake users

Snowflake System-Defined Roles

A Snowflake role, which is assigned to a user, is an entity to which privileges can be assigned. Assigned privileges do not come with the GRANT option, the ability to grant the assigned privilege to another role, unless specifically assigned. Roles can also be granted to other roles, which creates a *role hierarchy*. With this role hierarchy structure, privileges are also inherited by all roles above a particular role in the hierarchy. A user can have multiple roles and can switch between roles, though only one role can be active in a current Snowflake session. The exception would be if the USE SECONDARY ROLES option is used in an active session. As illustrated in Figure 5-12, there are a small number of system-defined roles in a Snowflake account.

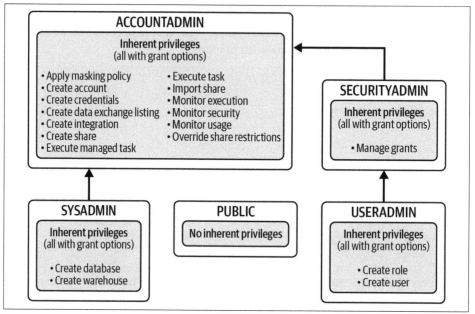

Figure 5-12. System-defined account roles

As shown in Figure 5-12, the account administrator (ACCOUNTADMIN) is at the top level of system-defined account roles and can view and operate on all objects in the account, with one exception. The account administrator will have no access to an object when the object is created by a custom role without an assigned system-defined role.

The ACCOUNTADMIN role can stop any running SQL statements and can view and manage Snowflake billing. Privileges for resource monitors are unique to the ACCOUNTADMIN role. None of the inherent privileges that come with the resource monitor privileges come with the GRANT option, but the ACCOUNTADMIN can assign the ALTER RESOURCE MONITOR privilege to another role. It is a best practice to limit the ACCOUNTADMIN role to the minimum number of users required to maintain control of the Snowflake account, but to no fewer than two users.

 Snowflake has no concept of a *super user* or a *super role*. All access to securable objects, even by the account administrator, requires access privileges granted explicitly when the ACCOUNTADMIN creates objects itself, or implicitly by being in a higher hierarchy role. As such, if a custom role is created without assignment to another role in a hierarchy that ultimately leads to the ACCOUNTADMIN role, any securable objects created by that role would be inaccessible by the ACCOUNTADMIN role.

In addition to ACCOUNTADMIN, other system-defined roles can manage security for objects in the system by using the inherent privileges assigned to them. Those privileges can be granted to other roles in Snowflake, including custom roles, to assign the responsibility for managing security in the system. An example of when the ACCOUNTADMIN assigns the Apply Masking Policy privilege to a custom role will be demonstrated later in the chapter.

The security administrator (SECURITYADMIN) is inherently given the MANAGE GRANTS privilege and also inherits all the privileges of the USERADMIN role. The user administrator (USERADMIN) is responsible for creating and managing users and roles.

The system administrator (SYSADMIN) role is a system-defined role with privileges to create virtual warehouses, databases, and other objects in the Snowflake account. The most common roles created by the USERADMIN are assigned to the SYSADMIN role, thus enabling the system or account administrator to manage any of the objects created by custom roles.

The PUBLIC role is automatically granted to every role and every user in the Snowflake account. Just like any other role, the PUBLIC role can own securable objects.

 It is important to remember that any privileges or object access provided to the PUBLIC role is available to all roles and all users in the account.

Creating Custom Roles

Creating and managing custom roles is one of the most important functions in Snowflake. Before creating custom roles, planning should be undertaken to design a custom role architecture that will secure and protect sensitive data but will not be unnecessarily restrictive. Involved in the planning discussion should be the data stewards, governance committee, staff who understand the business needs, and IT professionals. There is an example in this chapter of an approach for creating custom roles. The approach I've taken is to divide the custom roles into *functional-level custom roles*, which include business and IT roles, and *system-level custom roles*, which include service account roles and object access roles.

Let's look at the roles that exist in the Snowflake account we created in preparation for creating new custom roles. The command to show roles will return a list of the role names as well as some additional information:

```
USE ROLE USERADMIN;
SHOW ROLES;
```

In Figure 5-13, for the USERADMIN role, we see that the is_current status is Y and the is_inherited status is Y for the PUBLIC role. This means the USERADMIN role is the role currently in use and above the public role in the hierarchy; thus, it will inherit any privileges assigned to the PUBLIC role.

	name	is_default	is_current	is_inherited
1	ACCOUNTADMIN	Y	N	N
2	ORGADMIN	N	N	N
3	PUBLIC	N	N	Y
4	SECURITYADMIN	N	N	N
5	SYSADMIN	N	N	N
6	USERADMIN	N	Y	N

Figure 5-13. Showing the USERADMIN role as the current user

As shown in Figure 5-14, the security administrator role inherits privileges from the USERADMIN and PUBLIC roles. Here is the command to show the roles:

```
USE ROLE SECURITYADMIN;
SHOW ROLES;
```

	name	is_default	is_current	is_inherited
1	ACCOUNTADMIN	Y	N	N
2	ORGADMIN	N	N	N
3	PUBLIC	N	N	Y
4	SECURITYADMIN	N	Y	N
5	SYSADMIN	N	N	N
6	USERADMIN	N	N	Y

Figure 5-14. Showing SECURITYADMIN as the current user

Functional-Level Business and IT Roles

You'll notice that in Figure 5-15, a decision was made to use suffixes to differentiate between levels, such as *Sr* for senior analyst and *Jr* for junior analyst. A decision was also made to use prefixes for roles in which different environments might be needed, such as *SBX* for Sandbox, *DEV* for Development, and *PRD* for Production.

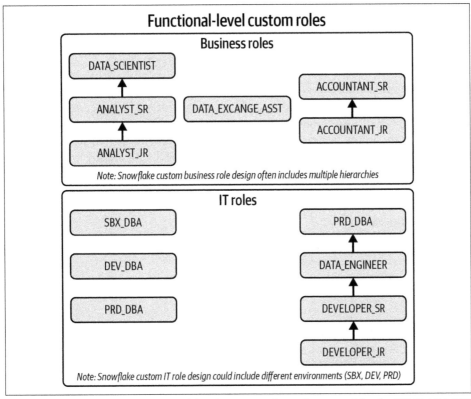

Figure 5-15. Example of functional-level custom roles to be created by the USERADMIN role

We use the USERADMIN role to create our 10 functional custom roles:

```
USE ROLE USERADMIN;
CREATE OR REPLACE ROLE DATA_SCIENTIST;
CREATE OR REPLACE ROLE ANALYST_SR;
CREATE OR REPLACE ROLE ANALYST_JR;
CREATE OR REPLACE ROLE DATA_EXCHANGE_ASST;
CREATE OR REPLACE ROLE ACCOUNTANT_SR;
CREATE OR REPLACE ROLE ACCOUNTANT_JR;
CREATE OR REPLACE ROLE PRD_DBA;
CREATE OR REPLACE ROLE DATA_ENGINEER;
CREATE OR REPLACE ROLE DEVELOPER_SR;
```

```
CREATE OR REPLACE ROLE DEVELOPER_JR;
SHOW ROLES;
```

By using the SHOW command, you'll find that none of the custom roles has been gran-ted to other roles. It is otherwise important to have all custom roles assigned to another role in the hierarchy with the top custom role being assigned to either the SYSADMIN role or the ACCOUNTADMIN role, unless there is a business need to isolate a custom role. Later in this chapter we'll complete the hierarchy of custom roles by assigning the custom roles to a system-defined role.

System-Level Service Account and Object Access Roles

For system-level custom roles (see Figure 5-16), I've created two different types of roles. The service account roles are typically roles used for loading data or connecting to visualization tools. The object access roles are roles for which data access privi-leges, such as the ability to view the data in a particular schema or to insert data into a table, will be granted. These object access roles then will be assigned to other roles higher in the hierarchy.

First let's use the USERADMIN role to create system service account roles:

```
USE ROLE USERADMIN;
CREATE OR REPLACE ROLE LOADER;
CREATE OR REPLACE ROLE VISUALIZER;
CREATE OR REPLACE ROLE REPORTING;
CREATE OR REPLACE ROLE MONITORING;
```

Next, we'll create the system object access roles:

```
USE ROLE USERADMIN;
CREATE OR REPLACE ROLE DB1_SCHEMA1_READONLY;
CREATE OR REPLACE ROLE DB1_SCHEMA1_ALL;
CREATE OR REPLACE ROLE DB2_SCHEMA1_READONLY;
CREATE OR REPLACE ROLE DB2_SCHEMA1_ALL;
CREATE OR REPLACE ROLE DB2_SCHEMA2_READONLY;
CREATE OR REPLACE ROLE DB2_SCHEMA2_ALL;

CREATE OR REPLACE ROLE RM1_MODIFY;

CREATE OR REPLACE ROLE WH1_USAGE;
CREATE OR REPLACE ROLE WH2_USAGE;
CREATE OR REPLACE ROLE WH3_USAGE;

CREATE OR REPLACE ROLE DB1_MONITOR;
CREATE OR REPLACE ROLE DB2_MONITOR;
CREATE OR REPLACE ROLE WH1_MONITOR;
CREATE OR REPLACE ROLE WH2_MONITOR;
CREATE OR REPLACE ROLE WH3_MONITOR;
CREATE OR REPLACE ROLE RM1_MONITOR;
```

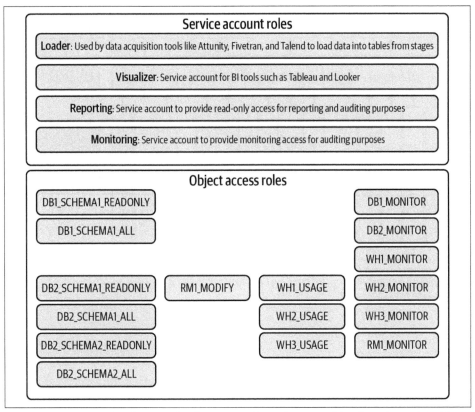

Figure 5-16. Example of system-level custom roles to be created by the USERADMIN role

Role Hierarchy Assignments: Assigning Roles to Other Roles

As discussed earlier, we want to assign the object access roles to other roles in the role hierarchy. As part of Figure 5-17, you'll see that it is necessary to also assign a virtual warehouse to any role that we expect would need the ability to run queries.

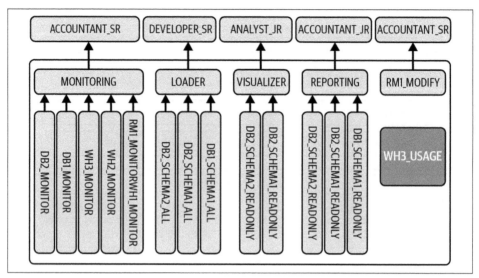

Figure 5-17. Assignment of system-level custom roles to be granted to other roles by the USERADMIN role

We'll now complete the system-level role hierarchy assignments:

```
USE ROLE USERADMIN;
GRANT ROLE RM1_MONITOR TO ROLE MONITORING;
GRANT ROLE WH1_MONITOR TO ROLE MONITORING;
GRANT ROLE WH2_MONITOR TO ROLE MONITORING;
GRANT ROLE WH3_MONITOR TO ROLE MONITORING;
GRANT ROLE DB1_MONITOR TO ROLE MONITORING;
GRANT ROLE DB2_MONITOR TO ROLE MONITORING;
GRANT ROLE WH3_USAGE TO ROLE MONITORING;

GRANT ROLE DB1_SCHEMA1_ALL TO ROLE LOADER;
GRANT ROLE DB2_SCHEMA1_ALL TO ROLE LOADER;
GRANT ROLE DB2_SCHEMA2_ALL TO ROLE LOADER;
GRANT ROLE WH3_USAGE TO ROLE LOADER;

GRANT ROLE DB2_SCHEMA1_READONLY TO ROLE VISUALIZER;
GRANT ROLE DB2_SCHEMA2_READONLY TO ROLE VISUALIZER;
GRANT ROLE WH3_USAGE TO ROLE VISUALIZER;

GRANT ROLE DB1_SCHEMA1_READONLY TO ROLE REPORTING;
GRANT ROLE DB2_SCHEMA1_READONLY TO ROLE REPORTING;
GRANT ROLE DB2_SCHEMA2_READONLY TO ROLE REPORTING;

GRANT ROLE WH3_USAGE TO ROLE REPORTING;
GRANT ROLE MONITORING TO ROLE ACCOUNTANT_SR;
GRANT ROLE LOADER TO ROLE DEVELOPER_SR;
GRANT ROLE VISUALIZER TO ROLE ANALYST_JR;
```

```
GRANT ROLE REPORTING TO ROLE ACCOUNTANT_JR;
GRANT ROLE RM1_MODIFY TO ROLE ACCOUNTANT_SR;
```

Completing the functional-level role hierarchy assignments means we'll also want to assign the top-level custom role to either the SYSADMIN or ACCOUNTADMIN role as a final step in the hierarchy assignment process. As before, we'll also want to assign a virtual warehouse to any role that we expect would need the ability to run queries. This is demonstrated in Figure 5-18.

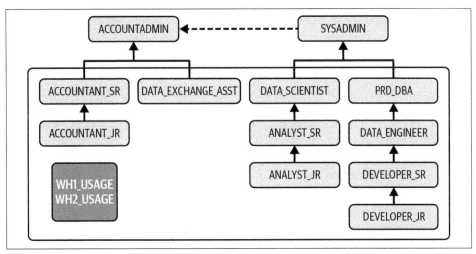

Figure 5-18. Assignment of functional-level custom roles to be granted to other roles by the USERADMIN role

The USERADMIN role is used to complete the functional role hierarchy assignments:

```
USE ROLE USERADMIN;
GRANT ROLE ACCOUNTANT_JR TO ROLE ACCOUNTANT_SR;
GRANT ROLE ANALYST_JR TO ROLE ANALYST_SR;
GRANT ROLE ANALYST_SR TO ROLE DATA_SCIENTIST;
GRANT ROLE DEVELOPER_JR TO ROLE DEVELOPER_SR;
GRANT ROLE DEVELOPER_SR TO ROLE DATA_ENGINEER;
GRANT ROLE DATA_ENGINEER TO ROLE PRD_DBA;
GRANT ROLE ACCOUNTANT_SR TO ROLE ACCOUNTADMIN;
GRANT ROLE DATA_EXCHANGE_ASST TO ROLE ACCOUNTADMIN;
GRANT ROLE DATA_SCIENTIST TO ROLE SYSADMIN;
GRANT ROLE PRD_DBA TO ROLE SYSADMIN;
```

Next, be sure to grant usage of virtual warehouse VW2_WH directly to IT roles and usage of virtual warehouse VW2_WH to business roles:

```
GRANT ROLE WH1_USAGE TO ROLE DEVELOPER_JR;
GRANT ROLE WH1_USAGE TO ROLE DEVELOPER_SR;

GRANT ROLE WH1_USAGE TO ROLE DATA_ENGINEER;
GRANT ROLE WH1_USAGE TO ROLE PRD_DBA;
```

```
GRANT ROLE WH2_USAGE TO ROLE ACCOUNTANT_JR;
GRANT ROLE WH2_USAGE TO ROLE ACCOUNTANT_SR;
GRANT ROLE WH2_USAGE TO ROLE DATA_EXCHANGE_ASST;
GRANT ROLE WH2_USAGE TO ROLE ANALYST_JR;
GRANT ROLE WH2_USAGE TO ROLE ANALYST_SR;
GRANT ROLE WH2_USAGE TO ROLE DATA_SCIENTIST;
```

Granting Privileges to Roles

Snowflake privileges are a defined level of access to a securable object. The granularity of access can be granted by using different distinct privileges. Privileges can also be revoked if necessary. Each securable object has a specific set of privileges which can be granted on it. For existing objects, these privileges must be granted on the individual object. To make grant management more flexible and simpler, future grants can be assigned on objects created in a schema. I've elected here to assign the following privileges to the roles shown in Figure 5-19. These particular privileges are privileges that only the ACCOUNTADMIN can assign.

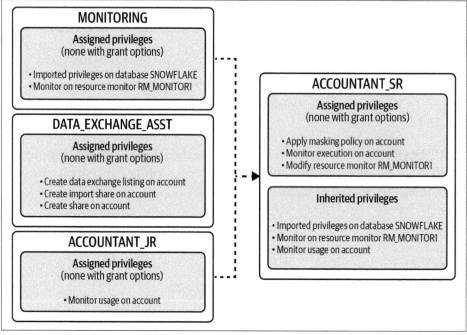

Figure 5-19. Snowflake-assigned privileges granted by the ACCOUNTADMIN role

The ACCOUNTADMIN role is required to grant direct global privileges to the functional roles. We also will need to use the ACCOUNTADMIN role to grant privileges to custom roles that only the ACCOUNTADMIN can grant:

```
USE ROLE ACCOUNTADMIN;
GRANT CREATE DATA EXCHANGE LISTING ON ACCOUNT TO ROLE DATA_EXCHANGE_ASST;
GRANT IMPORT SHARE ON ACCOUNT TO ROLE DATA_EXCHANGE_ASST;
GRANT CREATE SHARE ON ACCOUNT TO ROLE DATA_EXCHANGE_ASST;
GRANT IMPORTED PRIVILEGES ON DATABASE SNOWFLAKE TO ROLE MONITORING;
GRANT MONITOR ON RESOURCE MONITOR MONITOR1_RM TO ROLE MONITORING;
GRANT MONITOR USAGE ON ACCOUNT TO ROLE ACCOUNTANT_JR;
GRANT APPLY MASKING POLICY ON ACCOUNT TO ROLE ACCOUNTANT_SR;
GRANT MONITOR EXECUTION ON ACCOUNT TO ROLE ACCOUNTANT_SR;
GRANT MODIFY ON RESOURCE MONITOR MONITOR1_RM TO ROLE ACCOUNTANT_SR;
```

A number of different custom roles need privileges to interact with data in objects and need the ability to use a virtual warehouse to make that interaction. For the ability to view data in a table, a role needs privileges to use the database and schema in which the table resides as well as the ability to use the SELECT command on the table. The privileges will be assigned for any existing objects in the schema when these privileges are granted. We'll also want to consider assigning FUTURE GRANT privileges so that the role can access tables created in the future. Future grants can only be assigned by the ACCOUNTADMIN; therefore, we'll have to assign future grant access in a later step.

Following is a summarized list of assigned privileges. None of the privileges has a GRANT option. You'll notice that the object monitoring privilege is set at the database level; thus, the role will be able to monitor databases we created as well as all objects below the databases in the hierarchy:

DB1_SCHEMA1_READONLY
- USAGE on database DB1
- USAGE on schema DB1.DB1_SCHEMA1
- SELECT on all tables in schema DB1.DB1_SCHEMA1
- SELECT on future tables in schema DB1.DB1_SCHEMA1

DB2_SCHEMA1_READONLY
- USAGE on database DB2
- USAGE on schema DB2.DB2_SCHEMA1
- SELECT on all tables in schema DB2.DB2_SCHEMA1

DB2_SCHEMA2_READONLY
- USAGE on database DB2
- USAGE on schema DB2.DB2_SCHEMA2
- SELECT on all tables in schema DB2.DB2_SCHEMA2
- SELECT on future tables in schema DB2.DB2_SCHEMA1

DB1_SCHEMA1_ALL
- ALL on schema DB1.DB1_SCHEMA1
- SELECT on future tables in schema DB1.DB1_SCHEMA1

DB2_SCHEMA1_ALL
- ALL on schema DB2.DB1_SCHEMA1
- SELECT on future tables in schema DB2.DB1_SCHEMA1

DB2_SCHEMA2_ALL
- ALL on schema DB2.DB2_SCHEMA2
- SELECT on future tables in schema DB2.DB2_Schema2

DB1_MONITOR
- MONITOR on database DB1

DB2_MONITOR
- MONITOR on database DB2

WH1_MONITOR
- MONITOR on virtual warehouse VW1_WH

WH2_MONITOR
- MONITOR on virtual warehouse VW2_WH

WH3_MONITOR
- MONITOR on virtual warehouse VW3_WH

WH1_USAGE
- USAGE on virtual warehouse VW1_WH

WH2_USAGE
- USAGE on virtual warehouse VW2_WH

WH3_USAGE
- USAGE on virtual warehouse VW3_WH

Notice that the SYSADMIN role, not the USERADMIN role, is required to grant privileges. Use the SYSADMIN role to grant direct assigned privileges to system-level object access roles:

```
USE ROLE SYSADMIN;
GRANT USAGE ON DATABASE DB1 TO ROLE DB1_SCHEMA1_READONLY;
GRANT USAGE ON DATABASE DB2 TO ROLE DB2_SCHEMA1_READONLY;
GRANT USAGE ON DATABASE DB2 TO ROLE DB2_SCHEMA2_READONLY;
GRANT USAGE ON SCHEMA DB1.DB1_SCHEMA1 TO ROLE DB1_SCHEMA1_READONLY;
GRANT USAGE ON SCHEMA DB2.DB2_SCHEMA1 TO ROLE DB2_SCHEMA1_READONLY;
GRANT USAGE ON SCHEMA DB2.DB2_SCHEMA2 TO ROLE DB2_SCHEMA2_READONLY;
```

```
GRANT SELECT ON ALL TABLES IN SCHEMA DB1.DB1_SCHEMA1
    TO ROLE DB1_SCHEMA1_READONLY;
GRANT SELECT ON ALL TABLES IN SCHEMA DB2.DB2_SCHEMA1
    TO ROLE DB2_SCHEMA1_READONLY;
GRANT SELECT ON ALL TABLES IN SCHEMA DB2.DB2_SCHEMA2
    TO ROLE DB1_SCHEMA1_READONLY;

GRANT ALL ON SCHEMA DB1.DB1_SCHEMA1 TO ROLE DB1_SCHEMA1_ALL;
GRANT ALL ON SCHEMA DB2.DB2_SCHEMA1 TO ROLE DB2_SCHEMA1_ALL;
GRANT ALL ON SCHEMA DB2.DB2_SCHEMA2 TO ROLE DB2_SCHEMA2_ALL;

GRANT MONITOR ON DATABASE DB1 TO ROLE DB1_MONITOR;
GRANT MONITOR ON DATABASE DB2 TO ROLE DB2_MONITOR;
GRANT MONITOR ON WAREHOUSE VW1_WH TO ROLE WH1_MONITOR;
GRANT MONITOR ON WAREHOUSE VW2_WH TO ROLE WH2_MONITOR;
GRANT MONITOR ON WAREHOUSE VW3_WH TO ROLE WH3_MONITOR;

GRANT USAGE ON WAREHOUSE VW1_WH TO WH1_USAGE;
GRANT USAGE ON WAREHOUSE VW2_WH TO WH2_USAGE;
GRANT USAGE ON WAREHOUSE VW3_WH TO WH3_USAGE;
```

Use the ACCOUNTADMIN role to grant FUTURE direct assigned privileges:

```
USE ROLE ACCOUNTADMIN;
GRANT SELECT ON FUTURE TABLES IN SCHEMA DB1.DB1_SCHEMA1
    TO ROLE DB1_SCHEMA1_READONLY;
GRANT SELECT ON FUTURE TABLES IN SCHEMA DB2.DB2_SCHEMA1
    TO ROLE DB2_SCHEMA1_READONLY;
GRANT SELECT ON FUTURE TABLES IN SCHEMA DB2.DB2_SCHEMA2
    TO ROLE DB2_SCHEMA2_READONLY;
GRANT SELECT ON FUTURE TABLES IN SCHEMA DB1.DB1_SCHEMA1 TO ROLE DB1_SCHEMA1_ALL;
GRANT SELECT ON FUTURE TABLES IN SCHEMA DB2.DB2_SCHEMA1 TO ROLE DB2_SCHEMA1_ALL;
GRANT SELECT ON FUTURE TABLES IN SCHEMA DB2.DB2_SCHEMA2 TO ROLE DB2_SCHEMA2_ALL;
```

Assigning Roles to Users

We created four users earlier in the chapter. Now let's assign roles to each of those four users. It is possible to assign more than one role to each user, but only one role can be used at any given time (i.e., assigned roles cannot be "layered" or combined). Remember that for any role that is assigned for which there are roles below it in the hierarchy, the user has already inherited that role. For example, the Data Scientist role inherits the Analyst Sr and Analyst Jr roles and will see those roles in their account. Accordingly, it would be redundant to assign either of those two roles to a user who is assigned the Data Scientist role:

```
USE ROLE USERADMIN;
GRANT ROLE DATA_EXCHANGE_ASST TO USER USER1;
GRANT ROLE DATA_SCIENTIST TO USER USER2;
GRANT ROLE ACCOUNTANT_SR TO USER USER3;
GRANT ROLE PRD_DBA TO USER USER4;
```

Testing and Validating Our Work

Now is when we get to test and validate the work we completed to establish our access control security.

> When running any of the queries using any of the custom roles, you'll need to have a running virtual warehouse to complete the queries. If, at any time, you receive an error message that there is no running virtual warehouse, you can always use the SHOW command to find a list of available virtual warehouses for that role and the USE command to get the virtual warehouse running.

For example, the role PRD_DBA has available the VW1_WH virtual warehouse, which was assigned to the role, and the WV3_WH virtual warehouse, which was inherited. This is evidenced in Figure 5-20.

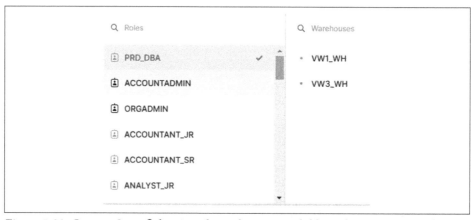

Figure 5-20. Current Snowflake virtual warehouses available to the PRD_DBA role

Now let's test to see if the access works as we had intended. We granted access to the SNOWFLAKE database to only a few people, as is a best practice. The ACCOUNTADMIN role has access to the SNOWFLAKE database, and earlier we used the ACCOUNTADMIN role to grant access to the senior accountant. Therefore, we would expect an error to be returned if the junior accountant role attempted to access the table:

```
USE ROLE ACCOUNTANT_JR;
SELECT * FROM SNOWFLAKE.ACCOUNT_USAGE.QUERY_HISTORY WHERE QUERY_TYPE = 'GRANT';
```

This is confirmed in Figure 5-21.

> ⚠
> Shared database is no longer available for use. It will need to be re-created if and when the publisher makes it available again.

Figure 5-21. An error is returned because the junior accountant role has not been granted access

You may want to refresh the Snowsight web UI screen or log out and log back in before attempting to test the custom roles.

If a user with the senior accountant role ran the same query, as shown in the following code, they would receive the query results shown in Figure 5-22:

```
USE ROLE ACCOUNTANT_SR;
USE WAREHOUSE VW2_WH;
SELECT * FROM SNOWFLAKE.ACCOUNT_USAGE.QUERY_HISTORY WHERE QUERY_TYPE ='GRANT';
```

	QUERY_TEXT	⋯	DATABASE_ID	DATABASE_NAME	SCHEMA_ID	SCHEMA_NAME	QUERY_TYPE
1	GRANT MONITOR ON DATABASE DB2 TO ROLE DB2_MONITOR;		95	DB1	223	DB1_SCHEMA1	GRANT
2	GRANT SELECT ON FUTURE TABLES IN SCHEMA DB2.DB2_SCHEMA1 TO ROLE DB2_SCHEM.		95	DB1	223	DB1_SCHEMA1	GRANT
3	GRANT SELECT ON FUTURE TABLES IN SCHEMA DB1.DB1_SCHEMA1 TO ROLE DB1_SCHEM.		95	DB1	223	DB1_SCHEMA1	GRANT
4	GRANT SELECT ON FUTURE TABLES IN SCHEMA DB2.DB2_SCHEMA1 TO ROLE DB2_SCHEM.		95	DB1	223	DB1_SCHEMA1	GRANT

Figure 5-22. Results shown because the senior accountant has been granted access

Right now, our Snowflake account has no tables created by us. Whenever the SYSADMIN role creates a new table, it must assign other roles the necessary privileges for that table or else they can't access the table. However, we used a future grants option earlier to grant access to any future objects, like tables, that we created in the three schemas. Therefore, no action is needed to assign privileges on a newly created table. Let's test to see if the future grants privilege we assigned will work as intended.

First, you can see that there are two databases accessible to the SYSADMIN role:

```
USE ROLE SYSADMIN;
SHOW DATABASES;
```

Now you can see that no tables currently exist in the DB1 schema:

```
USE SCHEMA DB1_SCHEMA1;
SHOW TABLES;
```

Let's create a simple table and confirm that the table was created, as shown in Figure 5-23:

```
CREATE OR REPLACE TABLE DB1.DB1_SCHEMA1.TABLE1 (a varchar);
INSERT INTO TABLE1 VALUES ('A');
SHOW TABLES;
```

	name	database_name	schema_name	kind
1	TABLE1	DB1	DB1_SCHEMA1	TABLE

Figure 5-23. Confirmation that the table was created

Next, we'll test to see if the REPORTING role can access the table we just created:

```
USE ROLE REPORTING;
USE WAREHOUSE VW3_WH;
SELECT * FROM DB1.DB1_SCHEMA1.TABLE1;
```

Based on the future grants privileges we assigned to the role that was then assigned to the REPORTING role, we expect that the REPORTING role should be able to access the table. This is confirmed in Figure 5-24.

Figure 5-24. Confirmation that the REPORTING role can access the newly created table

We did not grant DB1 access to the VISUALIZER role, so that role will not be able to see the table, as evidenced in Figure 5-25:

```
USE ROLE VISUALIZER;
SELECT * FROM DB1.DB1_SCHEMA1.TABLE1;
```

⚠

Database 'DB1' does not exist or not authorized.

Figure 5-25. The VISUALIZER role does not have access to the newly created table

Here are some additional queries you can try on your own that will give you some useful information:

```
USE ROLE ACCOUNTANT_SR;
USE WAREHOUSE VW3_WH;
SELECT * FROM SNOWFLAKE.ACCOUNT_USAGE.GRANTS_TO_USERS;
SHOW GRANTS ON ACCOUNT;
SHOW GRANTS ON DATABASE DB1;
SHOW GRANTS OF ROLE ANALYST_SR;
SHOW FUTURE GRANTS IN DATABASE DB1;
SHOW FUTURE GRANTS IN SCHEMA DB1.DB1_SCHEMA1;
```

Any of the global privileges, privileges for account objects, and privileges for schemas can be revoked from a role. As an example, we'll have the account administrator grant a role to the junior analyst and then the USERADMIN will revoke that role:

```
USE ROLE ACCOUNTADMIN;
GRANT MONITOR USAGE ON ACCOUNT TO ROLE ANALYST_JR;
USE ROLE USERADMIN;
REVOKE MONITOR USAGE ON ACCOUNT FROM ROLE ANALYST_JR;
```

During a session, a user can change their role if they are assigned more than one role. When a user attempts to execute an action on an object, Snowflake compares the privileges required to complete the action against any privileges that the current role inherited, or that were inherently given or assigned. The action is allowed if the role in the session has the necessary privileges.

User Management

A *User object* in Snowflake stores all the information about a user, including their login name, password, and defaults. A Snowflake user can be a person or a program. From previous discussions, we know that Snowflake users are created and managed by the USERADMIN system-defined role. The user name is required and should be unique when creating a user. Even though all other properties are optional, it is a best practice to include many of them. At a minimum, you should include some basic details and assign an initial password which you require the user to change at the next login. Here is an example:

```
USE ROLE USERADMIN;
CREATE OR REPLACE USER USER10
PASSWORD='123'
LOGIN_NAME = ABARNETT
DISPLAY_NAME = AMY
FIRST_NAME = AMY
LAST_NAME = BARNETT
EMAIL = 'ABARNETT@COMPANY.COM'
MUST_CHANGE_PASSWORD=TRUE;
```

You can add new properties or change existing user properties by using the ALTER command. For example, you may have a user to whom you want to grant temporary access to your Snowflake account. That can be accomplished by setting up an expiration time for the user:

```
USE ROLE USERADMIN;
ALTER USER USER10 SET DAYS_TO_EXPIRY = 30;
```

Adding defaults for the user makes it easier for the user. You can make it so that the user has a default role or default virtual warehouse, for example.

Adding a default virtual warehouse for the user does not verify that the virtual warehouse exists. We never created a WAREHOUSE52, yet the code to assign that virtual warehouse as a default will be executed successfully with no errors or warning:

```
USE ROLE USERADMIN;
ALTER USER USER10 SET DEFAULT_WAREHOUSE=WAREHOUSE52_WH;
```

We also can attempt to assign to a user a default role that does exist:

```
USE ROLE USERADMIN;
ALTER USER USER10 SET DEFAULT_ROLE=IMAGINARY_ROLE;
```

However, if we did not previously grant that role to the user, we cannot make it the default role. In other words, setting a default role does not assign the role to the user. The same thing applies for access to a database. When we attempt to assign defaults that have not previously been assigned to a user, no warning is given, but the command is not actually executed successfully.

To see for yourself, log out of your Snowflake account and log in as USER10. Remember that when we created the user ABARNETT we required the user to reset the password. As a result, you'll need to create a new acceptable password for USER10 (Figure 5-26 shows the UI for creating a new password).

❄

Password expired

Your password for **ABARNETT** has expired

New password

[   ]

Your password must be 8 - 256 characters and contain at least 1
number(s), 0 special character(s), 1 uppercase and 1 lowercase letter(s).

Confirm password

[   ]

[Submit]

Figure 5-26. A new password is required for USER10 when signing in for the first time

When you create a new password and attempt to log in, you'll receive an error message because there is a default role set for ABARNETT that hasn't been granted to the user. As such, login will fail. Go ahead and log back in as yourself and we'll make the needed corrections.

Let's set some defaults for USER10 that are correct, as shown in Figure 5-27. We'll log back out of our admin account and log back in as USER10 once we're done:

```
USE ROLE USERADMIN;
GRANT ROLE ACCOUNTANT_SR TO USER USER10;
ALTER USER USER10 SET DEFAULT_NAMESPACE=SNOWFLAKE.ACCOUNT_USAGE;
ALTER USER USER10 SET DEFAULT_WAREHOUSE=VW2_WH;
ALTER USER USER10 SET DEFAULT_ROLE = ACCOUNTANT_SR;
ALTER USER USER10 UNSET DEFAULT_WAREHOUSE;
```

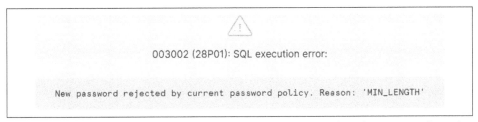

Figure 5-27. USER10 has been granted the default role of ACCOUNTANT_SR

A common user management problem is users who are unable to log in to their account. The Snowflake system will lock out a user who failed to log in successfully after five consecutive attempts. The Snowflake system will automatically clear the lock after 15 minutes. If the user cannot wait, the timer can immediately be reset:

```
USE ROLE USERADMIN;
ALTER USER USER10 SET MINS_TO_UNLOCK=0;
```

Note that the original method we used to create the password will not work, because 123 is not an acceptable password:

```
USE ROLE USERADMIN;
ALTER USER USER10 SET PASSWORD = '123'
MUST_CHANGE_PASSWORD = TRUE;
```

If we try to use the 123 password, an error will be returned, as shown in Figure 5-28.

003002 (28P01): SQL execution error:

New password rejected by current password policy. Reason: 'MIN_LENGTH'

Figure 5-28. The password was rejected because the minimum length was not achieved

The password submitted by the USERADMIN to reset a forgotten password must be at least eight characters in length, and contain at least one digit, one uppercase letter, and one lowercase letter:

```
USE ROLE USERADMIN;
ALTER USER USER10 SET PASSWORD = '123456Aa'
MUST_CHANGE_PASSWORD = TRUE;
```

Keep in mind that because the USERADMIN role rolls up to the SECURITYADMIN role, which itself rolls up to the ACCOUNTADMIN role, the two higher roles can also run any command that the USERADMIN role can run. Here is an example:

```
USE ROLE SECURITYADMIN;
ALTER USER USER10 SET PASSWORD = '123456Bb'
MUST_CHANGE_PASSWORD = TRUE;
```

There may be a time when it is necessary to abort a user's currently running queries and prevent the person from running any new queries. To accomplish this and to immediately lock the user out of Snowflake, use the following command:

```
USE ROLE USERADMIN;
ALTER USER USER10 SET DISABLED = TRUE;
```

To describe an individual user and get a listing of all the user's property values and default values, use the DESCRIBE command:

```
USE ROLE USERADMIN;
DESC USER USER10;
```

The results are shown in Figure 5-29.

	property	value	...	default	description
1	NAME	USER10		null	Name
2	COMMENT	null		null	user comment associated to an object in the dictionary
3	DISPLAY_NAME	AMY		null	Display name of the associated object
4	LOGIN_NAME	ABARNETT		null	Login name of the user
5	FIRST_NAME	AMY		null	First name of the user
6	MIDDLE_NAME	null		null	Middle name of the user
7	LAST_NAME	BARNETT		null	Last name of the user
8	EMAIL	ABARNETT@COMPANY.COM		null	Email address of the user
9	PASSWORD	********		null	Password of the user
10	MUST_CHANGE_PASSWORD	true		false	User must change the password
11	DISABLED	true		false	Whether the user is disabled
12	SNOWFLAKE_LOCK	false		false	Whether the user or account is locked by Snowflake
13	SNOWFLAKE_SUPPORT	false		false	Snowflake Support is allowed to use the user or account
14	DAYS_TO_EXPIRY	29.990625		null	User record will be treated as expired after specified number of days

Figure 5-29. Description of USER10

To reset one of the property values of the user back to the default value, you can use this command:

```
USE ROLE USERADMIN;
ALTER USER USER10 SET DEFAULT_WAREHOUSE = DEFAULT;

USE ROLE USERADMIN;
DESC USER USER10;
```

We discovered earlier that the SECURITYADMIN role, not the USERADMIN role, has inherent privileges to see a list of all users. The relevant code follows, and the results are shown in Figure 5-30:

```
USE ROLE SECURITYADMIN;
SHOW USERS;
```

	name	created_on	login_name	display_name
1	JKA2022	.945 -0700	JKA2022	JKA2022
2	SNOWFLAKE	.959 -0700	SNOWFLAKE	SNOWFLAKE
3	USER1	.092 -0700	ARNOLD	USER1
4	USER10	.785 -0700	ABARNETT	AMY
5	USER2	.426 -0700	BEATRICE	USER2
6	USER3	.914 -0700	COLLIN	USER3
7	USER4	.244 -0700	DIEDRE	USER4

Figure 5-30. A list of users in the Snowflake account

You'll notice that the list of users includes the initial user that set up the account and all the users that you created. In addition, there is one more user that came with the account. The SNOWFLAKE user is a special user that is only used by Snowflake support with the permission of the ACCOUNTADMIN when there is a need to troubleshoot account issues.

 It is possible to delete the SNOWFLAKE user, but once it's deleted, you can't simply create another SNOWFLAKE user that can be used for support. Therefore, it is highly recommended that you do not delete this user.

Wildcards are supported when using the SHOW command. You can use the LIKE command with an underscore to match any single character and with a percent sign to match any sequence of zero or more characters. The following is an example:

```
USE ROLE SECURITYADMIN;
SHOW USERS LIKE 'USER%';
```

Just as users can be created, they can also be dropped. Notice that nothing needs to be done to anything prior to dropping the user, such as revoking their role. Just issue the DROP command:

```
USE ROLE USERADMIN;
DROP USER USER10;
```

 The ACCOUNTADMIN has access to a list of all users by querying the SNOWFLAKE.ACCOUNT_USAGE.USERS table, including those users who have been deleted.

Thus far, we've been using the Snowflake worksheet for user management. There is another place for us to manage users, too. Navigate to the Main menu by clicking the Home icon. Once at the Main menu, change your role to SECURITYADMIN and then click Admin → Users & Roles. You'll see a list of six users including your user account, the SNOWFLAKE user, and users 1 through 4. If you click the ellipsis on the far-right side, for USER4, you'll see a list of options (as shown in Figure 5-31).

Figure 5-31. Menu options for managing users

You'll notice how easy it is to grant a role to a user or to disable or drop the user. Let's click Edit to see the Edit User screen (as shown in Figure 5-32).

Figure 5-32. The Edit User screen

From this screen, you can assign a default role and/or a default virtual warehouse. Setting a default role and virtual warehouse determines the role and virtual warehouse associated with the user at the time the Snowflake session is initiated by the user. However, users can change roles or select a different virtual warehouse at any time.

Role Management

In addition to managing users from the Admin menu, you can also manage roles (as shown in Figure 5-33).

Figure 5-33. Role management in the Admin menu

Within the Roles submenu, you have the choice to manage roles via graph or table. The Graph view can be especially useful (as shown in Figure 5-34).

Take some time to navigate both the Graph and Table sections of the Roles submenu. You'll notice that you can edit the roles you've already created. In addition, there is a + Role button in the upper-right corner of the screen where you can create a new role.

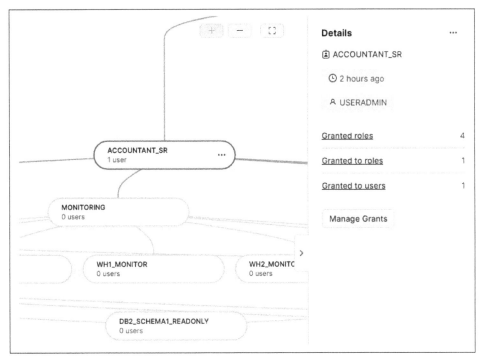

Figure 5-34. The Graph view and details for the ACCOUNTANT_SR role

Previously, it was mentioned that a default role can be designated for any user. When a user first logs in, their primary role is whatever default role was assigned to them. A user's current role in a session is considered their primary role.

If a Snowflake user was assigned more than one role, they can switch between the roles. There are only primary and secondary roles: any role not being used as the primary is a secondary role.

Secondary roles can be handled in different ways. One way is to keep all roles separate so the user can only use one role at a time. Another way is to grant a secondary role to a primary role, in effect creating a *persistent access layering of a specific secondary role to a primary role* for everyone who uses the primary role. We'll see an example of that in Chapter 7. If, instead, some secondary roles should be granted only to select users, then it is possible to implement a *session-based access layering of all secondary roles* by employing the USE SECONDARY ROLES statement.

Snowflake Multi-Account Strategy

In this chapter, we've explored how to manage a single Snowflake account. There are many times, however, when it makes sense to have a multi-account strategy to take advantage of the separation of accounts. One use case for needing multiple accounts is to use different accounts for different environments, such as development, testing, and production. While it is certainly possible to use a single account to accomplish separation of environments, choosing a multi-account approach means different environments can have different security features selected. This makes it possible to balance differently how productivity versus security risk is handled for each account. There is also the ability to save money by using a higher-grade feature set only for production and not for development or testing. This is possible when using a multi-account strategy.

Sometimes a company faces regulatory constraints that prevent it from using a specific cloud provider or region in one subsidiary. In that case, a new Snowflake account can be created for that particular subsidiary whereby an acceptable cloud provider and region can be selected. Other times, multi-account choices are made for many different strategic reasons. Many of today's organizations are global and need their data located geographically in certain regions. Sometimes organizations opt for a multicloud approach to reduce dependency on a single vendor or to make it easier to merge with an acquired company that operates on a different cloud provider.

Snowflake makes it easy for companies to adopt a multi-account strategy with the Snowflake organization object and the ORGADMIN role. A Snowflake organization simplifies account management and billing, database replication and failover/failback, Secure Data Sharing, and other administrative tasks.

> An ORGADMIN can create a new Snowflake account and can view account properties. However, an ORGADMIN does not have access to the account data by default.

It takes approximately 30 seconds for the DNS changes to propagate before you can access a newly created Snowflake account. The maximum number of accounts in a Snowflake organization cannot exceed 25 by default; however, you can contact Snowflake support to have the limit raised.

Managing Users and Groups with SCIM

Snowflake supports SCIM 2.0 for integration with identity providers Okta and Microsoft Azure AD as well as with other identity providers which require customization.

The specific Snowflake SCIM role must own any users and roles that are imported from the identity provider. If the Snowflake SCIM role does not own the imported users or roles, updates in the identity provider will not be synced to Snowflake. Also, ensure that you do not make user and group changes in Snowflake if using an identity provider, because those changes made directly in Snowflake will not synchronize back to the identity provider.

Code Cleanup

Let's perform code cleanup so that you can remove the objects in your Snowflake account in preparation for working on another chapter example.

Note that there is no need to drop objects in the hierarchy below the database before dropping the databases, nor to revoke the virtual warehouse usage privileges before dropping the virtual warehouses:

```
USE ROLE SYSADMIN;
DROP DATABASE DB1;
DROP DATABASE DB2;
SHOW DATABASES;
DROP WAREHOUSE VW1_WH; DROP WAREHOUSE VW2_WH; DROP WAREHOUSE VW3_WH;
SHOW WAREHOUSES;
```

Just as the ACCOUNTADMIN had to create resource monitors, the same role must be used to drop resource monitors. After you drop the resource monitor and use the SHOW command, you'll see there is no longer a resource monitor on the account:

```
USE ROLE ACCOUNTADMIN;
DROP RESOURCE MONITOR MONITOR1_RM;
SHOW RESOURCE MONITORS;
```

Next, the USERADMIN role will want to drop all the custom roles that were created:

```
USE ROLE USERADMIN;
DROP ROLE DATA_SCIENTIST; DROP ROLE ANALYST_SR; DROP ROLE ANALYST_JR;
DROP ROLE DATA_EXCHANGE_ASST; DROP ROLE ACCOUNTANT_SR; DROP ROLE ACCOUNTANT_JR;
DROP ROLE PRD_DBA; DROP ROLE DATA_ENGINEER; DROP ROLE DEVELOPER_SR; DROP
ROLE DEVELOPER_JR; DROP ROLE LOADER; DROP ROLE VISUALIZER; DROP ROLE REPORTING;
DROP ROLE MONITORING;  DROP ROLE RM1_MODIFY; DROP ROLE WH1_USAGE;
DROP ROLE WH2_USAGE; DROP ROLE WH3_USAGE; DROP ROLE DB1_MONITOR; DROP
ROLE DB2_MONITOR; DROP ROLE WH1_MONITOR; DROP ROLE WH2_MONITOR; DROP ROLE
WH3_MONITOR; DROP ROLE RM1_MONITOR; DROP ROLE DB1_SCHEMA1_READONLY; DROP ROLE
DB1_SCHEMA1_ALL; DROP ROLE DB2_SCHEMA1_READONLY; DROP ROLE DB2_SCHEMA1_ALL;
DROP ROLE DB2_SCHEMA2_READONLY; DROP ROLE DB2_SCHEMA2_ALL;
SHOW ROLES;
```

And now we are able to drop the users we created:

```
USE ROLE USERADMIN;
DROP USER USER1; DROP USER USER2; DROP USER USER3;DROP USER USER4;
```

We can confirm that all the users have now been dropped:

```
USE ROLE SECURITYADMIN;
SHOW USERS;
```

Summary

In this chapter, we learned about Snowflake's access control model. With many hands-on examples, we created securable objects and custom roles, we assigned role hierarchies, and we granted privileges to roles. Afterward, we assigned roles to users and then tested and validated our work before performing user management and seeing where we could perform role management in the Snowsight web UI.

Throughout, we also came to understand some best practices when using role-based access control (RBAC) and discretionary access control (DAC). In future chapter examples, you'll notice how we use some of these best practices, such as making sure to create new securable objects with the standard SYSADMIN role unless a custom role is created and used for that purpose.

In the next chapter, we'll start by using the SYSADMIN role to create some objects in Snowsight as part of our prep work. We'll also get introduced to SnowSQL, Snowflake's command-line interface (CLI). With the SnowSQL CLI, we'll have to set the context for roles using SQL as there is no intuitive web interface with drop-down menus in SnowSQL like there is in Snowsight. The easy and intuitive Snowsight web user interface is where you'll likely spend most of your time as a Snowflake user, but there are times when SnowSQL is necessary, most often when you're focused on loading and unloading data.

Knowledge Check

The following questions are based on the information contained in this chapter:

1. How would you define inherent privileges? Give a few examples.

2. Can you name all the Snowflake system-defined account roles? To which of the system-defined roles should most custom roles be assigned in the role hierarchy?

3. What are some of the important considerations to keep in mind when assigning defaults, such as default role or default virtual warehouse, to a user?

4. What is one thing that an ACCOUNTADMIN role can do that no other role can ever do?

5. Can you name the privileges a role needs in order to view the contents of a table?

6. What is unique about the SNOWFLAKE database that is included in the account?

7. How many Snowflake accounts can an entity create?

8. What does it mean if privileges come with GRANT options?

9. Under what circumstances can a user execute either the SHOW WAREHOUSES or SHOW DATABASES command and get different results?

10. Does Snowflake have the concept of a super user or super role? Explain.

Answers to these questions are available in Appendix A.

Data Loading and Unloading

Data engineers are responsible for managing the ingestion and transformation of raw data sets from various disparate sources to deliver the data in a state that end users need in order to gain actionable insights. This chapter provides the foundational knowledge anyone can use to learn more about how to achieve the best data engineering results on the Snowflake cloud data platform.

The chapter begins with a summary of basic concepts of Snowflake data loading and unloading, including data types, compression methods, file format types, and Snowflake stages. In the data loading tools section, we'll take a deep dive into learning how to use SQL insert statements in the Snowflake worksheet to load both structured and semi-structured data. We'll also learn how to load data using the web UI Load Data wizard and the SnowSQL command-line interface (CLI). For a more automated approach to data loading, we can use data pipelines, connectors, and third-party tools. We'll explore some of these automated data loading options later in the chapter. In addition, we'll look at some alternatives to data loading, such as creating materialized views on external stages and accessing shared data. Finally, we'll discuss unloading data files from Snowflake.

For our hands-on examples, we'll be completing most of the work in Snowsight, the default web UI. However, we'll need to switch to the Snowflake Classic Console briefly to use the Load Data wizard and when we need to download SnowSQL. Before diving in, let's first take care of the prep work needed for the hands-on examples in this chapter.

Prep Work

Create a new worksheet titled *Chapter6 Data Loading and Unloading*. Refer to "Navigating Snowsight Worksheets" on page 8 if you need help creating a new worksheet. To set the worksheet context, make sure you are using the SYSADMIN role and the COMPUTE_WH virtual warehouse.

In this chapter, all our work will be completed in one database. For each uploading type, we'll create a separate schema. Also, we'll be including comments throughout for all our CREATE statements. Execute the following SQL statements from within the Snowsight web UI worksheet:

```
USE ROLE SYSADMIN;
USE WAREHOUSE COMPUTE_WH;
CREATE OR REPLACE DATABASE DEMO6_DB
    COMMENT = "Database for all Chapter 6 Examples";
CREATE OR REPLACE SCHEMA WS COMMENT = "Schema for Worksheet Insert Examples";
CREATE OR REPLACE SCHEMA UI COMMENT = "Schema for Web UI Uploads";
CREATE OR REPLACE SCHEMA SNOW COMMENT = "Schema for SnowSQL Loads";
CREATE OR REPLACE WAREHOUSE LOAD_WH
    COMMENT = "Warehouse for CH 6 Load Examples";
```

You'll also need a CSV file to upload using the web UI Load Data wizard and the SnowSQL CLI. There are files on GitHub for this chapter, including the CSV file, that you can download and use. Alternatively, you can create your own file by using the data in Table 6-1. You can save the table as a CSV comma-delimited file named TABLE20.

Table 6-1. Data for the CSV file to be used in the chapter's hands-on exercises

ID	F_NAME	L_NAME	CITY
1	Anthony	Robinson	Atlanta
2	Peggy	Mathison	Birmingham
3	Marshall	Baker	Chicago
4	Kevin	Cline	Denver

Basics of Data Loading and Unloading

Before we get to our hands-on examples for data loading and unloading, we need to review a few important concepts. In this section, we'll spend some time learning about the data types for semi-structured data. We'll also learn about the file format types and data file compression methods supported by Snowflake. In addition, we'll discuss the difference in the frequency of data load options, and review Snowflake stages and how we reference different types of stages in our SQL statements. Finally, we'll make note of some of the different data sources that are applicable for data loading.

Data Types

Snowflake data types were introduced in Chapter 4, where we took a deep dive into Snowflake data types that support structured data. In this chapter, we'll be using several data types for structured data, and we'll be diving deeper into the semi-structured data types of VARIANT, OBJECT, and ARRAY.

Semi-structured data types

Snowflake provides flexible schema data types for loading semi-structured data. No transformations are needed prior to loading semi-structured data because Snowflake automatically converts semi-structured data to allow for SQL querying of the data in a fully relational manner.

Three Snowflake data types are used to support semi-structured data types: VARIANT, OBJECT, and ARRAY. Interestingly, the VARIANT data type can store the values of any other Snowflake data type, including OBJECT and ARRAY. Thus, VARIANT is considered a universal data type.

The VARIANT data type has a size limit of 16 MB of compressed data. Therefore, it is recommended that you flatten your object and key data into separate relational columns if your semi-structured data stored in a VARIANT data type column includes arrays, numbers with strings, or dates and timestamps. This is especially important for dates and timestamps loaded into a VARIANT data type, because those data types end up being stored as strings in a VARIANT column.

The Snowflake VARIANT data type is a good choice if you are not yet sure what types of operations you want to perform on the semi-structured data you load into Snowflake.

The Snowflake OBJECT data type represents collections of key-value pairs, where the key is a nonempty string and the values are of a VARIANT data type. The Snowflake ARRAY data type represents dense or sparse arrays of an arbitrary size, where the index is a non-negative integer and the values are of a VARIANT data type.

File Formats

File formats are Snowflake objects that can be used with COPY commands. A file format defines the data file with parameters such as compression and file type. It also defines format options such as trim space and field delimiter for CSV files, and strip outer array for JSON files. A listing of different file format parameters for CSV and JSON files is presented later in this section.

Snowflake-supported file format types for data unloading include JSON and Parquet for semi-structured data, and delimited file formats such as CSV and TSV for structured data. Data loading file format types supported by Snowflake include the same format types for unloading, plus XML, Avro, and ORC.

When loading data into Snowflake from delimited files such as CSV or TSV files, the default character set is UTF-8; other character sets are accepted for delimited files, but they are converted by Snowflake to UTF-8 before being stored in tables. For all other supported file formats, UTF-8 is the only supported character set when loading data. For unloading data, UTF-8 is the only supported character set no matter the file format type.

 Snowflake supports both the Newline delimited JSON (NDJSON) standard format, and the comma-separated JSON format for loading data into Snowflake tables. When unloading to files, Snowflake outputs only to the NDJSON format.

Many format options are available when loading and unloading data into and out of Snowflake. The format options available depend on the type of file format. Table 6-2 includes the format options for the CSV file format type.

Table 6-2. Format options for the CSV file format type

Format options	Parameters	Loading/ unloading	Description	Default
ENCODING =	'<string>' | UTF8	Loading	String that specifies the character set of source data	UTF8
ERROR_ON_COLUMN _COUNT_MISMATCH =	TRUE | FALSE	Loading	Boolean that specifies whether to generate a parsing error if the number of delimited columns in an input file doesn't match the number of columns in the corresponding table	TRUE
REPLACE_INVALID _CHARACTERS =	TRUE | FALSE	Loading	Boolean that specifies whether to replace invalid UTF-8 characters with Unicode replacement characters	FALSE
SKIP_BLANK_LINES =	TRUE | FALSE	Loading	Specifies whether to skip blank lines in the files	FALSE
SKIP_BYTE_ORDER_MARK =	TRUE | FALSE	Loading	Boolean that specifies whether to skip the byte order mark	TRUE
VALIDATE_UTF8 =	TRUE | FALSE	Loading	Boolean that specifies whether to validate UTF-8 character encoding	TRUE

Format options	Parameters	Loading/ unloading	Description	Default
SKIP_HEADER=	`<integer>`	Loading	Number of lines at the start of the file to skip	0
TRIM_SPACE =	TRUE | FALSE	Loading	Boolean that specifies whether to remove whitespace from fields	FALSE
BINARY_FORMAT =	HEX | BASE64 | UTF8	Loading, unloading	Defines the encoding format for binary input and output	HEX
DATE_FORMAT =	`'<string>'` | AUTO	Loading, unloading	Defines the format of date values	AUTO
EMPTY_FIELD_AS_NULL =	TRUE | FALSE	Loading, unloading	Specifies whether to insert SQL NULL for empty fields in a file	TRUE
ESCAPE =	`'<character>'` | NONE	Loading, unloading	Single character string used as the escape character for enclosed and unenclosed values	NONE
ESCAPE_UNENCLOSED _FIELD =	`'<character>'` | NONE	Loading, unloading	Single character string used as the escape character for unenclosed values only	/ (backslash)
FIELD_DELIMITER =	`'<character>'` | NONE	Loading, unloading	One or more characters that separate fields in a file	, (comma)
FIELD_OPTIONALLY _ENCLOSED_BY =	`'<character>'` | NONE	Loading, unloading	Character used to enclose strings, often used with Escape	NONE
NULL_IF =	`('<string> [ , '<string>, …} )`	Loading, unloading	String used to convert to and from SQL NULL	NULL (\\N)
RECORD_DELIMITER =	`'<character>'` | NONE	Loading, unloading	One or more characters that separate records in a file	Newline character
TIME_FORMAT =	`'<string>'` | AUTO	Loading, unloading	Defines the format of time values	AUTO
TIMESTAMP_FORMAT =	`'<string>'` | AUTO	Loading, unloading	Defines the format of timestamp values	AUTO
FILE_EXTENSION =	`'<string>'`	Unloading	Specifies the extension for files unloaded to a stage	NULL

Table 6-3 includes the format options for the JSON file format type. The JSON file format type is one of several semi-structured data types supported by Snowflake. Format type options for other semi-structured data types, such as Avro, ORC, Parquet, and XML, can be found in the Snowflake online documentation (*https://oreil.ly/F1BvG*).

Table 6-3. Format options for the JSON file format type

Format options	Parameters	Loading/ unloading	Description	Default
ALLOW_DUPLICATE	TRUE | FALSE	Loading	Boolean that specifies whether to allow duplicate object field names (only the last one is preserved)	FALSE
BINARY_FORMAT =	HEX | BASE64 | UTF8	Loading	Defines the encoding format for binary string values	HEX
DATE_FORMAT =	'<string>' | AUTO	Loading	Defines the format of date values	AUTO
ENABLE_OCTAL =	TRUE | FALSE	Loading	Boolean that enables parsing of octal numbers	FALSE
IGNORE UTF8_ERRORS =	TRUE | FALSE	Loading	Boolean that specifies whether UTF-8 encoding errors produce conditions	FALSE
NULL_IF =	('<string> [, '<string>, …})	Loading	String used to convert to and from SQL NULL	NULL (\\N)
REPLACE_INVALID _CHARACTERS =	TRUE | FALSE	Loading	Boolean that specifies whether to replace invalid UTF-8 characters with Unicode replacement characters	FALSE
SKIP_BYTE_ORDER_MARK =	TRUE | FALSE	Loading	Boolean that specifies whether to skip the byte order mark	TRUE
STRIP_NULL_VALUES =	TRUE | FALSE	Loading	Boolean that instructs the JSON parser to remove object fields or array elements containing null values	FALSE
STRIP_OUTER_ARRAY =	TRUE | FALSE	Loading	Boolean that instructs the JSON parser to remove outer brackets	FALSE
TIME_FORMAT =	'<string>' | AUTO	Loading	Defines the format of time values	AUTO
TIMESTAMP_FORMAT =	'<string>' | AUTO	Loading	Defines the format of timestamp values	AUTO
TRIM_SPACE =	TRUE | FALSE	Loading	Boolean that specifies whether to remove whitespace from strings	FALSE
FILE_EXTENSION =	'<string>'	Unloading	Specifies the extension for files unloaded to a stage	NULL

Creating file formats for Snowflake data loading is optional. It is recommended that you create file format objects if you foresee that you'll be able to reuse them with COPY commands for loading similarly structured files.

Data File Compression

You can load compressed and uncompressed data into Snowflake. All data stored in Snowflake by default is compressed using gzip, without you having to select the columns or choose a compression algorithm. You can compress your data files prior to loading the data into Snowflake; it is recommended that you compress your files if they are large in size. Snowflake supports the GZIP, BZIP2, DEFLATE, RAW_DEFLATE, BROTLI, and ZSTANDARD (ZSTD) compression methods, and can automatically detect all of them except for BROTLI and ZSTANDARD (ZSTD). For those compression methods, you'll need to specify the compression method at the time of data load.

> Snowflake also supports the Lempei-Ziv-Oberhumer (LZO) and SNAPPY compression methods for the Parquet file format type.

Frequency of Data Processing

Data processing begins with raw data that is prepared, processed, and then stored. It is possible to stream live data to storage for immediate availability, but more frequently, data is processed in near-real time. Sometimes data is processed in batches. Let's take a look at the differences between the types of data processing.

Batch processing

Batch processing involves automatically processing a large amount of data that has accumulated over a specified period of time. Payroll systems are a good example of batch processing since the data may only need to be processed biweekly. Any data that is only accessible to you in batches, situations where data freshness is not mission critical, and anytime you are working with complex algorithms on large data sets may be good use cases for batch processing. The most important benefit of batch processing is that it's typically less expensive than the other types of data processing. It's less expensive because compute resources are only used when the processing is executed, and since batch processes execute less frequently than near–real-time processing, the overall cost is less. The trade-off, though, is data freshness.

Streaming, continuous loading, and micro-batch processing

The terms *streaming*, *stream processing*, *continuous loading*, *near–real-time processing*, and *micro-batch processing* are often used interchangeably because in practice they achieve similar results. Continuous loading, near–real-time processing, and micro-batch processing are synonymous; however, there are differences between those three terms and the terms *streaming* and *stream processing*.

For micro-batch processing implementations, batch processes are executed on small amounts of data which can be processed in less than 60 seconds. If the data routinely takes longer than 60 seconds to load, you may want to consider reducing the size of each batch. The time between loading each micro-batch could be greater than 60 seconds but is usually no more than a few minutes between loads. This achieves near–real-time results.

In contrast, pure-play stream processing solutions would use tools such as a Kafka Streams API or Confluent's KSQL in situations in which actual real-time data is critical. Examples of when real-time data is important include security situations in which data applications provide immediate fraud detection capabilities, and operational situations in which it is important to have a real-time view of ecommerce data or Internet of Things (IoT) data, such as security cameras or patient medical devices.

In the next section, we'll discuss ways to load data using all methods, but we'll focus mostly on continuous loading implementations. Unlike batch processing, continuous loading has either a small state or no state at all and typically involves relatively simple transformations. Continuous loading is most often used when we need fresh, near–real-time data without needing to know what happened in the last two or three seconds. Some situations when we might want to use continuous loading are for web analytics and human resources systems.

Snowflake Stage References

Snowflake stages were introduced in Chapter 3. We'll briefly review a few important things about stages here, since they are an important part of Snowflake data loading and unloading.

Snowflake stages are temporary storage spaces used as an intermediate step to lead files to Snowflake tables or to unload data from Snowflake tables into files. There are two main types of stages: internal and external. For external stages, the files are stored in an external location such as an S3 bucket, and they are referenced by the external stage. Access to these external locations was previously managed through cloud identity and access management (IAM) roles and access control lists (ACLs). Today, however, the best practice is to create a storage integration. A *storage integration* is a Snowflake object that stores a generated IAM entity for external cloud storage and optionally includes allowed or blocked storage locations for Amazon S3, Google Cloud Storage, or Microsoft Azure.

Internal stage types include internal named stages, user stages, and table stages. Note that all stage types in Snowflake are referred to using the @ symbol.

Named stages

Internal named stages are database objects; thus, they can be used by any user who has been granted a role with the appropriate privileges. SQL statements in which a named stage is referenced will need the @ symbol along with the name of the stage. To list named stages, you can run the LIST @*<stage name>* statement.

User stages

Each Snowflake user has a stage for storing files which is accessible only by that user. A user stage is not a separate database object, and it cannot be altered or dropped. The data in a user stage is accessible only to the specific user who executed the SQL commands. SQL statements in which a user stage is referenced will need the @~ symbols. The LIST @~ SQL statement can be used to list user stages. Once you run the list command for a user stage, your results should be similar to those shown in Figure 6-1.

	name	size	md5	...
1	worksheet_data/c1bccd70-c8cc-4c30-9f2e-b0559dc641af	720	f3112daba61c8171102aa2376cd41ee3	
2	worksheet_data/metadata	400	5dd847674966f16131fafae3ad696971	

Figure 6-1. Results of the list command for the user stage

Table stages

A table stage is not a separate database object; rather, it is an implicit stage tied to the table itself. Just like user stages, a table stage cannot be altered or dropped. Additionally, the data in table stages is accessible only to those Snowflake roles which have been granted the privileges to read from the table. SQL statements in which a table stage is referenced will need the @% symbols as well as the name of the table. LIST @% *<name of table>* is the statement you can use to list table stages.

Data Sources

Data can be loaded into Snowflake from a local file system, Amazon S3 bucket, Azure container, or GCP bucket. Loading your data from different sources is not limited by the cloud platform that hosts your Snowflake account. With the exception of some auto-ingest Snowpipe use cases, you can load data from any of the sources previously mentioned, whether your Snowflake account is hosted on Amazon, Azure, or GCP.

Using Snowflake or third-party tools, you can load data into Snowflake from virtually any data source, including files, APIs, enterprise applications, and databases.

In this chapter, we'll get hands-on experience with inserting and loading structured and semi-structured data, and we'll discover ways to ingest other data sources, such as IoT and web/log data, by using the Kafka Connector, Snowpipe, and/or third-party tools.

Data Loading Tools

In this section, we'll explore five different ways to load data into Snowflake. The first way, which we've been using throughout the chapters thus far, is to insert data into tables via SQL command statements in the Snowflake worksheets. Next, we'll learn how to upload files directly in the web UI. We'll also explore the SnowSQL CLI, where we'll use COPY INTO and PUT commands. Rounding out this section on data loading, we'll learn about data pipelines and third-party ETL and ELT tools.

Snowflake Worksheet SQL Using INSERT INTO and INSERT ALL Commands

We'll begin our data loading examples by using the SQL INSERT command in the Snowflake worksheet. We have frequently used the INSERT INTO command in our chapter examples because it is the quickest way to insert data into tables when you have just a few rows of data. So, the examples in this section should be familiar to you.

For all examples in this section, we'll use one schema within which we'll create all the necessary tables. In preparation, we'll execute the following two USE commands. Be sure to execute these commands again if you create a new worksheet as you work to complete examples in this section:

```
USE WAREHOUSE LOAD_WH;
USE DATABASE DEMO6_DB;
USE SCHEMA WS;
```

 All the INSERT commands we'll be demonstrating in this chapter are Data Manipulation Language (DML) commands, not to be confused with the Snowflake INSERT string and binary function.

Single-row inserts for structured and semi-structured data

We'll first create our TABLE1 table for the single-row insert example for structured data. Then we'll insert one row using explicitly specified values in the INSERT INTO command:

```
CREATE OR REPLACE TABLE TABLE1
    (id integer, f_name string, l_name string, city string)
COMMENT = "Single-Row Insert for Structured Data
    using Explicitly Specified Values";

INSERT INTO TABLE1 (id, f_name, l_name, city)
VALUES (1, 'Anthony', 'Robinson', 'Atlanta');
SELECT * FROM TABLE1;
```

You should now see that one record has been entered into the table. Let's go ahead and insert another single row:

```
INSERT INTO TABLE1 (id, f_name, l_name, city)
VALUES (2, 'Peggy', 'Mathison', 'Birmingham');
SELECT * FROM TABLE1;
```

Now let's turn our attention to learning how we would insert semi-structured data in Snowflake. For the semi-structured data examples in this chapter, we'll use JSON data.

For a single-row data insert for semi-structured data, we can't use the VALUES clause like we did for structured data. Instead, we'll use a query clause as an alternative. Notice that VARIANT is our data type:

```
CREATE OR REPLACE TABLE TABLE2
    (id integer, variant1 variant)
COMMENT = "Single-Row Insert for Semi-Structured JSON Data";

INSERT INTO TABLE2 (id, variant1)
SELECT 1, parse_json(' {"f_name": "Anthony", "l_name": "Robinson",
    "city": "Atlanta" } ');
SELECT * FROM TABLE2;
```

We now have one single row of semi-structured data in our TABLE2 table. Let's go ahead and insert one more JSON record:

```
INSERT INTO TABLE2 (id, variant1)
SELECT 2, parse_json(' {"f_name": "Peggy", "l_name": "Mathison",
    "city": "Birmingham" } ');
SELECT * FROM TABLE2;
```

The results of your SELECT statement should show two rows, as seen in Figure 6-2.

	ID	VARIANT1	...
1	1	{ "city": "Atlanta", "f_name": "Anthony", "l_name": "Robinson" }	
2	2	{ "city": "Birmingham", "f_name": "Peggy", "l_name": "Mathison" }	

Figure 6-2. Results of inserting two semi-structured data rows into the TABLE2 table

Our examples thus far have demonstrated how to add a single row of data, either structured or semi-structured, to a Snowflake table. Next, we'll take a look at how to add multiple rows of data at a time with one SQL statement.

Multirow inserts for structured and semi-structured data

First we'll create a new table and then insert two rows with one SQL statement:

```
CREATE OR REPLACE TABLE TABLE3
    (id integer, f_name string, l_name string, city string)
COMMENT = "Multi-row Insert for Structured Data using Explicitly Stated Values";
INSERT INTO TABLE3 (id, f_name, l_name, city) VALUES
    (1, 'Anthony', 'Robinson', 'Atlanta'), (2, 'Peggy', 'Mathison',
    'Birmingham');
SELECT * FROM TABLE3;
```

Your results should look like those shown in Figure 6-3.

	ID	F_NAME	L_NAME	CITY	...
1	1	Anthony	Robinson	Atlanta	
2	2	Peggy	Mathison	Birmingham	

Figure 6-3. Results of inserting two records, with a structured data type, using one INSERT command

Now let's try inserting data into a new table from an existing table. We'll create the new table with exactly the same columns as the existing table. Notice that we'll apply a condition so that only specific records from the existing table are inserted into the new table:

```
CREATE OR REPLACE TABLE TABLE4
    (id integer, f_name string, l_name string, city string)
COMMENT = "Multi-row Insert for Structured Data using Query, All Columns Same";
INSERT INTO TABLE4 (id, f_name, l_name, city)
    SELECT * FROM TABLE3 WHERE CONTAINS (city, 'Atlanta');
SELECT * FROM TABLE4;
```

You can see the results of the INSERT command in Figure 6-4. Only one row was inserted into the new table because only that row met the criteria. More than one row would have been inserted if more than one row in the existing table had met the conditions for selection.

	...	ID	F_NAME	L_NAME	CITY
1		1	Anthony	Robinson	Atlanta

Figure 6-4. Results of inserting data into a new table from an existing table where a condition was applied

In this next example, we'll create another table with the same rows as an existing table, but we'll insert fewer column values into the new table than are available in the existing table:

```
CREATE OR REPLACE TABLE TABLE5
    (id integer, f_name string, l_name string, city string)
COMMENT = "Multi-row Insert for Structured Data using Query, Fewer Columns";
```

If we attempt to use a SELECT * command, as we did in the previous example, an error will be returned:

```
INSERT INTO TABLE5
    (id, f_name, l_name) SELECT * FROM TABLE3 WHERE CONTAINS (city, 'Atlanta');
```

Our INSERT INTO command will be successful if we specify in the SELECT command the columns we want to insert:

```
INSERT INTO TABLE5 (id, f_name, l_name)
    SELECT id, f_name, l_name FROM TABLE3 WHERE CONTAINS (city, 'Atlanta');
SELECT * FROM TABLE5;
```

The results of the SELECT command for the TABLE5 table, shown in Figure 6-5, include a null value for the CITY column. This is because we didn't insert that column value from the existing table.

	ID	F_NAME	...	L_NAME	CITY
1	1	Anthony		Robinson	

Figure 6-5. Results of inserting fewer columns from an existing source table into a new target table

Our next example will demonstrate how multiple rows for structured data can be inserted into a table using a common table expression (CTE), a named subquery defined in a WITH clause. A CTE functions as a temporary view in a statement, except it does not store the definition in metadata. In order to demonstrate this example, we'll first need to create a table that will be used as part of the next demo:

```
CREATE OR REPLACE TABLE TABLE6
    (id integer, first_name string, last_name string, city_name string)
COMMENT = "Table to be used as part of next demo";

INSERT INTO TABLE6 (id, first_name, last_name, city_name) VALUES
    (1, 'Anthony', 'Robinson', 'Atlanta'),
    (2, 'Peggy', 'Mathison', 'Birmingham');
```

Now we'll create a new table, TABLE7, into which we will insert data by using a CTE which gets data from the TABLE6 table:

```
CREATE OR REPLACE TABLE TABLE7
    (id integer, f_name string, l_name string, city string)
COMMENT = "Multi-row Insert for Structured Data using CTE";

INSERT INTO TABLE7 (id, f_name, l_name, city)
    WITH CTE AS
    (SELECT id, first_name as f_name, last_name as l_name,
        city_name as city FROM TABLE6)
    SELECT id, f_name, l_name, city
    FROM CTE;
SELECT * FROM TABLE7;
```

Figure 6-6 displays the results of the INSERT command from the CTE example. CTEs are used to improve code readability, to make it easier to maintain code, and to take advantage of recursive programming.

	ID	F_NAME	L_NAME	...	CITY
1	1	Anthony	Robinson		Atlanta
2	2	Peggy	Mathison		Birmingham

Figure 6-6. Results of the INSERT command from the CTE example

Next, we'll explore how to insert records into a new table by creating an inner join on two tables using a zip code column. We first need to create the two tables from which we will create an inner join. The first table will include an identifier column, first and last names, and a zip code column:

```
CREATE OR REPLACE TABLE TABLE8
    (id integer, f_name string, l_name string, zip_code string)
COMMENT  = "Table to be used as part of next demo";
INSERT INTO TABLE8 (id, f_name, l_name, zip_code)
VALUES (1, 'Anthony', 'Robinson', '30301'), (2, 'Peggy', 'Mathison', '35005');
```

The next table will include identifier, zip code, city, and state columns:

```
CREATE OR REPLACE TABLE TABLE9
(id integer, zip_code string, city string, state string)
COMMENT = "Table to be used as part of next demo";
INSERT INTO TABLE9 (id, zip_code, city, state) VALUES
    (1, '30301', 'Atlanta', 'Georgia'),
    (2, '35005', 'Birmingham', 'Alabama');
```

Now we'll create a new table which we will use to insert records using an inner join from the two new tables we just created:

```
CREATE OR REPLACE TABLE TABLE10
    (id integer, f_name string, l_name string, city string,
    state string, zip_code string)
COMMENT = "Multi-row inserts from two tables using an Inner JOIN on zip_code";

INSERT INTO TABLE10 (id, f_name, l_name, city, state, zip_code)
SELECT a.id, a.f_name, a.l_name, b.city, b.state, a.zip_code
FROM TABLE8 a
    INNER JOIN TABLE9 b on a.zip_code = b.zip_code;
SELECT *FROM TABLE10;
```

Figure 6-7 shows the results of the INSERT command using an inner join.

	ID	F_NAME	L_NAME	...	CITY	STATE	ZIP_CODE
1	1	Anthony	Robinson		Atlanta	Georgia	30301
2	2	Peggy	Mathison		Birmingham	Alabama	35005

Figure 6-7. Results of the INSERT command in a new table using an inner join on two existing tables

Until now, our examples for multirow inserts have all been with structured data. Let's take a look at an example for a multirow insert with semi-structured data:

```
CREATE
OR REPLACE TABLE TABLE11
    (variant1 variant)
COMMENT = "Multi-row Insert for Semi-structured JSON Data";
```

You'll notice that for our next INSERT command, we'll include an underscore in front of the ID column for the first value. For the second value, we will not put an underscore in front of the ID column:

```
INSERT INTO TABLE11
    select parse_json(column1)
    from values
    ('{ "_id": "1",
     "name": { "first": "Anthony", "last": "Robinson" },
     "company": "Pascal",
     "email": "anthony@pascal.com",
     "phone": "+1 (999) 444-2222"}'),
    ('{ "id": "2",
     "name": { "first": "Peggy", "last": "Mathison" },
     "company": "Ada",
     "email": "Peggy@ada.com",
     "phone": "+1 (999) 555-3333"}');
SELECT * FROM TABLE11;
```

The results of the INSERT command are shown in Figure 6-8. You'll notice that the columns appear in alphabetical order, not in the order in which they were listed in the INSERT statement. Because the ID column for the first record has an underscore in front of it, the ID column is the first column listed.

	VARIANT 1	...
1	{ "_id": "1", "company": "Pascal", "email": "anthony@pascal.com", "name": { "first": "Anthony", "last": "Robinson" }, "
2	{ "company": "Ada", "email": "Peggy@ada.com", "id": "2", "name": { "first": "Peggy", "last": "Mathison" }, "phone": "+

Figure 6-8. Results of a multirow insert for semi-structured JSON data

In our prior examples, we've been inserting data into a single table. In the next section, we'll learn how to insert data into more than one table at a time.

Multitable inserts

It is possible to update multiple tables at a time by inserting one or more rows into the tables using a query statement. The inserts can be unconditional or conditional. Conditional multitable inserts create inserts by using WHEN-ELSE clauses to determine the table(s) into which each row will be inserted.

The first example will demonstrate how an unconditional multitable insert works. First we'll create the source table:

```
CREATE OR REPLACE TABLE TABLE12
(id integer, first_name string, last_name string, city_name string)
COMMENT = "Source Table to be used as part of next demo for Unconditional Table
Inserts";
INSERT INTO TABLE12 (id, first_name, last_name, city_name) VALUES
(1, 'Anthony', 'Robinson', 'Atlanta'), (2, 'Peggy', 'Mathison', 'Birmingham');
```

Let's create the two target tables:

```
CREATE OR REPLACE TABLE TABLE13
(id integer, f_name string, l_name string, city string)
COMMENT = "Unconditional Table Insert  - Destination Table 1 for unconditional
    multi-table insert";

CREATE OR REPLACE TABLE TABLE14
(id integer, f_name string, l_name string, city string)
COMMENT = "Unconditional Table Insert  - Destination Table 2 for unconditional
    multi-table insert";
```

We can now use the data in the TABLE12 table to insert into the two new tables. You'll notice that we have several commands that will insert data into the tables. First we'll insert all the data from the TABLE12 table into the TABLE13 table. Then we'll insert select values into the TABLE13 and TABLE14 tables. Pay particular attention to the INSERT ALL statement lines:

```
INSERT ALL
    INTO TABLE13
    INTO TABLE13 (id, f_name, l_name, city)
            VALUES (id, last_name, first_name, default)
    INTO TABLE14 (id, f_name, l_name, city)
    INTO TABLE14 VALUES (id, city_name, last_name, first_name)
SELECT id, first_name, last_name, city_name FROM TABLE12;
```

Let's see what our INSERT ALL statement accomplished. First, take a look at the data in the original table by using the SELECT * FROM TABLE12; statement.

Next, take a look at what data exists in the TABLE13 table by using the SELECT * FROM TABLE13; statement. You'll see in Figure 6-9 that four records were inserted into the TABLE13 table. Notice that the third and fourth records have no values in the CITY column.

	ID	F_NAME	L_NAME	CITY
1	1	Anthony	Robinson	Atlanta
2	2	Peggy	Mathison	Birmingham
3	1	Robinson	Anthony	
4	2	Mathison	Peggy	

Figure 6-9. One of two target tables of a multitable INSERT statement

What about the TABLE14 table? Use the SELECT * FROM TABLE14; statement to see what exists in that table (as shown in Figure 6-10).

	ID	F_NAME	L_NAME	CITY	...
1	1	Anthony	Robinson	Atlanta	
2	2	Peggy	Mathison	Birmingham	
3	1	Atlanta	Robinson	Anthony	
4	2	Birmingham	Mathison	Peggy	

Figure 6-10. The second of two target tables of a multitable INSERT statement

We can see that there are also four rows in the TABLE14 table. The first two records are the same as those that exist in the TABLE12 and TABLE13 tables. However, rows 3 and 4 are different. Review the previous INSERT statement to see how the different values were inserted into the various rows.

Our previous example demonstrated an unconditional multitable insert example. Now we'll look at a conditional multitable insert example. Let's create the source table for this example:

```
CREATE OR REPLACE TABLE TABLE15
(id integer, first_name string, last_name string, city_name string)
```

```
COMMENT = "Source Table to be used as part of next demo for
    Conditional multi-table Insert";
INSERT INTO TABLE15 (id, first_name, last_name, city_name)
VALUES
(1, 'Anthony', 'Robinson', 'Atlanta'),
(2, 'Peggy', 'Mathison', 'Birmingham'),
(3, 'Marshall', 'Baker', 'Chicago'),(4, 'Kevin', 'Cline', 'Denver'),
(5, 'Amy', 'Ranger', 'Everly'),(6, 'Andy', 'Murray', 'Fresno');
```

Next, we will create the two target tables:

```
CREATE OR REPLACE TABLE TABLE16
    (id integer, f_name string, l_name string, city string)
COMMENT = "Destination Table 1 for conditional multi-table insert";

CREATE OR REPLACE TABLE TABLE17
    (id integer, f_name string, l_name string, city string)
COMMENT = "Destination Table 2 for conditional multi-table insert";
```

We are now ready to demonstrate a conditional multitable insert:

```
INSERT ALL
    WHEN id <5 THEN
        INTO TABLE16
    WHEN id <3 THEN
        INTO TABLE16
        INTO TABLE17
    WHEN id = 1 THEN
        INTO TABLE16 (id, f_name) VALUES (id, first_name)
    ELSE
        INTO TABLE17
SELECT id, first_name, last_name, city_name FROM TABLE15;
```

Using the SELECT * FROM TABLE16 statement, we can see seven rows were inserted
into the table (as shown in Figure 6-11).

	ID	F_NAME	L_NAME	CITY	...
1	1	Anthony	Robinson	Atlanta	
2	2	Peggy	Mathison	Birmingham	
3	3	Marshall	Baker	Chicago	
4	4	Kevin	Cline	Denver	
5	1	Anthony	Robinson	Atlanta	
6	2	Peggy	Mathison	Birmingham	
7	1	Anthony			

Figure 6-11. Results of a conditional multitable insert into the first target table

From the previous INSERT statement, you'll notice that the TABLE16 table was
included in three different conditional statements. One of those conditional

statements inserted values into two of the four columns, which is why there are two null values for the last record.

Using the `SELECT * FROM TABLE17` statement, we can see in Figure 6-12 that those four rows were inserted into the table.

	ID	F_NAME	...	L_NAME	CITY
1	1	Anthony		Robinson	Atlanta
2	2	Peggy		Mathison	Birmingham
3	5	Amy		Ranger	Everly
4	6	Andy		Murray	Fresno

Figure 6-12. Results of a conditional multitable insert into the second target table

You'll notice that the records with the IDs for 5 and 6 only appear in the second target table. Those two records were inserted as a result of the `ELSE` portion of the `INSERT` statement.

In the examples thus far, we've loaded structured data and semi-structured data. The semi-structured data we loaded was in the JSON file format type and we used the Snowflake `VARIANT` data type to load the data. The `VARIANT` type is just one data type for semi-structured data. There are two other Snowflake data types for semi-structured data. We'll first look at an example for the `ARRAY` data type and then the `OBJECT` data type; we'll load data for an `ARRAY` and an `OBJECT` using the `VARIANT` universal data type.

ARRAY_INSERT

The `ARRAY_INSERT` Snowflake function provides us with a way to directly insert data into a table. We'll create a new table which we can use to demonstrate the `ARRAY_INSERT` data function:

```
CREATE OR REPLACE TABLE TABLE18
    (Array variant)
COMMENT = "Insert Array";
```

The syntax for the `ARRAY_INSERT` function is as follows:

```
ARRAY_INSERT (<array>, <position>, <new element>)
WHERE <array> INCLUDES ARRAY_CONSTRUCT(<values>)
```

As you can see, the `ARRAY_INSERT` function inserts an array followed by a new array value in a specific position in the array. We'll use two different examples to see how it works. First, let's insert an array with a new value that would naturally come next in the array:

```
INSERT INTO TABLE18
SELECT ARRAY_INSERT(array_construct(0, 1, 2, 3), 4, 4);
```

Run a SELECT * statement on the TABLE18 table and you'll get the result shown in Figure 6-13.

Figure 6-13. Result of using the ARRAY_INSERT command

Now let's see what happens if we insert the value that would naturally come next in the array, but insert it into a different position:

```
INSERT INTO TABLE18
SELECT ARRAY_INSERT(array_construct(0, 1, 2, 3), 7, 4);
```

If we run a SELECT * statement again, we'll see the results shown in Figure 6-14.

	ARRAY
1	[0, 1, 2, 3, 4]
2	[0, 1, 2, 3, undefined, undefined, undefined, 4]

Figure 6-14. Results of using the ARRAY_INSERT command a second time

As shown in Figure 6-14, the number 4 was inserted into the seventh position. For positions four through six, there is an *undefined* value since no values were given for those positions.

OBJECT_INSERT

OBJECT_INSERT is a Snowflake semi-structured data function. To demonstrate how the function works, let's first create a new table:

```
CREATE OR REPLACE TABLE TABLE19
    (Object variant)
COMMENT = "Insert Object";
```

The syntax for the OBJECT_INSERT function is as follows:

```
OBJECT_INSERT (<object>, <key>, <value>)
WHERE <object> INCLUDES OBJECT_CONSTRUCT(<key-value pairs>)
```

Now let's insert into a new table some key-value pairs using the OBJECT_INSERT function:

```
INSERT INTO TABLE19
    SELECT OBJECT_INSERT(OBJECT_CONSTRUCT('a', 1, 'b', 2, 'c', 3), 'd', 4);
SELECT * FROM TABLE19;
```

As shown in Figure 6-15, the key-value pairs were inserted as expected.

	OBJECT
1	{ "a": 1, "b": 2, "c": 3, "d": 4 }

Figure 6-15. Result of using the OBJECT_INSERT function

Next, we'll use OBJECT_INSERT to see how null values are handled. First we'll insert a blank value, a null value with the word *null* enclosed in quotes, and then a null value without the quotes:

```
INSERT INTO TABLE19 SELECT
    OBJECT_INSERT(object_construct('a', 1, 'b', 2, 'c', 3), 'd', ' ');
INSERT INTO TABLE19 SELECT
    OBJECT_INSERT(object_construct('a', 1, 'b', 2, 'c', 3), 'd', 'null');
INSERT INTO TABLE19 SELECT
    OBJECT_INSERT(object_construct('a', 1, 'b', 2, 'c', 3), 'd', null);
INSERT INTO TABLE19 SELECT
    OBJECT_INSERT(object_construct('a', 1, 'b', 2, 'c', 3), null, 'd');
SELECT * FROM TABLE19;
```

The results of all the INSERT commands can be seen in Figure 6-16. You'll notice from the last two inserted records that whenever the key-value pair includes a null value, the key-value pair is not inserted.

	OBJECT
1	{ "a": 1, "b": 2, "c": 3, "d": 4 }
2	{ "a": 1, "b": 2, "c": 3, "d": " " }
3	{ "a": 1, "b": 2, "c": 3, "d": "null" }
4	{ "a": 1, "b": 2, "c": 3 }
5	{ "a": 1, "b": 2, "c": 3, "d": " " }
6	{ "a": 1, "b": 2, "c": 3, "d": "null" }
7	{ "a": 1, "b": 2, "c": 3 }
8	{ "a": 1, "b": 2, "c": 3 }

Figure 6-16. Results of inserting rows using the OBJECT_INSERT function

We've taken a look at several different ways data can be inserted into a Snowflake table using SQL statements in the Snowflake worksheet. We used the Snowflake worksheet to demonstrate many of the concepts because it is simple to use. Many of the concepts we learned about in this section are also applicable when we use the Snowflake web UI to load data files or when it makes sense to use the SnowSQL CLI.

In the next section, we're going to use the web UI Load Data wizard to load both structured data files and semi-structured data files. The wizard is intended only for manually loading a few small files at a time.

Before we move on to a different schema, let's review the table comments for all the tables we've been working with in this schema:

```
SHOW TABLES LIKE '%TABLE%';
```

We've been using comments for all the tables we've created in this chapter. If we wanted, we could also use comments for any individual field that we create within a table.

Web UI Load Data Wizard

In prior examples of inserting data into Snowflake tables, we used SQL statements to insert data directly into the tables. We're now going to explore one way we can load files of data. In this section, we'll load some structured data and semi-structured data files, each of them less than 50 MB in size.

 It is important to adhere to the small file size recommendation when using the Snowflake web UI Load Data wizard. Doing so will help to ensure better performance. It will also prevent your browser from crashing, because as the file size increases, more memory consumption will be required to encrypt the files. If you need to load larger files, please refer to the next section, which describes how to use the Snowflake SnowSQL CLI.

Whereas we previously loaded data directly into a Snowflake table using an INSERT command, the wizard indirectly loads the data into a Snowflake table by seamlessly combining two phases: one phase to stage the files and the next phase to load the staged files into a table (as shown in Figure 6-17).

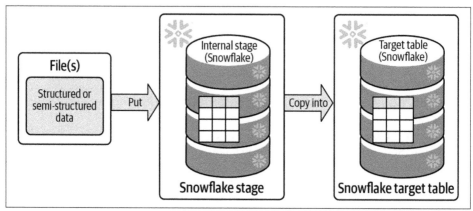

Figure 6-17. Loading file(s) into a Snowflake target table via a Snowflake stage

To accomplish this, the wizard uses the PUT and COPY commands behind the scenes. The PUT command places the file(s) in a stage and the COPY command moves the data from the Snowflake stage to the Snowflake table. When done loading the data into a Snowflake table from the stage, the wizard then deletes all the staged files.

At this time, the Snowflake web UI Load Data wizard is available only in the Classic Console. It is anticipated that the wizard will be available for Snowsight sometime in early 2023.

While we are still in Snowsight, let's go ahead and create the table we'll need for our hands-on examples. Be sure to use the UI schema for this example:

```
USE SCHEMA UI;
CREATE OR REPLACE TABLE TABLE20
    (id integer, f_name string, l_name string, city string)
COMMENT = "Load Structured Data file via the Web UI wizard";
```

Now we'll need to navigate to the Classic Console to complete the examples in this section. In the upper-left corner of your screen, click the Home icon and then click the Classic Console button (as shown in Figure 6-18).

Figure 6-18. Clicking the Home Icon and the Classic Console button to navigate from Snowsight to the Classic Console

Once in the Classic Console, click the Databases tab and then drill down into the DEMO6_DB database. Next, click the TABLE20 table name, which is what we will be using to insert a file with structured data. Your screen should now look like what is shown in Figure 6-19.

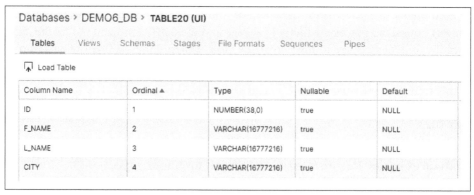

Figure 6-19. The Classic Console after clicking the Databases tab, DEMO6_DB database, and TABLE20 table

You will notice the Load Table upload icon. That is what we'll use to upload a file with structured data to the TABLE20 Snowflake table.

Structured data example

We're ready to proceed with our structured data example. Once you click the Load Table icon, you'll be asked to select the virtual warehouse you want to use to load the files (as shown in Figure 6-20).

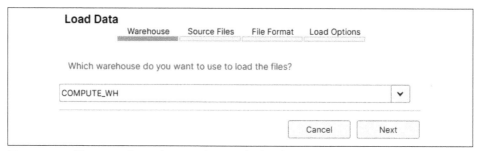

Figure 6-20. The virtual warehouse selection for loading the file using the wizard

Select the LOAD_WH virtual warehouse we created at the beginning of this chapter and then click the Next button. Select the CSV file from your computer by clicking the Select Files button and then selecting the *TABLE20* CSV file saved on your computer as shown in Figure 6-21. Click the Next button.

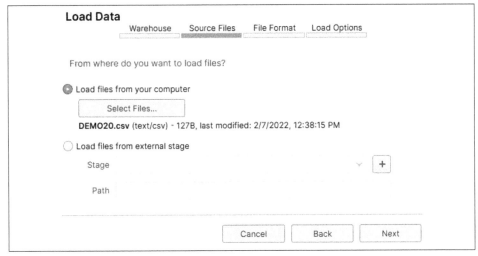

Figure 6-21. Selecting the CSV file from your computer using the wizard

Now is when we'll have to select the file format, if we have one that is already created. Otherwise, we'll create a new file format. In our examples, we have not created any file formats thus far, so we'll need to create a new file format. To create a new file format, click the + (plus sign) button (as shown in Figure 6-22).

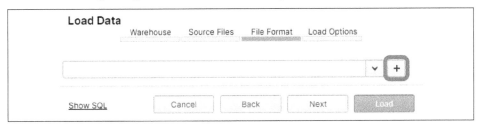

Figure 6-22. Creating a new file format in the wizard

Once we click the + button, we'll have the option to make choices about the file format we want to create. The file format options in Figure 6-23 should be familiar to you. Refer back to Table 6-2 to see these same options, which can be selected if you choose to create a new file format using SQL in a worksheet.

Create File Format

Name*	CSV_FF
Schema Name	PUBLIC
Format Type	CSV
Compression Method	Auto
Column separator	Comma
Row separator	New Line
Header lines to skip	1
Field optionally enclosed by	None
Null String	\\N

☐ Trim space before and after ⑦

Show SQL   Cancel   Finish

Figure 6-23. Creating a file format from within the Snowflake Load Data wizard

Because our CSV file has a header, we'll want to change the "Header lines to skip" option from 0 to 1. If you were to click the Show SQL link, the SQL code shown in Figure 6-24 would be revealed.

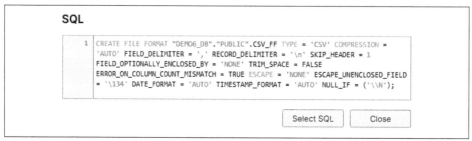

```
1  CREATE FILE FORMAT "DEMO6_DB"."PUBLIC".CSV_FF TYPE = 'CSV' COMPRESSION =
   'AUTO' FIELD_DELIMITER = ',' RECORD_DELIMITER = '\n' SKIP_HEADER = 1
   FIELD_OPTIONALLY_ENCLOSED_BY = 'NONE' TRIM_SPACE = FALSE
   ERROR_ON_COLUMN_COUNT_MISMATCH = TRUE ESCAPE = 'NONE' ESCAPE_UNENCLOSED_FIELD
   = '\134' DATE_FORMAT = 'AUTO' TIMESTAMP_FORMAT = 'AUTO' NULL_IF = ('\\N');
```

Select SQL   Close

Figure 6-24. The SQL code to create a Snowflake file format with the default options from the wizard

Click the Close button if you took a look at the SQL, and then click the Finish button and then the Next button. At this time, you'll see what load options you have available for error handling (as shown in Figure 6-25).

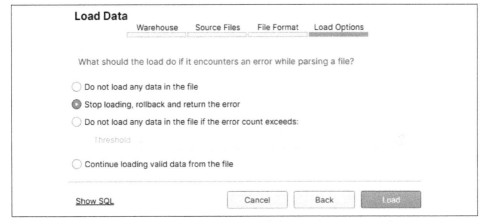

Figure 6-25. Error handling options in the Snowflake Load Data wizard

I recommend you click each option and then select the Show SQL option so that you can see how you'd write the SQL code, if needed.

> If you are working in the SnowSQL CLI and are unsure how to write the SQL needed to create a particular file format, or if you want more help with creating the error handling, you can return to the Snowflake Load Data wizard by making your selections and then clicking the Show SQL option.

Now click the Load button and you'll see messaging stating that Snowflake is in the process of staging the file (as shown in Figure 6-26).

Figure 6-26. Messaging indicating that Snowflake has encrypted the file and is in the process of putting it in a stage

Once Snowflake has completed the data load, you'll see the load results that indicate four rows were parsed and loaded. Let's go ahead and return to Snowsight by clicking the Snowsight tab in the upper-right corner of the screen (as shown in Figure 6-27).

Figure 6-27. The Snowsight tab from the Snowflake Classic Console

Navigate back to the worksheet and execute the following commands:

```
USE DATABASE DEMO6_DB;
USE SCHEMA UI;
SELECT * FROM TABLE20;
```

By running a SELECT * command using the DEMO6_DB database and the UI schema, you'll notice that four records were successfully inserted into the TABLE20 table.

In the next section, we'll use the same CSV data file, but this time we will upload the file using the SnowSQL CLI.

SnowSQL CLI SQL PUT and COPY INTO Commands

SnowSQL is the CLI for connecting to Snowflake. It can be used to execute SQL queries and perform all Data Definition Language (DDL) and DML operations. SnowSQL can be downloaded from the Snowflake Classic Console by clicking the Help tab and then selecting the Download option. You'll then have the option to download the SnowSQL CLI for Linux, Windows, or macOS. Instructions on how to install SnowSQL for each operating system can be found in the Snowflake online documentation (*https://oreil.ly/Vqfxr*).

After you download and install SnowSQL, you can log in to SnowSQL from your command prompt by using the following as an example. Note that JKAVILA2022 is my username and dx58224.us-central11.gcp is my Snowflake account name. The -a option is to indicate your Snowflake account and -u is to identify the username to connect to Snowflake. The account name and username shown here are just examples. They are not actual usable information but were from when I previously created a trial Snowflake account:

```
c:\>snowsql -a dx58224.us-central1.gcp -u JKAVILA2022 <enter>
Password: ********* <enter>
```

Let's get started in SnowSQL by indicating the role, virtual warehouse, database, and schema we want to use for this example:

```
USE ROLE ACCOUNTADMIN;
USE WAREHOUSE LOAD_WH;
USE DATABASE DEMO6_DB;
USE SCHEMA SNOW;
```

You can see the last SQL statement and the result of all the previous SQL statements, which shows the command-line prompt of *<username>#<virtual ware house>@<database>.<schema>* (Figure 6-28).

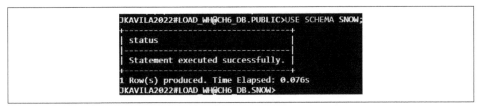

Figure 6-28. Result of using the stated role, virtual warehouse, database, and schema

Now let's create a new table using the following SQL statement:

```
CREATE OR REPLACE TABLE TABLE20 (id integer, f_name string,
    l_name string, city string);
```

Once you have created the table, you are ready to use the PUT command to load the CSV file into the table stage:

```
Put file:///users/joyce/documents/TABLE20.csv @"DEMO6_DB"."SNOW".%"TABLE20";
```

Be sure to replace users/joyce/documents with your own file path. Also be sure to place a space between the file path on your computer and the @ symbol. Figure 6-29 shows the result of using the PUT command to load the CSV file into the table stage.

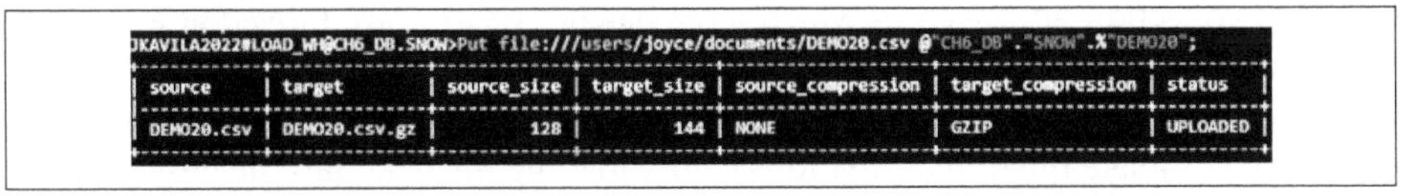

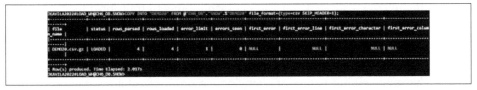

Figure 6-29. Result of using the PUT command to load the CSV file into the table stage

Next, we'll copy the files from the table stage with the result shown in Figure 6-30:

```
COPY INTO "TABLE20" FROM @"DEMO6_DB"."SNOW".%"TABLE20"
    file_format=(type=csv SKIP_HEADER=1);
```

Figure 6-30. Result of using the COPY INTO command to load data from the stage into the target table

For this example, we put the files into the table stage because we were loading into a single table. We could just as easily have created an internal named stage and put the files there instead. It is recommended to use an internal named stage if you share files with multiple users or if files are loaded into multiple tables.

While using the COPY INTO command, it is possible to perform basic transformations such as reordering columns or performing casts using a SELECT command. More information about transforming during a load can be found in the Snowflake documentation (*https://oreil.ly/uMeaE*).

We've seen how we can use the web UI Load Data wizard and SnowSQL to take files and manually load them into Snowflake tables by first putting them into a stage and then copying the data from the stage to the Snowflake table. In the next section, we'll discover how to have data automatically loaded into Snowflake.

Data Pipelines

A *data pipeline* is a data transportation conduit that uses automated processing steps to move data to a target repository. A pipeline's data origin, sometimes referred to as the *data pipeline definition*, is the final point of data collection before the data is moved through the pipeline. The movement of the data through the pipeline is known as the *dataflow*. Pipeline architecture can be of either a batch processing or a stream processing type, with continuous loading architecture somewhere between the two.

One data collection approach in which large batches of data are moved at a specific time and different storage areas preserve the data as it moves through the pipeline is known as an extract, transform, load (ETL) approach. ETL tools need processing engines to complete the transformations before loading the data into the target repository. ETL can be an ideal solution when the destination requires a specific data format that is different from the pipeline definition.

As an alternative to ETL, there is a data pipeline process known as extract, load, transform (ELT), which uses processing engines at the destination to transform the data once it is within the repository. This is a more streamlined approach because it removes the intermediate step and allows organizations to transform their raw data only when necessary. The ELT approach is often the preferred approach when the destination is a cloud native data warehouse.

In an ELT approach, a Snowflake Snowpipe is the *extract* part. Some transformations, such as changing column names or changing the order of columns, can be accomplished, and then the COPY INTO command loads the data into the target destination.

 Semi-structured data types, such as JSON and Avro, are supported by Snowpipe.

To complete the ELT data pipeline using Snowpipe, we would also need to use Snowflake objects such as streams and tasks to transform data in which things such as string concatenation or number calculations are required.

When using Snowflake's Snowpipe, there are two different mechanisms for detecting when the staged files are available: automate Snowpipe using cloud messaging and call Snowpipe REST endpoints.

One thing to note is that you can speed up Snowpipe by ingesting smaller data files. Chunking large files into smaller ones not only allows Snowflake to process the data more quickly but also makes the data available sooner.

As a rule of thumb, the optimal file size for loading into Snowpipe is 100 to 250 MB of compressed data. Try to stage the data within 60-second intervals if the data arrives continuously. Remember, it is possible to create a Snowpipe in such a way that latency can be decreased and throughput can be significantly increased, but the architectural design needs to be weighed against the increased Snowpipe costs that occur as more frequent file ingestions are triggered.

While Snowpipe latency reduction may be good enough for most near–real-time situations, there are times when Snowpipe might not be fast enough. Ecommerce and IoT are two examples in which actual real-time data processing might be needed. In these cases, we'd need to utilize a pure-play stream processing tool such as Confluent's KSQL, which processes data directly in a Kafka Stream, or Apache Flink and Apache Flume.

The next sections will provide more detail about Kafka and Snowpipe, the most common choices for continuously loading data pipelines.

There are a few different considerations when deciding between the two Snowpipe methods of auto-ingest or REST API. In situations where files arrive continuously, you can use Snowflake's auto-ingest feature to create an event notification. Snowpipe auto-ingest is the more scalable approach. REST API is the better option for use cases in which data arrives randomly and/or if preprocessing needs require using an ETL or ELT tool, or in situations in which an external stage is unavailable.

Using Apache Kafka

Apache Kafka is a framework for connecting Kafka to external systems. Kafka was originally created to enable messaging queue workloads which included producers and consumers in a publisher and subscriber model (as shown in Figure 6-31). The

Kafka Producer and Consumer APIs are known for their simplicity. Data is sent asynchronously, which results in a callback. Although the Kafka Producer API can be extended and built upon, it isn't recommended to use the Kafka Producer or Consumer API for an ETL approach. Instead, you should consider using the Kafka Connect source API.

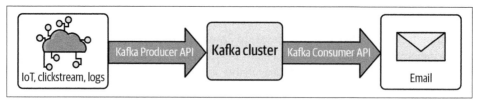

Figure 6-31. Kafka Producer and Consumer workloads

Today the Kafka architecture includes other workloads. The Kafka Streams API and KSQL can be used for applications wanting to consume from Kafka and produce back into Kafka (as shown in Figure 6-32). The Kafka Streams API is a stream processing library written in the Java language and is recommended if you expect you'll be writing complex logic. Alternatively, you can use KSQL if you want to write a real-time SQL-like job.

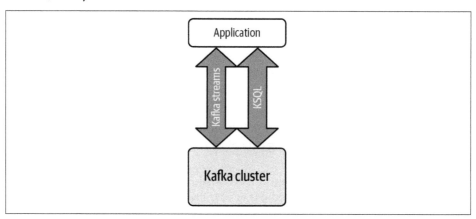

Figure 6-32. Kafka Streams and KSQL for real-time jobs

Kafka Streams requires that custom coding be undertaken, and it does come with joins and aggregations. Unlike the Kafka Connector, the Kafka Streams include exactly-once processing native capabilities. Apache Kafka also works with external processing systems such as Apache Flink, Apache Spark, and Apache NiFi for stream processing.

Another Kafka approach is the Kafka Connector source, typically used for bridging between Kafka and a datastore such as Twitter, and the Kafka Connector sink. The Kafka Connector, illustrated in Figure 6-33, is what we'll focus on in this section.

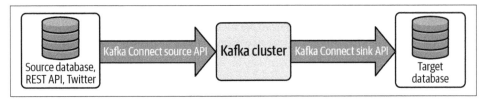

Figure 6-33. The Kafka Connector source API and Kafka Connector sink API

Kafka runs on a cluster of one or more servers, known as brokers, and partitions all Kafka topics to be distributed across cluster nodes. A Kafka topic is a category, or feed name, to which rows of records are stored.

One Kafka topic processes a stream of messages, consisting of rows, which are then inserted into a Snowflake table. Within the Kafka configuration, a topic can be mapped to an existing Snowflake table (as shown in Figure 6-34). For any unmapped topics, the Kafka Connector creates a new Snowflake table using the topic name.

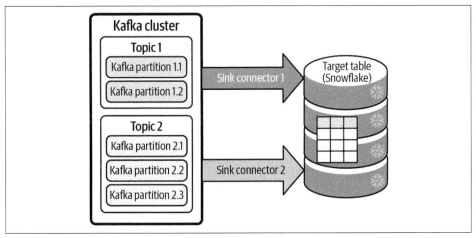

Figure 6-34. Kafka Topic 1 is mapped to an existing Snowflake table, while the unmapped Topic 2 will result in a new table created by the Kafka Connector

The Kafka Connector will use the following rules to convert a topic name to a Snowflake table name when creating a new table:

- Lowercase topic names are converted to uppercase table names.
- The Connector prepends an underscore to the table name unless the first character in the topic is an upper- or lowercase letter, or an underscore character.
- An underscore character replaces any topic name character that is not a Snowflake table name legal character.

It is recommended that any Kafka topic names you create should follow the rules for Snowflake identifier names. That way, underscore characters won't be needed to replace Snowflake table name illegal characters.

Now that we have a basic understanding of Kafka Connect, let's look at the complete Kafka ingest flow to a Snowflake table using a Kafka Connector (as shown in Figure 6-35). It's important to note that you configure the Kafka Connector by creating a file with specified parameters for things such as the Snowflake login credential, topic name(s), Snowflake table name(s), and more.

 A Kafka Connector can ingest messages from multiple topics, but the corresponding tables for connectors listed in one configuration file must all be stored in a single database and schema.

Using the Kafka Connector does not itself incur any charges. However, there are Snowpipe charges because Snowpipe is used to load the data that is read from the Kafka Connector.

 Some important things to remember about Snowpipe billing is that Snowpipe doesn't require a virtual warehouse, because it is a serverless model. In a serverless model, Snowflake provides and automatically manages compute resources based on the load. Also, there is a utilization cost of 0.06 credits per 1,000 files notified. The utilization cost applies to both Snowpipe REST and Snowpipe AUTO_INGEST.

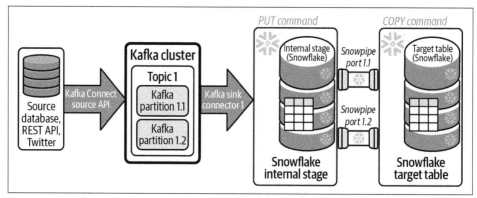

Figure 6-35. The Kafka ingest flow to a Snowflake table using the Kafka Connector

---

From Figure 6-35, we can see that the Kafka Connect source API receives records from a source database, REST API, or application such as Twitter. The Kafka cluster receives those records and splits each topic into one or more Kafka partitions. It is important to note that, in our example, we're including only one topic and sink connector in Figure 6-35, but a Kafka cluster could have multiple topics and, thus, would use multiple sink connectors.

Once a certain time has passed or a certain number of records have been received, the Kafka sink connector writes the messages to a Snowflake internal named stage using the PUT command. The sink connector then triggers Snowpipe to ingest the staged files. You'll notice in Figure 6-35 that there are two Snowpipes because there are two Kafka topic partitions.

A Snowflake Snowpipe serverless compute cluster will use the COPY command to load the data into a Snowflake table from the internal Snowflake stage. After confirming the data was successfully loaded, the files in the internal stage will be deleted.

When the Snowflake table is created by the Kafka Connector, two columns of the VARIANT data type will be created. The first column is the RECORD_CONTENT column which contains the Kafka message.

Kafka messages are passed to Snowflake in either a JSON or Avro format and each message is stored in one VARIANT column, without the data being parsed. The field names and values within the message are case sensitive.

The second VARIANT column created is the RECORD_METADATA column which has the metadata about the message. Among other things, the metadata includes the topic and the number of Kafka partitions within the topic.

It is possible to create custom Kafka code for performing in-flight transformations or for making data available more quickly. In those situations, the sink connector would be replaced by the custom code using JDBC batch insert statements.

The Kafka Connector is but one of the many connectors available for data integration. For complete information about Snowflake connectors and drivers, you can view the Snowflake developer documentation (*https://oreil.ly/VXxLv*).

Automating Snowpipe using cloud messaging and optional on-premises Kafka clusters

Snowflake Snowpipe can be automated using cloud messaging from AWS, Azure, or GCP. The auto-ingestion method uses cloud message event notification and a Snowflake external stage. The external stage is important because an automated Snowpipe only works with a Snowflake external stage object.

 Optionally, in conjunction with automated Snowpipe using cloud messaging, it is possible to utilize on-premises Kafka clusters to stream topics to one of the cloud providers, where messages are collected and stored and are then auto-ingested using event notification.

For each of the three cloud providers upon which Snowflake is built, there is an associated event notification type (as shown in Figure 6-36) that can be used for cloud messaging.

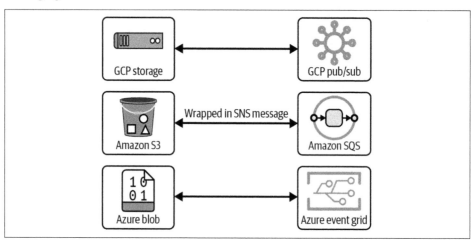

Figure 6-36. Event notification types for GCP, AWS, and Microsoft

The cloud messaging service notifies Snowpipe of the arrival of new data files. In a continuous serverless fashion, Snowpipe loads the data into the target table (as shown in Figure 6-37).

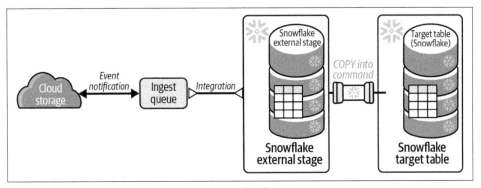

Figure 6-37. Snowpipe auto-ingestion using cloud messaging

Let's consider an example of how to use Snowpipe auto-ingestion for loading data into Snowflake. We'll use Microsoft Azure as an example by considering, at a high level, the pieces of information we need, and then we'll look at the steps required.

First, you'll need several pieces of information that are assigned from Azure:

- Tenant ID
- Storage queue notification URL, which will be in a form similar to *https://sflakesnowpipe.queue.core.windows.net/snowdata-queue*
- Application name, which will be in a form similar to SnowflakePACInt1025
- Primary Azure blob storage endpoint, which will be in a form similar to *https://sflakesnowpipe.blob.core.windows.net/*
- Blob services shared access signature, which will be in a form similar to *https://sflakesnowpipe.blob.core.windows.net/xxxx*

Within Azure, you'll need to create the following items: resource group, storage account name, container name, queue name, event subscription name, and system topic name.

You'll also need to obtain the Azure consent URL assigned in Snowflake. It will be in a form similar to *https://login.microsoftonline.com/xxxx*.

In Snowflake, you'll need to make sure you have a database, schema, table with fields, and stage created. You'll also need to create an integration and pipe in Snowflake.

 The stage link to a Snowflake integration is created using a hidden ID rather than the name of the integration. Therefore, the association between a Snowflake integration and any stage that references it will be broken if the integration is re-created, even with the same name.

Here are the steps you'd need to take to create a Snowpipe auto-ingestion approach for loading data from Microsoft Azure:

1. Log in to your Azure account and obtain your tenant ID.

2. In Azure, create the following items if they do not already exist: resource group, storage account within the resource group, container, queue, and event subscription.

3. In Azure, get the queue URI.

4. In Snowflake, create the following items if they do not already exist: database, schema, and table.

5. In Snowflake, set your role to ACCOUNTADMIN and create a notification integration:

```
CREATE NOTIFICATION INTEGRATION <integration name>
    ENABLED=TRUE
    TYPE= QUEUE
    NOTIFICATION_PROVIDER=AZURE_STORAGE_QUEUE
    AZURE_STORAGE_QUEUE_PRIMARY_URI = '<URI>'
    AZURE_TENANT_ID = '<tenant id>';
```

6. In Snowflake, get the AZURE CONSENT URL:

```
DESC NOTIFICATION INTEGRATION <integration name>;
```

7. In Azure, add the role assignment and get the endpoint.

8. In Azure, generate the shared access signature.

9. In Snowflake, create an external stage.

10. In Snowflake, create a Snowpipe:

```
CREATE PIPE <database.schema.pipe_name>
    AUTO_INGEST=TRUE
    INTEGRATION=<integration name>
    AS
    COPY INTO <database.schema.target_table_name>
    FROM @<database.schema.external_stage_name>
    FILE_FORMAT=(TYPE='JSON');
```

> To resolve data load errors related to data issues, it is strongly recommended that you use the VALIDATE function as part of a postload validation process to ensure that all files have been successfully loaded into target tables.

This section has provided the basic information about auto-ingest Snowpipe. You can find more detailed information on the Snowflake website (*https://oreil.ly/jT4OR*), where you'll be able to learn more about cloud storage service support for automated Snowpipe. It is important to note that cross-cloud support is currently available only to accounts hosted on Amazon Web Services.

In addition to auto-ingest Snowpipe, Snowflake provides a REST API option to trigger data to Snowpipe. One important note is that Snowpipe REST APIs work with internal as well as external Snowflake stages.

Calling Snowpipe REST endpoints

Another way to trigger a data loading event is by using Snowflake's Snowpipe REST API method. Using this method, a public REST endpoint with the name of a pipe and a list of filenames is called. If new data files matching the filenames list are discovered, they are queued for loading. Snowpipe serverless compute resources will then load the queued files into the Snowflake target table.

Cloud storage service support for Snowpipe REST API calls from Snowflake accounts allows for cross-cloud support for all accounts hosted on Amazon Web Services, Google Cloud Platform, or Microsoft Azure.

Table 6-4 describes the differences between the two methods for using Snowpipe.

Table 6-4. Differences between Snowpipe REST and Snowpipe AUTO_INGEST

Snowpipe REST	Snowpipe AUTO_INGEST
Available for use with internal and external stages	Available for use with external stages only
Manually call Snowpipe REST API endpoint, with the name of a pipe and a list of filenames	A notification is received from cloud provider when a new file arrives
Pass a list of files in the stage location	Process new files when awakened

Snowflake offers a Getting Started with Snowpipe Quickstart (*https://oreil.ly/LE7Vn*) if you'd like to learn more about Snowpipe.

As we've learned, Snowpipe can add latency to your streaming data. It also requires you to store your data in a stage prior to loading the data into a table, which increases the storage costs. To help solve those problems, Snowflake has created a new streaming API. This new API allows you to use a Streaming Ingest SDK, which can be implemented using Java. It is then possible to create a mapping of values and rows to be inserted. If you're currently using Kafka as part of your solution, it is relatively easy to change the properties and begin taking advantage of the new Snowpipe Streaming functionality.

Third-Party ETL and ELT Tools

Snowflake supports tools that transform data during loading (ETL) as well as tools that transform data after loading (ELT). Many different third-party integration tools are supported natively by Snowflake, including Fivetran, Informatica, Matillion, Talend, and more. You can view a list of Snowflake-supported integration tools in the Snowflake developer documentation pages (*https://oreil.ly/0S8tw*).

Alternatives to Loading Data

Queries can be executed on data that isn't loaded into Snowflake. One example would be external tables created on data within a data lake. Using Snowflake external tables allows you to query the existing data stored in external cloud storage, where the data remains as the source of truth, without needing to load the data into Snowflake. This solution is frequently used when large amounts of data exist in external cloud storage but only a portion of the data is needed for analysis. In this case, we can create a materialized view on the external table so that only a subset of the data is used; this leads to improved query performance.

External tables and materialized views were introduced in Chapter 4. More detail about materialized views is also included in Chapter 9.

Another alternative to loading data into a table is to use Snowflake data sharing to access data that is owned by someone else and shared with you. The Snowflake Marketplace includes many data offerings available to the public. Chapter 10 includes the details for all the Snowflake secure data sharing options.

One other alternative to data loading would be to clone a table. Cloning a table with the CREATE command results in a new table being created with the same data as the existing table. It is also possible to replicate a table with existing data. An example of a statement to clone a table would be as follows:

```
USE ROLE SYSADMIN; USE SCHEMA WS;
CREATE TABLE DEMO_CLONE CLONE TABLE1;
```

Finally, one newer alternative to loading data is to use Snowflake's Snowpark functionality. Snowpark offers the ability to query and process data in a data pipeline without moving data to the system where the application code runs. Snowpark is described in more detail in Chapter 12.

Tools to Unload Data

The process for unloading data from Snowflake is the same as the data loading process, except in reverse. When the target location is a local file system, data is first unloaded to a Snowflake internal stage using the COPY INTO command. The GET command is then used to download from the internal stage to the local file system (as shown in Figure 6-38).

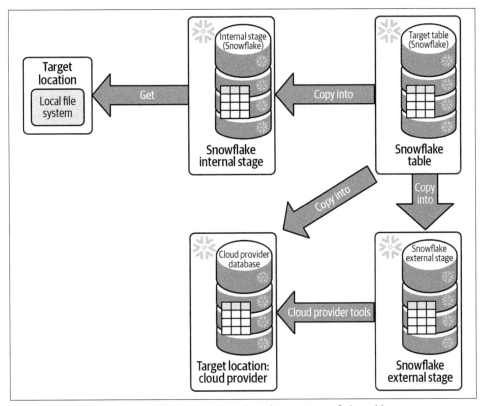

Figure 6-38. Multiple ways of downloading data from a Snowflake table to a target location

For data being unloaded to one of the three major cloud providers, there are two options. Data files can be unloaded directly into a storage location for the cloud provider for whom the Snowflake account is built upon. For example, if you selected Google Cloud as your Snowflake provider, you could unload files directly to a GCP container and then use Google Cloud Storage utilities to download locally. Alternatively, you can use the COPY INTO command to extract files from a Snowflake table into a Snowflake external stage and then use cloud provider tools to download into storage.

Data Loading Best Practices for Snowflake Data Engineers

This chapter has provided detailed information about loading data into Snowflake. Some recommendations and tips were offered throughout the chapter, but it makes sense to summarize a few best practices for Snowflake data engineers in this section.

Select the Right Data Loading Tool and Consider the Appropriate Data Type Options

Your choice of data loading tool is influenced by many factors: whether the load is intended to be a repeat process or a one-time load, whether the data is needed in real time or near-real time by end users, the data type of the data to be loaded, the existing skill set of your team, and more. Keeping these factors in mind, general best practice recommendations can still be made.

In an ETL approach, it is possible to use third-party tools to transform data prior to it being loaded into Snowflake. It often makes more sense, though, to take an ELT approach to data loading rather than an ETL approach because of Snowflake's ability to scale out. In an ELT approach, some transformations, such as changing column names or changing the order of columns, can be accomplished. After the data has been ingested, more complex data transformations, such as string concatenation or number calculations, can be accomplished with Snowflake streams and tasks or stored procedures. Powerful options also exist for transforming data using the Snowpark API and Java UDFs.

JDBC and ODBC connectors are good choices in some situations, but they should not be the tool of choice for large, regular data loads.

When considering the data being loaded, it is important to choose the appropriate data type when creating your Snowflake table. For example, date and timestamp data types are stored more efficiently in Snowflake than the VARCHAR data type.

Data file size limitations and recommendations, especially for semi-structured data, should be adhered to. Parquet files greater than 3 GB could time out, so it is recommended they be split into 1 GB sizes or smaller.

Having awareness of some unique ways to natively load data into Snowflake is important because it opens up the possibilities of the tools you can consider. Two examples of unique Snowflake tools available to you that you should consider are Snowpipe and file formats for the many semi-structured data types supported by Snowflake.

Avoid Row-by-Row Data Processing

Query performance is greatly impacted in situations involving row-by-row data processing. Given that Snowflake is built to ingest and process billions of rows with ease, the data process you design should focus on processing the entire data set, rather than one row at a time. The negative impact of row-by-row data processing cannot be emphasized strongly enough.

Choose the Right Snowflake Virtual Warehouse Size and Split Files as Needed

To prevent resource contention, be sure to isolate data load jobs from queries by dedicating separate virtual warehouses for each. Rather than assuming a larger virtual warehouse will necessarily load massive data files any faster than a smaller virtual warehouse (it likely won't), make sure to instead try splitting large files into smaller files of about 100 to 250 MB in size. Remember that the number of files being loaded and the size of each file influences performance more than the size of the virtual warehouse.

That said, it's important to note that choosing the right Snowflake virtual warehouse size is necessary when using the COPY command. However, a serverless approach could be more ideal depending on the use case. If a serverless approach is desired, Snowpipe could be used. In that case, there is no need to worry about virtual warehouse sizing.

Transform Data in Steps and Use Transient Tables for Intermediate Results

When appropriate, transform data in multiple steps rather than having massive SQL statement(s). This should result in simpler code and makes it possible to test intermediate results. For the intermediate results, it is recommended that you use transient tables and truncate them prior to the next data load so that the Time Travel storage fees will be reduced.

Code Cleanup

Because we created all our tables in one database, DEMO6_DB, our cleanup is simple. We can't drop a virtual warehouse we are currently using; thus, we'll need to change the virtual warehouse first:

```
USE WAREHOUSE COMPUTE_WH;
DROP DATABASE DEMO6_DB;
DROP WAREHOUSE LOAD_WH;
```

Summary

In this chapter, we took a deep dive into several different types of data loading tools for both manually inserting a few rows of data into tables and creating automated processes which we can use to load data files of a massive size. We also considered some data load best practices for Snowflake data engineers.

Knowing how to best load data into Snowflake is not enough, though. We also need to make sure we have a good understanding and appreciation for the ways we can protect our data. The next chapter provides important next steps that are needed to gain a broader understanding and appreciation for data governance and data security.

Knowledge Check

The following questions are based on the information contained in this chapter:

1. What are the three Snowflake data types used for semi-structured data? Which one of the three is the universal data type?

2. What are the types of Snowflake stages? Are stages Snowflake objects? Explain.

3. In what instances is the INSERT ALL SQL statement used?

4. What happens when a key-value pair includes a null value at the time of insertion?

5. When using the Load Data wizard, what are the error handling options and which one is the default?

6. Is it possible to perform transformations while using the COPY INTO command?

7. What are the semi-structured data types supported by Snowflake for loading and unloading?

8. Of the two Snowpipe methods, which is the more scalable approach? When would it be best to use each approach?

9. What is an example of a best practice for data loading, as it specifically relates to virtual warehouses?

10. What is the Snowflake command to load data into a stage and the command to unload data from a stage?

Answers to these questions are available in Appendix A.

Implementing Data Governance, Account Security, and Data Protection and Recovery

Much has been written about data governance and account security—two very broad topics. While this chapter isn't intended to make you an expert on these topics, it will introduce you to many Snowflake data security features and governance tools which will give you a broader understanding and appreciation for the many ways you can implement data governance and security policies in Snowflake.

Traditionally, data governance was focused on having the right people available to execute the right processes with the right data, at the right time and with the right technology. The Data Governance 2.0 Framework, shown in Figure 7-1, extends that focus by also emphasizing business value propositions. Specifically, the area of data sharing as it relates to data discoverability offers so much business value that Chapter 11 is devoted to the topic.

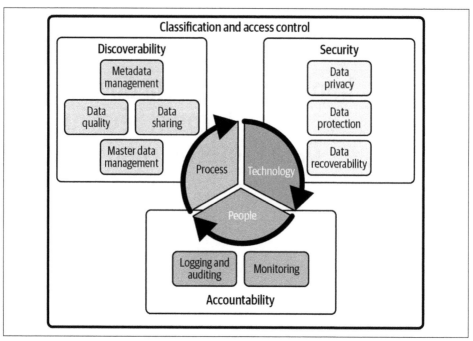

Figure 7-1. The Data Governance 2.0 Framework

The focus of this chapter is to implement concepts from the Data Governance 2.0 Framework within Snowflake by using powerful but easy-to-use Snowflake features. For example, you'll learn how to manage network security policies and firewall access. You'll also learn more about Time Travel and fail-safe, database replication, and failover/failback. In addition, this chapter includes many examples of ways you can democratize data with data governance controls such as object tagging, classification, data masking, row access policies, external tokenization, and anonymization. Several hands-on examples throughout the chapter were designed to deepen your knowledge and understanding of data governance, account security, and data protection and recovery in Snowflake.

Prep Work

We'll be working through some examples to demonstrate how Time Travel, object tagging, dynamic data masking, and row-level security work in Snowflake. Before we get to each of those sections, we'll need to do some setup work to create some roles and tables and assign some permissions. This will also exercise some of the skills you learned in earlier chapters.

Create a new folder titled *Chapter 7 Security, Protection, Data Recovery*. Refer to "Navigating Snowsight Worksheets" on page 8 if you need help creating a new folder and worksheet. To set the worksheet context, make sure you are using the SYSADMIN role and the COMPUTE_WH virtual warehouse.

In the example in this chapter, we follow a new user named Adam, and use his credentials to confirm that appropriate access was given.

 You'll need to replace ' *YOUREMAIL@EMAIL.COM* ' with your actual email address or the following code will not work as intended. Be sure to leave the single quotes around your email address.

Let's now create a new user account for Adam:

```
USE ROLE USERADMIN;
CREATE OR REPLACE USER ADAM
PASSWORD = '123'
LOGIN_NAME=ADAM
DISPLAY_NAME=ADAM
EMAIL= ' YOUREMAIL@EMAIL.COM '
MUST_CHANGE_PASSWORD=TRUE;
```

We also need a few new roles. We'll be using the Human Resources role, HR_ROLE, to test out our dynamic data masking. The two AREA roles will be used later to demonstrate row-level security:

```
USE ROLE USERADMIN;
CREATE OR REPLACE ROLE HR_ROLE;
CREATE OR REPLACE ROLE AREA1_ROLE;
CREATE OR REPLACE ROLE AREA2_ROLE;
```

The SYSADMIN role will be used to create some of the objects we'll be using:

```
USE ROLE SYSADMIN;
USE WAREHOUSE COMPUTE_WH;
CREATE OR REPLACE DATABASE DEMO7_DB;
CREATE OR REPLACE SCHEMA TAG_LIBRARY;
CREATE OR REPLACE SCHEMA HRDATA;
CREATE OR REPLACE SCHEMA CH7DATA;
CREATE OR REPLACE TABLE DEMO7_DB.CH7DATA.RATINGS
(EMP_ID integer, RATING integer, DEPT_ID varchar, AREA integer);
```

We'll also want to insert some arbitrary data:

```
INSERT INTO DEMO7_DB.CH7DATA.RATINGS VALUES
(1, 77, '100', 1),
(2, 80, '100', 1),
(3, 72, '101', 1),
(4, 94, '200', 2),
(5, 88, '300', 3),
(6, 91, '400', 3);
```

Next, we'll grant some permissions to roles and then assign those roles to our new user. We'll use the SECURITYADMIN role to grant virtual warehouse usage to the three new roles so that they are able to perform query operations:

```
USE ROLE SECURITYADMIN;
GRANT USAGE ON WAREHOUSE COMPUTE_WH TO ROLE HR_ROLE;
GRANT USAGE ON WAREHOUSE COMPUTE_WH TO ROLE AREA1_ROLE;
GRANT USAGE ON WAREHOUSE COMPUTE_WH TO ROLE AREA2_ROLE;
```

We also need to grant those roles usage to the necessary objects:

```
GRANT USAGE ON DATABASE DEMO7_DB TO ROLE HR_ROLE;
GRANT USAGE ON DATABASE DEMO7_DB TO ROLE AREA1_ROLE;
GRANT USAGE ON DATABASE DEMO7_DB TO ROLE AREA2_ROLE;
GRANT USAGE ON SCHEMA DEMO7_DB.CH7DATA TO ROLE HR_ROLE;
GRANT USAGE ON SCHEMA DEMO7_DB.HRDATA TO ROLE HR_ROLE;
GRANT USAGE ON SCHEMA DEMO7_DB.CH7DATA TO ROLE AREA1_ROLE;
GRANT USAGE ON SCHEMA DEMO7_DB.CH7DATA TO ROLE AREA2_ROLE;
GRANT SELECT ON ALL TABLES IN SCHEMA DEMO7_DB.CH7DATA TO ROLE HR_ROLE;
GRANT SELECT ON ALL TABLES IN SCHEMA DEMO7_DB.CH7DATA TO ROLE AREA1_ROLE;
GRANT SELECT ON ALL TABLES IN SCHEMA DEMO7_DB.CH7DATA TO ROLE AREA2_ROLE;
```

And finally, we'll want to assign the three roles to our new user. Two of the roles will also be assigned back to the SYSADMIN role. We've chosen not to assign the HR_ROLE back to the SYSADMIN role:

```
GRANT ROLE HR_ROLE TO USER ADAM;
GRANT ROLE AREA1_ROLE TO USER ADAM;
GRANT ROLE AREA2_ROLE TO USER ADAM;
GRANT ROLE AREA1_ROLE TO ROLE SYSADMIN;
GRANT ROLE AREA2_ROLE TO ROLE SYSADMIN;
```

We will now need to use the ACCOUNTADMIN role to grant future select and insert privileges to the HR_ROLE. Afterward, let's reset the role back to the SYSADMIN role:

```
USE ROLE ACCOUNTADMIN;
GRANT SELECT ON FUTURE TABLES IN SCHEMA DEMO7_DB.HRDATA TO ROLE HR_ROLE;
GRANT INSERT ON FUTURE TABLES IN SCHEMA DEMO7_DB.HRDATA TO ROLE HR_ROLE;
USE ROLE SYSADMIN;
```

Snowflake Security

Keeping your Snowflake account and data secure is a collaborative effort between Snowflake and you. Snowflake takes responsibility for the security of data in transit to and from the Data Cloud as well as the security of data at rest, stored in tables. This is accomplished by using strong encryption methods to protect data from external parties. Snowflake provides Soc 1 Type II and Soc 2 Type II compliance security validations for all Snowflake accounts. In addition, Snowflake performs many penetration tests each year and offers support for HIPAA compliance, PCI DSS compliance, and

FedRAMP Moderate compliance for Snowflake's Business Critical Edition and higher in certain regions. Snowflake is FedRAMP authorized Moderate with agencies such as the Centers for Medicare & Medicaid Services, the GSA, and the Department of Health and Human Services. Snowflake supports ITAR compliance, audited by a third-party organization. Snowflake is in the process of obtaining FedRAMP High authorization, which is expected winter of 2022 and based on agency and PMO availability. In parallel, Snowflake is pursuing IL4, with the intention of being IL4 authorized in 2023. Snowflake is also part of the HITRUST Shared Responsibility and Inheritance Program (SRM) and has earned the HITRUST certification. The HITRUST CSF is the leading information security framework for the healthcare industry.

Snowflake also provides the tools you need to keep your site access secure, protect your data, monitor user activity, and recover data, should it become necessary. In this section, we'll explore many of those tools, including native Snowflake authentication methods, network security policies, Snowflake query monitoring via access history, Time Travel, fail-safe, and replication and failover.

Controlling Account Access

Users wanting access to Snowflake need to identify and authenticate themselves, demonstrating proof of who they are. That proof is used to authenticate, or verify, that the user is indeed who they claim to be. In addition to authenticating users so that only allowed users are granted access, Snowflake gives administrators the ability to create security policies to also limit the location from where users can log in.

Of course, having too few access controls leads to increased risk. However, requiring users to jump through too many hoops also creates risk. When users experience excessive user authentication friction or other overly restrictive access controls, there is a tendency to avoid the complexity by engaging in shadow IT activities which most often results in information silos. While these shadow IT activities would most likely be discovered at some point, it is better to consider how to strike the right balance between implementing too many and not enough controls.

Authentication and user management

Snowflake supports authentication methods that can easily accommodate the different ways users can log in to Snowflake. Thus far, we've demonstrated how users can attempt to access Snowflake data *directly*. Alternatively, users can *indirectly* access Snowflake. Indirect access to Snowflake through business intelligence (BI) tools is one example. *Integration users* can also be established to provide a more secure and auditable way to move data in and out of Snowflake without relying on an existing user's account. Creating an integration user for Snowpipe, for example, is a best practice. For integration users, key pair is the preferred authentication method.

For users accessing Snowflake data through third-party applications, OAuth integration is the preferred choice because it enables access to data without sharing the user's password and it decouples authentication and authorization. Credentials do not need to be stored, because a token is used and tied to a Snowflake role instead.

When users need direct access to work within Snowflake, they can authenticate using federated authentication. For federated authentication, a user is authenticated with single sign-on (SSO) using an identity provider (IdP) such as Okta or Microsoft Active Directory Federation Services (AD FS).

For Snowflake accounts not using SSO, Snowflake offers a multifactor authentication (MFA) native solution which supports connection via the web UI, connections using the SnowSQL command-line interface (CLI), and JDBC and ODBC client connections. MFA is intended to be used in addition to strong passwords. Snowflake offers self-service MFA to all account levels so that users can enroll themselves.

To enroll in MFA from the web UI, use the Home icon to go to the Main menu. From there, in the upper-left corner, click the down arrow to the right of your name. Select Profile, then click the Enroll button next to "Multi-factor authentication." Next, click the "Start setup" button (as shown in Figure 7-2).

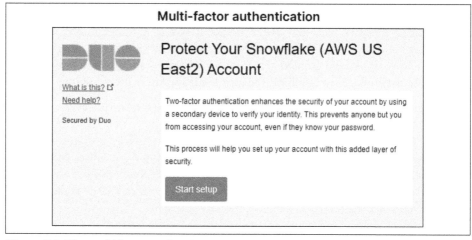

Figure 7-2. The multifactor authentication setup screen

From there, you can indicate what type of device you want to add. As you go through the enrollment process, you'll need to install the Duo Mobile application (see Figure 7-3) and scan a QR code.

Authentication helps to control account access but is just one part of what is needed to keep data secure. Once users are authenticated, the data they can see and the activities they can perform within Snowflake, such as creating tables and using the SELECT command to view the data, need to be controlled as well. In Snowflake, we can

---

accomplish this by using role-based access controls (RBACs). Chapter 5 is devoted to RBAC due to the importance of limiting data access.

Figure 7-3. The Duo Mobile setup screen for multifactor authentication

In Chapter 5, we discussed best practices. One example of a best practice that we recommended is that custom roles be granted back to the system administrator role. However, you may want to consider some exceptions to that practice for roles used to access sensitive data, such as HR, financial, or medical data. Earlier in this chapter, we created three new custom roles and we assigned two of those roles back to the system administrator. However, you'll notice we did not grant the HR role to an administrator. This was not an oversight, but intended, because there could be sensitive HR data that not even the Snowflake administrator should be allowed to access. As a reminder, you can see role relationships by using the role hierarchy visualization explorer that was introduced in Chapter 5.

Managing network security policies and firewall access

By default, users can connect to Snowflake from any location. However, to reduce security risks or to meet compliance requirements, you may need to restrict how and where users can connect to Snowflake. This can be achieved by creating network policy objects. For example, network policies can be created to allow traffic from certain IP addresses or your organization's virtual private networks (VPNs) and virtual private clouds (VPCs). You can specify a list of IP ranges to allow or disallow.

Any defined blocked IP ranges should be a subset of the list of allowed IP addresses because anything outside the list of allowed IP ranges would automatically be disallowed anyway.

There are two types of network policies: account-level network policies and user-level network policies. Account-level network security policies can be created via the web interface or by using SQL. In contrast, user-level network policies can only be formed using SQL.

You'll need to use the account administrator role to set up a network policy. As an account administrator, you can click Admin → Security from the Main menu. Make sure your role is set to ACCOUNTADMIN. In the upper-right corner, click the + Network Policy button. This will provide a screen, shown in Figure 7-4, where you can create a new network policy.

New network policy

Creating as ⓘ ACCOUNTADMIN

Enter a valid IPv4 address and optional CIDR or multiple addresses in a comma-separated list.

Policy Name

Allowed IP Addresses

```
1.1.1.1, 2.2.2.2/3...
```

Blocked IP Addresses (optional)

```
1.1.1.1, 2.2.2.2/3...
```

Cancel   Create network policy

Figure 7-4. The network policy creation screen

After an account-level network policy is created, it will need to be activated by associating the policy to your Snowflake account. On the right side of the screen is an Activate Policy button.

A SECURITYADMIN or ACCOUNTADMIN role can create an account-level network policy, but only one network policy can be activated at a time. Similarly, a user-level network policy also needs to be activated before Snowflake will enforce the policy, and only one user-level policy per user can be activated at a time. For any user having both an account-level and user-level network policy, the user-level policy will take precedence.

You can use the SHOW NETWORK POLICIES statement to see a list of all network policies in your Snowflake account. Make sure you use the ACCOUNTADMIN role to execute the statement. Executing the command does not require a running warehouse.

For firewall egress traffic, you can allow your organization's firewall to connect client applications to Snowflake, if your network has a firewall for egress traffic. If you're allowing a public endpoint, you can execute the SELECT SYSTEM$WHITELIST() function. If you have an accessible private endpoint, you can execute the SELECT SYSTEM $WHITELIST_PRIVATELINK() function. Note that if you are using a network proxy to inspect egress traffic, you can set it up for SSL passthrough.

SSL terminating proxies are not supported by Snowflake.

Diagnosing and troubleshooting network connection issues can be accomplished with the Snowflake Connectivity Diagnostic Tool, SnowCD. SnowCD leverages the Snowflake hostname IP address and ports that were listed by the previous system functions to run a series of connection checks to evaluate and help troubleshoot the network connection to Snowflake. For instructions on how to download and install SnowCD, review the Snowflake user guide documentation (*https://oreil.ly/0S8tw*).

Monitoring Activity with the Snowflake ACCESS_HISTORY Account Usage View

Designing and implementing access controls to limit access to certain data is a critical piece of account security. In addition, a Snowflake tool exists that can be used to monitor access. The Snowflake ACCESS_HISTORY view monitors access to enable companies to satisfy their compliance audits and comply with regulatory requirements. While performing monitoring for security reasons, it is recommended to use the ACCESS_HISTORY view to also identify any unused tables or columns which could be removed to optimize storage costs.

The Snowflake ACCESS_HISTORY view is used to query the access history of Snowflake objects within the previous 365 days. It is accessible to the Snowflake

ACCOUNTADMIN role by default. The ACCESS_HISTORY view supports SQL read and write operations. Columns in this view include QUERY_ID, the name of the user who ran the query, the start time of the query, and the objects that were accessed or modified by the user. Notice that the output for the accessed objects is given in JSON form, as shown in Figure 7-5. As a result, we'll want to flatten the output. We first learned about the FLATTEN function in Chapter 4.

DIRECT_OBJECTS_ACCESSED				BASE_OBJECTS_ACCESSED				↑ ...
[{ "columns": [	{	"columnId": 9225,	"columnName": "DEPT_ID"	}, [{ "columns": [	{	"columnId": 10242,	"columnName": "RATING"	},
[{ "columns": [	{	"columnId": 9225,	"columnName": "DEPT_ID"	}, [{ "columns": [	{	"columnId": 10242,	"columnName": "RATING"	},
[{ "columns": [	{	"columnId": 9225,	"columnName": "DEPT_ID"	}, [{ "columns": [	{	"columnId": 10242,	"columnName": "RATING"	},
[{ "columns": [	{	"columnId": 9225,	"columnName": "DEPT_ID"	}, [{ "columns": [	{	"columnId": 10242,	"columnName": "RATING"	},
[{ "columns": [	{	"columnId": 10242,	"columnName": "RATING"	} [{ "columns": [	{	"columnId": 10242,	"columnName": "RATING"	},
[{ "columns": [	{	"columnId": 10242,	"columnName": "RATING"	} [{ "columns": [	{	"columnId": 10242,	"columnName": "RATING"	},
[{ "columns": [	{	"columnId": 10258,	"columnName": "DEPT"	}, [{ "columns": [	{	"columnId": 10258,	"columnName": "DEPT"	},
[{ "columns": [	{	"columnId": 10258,	"columnName": "DEPT"	}, [{ "columns": [	{	"columnId": 10258,	"columnName": "DEPT"	},
[{ "columns": [	{	"columnId": 10259,	"columnName": "ROLE_NAME"	[{ "columns": [	{	"columnId": 10259,	"columnName": "ROLE_NAME"	
[{ "columns": [	{	"columnId": 10261,	"columnName": "ROLE_NAME"	[{ "columns": [	{	"columnId": 10261,	"columnName": "ROLE_NAME"	

Figure 7-5. Output for accessed objects is in JSON form

The Snowflake ACCESS_HISTORY view supports most write operation commands, including GET, PUT, DELETE, INSERT, MERGE, UPDATE, COPY INTO, and CREATE. The operations to populate views or streams, as well as data movement resulting from replication, are not included in the ACCESS_HISTORY view.

Let's consider what specific information the ACCESS_HISTORY view can provide for us. We can run a query to see the number of queries each user has run. We'll list the user with the most frequent number of queries first:

```
USE ROLE ACCOUNTADMIN;
SELECT USER_NAME, COUNT(*) USES FROM SNOWFLAKE.ACCOUNT_USAGE.ACCESS_HISTORY
GROUP BY USER_NAME ORDER BY USES DESC;
```

We can also query the Snowflake ACCESS_HISTORY view to find out the most frequently used tables:

```
SELECT OBJ.VALUE:objectName::STRING TABLENAME,
COUNT(*) USES FROM SNOWFLAKE.ACCOUNT_USAGE.ACCESS_HISTORY,
TABLE(FLATTEN(BASE_OBJECTS_ACCESSED)) OBJ GROUP BY TABLENAME ORDER BY USES DESC;
```

While both pieces of information are interesting, the information isn't particularly useful without some additional context. What we'd really like to know is what tables are being accessed, by whom, and how frequently. This next statement will give us that information:

```
SELECT OBJ.VALUE:objectName::string TABLENAME, USER_NAME,
COUNT(*) USES FROM SNOWFLAKE.ACCOUNT_USAGE.ACCESS_HISTORY,
TABLE(FLATTEN(BASE_OBJECTS_ACCESSED)) OBJ GROUP BY 1, 2 ORDER BY USES DESC;
```

The SNOWFLAKE ACCOUNT_USAGE schema includes other views useful for monitoring. The LOGIN_HISTORY view is a log of every connection established with Snowflake so that you can determine who logged in from where and using what authentication method. The QUERY_HISTORY view provides a log of every query run in Snowflake, including queries against metadata such as users or roles as well as queries against data.

Data Protection and Recovery

Snowflake offers several native data protection and high availability features. Many of those features, such as encryption and key management, are automatic and require no involvement from you to function fully. Other data protection and recovery features, such as Time Travel and fail-safe, exist within Snowflake automatically and are available for you to take advantage of them anytime you find it necessary. Lastly, there are some Snowflake data protection and recovery native features, such as replication and failover, that require some planning and implementation on your part to take advantage of them. That said, let's take a deeper dive into each of the three categories of data protection and recovery features just mentioned.

Encryption and key management

Snowflake automatically provides end-to-end encryption (E2EE) for all Snowflake editions, regardless of the edition type, so that not even the cloud provider on which your Snowflake account is deployed can access your data. When you store a Snowflake table, one or more files are created and stored using the cloud provider's storage service. Snowflake encrypts each file with a different key and then "wraps" each file and file key together by encrypting them with a higher-level table master key. One reason for this is to avoid having to store many individual file keys in a secure location. Table master keys, used to encrypt and decrypt the file keys, are themselves encrypted with a higher-level account master key and stored in the table's metadata. Similarly, an account master key, used to encrypt and decrypt table master keys, is encrypted with the root key. The root key, the only key stored in clear text, is used to encrypt and decrypt an account master key.

To summarize, Snowflake's hierarchical key model consists of the root key, account master keys, table master keys, and file keys. An account key or table key is rotated by Snowflake when the key is more than 30 days old. Note that result master keys and stage master keys also exist at the table master key level.

Snowflake's root key is in a hardware security module (HSM). Snowflake offers the Tri-Secret Secure feature for organizations that need more control over keys and have the Snowflake Business Critical Edition or higher. This feature allows you to generate your own root key using a cloud provider's key management service such that two account master keys are used instead of just one. Each master key is wrapped by a root key; your root key wraps one account master key and Snowflake's root key wraps the other. As shown in Figure 7-6, both master keys are needed to decrypt the table, result, or stage master keys.

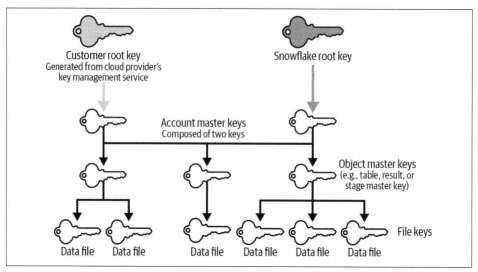

Figure 7-6. The Tri-Secret Secure hierarchy of keys

With the Business Critical edition and higher, Snowflake can encrypt all data transmitted over the network within a VPC. Query statement encryption is supported on Enterprise for Sensitive Data (ESD) accounts.

Time Travel and fail-safe retention periods, described in the next section, are not affected by rekeying. Rekeying is transparent to both features. However, some additional storage charges are associated with rekeying of data in fail-safe.

Time Travel and fail-safe

Snowflake provides native change data capture (CDC) features to ensure, for a specified period of time, the continued availability of important data that has been changed or deleted. Historical data in permanent databases and database objects can be queried, cloned, and restored for a maximum of 90 days. Data in temporary and transient objects can be accessed up to a maximum of 24 hours. Beyond those Time Travel access periods, historical data in permanent databases and database objects can be recovered by a Snowflake employee up to seven days later. The seven days of recoverability are known as the fail-safe period.

Using the Time Travel feature, a Snowflake administrator can query data in the past that has since been updated or deleted, and can create clones of entire tables, schemas, and databases at or before specific points in the past. Having Time Travel offers protection from accidental data operations such as dropping a column or table by mistake.

Time Travel is available for permanent, temporary, or transient tables, but not external tables. The following commands can be used for Time Travel: SELECT At/Before, CLONE At/Before, and UNDROP. With Time Travel, a user can use the SELECT command to query objects in one of three ways:

- Querying can be accomplished using a timestamp to see what an object looked like before a given point in time.

- Querying can be accomplished using a time offset to see what an object looked like previously based on a certain amount of time that has passed.

- It is possible to use Time Travel to view what an object looked like before running a specific query. To obtain any query ID, you can click the Activity → Query History menu option where you will then be able to see a listing of all queries, including the query ID and status, as shown in Figure 7-7.

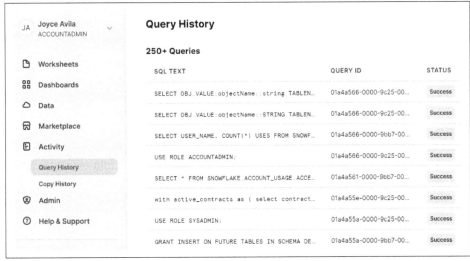

Figure 7-7. Query history as seen from the Query History submenu

The Time Travel retention period is automatically enabled for all Snowflake accounts, and the default is 24 hours, or one day; however, it can be set to zero at the account and object levels. For Snowflake Enterprise Edition and higher orgs, the retention period can be set up to 90 days for permanent databases, schemas, and tables. Let's go ahead and set the retention period for our database to 90 days. Navigate back to the worksheet and execute the following command:

```
USE ROLE SYSADMIN;
ALTER DATABASE DEMO7_DB SET DATA_RETENTION_TIME_IN_DAYS = 90;
```

By setting the retention time as 90 days for the database, all the database objects will also have a 90-day retention time period. We can confirm this by taking a look at the database's INFORMATION_SCHEMA TABLES view:

```
USE ROLE SYSADMIN;
SELECT TABLE_CATALOG, TABLE_SCHEMA, TABLE_NAME, RETENTION_TIME
FROM DEMO7_DB.INFORMATION_SCHEMA.TABLES;
```

You'll then be able to see that the RATINGS table has a 90-day retention time, as shown in Figure 7-8.

	TABLE_CATALOG	TABLE_SCHEMA	TABLE_NAME	RETENTION_TIME
1	DEMO7_DB	CH7DATA	RATINGS	90

Figure 7-8. Details of the information schema showing a 90-day retention time for the RATINGS table

While Time Travel cannot be disabled for an account, you can effectively disable Time Travel for specific databases, schemas, or tables by changing the default data retention time from one day to zero days. Information about dropped objects can still be seen in Snowflake account usage but not the information schema.

There are nuances to be aware of if you change the retention periods. Changing the data retention time at the schema level will result in all tables in the schema inheriting the schema's retention period unless the table is explicitly given a different retention period. Another thing you should keep in mind is that the order in which you drop objects does affect the retention period if there are differences. When you drop a schema, all the existing tables will be available for the same time period as the schema. If you want to make sure the data retention period for child objects is honored, you'll need to drop the child objects prior to dropping the parent object.

Let's now look at some examples to see how Time Travel works. Let's assume we make a mistake and update all the values in a column, rather than just updating one value. That could look something like the following statement:

```
USE ROLE SYSADMIN;
UPDATE DEMO7_DB.CH7DATA.RATINGS AREA SET AREA=4;
```

When we take a look at the table after the previous statement, we see that we did indeed make a mistake. Using the SELECT * statement, we see that all the area values have been changed to a value of 4 instead of just the value for one employee:

```
SELECT * FROM DEMO7_DB.CH7DATA.RATINGS;
```

We have a couple of ways we can revert the AREA column back to its previous values. We can use one of the two approaches based on time values, either by using a specific time in the past or by going back a certain amount of time from now, or we can use a query ID. Since we realized our mistake right away, any of the three would be easy to implement. For our example, we'll go ahead and travel back in time by five minutes. Let's first confirm that going back in time five minutes will yield the result we want:

```
SELECT * FROM DEMO7_DB.CH7DATA.RATINGS at (offset => -60*5);
```

If the table looks correct, go ahead and proceed with the next statement. If not, adjust the number of minutes until you find the correct time needed and then proceed with the next statement:

```
CREATE OR REPLACE TABLE DEMO7_DB.CH7DATA.RATINGS
AS SELECT * FROM DEMO7_DB.CH7DATA.RATINGS at (offset => -60*5);
```

If we check now, we'll see that the table has the previous values before we made the update:

```
SELECT * FROM DEMO7_DB.CH7DATA.RATINGS;
```

Rather than going back in time using a time offset, we could've accomplished the same thing by using a query ID from our history. That statement would look like this:

```
SELECT * from DEMO7_DB.CH7DATA.RATINGS before(statement =>
    '<Query ID from History>');
```

Something else that could possibly happen is that we might drop a table by mistake and then, after realizing our mistake, we'll want to go back in time before the table was dropped. Let's see how that would look. We'll first drop the table:

```
DROP TABLE DEMO7_DB.CH7DATA.RATINGS;
```

Try running a SELECT * command and you'll see that the table no longer exists. Now UNDROP the table and try running the SELECT * command again:

```
UNDROP TABLE DEMO7_DB.CH7DATA.RATINGS;
```

It is important to remember that Time Travel works on permanent, transient, and temporary objects, such as databases and database objects. It doesn't work on users or warehouses. If you drop a user, for example, you'll have to re-create that user.

Whereas Time Travel allows a Snowflake user to access the data for a certain period of time, only a Snowflake employee may be able to recover data from fail-safe storage. Fail-safe storage exists as a best effort emergency measure that may be able to protect data loss in permanent tables due to a catastrophic event such as a security breach or system failure.

Next, we'll summarize how Time Travel and fail-safe work together for permanent tables and how that compares to how Time Travel works for transient and temporary tables. In Figure 7-9, we can visualize a Time Travel and fail-safe timeline for permanent objects.

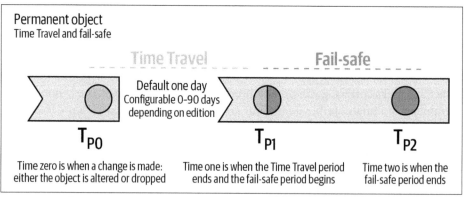

Figure 7-9. The permanent object Time Travel and fail-safe timeline

It is possible to increase the Time Travel retention period for permanent objects. When that is done, the data that exists in the current Time Travel retention period will now be retained longer before moving to fail-safe. However, data that had previously exceeded the current retention period and was already moved into the fail-safe seven-day period will not be affected. It is not possible for data to move from the fail-safe period back to the Time Travel period.

When a Time Travel retention period is reduced for permanent objects, the data in fail-safe is not affected. The data in Time Travel will be affected. Any Time Travel data whose time exceeds the new retention period will be moved to fail-safe where it will be stored for seven days.

Snowflake transient objects are like permanent objects, except transient objects have no fail-safe period. In addition, the maximum default Time Travel period for transient objects is only one day, which is much less than the 90-day Time Travel period possible for permanent objects. See Figure 7-10 for a visualization of the timeline.

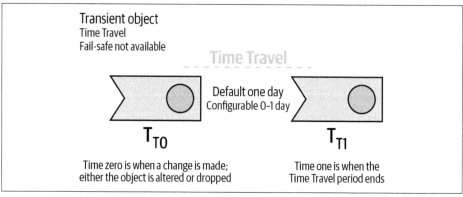

Figure 7-10. The transient object Time Travel timeline

Temporary objects have the same Time Travel default and maximum values as transient objects. Just like transient objects, there is no fail-safe for temporary objects. The difference between temporary objects and transient objects is that when the session ends, the data in transient objects is no longer accessible through the Time Travel feature. See Figure 7-11 for the timeline visualization for temporary Snowflake objects.

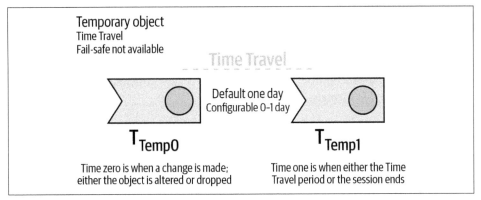

Figure 7-11. The temporary object Time Travel timeline

Both Time Travel and fail-safe, along with active storage, are part of the total calculated storage that incurs storage costs. You can use the following statement to see how much storage, in bytes, is attributed to each table in each of the three sections:

```
USE ROLE ACCOUNTADMIN;
SELECT TABLE_NAME,ACTIVE_BYTES,TIME_TRAVEL_BYTES,FAILSAFE_BYTES
FROM SNOWFLAKE.ACCOUNT_USAGE.TABLE_STORAGE_METRICS;
```

Replication and Failover

Healthcare, financial, and retail businesses are just a few types of organizations in which no downtime is acceptable. Yet these organizations face a variety of challenges, including natural disasters, network issues, and viruses, in maintaining 24/7 system and data availability. This is where Snowflake replication and failover can help.

Snowflake replication, supported across regions and across cloud platforms, enables an organization to replicate databases between Snowflake accounts. As such, replication and failover almost instantly synchronize Snowflake data and, because cross-cloud and cross-region replication is asynchronous, there is little to no performance impact on primary databases.

Snowflake encrypts files for replication with a random unique key.

It is important to be aware that cloned Snowflake objects are replicated physically, rather than logically, to secondary databases. This means that there will be additional data storage costs for any cloned objects. Replication charges also include data transfer costs and the cost of compute resources. Replication supports incremental refreshes, and customers can determine the frequency at which the replication runs. It is important to know that these charges will be billed on the target account.

Both permanent and transient primary databases can be replicated. When one of these primary database types is replicated, the following items are also replicated to the secondary database: automatic cluster of clustered tables, views including materialized views, stored procedures, masking and row access policies, tags, user-defined functions (UDFs), file formats, and sequences.

Snowflake replication is supported for databases, but if an external table exists in the primary database, it's not possible to create or refresh a secondary database with an external table. In addition, the following individual objects cannot be replicated: warehouses, resource monitors, roles, users, pipes, and streams. Note that account-level replication and the ability to create failover groups are available.

 Before you replicate a database to a different geographic region or country, it is recommended that you research whether your organization has any legal or regulatory restrictions as to where your data can be hosted.

Democratizing Data with Data Governance Controls

One goal of data governance is to establish effective controls to better manage risks by identifying sensitive data and protecting it while continually monitoring the effectiveness of the controls. Increased governmental regulations and regulatory compliance requirements have made it more important than ever to focus on data governance. As you would expect, data governance comes with an associated cost. While it is tempting to think of data governance as something that comes at a cost without providing any real positive benefits, that's simply not true. In fact, well-designed data governance controls provide the necessary framework to support data democratization, one of the most competitive advantages an organization can achieve.

Protecting sensitive data was often achieved by simply prohibiting access to all the data for which the sensitive data was a part or by creating separate data storages absent the sensitive data. This created data silos that often consisted of stale data and came at a high cost to implement and maintain. In many cases, it was too time-consuming or costly to provide the nonsensitive data to others in the organization. As a result, it was not unusual for organizational groups to create their own non–IT-approved data solutions. Not only was there poor decision-making based on stale, incomplete data, but there was also increased risk about which the organization was often unaware. It is not surprising that data governance has been viewed with such negativity. Snowflake provides tools to help address these issues.

With Snowflake's improved tools and methods available today, replicating data to achieve data governance goals is neither required nor recommended. With Snowflake's many governance-related features, data can quickly and easily be secured to allow for open access to real-time data. By providing access to data that is fresh and complete, Snowflake makes it possible for data democratization to exist and thrive within an organization. Because of effective data governance, data democratization can increase access to data for all knowledge workers within an organization. If sensitive data exists within the data, we can simply identify it and restrict access to the actual data but not the metadata.

The tangible benefits of all stakeholders in a data-driven organization being able to make insightful data-driven decisions in real time cannot be overstated. It all starts with embracing data governance as the framework for data democratization as well as the necessary vehicle for data security, ensuring privacy, and adhering to regulatory and compliance requirements.

Previously, we discussed Snowflake ACCESS_HISTORY, one of the main governance features. Just like Snowflake ACCESS_HISTORY, the governance features described in this section are available in Enterprise Edition and higher Snowflake orgs. In this section, we'll describe more governance features including the INFORMATION_SCHEMA Data Dictionary, object tagging, data masking, row access policies, row-level security, external tokenization, and secure views.

INFORMATION_SCHEMA Data Dictionary

The INFORMATION_SCHEMA, also known as the Snowflake Data Dictionary, includes usage metrics and metadata information. The information in the INFORMATION_SCHEMA includes views at the account and database levels. The INFORMATION_SCHEMA was covered in detail in Chapter 3.

Object Tagging

Protecting data in Snowflake begins with understanding the type of data that is stored in an object and annotating that information so that the necessary steps can be taken to secure and protect the data. To help with the annotation process, Snowflake provides a native feature that can be used to create a library of custom tags. These tags can then be associated to Snowflake objects.

A Snowflake tag is a schema-level object that can be associated to different object types, including columns as well as schema-, database-, and account-level objects.

The tag is stored as a key-value pair where the tag is the key, and each tag can have many different string values. A tag identifier must be unique within each schema. Snowflake limits the number of tags to 10,000 per account.

If you enclose an identifier in double quotes, it is case sensitive and can include blank spaces. If an identifier is unquoted, it cannot be case sensitive, cannot contain blank spaces, and must begin with a letter or underscore.

To demonstrate how Snowflake object tagging works, we'll start by creating a taxonomy of the tags we intend to use:

```
USE ROLE SYSADMIN;
CREATE OR REPLACE SCHEMA DEMO7_DB.TAG_LIBRARY;
```

The first tag we want to set up is a tag associated at the table level to describe whether the table will be classified as confidential, restricted, internal, or public. Notice that we make sure to include a comment to list out the possible values we'd like to use for that tag:

```
CREATE OR REPLACE TAG Classification;
ALTER TAG Classification set comment =
    "Tag Tables or Views with one of the following classification values:
    'Confidential', 'Restricted', 'Internal', 'Public'";
```

Next, we'll create a tag associated at the column level that will identify fields that contain personally identifiable information (PII):

```
CREATE OR REPLACE TAG PII;
ALTER TAG PII set comment = "Tag Tables or Views with PII with one or more
    of the following values: 'Phone', 'Email', 'Address'";
```

And finally, we'll create a tag associated at the column level that will identify fields that contain sensitive PII such as Social Security numbers, passport information, and medical information:

```
CREATE OR REPLACE TAG SENSITIVE_PII;
ALTER TAG SENSITIVE_PII set comment = "Tag Tables or Views with Sensitive PII
    with one or more of the following values: 'SSN', 'DL', 'Passport',
        'Financial', 'Medical'";
```

We'll continue using the administrator roles to create a new EMPLOYEES table. Remember that earlier we granted the HR role the ability to use the SELECT statement on future tables in the HRDATA schema so that that role will have access to this new table we are creating:

```
USE ROLE SYSADMIN;
CREATE OR REPLACE TABLE DEMO7_DB.HRDATA.EMPLOYEES (emp_id integer,
    fname varchar(50), lname varchar(50), ssn varchar(50), email varchar(50),
    dept_id integer, dept varchar(50));
INSERT INTO DEMO7_DB.HRDATA.EMPLOYEES (emp_id, fname, lname, ssn, email,
    dept_id, dept) VALUES
    (0, 'First', 'Last', '000-00-0000', 'email@email.com', '100', 'IT');
```

After creating the new EMPLOYEES table, we'll assign tags by using the ALTER command. First we assign the classification tag, with the value of "Confidential", to the entire table:

```
ALTER TABLE DEMO7_DB.HRDATA.EMPLOYEES
    set tag DEMO7_DB.TAG_LIBRARY.Classification="Confidential";
```

Next, we'll assign two tags to two individual columns:

```
ALTER TABLE DEMO7_DB.HRDATA.EMPLOYEES MODIFY EMAIL
    set tag DEMO7_DB.TAG_LIBRARY.PII = "Email";
ALTER TABLE DEMO7_DB.HRDATA.EMPLOYEES MODIFY SSN
    SET TAG DEMO7_DB.TAG_LIBRARY.SENSITIVE_PII = "SSN";
```

 In addition to tags directly assigned to an object, objects can also have inherited tags based on the Snowflake object hierarchy. For example, any tag that is applied to a table is also applied to the columns in that table.

You can use the SHOW TAGS statement to see that all three tags were created. Figure 7-12 shows the results.

	created_on	name	database_name	schema_name	owner
1	.004 -0700	CLASSIFICATION	DEMO7_DB	TAG_LIBRARY	SYSADMIN
2	.596 -0700	PII	DEMO7_DB	TAG_LIBRARY	SYSADMIN
3	.686 -0700	SENSITIVE_PII	DEMO7_DB	TAG_LIBRARY	SYSADMIN

Figure 7-12. Results of the SHOW TAGS statement

You can also query a table or column to see if a particular tag value is associated with the table or column. First, let's see if any Classification tag value is associated with our EMPLOYEES table:

```
SELECT SYSTEM$GET_TAG('Classification', 'DEMO7_DB.HRDATA.EMPLOYEES', 'table');
```

We see that the `Confidential` tag value is associated. Now let's see if any `SENSITIVE_PII` tag is associated with a column. You'll notice that we have to specify the column we want to check:

```
SELECT SYSTEM$GET_TAG('SENSITIVE_PII', 'DEMO7_DB.HRDATA.EMPLOYEES.SSN',
    'column');
```

The SSN tag value is associated with the SSN column, as expected. Let's see what happens if we try checking for a tag value that doesn't exist in a column:

```
SELECT SYSTEM$GET_TAG('SENSITIVE_PII', 'DEMO7_DB.HRDATA.EMPLOYEES.EMAIL',
    'column');
```

We'll get a `NULL` value returned when there is no tag value in a column associated with the specific tag we are inquiring about. In our example, we got the `NULL` value because there is no `SENSITIVE_PII` tag in the EMAIL column. There is, however, a `PII` tag in the EMAIL column, which you can confirm by changing the query.

Appropriately setting tags for tables, views, and columns allows us to query based on tags to discover which database objects and columns contain sensitive information. Then, data stewards can implement data masking policies or row access policies as needed.

Let's create a SQL statement to locate any object or column that has been tagged with a `PII` or `SENSITIVE_PII` tag but does not have a masking policy. Let's see what happens when we run the following statement:

```
//Audit all columns with a sensitive tag without a masking policy
//Note that Latency may be up to 2 hours for tag_references
USE ROLE ACCOUNTADMIN;
WITH column_with_tag
AS (SELECT object_name table_name,
    column_name column_name,
    object_database db_name,
    object_schema schema_name
    FROM snowflake.account_usage.tag_references
    WHERE tag_schema='TAG_LIBRARY'
    AND (tag_name='SENSITIVE_PII' OR tag_name = 'PII')
    AND column_name is not null),
        column_with_policy
AS (SELECT ref_entity_name table_name,
    ref_column_name column_name,
    ref_database_name db_name,
    ref_schema_name schema_name
    FROM snowflake.account_usage.policy_references
    WHERE policy_kind='MASKING POLICY')
    SELECT *
    FROM column_with_tag
    MINUS
    SELECT *
    FROM column_with_policy;
```

Most likely, the query was run successfully but returned no results. That is because there exists up to a two-hour latency before you are able to query the Snowflake database for tag references. Thus, you'll want to continue on with the rest of the chapter, but remember to come back and rerun this statement later to see the results, as shown in Figure 7-13.

	TABLE_NAME	COLUMN_NAME	DB_NAME ···	SCHEMA_NAME
1	EMPLOYEES	EMAIL	DEMO7_DB	HRDATA
2	EMPLOYEES	SSN	DEMO7_DB	HRDATA

Figure 7-13. Results showing which tagged columns do not have a masking policy

The way Snowflake tags are designed allows for different management approaches. In a centralized approach, the administrator is responsible for creating and applying tags to Snowflake objects. The administrator could create a TAG_ADMIN role to delegate the handling of that responsibility. Alternatively, a TAG_ADMIN role could be used in a decentralized manner such that individual teams apply tags to Snowflake objects.

In a later section of this chapter, we will discuss replication. For now, we'll just mention that when a Snowflake primary database is replicated, the tags are also replicated to the secondary database.

Snowflake classification is a new capability that automatically detects PII in a table, view, or column and tags it. Once the tags produced by classification have been assigned, they can be used for data governance, data sharing, and data privacy purposes.

In this section, we focused on security concerns for our object tagging example. Object tagging is also frequently used for tracking data and warehouse consumption for cost reporting purposes. See Chapter 8 for that object tagging example.

Classification

Snowflake's Data Classification analyzes columns in structured data for personal information that may be considered sensitive. Classification functionality is built into the Snowflake platform and includes predefined system tags to assist with classifying the data. Once data has been classified, it is discoverable by querying the INFORMATION_SCHEMA. Then, classified data access can be audited through the ACCESS_HISTORY view to ensure that the proper role-based policies and anonymization have been put in place.

Classification category types

There are two category classification types: semantic and privacy. A semantic category identifies a column that is storing personal attributes, such as name, address, age, or gender. Any column for which a semantic category is identified is further classified with a privacy category.

 Classification is available to all Enterprise Edition accounts and above. To classify data in a table or view, the role used to classify data must have the IMPORTED PRIVILEGES privileges on the SNOWFLAKE database. Additionally, the USAGE privilege on the database and schema is needed along with at least the SELECT privilege on the table or view. Because the classification feature uses tags, it is also necessary to have the APPLY TAG global privilege.

Snowflake classification supports three privacy categories as follows:

Identifier
Also known as a direct identifier. A direct identifier identifies an individual. Examples of direct identifiers include name, Social Security number, and phone number.

Quasi-identifier
Also known an indirect identifier. When combined with other attributes, quasi-identifiers can be used to uniquely identify an individual. An example in which an individual could be uniquely identified using quasi-identifiers is if a person's age, gender, and zip code were available.

Sensitive information
Includes personal attributes that aren't directly or indirectly identifying, but are private and thus shouldn't be disclosed. Examples include salary details and medical status.

 At this time, data in Snowflake can only be classified as sensitive or as a direct/indirect identifier, but not both. Knowing this could affect how you design rules for governed access.

Once a Snowflake table or view has been analyzed, the values for the system tags are returned. To analyze columns in a table or view, generate semantic and privacy categories using Snowflake's EXTRACT_SEMANTIC_CATEGORIES function. Next, the columns with semantic or privacy categories will need to be automatically or manually tagged. We learned about manual tagging in the previous section. To automatically tag columns that have semantic or privacy categories associated with them, you can use the ASSOCIATE_SEMANTIC_CATEGORY_TAGS stored procedure.

Classification can be performed on all table and view types, including external tables, materialized views, and secure views. Snowflake supports classifying data for all data types except the GEOGRAPHY, BINARY, and VARIANT data types.

Data Masking

Revealing certain data to all users could have consequences, especially in situations where there are legal and compliance requirements for keeping the data private and secure. Restricting internal access to private or sensitive data reduces the risk that the data could be leaked intentionally or unintentionally. Using object tagging is a necessary first step to identify data that needs to be secured. We can then use Snowflake's native governance controls such as data masking, column-level security, and row-level policies. Row-level access controls will be discussed in the next section.

Snowflake masking policies are schema-level objects applied to individual columns in tables or views. As such, a database and schema must exist before a masking policy can be applied to a column. This column-level security feature uses the masking policy to selectively mask plain-text data with either a partially masked value or a fully masked value.

Dynamic data masking

Using dynamic data masking, the masking policy is applied to the column at query runtime. The masking policy can incorporate role hierarchy and/or be based on things like network security policies. Also, dynamic data masking can be used with data sharing whereas external tokenization cannot.

In our first data masking example, we are going to create a role-based masking policy. We want to allow the HR role to view the plain-text data while all others will see a fully masked value. Remember that we'll need to use the account administrator role to create a masking policy:

```
USE ROLE ACCOUNTADMIN;
CREATE OR REPLACE masking policy DEMO7_DB.HRDATA.emailmask
    AS (val string) returns string ->
        CASE WHEN current_role() in ('HR_ROLE') THEN val
        ELSE '**MASKED**' END;

ALTER TABLE DEMO7_DB.HRDATA.EMPLOYEES modify column EMAIL
    set masking policy DEMO7_DB.HRDATA.emailmask;
```

Now that we've created an email masking policy, we'll want to create a second masking policy for Social Security numbers:

```
CREATE OR REPLACE masking policy DEMO7_DB.HRDATA.SSNmask
    AS (val string) returns string ->
    CASE WHEN current_role() in ('HR_ROLE') THEN val
        ELSE '**MASKED**' END;

ALTER TABLE DEMO7_DB.HRDATA.EMPLOYEES modify column SSN
    set masking policy DEMO7_DB.HRDATA.SSNmask;
```

If we view the data with the ACCOUNTADMIN role, which has not been granted the HR_ROLE, we'll see masked data. This is intentional because Snowflake has removed the concept of a Snowflake super user who has access to all data. This unique feature greatly reduces risk because it allows for thoughtful consideration of who should be granted access to different pieces of sensitive information:

```
USE ROLE ACCOUNTADMIN;
SELECT * FROM DEMO7_DB.HRDATA.EMPLOYEES;
```

Let's confirm that the HR role can actually see the data. *Be sure to log in as Adam*, the new user, before issuing the following SQL statements. If you do not log in as Adam, you'll receive an error message if you try to execute the command. That is because the user you are logged in as was not granted the HR_ROLE and, thus, you cannot use that role:

```
USE ROLE HR_ROLE;
USE WAREHOUSE COMPUTE_WH;
SELECT * FROM DEMO7_DB.HRDATA.EMPLOYEES;
```

Now that we feel confident that the HR data will be masked appropriately, let's insert some data into the table. You should still be logged in as the user Adam:

```
INSERT INTO DEMO7_DB.HRDATA.EMPLOYEES (emp_id, fname, lname, ssn, email,
dept_id, dept) VALUES
(1, 'Harry', 'Smith', '111-11-1111', 'harry@coemail.com', '100', 'IT'),
(2, 'Marsha', 'Addison', '222-22-2222', 'marsha@coemail.com', '100','IT'),
(3, 'Javier', 'Sanchez', '333-33-3333', 'javier@coemail.com', '101',
    'Marketing'),
(4, 'Alicia', 'Rodriguez', '444-44-4444', 'alicia@coemail.com', '200',
    'Finance'),
(5, 'Marco', 'Anderson', '555-55-5555', 'marco@coemail.com', '300', 'HR'),
(6, 'Barbara', 'Francis', '666-66-6666', 'barbara@coemail.com', '400', 'Exec');
SELECT * FROM DEMO7_DB.HRDATA.EMPLOYEES;
```

Because Adam has been granted the HR role, he sees all the data. Now let's go back to the main Snowflake account so that we'll be ready to continue with our hands-on example.

A role that can view an unmasked data column has the ability to insert unmasked data into another column which might not be protected by data masking.

Conditional masking

Conditional masking specifies two arguments, using one column to determine whether data in another column should be masked. The first argument indicates which column will be masked whereas the second and subsequent arguments are used as conditional columns.

In our example, we'll want the employee ID to always be seen by the HR role, but the employee ID for IT personnel should be the only employee IDs available to everyone. All employee ID numbers other than IT should be masked to everyone except HR:

```
USE ROLE ACCOUNTADMIN;
CREATE OR REPLACE masking policy DEMO7_DB.HRDATA.namemask
    AS (EMP_ID integer, DEPT_ID integer) returns integer ->
    CASE WHEN current_role() = 'HR_ROLE'
            then EMP_ID WHEN DEPT_ID = '100'
            then EMP_ID
            ELSE '**MASKED**' END;
```

Use the SELECT * command in both the main Snowflake account and as the user Adam to see the difference in how the employee ID numbers are seen.

Static masking

Static masking is another way to mask Snowflake data. Rather than creating the masking dynamically, we use ETL tools to transform a set of data to create one or more tables that always have certain columns masked. We're then able to grant access to each table, built upon the same set of underlying data, based on specific roles. Static masking allows for a clear separation of roles, but there is an increased cost, in terms of time and money, due to additional table maintenance and the need to create multiple, different tables.

Row Access Policies and Row-Level Security

Whereas data masking is column-based security, row access policies provide dynamic row-level security. It is important to design these policies in tandem because a column cannot have both a masking policy and a row access policy at the same time. That is precisely why we want to keep the examples separate by using two different schemas and tables to demonstrate masking policies and row access policies.

Added to a table or view when created or after the object is created, row access policies restrict the rows returned in the query result based on information such as role and/or geographic region. While row access policies can prevent rows from being returned in a query, they cannot prevent existing rows from being updated or new rows from being inserted.

One policy can be set on different tables and views, and row access policies can range from simple to complex. An example of a complex row access policy would be a mapping table. To illustrate how row policies work, we'll create a row-level security example based on how two different roles would be given access to the same data. First we'll create a mapping table:

```
USE ROLE SYSADMIN;
USE DATABASE DEMO7_DB;
USE SCHEMA CH7DATA;
CREATE OR REPLACE TABLE AreaFiltering (role_name text, area_id integer);
INSERT INTO AreaFiltering (role_name, area_id) VALUES
    ('AREA1_ROLE', 1), ('AREA2_ROLE', 2);
SELECT * FROM AreaFiltering;
```

Next, we'll create a secure view to hold the data from the RATINGS table so that that role can access specific roles for which it is allowed access:

```
USE ROLE SYSADMIN;
CREATE OR REPLACE SECURE VIEW V_RATINGS_SUMMARY AS
SELECT emp_id, rating, dept_id, area
FROM RATINGS
WHERE area= (SELECT area_id FROM AreaFiltering
WHERE role_name=CURRENT_ROLE());
```

We are still using the SYSADMIN role, so we won't see the data in the secure view. To confirm, be sure to run the following SELECT statement:

```
SELECT * FROM v_ratings_summary;
```

Now let's give the AREA1_ROLE the ability to see data in the secure view. The AREA1-ROLE will be able to see the data when the value in the area column from the DEMO7_DB.CH7DATA.RATINGS table is equal to AREA1:

```
GRANT SELECT ON ALL TABLES IN SCHEMA CH7DATA TO ROLE AREA1_ROLE;
GRANT SELECT ON AreaFiltering TO ROLE AREA1_ROLE;
GRANT SELECT ON v_ratings_summary TO ROLE AREA1_ROLE;
```

As the new user Adam, let's try viewing the data using the AREA1 role:

```
USE ROLE AREA1_ROLE;
USE DATABASE DEMO7_DB;
USE SCHEMA CH7DATA;
SELECT * FROM v_ratings_summary;
```

Because there are three rows of data associated with AREA1, we expect that Adam will be able to see three rows of data by using the AREA1_ROLE, and that is exactly the result we get (see Figure 7-14).

	EMP_ID	RATING	DEPT_ID	...	AREA
1	1	77	100		1
2	2	80	100		1
3	3	72	101		1

Figure 7-14. Result for the AREA1 role when accessing the secure view

Now let's switch back to the main Snowflake user and grant privileges to the AREA2 role:

```
USE ROLE SYSADMIN;
GRANT SELECT ON ALL TABLES IN SCHEMA CH7DATA TO ROLE AREA2_ROLE;
GRANT SELECT ON AreaFiltering TO ROLE AREA2_ROLE;
GRANT SELECT ON v_ratings_summary TO ROLE AREA2_ROLE;
```

We can once again switch back to Adam's user account and confirm that we can use the AREA2 role to view the data associated with AREA2:

```
USE ROLE AREA2_ROLE;
USE DATABASE DEMO7_DB;
USE SCHEMA CH7DATA;
SELECT * FROM v_ratings_summary;
```

While it is possible for Adam to use the two area roles to view the data in the secure view, it would be better if Adam could see at one time all the data that he should be able to see. Fortunately, we have a way in Snowflake to make that happen. We'll replace the original secure view with a new secure view that allows for a multicondition query. Be sure you are in the main Snowflake user account and run the following statement.

We need to drop the secure view first:

```
USE ROLE SYSADMIN;
DROP VIEW v_ratings_summary;
```

Next, we will create a new secure view that uses the multicondition query:

```
USE ROLE SYSADMIN;
USE DATABASE DEMO7_DB;
USE SCHEMA CH7DATA;
CREATE SECURE VIEW v_ratings_summary AS
    SELECT emp_id, rating, dept_id, area
    FROM RATINGS
    WHERE area IN (SELECT area_id FROM AreaFiltering
    WHERE role_name IN
        (SELECT value FROM TABLE(flatten(input =>
        parse_json(CURRENT_AVAILABLE_ROLES()))))) );
```

And finally, we'll give the necessary privileges to the roles:

```
GRANT SELECT ON AreaFiltering TO ROLE AREA1_ROLE;
GRANT SELECT ON v_ratings_summary TO ROLE AREA1_ROLE;
GRANT SELECT ON AreaFiltering TO ROLE AREA2_ROLE;
GRANT SELECT ON v_ratings_summary TO ROLE AREA2_ROLE;
```

Now for the interesting part! Go to Adam's user account and see what happens if we use either of the AREA roles:

```
USE ROLE AREA1_ROLE;
USE DATABASE DEMO7_DB;
USE SCHEMA CH7DATA;
SELECT * FROM v_ratings_summary;
```

Using either of the AREA roles, Adam will be able to see the combined results from both the AREA1 and AREA2 query results (as shown in Figure 7-15).

	EMP_ID	RATING	DEPT_ID	...	AREA
1	1	77	100		1
2	2	80	100		1
3	3	72	101		1
4	4	94	200		2

Figure 7-15. Combined results from the AREA1 and AREA2 query results

Let's see what happens if we use Adam's other role to query the secure view:

```
USE ROLE HR_ROLE;
USE DATABASE DEMO7_DB;
USE SCHEMA CH7DATA;
SELECT * FROM v_ratings_summary;
```

Adam receives the message that the view does not exist, or he is not authorized. This confirms for us that Adam can get full access to the results if he uses a role that has access to the view. If, instead, Adam uses a role which does not have access to the view, he will not be able to see any results.

External Tokenization

External tokenization functionality, which uses external functions, is available in the Snowflake Standard Edition and above. If you want to integrate your tokenization provider with Snowflake external tokenization, you'll need to have Snowflake Enterprise Edition or higher.

Secure Views and UDFs

It is a best practice to use secure views and secure UDFs instead of directly sharing Snowflake tables if sensitive data exists in a database. In Chapter 3, we worked through a market basket analysis example using a secure SQL UDF. Secure data sharing approaches are covered in detail in Chapter 10, where we will learn how to use a mapping table to share data in a base table with many different accounts where we want to share specific rows in the table with specific accounts.

We've previously been introduced to the PUBLIC schema available in all Snowflake databases. It is a best practice to use a public schema for secure views and a private schema for base tables.

Object Dependencies

The Snowflake object dependencies feature allows you to identify dependencies among Snowflake objects and is frequently used for impact analysis, data integrity assurance, and compliance purposes.

An object dependency is established when an existing object has to reference some metadata on its behalf or for at least one other object. A dependency can be triggered by an object's name, its ID value, or both. One example of an object dependency is a Snowflake external stage where the ID is used as a reference to the external storage location.

It is important for data engineers to be aware of the object dependencies before making changes to Snowflake architecture. Before an engineer renames a table or drops a table, for example, they could notify users of downstream views which are dependent on those tables. In this way, the engineer could get the feedback necessary to assess the impact of modifications before actually making changes.

Additionally, data analysts and data scientists can look upstream to see the lineage of a view. Being able to do so now, with object dependencies functionality, gives them the confidence that the view is backed by a trustworthy object source. Finally, the new object dependencies feature is important for compliance officers and auditors who need to be able to trace data from a given object to its original data source to meet compliance and regulatory requirements.

Object dependencies appears as a view in the Snowflake Account Usage schema. A Snowflake Account Administrator can query the OBJECT_DEPENDENCIES view and the output can include the object name path, the referencing object name and domain, along with the referenced object name and domain.

Snowflake's object dependencies feature is one of the many comprehensive data governance–native features provided by Snowflake. This suite of features makes it easy to efficiently know and protect your data. This is important because governing your data is critical to ensure that your data is secure, trustworthy, and compliant with regulatory requirements.

Code Cleanup

We can quickly and easily clean up our Snowflake org by dropping the Chapter 7 database and the new user we created:

```
USE ROLE ACCOUNTADMIN;
DROP DATABASE DEMO7_DB;
DROP USER ADAM;
```

Summary

In this chapter, information was provided to help you more effectively understand your Snowflake data and to better protect it. We learned how classification and object tagging help us understand what data exists in our Snowflake account, where it is stored, and how it is accessible to different roles. We also learned how to manage network security policies and firewall access as well as how to monitor user activity with Snowflake's ACCOUNT_USAGE view. In addition, many ways to protect data were presented: Time Travel, fail-safe, replication, failover/failback, data masking, row access policies, external tokenization, and secure views and UDFs.

Better understanding what data you have in Snowflake and more effectively and efficiently protecting it not only reduces risk but decreases the time it takes to locate the data, when needed. Reducing risk, saving time, and improving service levels ultimately results in lower overall costs and better performance. Chapter 8 will uncover more techniques to help manage costs.

More specifically, in that chapter you'll learn about tools and techniques to help manage your Snowflake account costs. Some new tools discussed in the chapter are resource monitors, to help control virtual warehouse costs and avoid unexpected credit usage, and business intelligence dashboards to monitor Snowflake usage and costs. In addition, you'll discover that ACCOUNT_USAGE views and object tagging, used in this chapter for security and protection reasons, are also tools that can be used to help manage costs.

Knowledge Check

The following questions are based on the information contained in this chapter:

1. When should multifactor authentication be used and how do users enroll?

2. Is there a limit to the number of network policies that can exist?

3. What are some of the unique features of a root encryption key?

4. Describe the different types of data masking and the main difference between data masking policies and row access policies. What is the most important restriction when using these two policies?

5. Can a Time Travel retention period be increased or reduced? If so, what happens as a result?

6. Do object tags need to be enclosed in quotes, double quotes, or no quotes? Explain. What are the two automatic data tagging features now offered by Snowflake?

7. For what reason do we need to flatten query output? Describe how we used the FLATTEN command in this chapter.

8. How are cloned objects handled in database replication?

9. What are the different ways we can use Time Travel to access historical data?

10. What are the associated costs to consider for Time Travel? What about for replication and failover?

Answers to these questions are available in Appendix A.

Managing Snowflake Account Costs

Organizations create business plans and budgets using the most current and accurate information possible. Knowing the amount to budget for an on-premises virtual warehouse is relatively easy because, for the most part, the costs are fixed. A usage-based cost approach, such as Snowflake's current pricing model, may initially seem intimidating. Indeed, understanding any usage-based cost model requires a clear understanding in advance of how costs are computed and what guardrails can be added to control for greater elasticity so that you don't experience runaway costs. Snowflake includes tools, such as resource monitors, which allow you to cap actual costs based on your initial plan. Going beyond a basic understanding of usage-based pricing and positioning your organization to take advantage of it can yield many positive results.

One of the greatest benefits of usage-based pricing is that it provides you an opportunity to transparently see and understand how your organization is charged for storing and using data. This often leads to changes that will immediately begin to lower costs. Snowflake's usage-based billing and Snowflake object tagging make it easy to assign appropriate costs to the appropriate accounts or departments. This means there is more cost accountability for each team and workload. With more accountability at a granular level, there will likely be more consideration about how resources are consumed and, thus, more action will be taken to become more efficient.

Snowflake's pricing model is straightforward, transparent, and easy to understand. In addition to the many benefits that are possible with any cloud technology usage-based cost approach, Snowflake has unique functionality which can result in decreased costs. One example is zero-copy cloning, which offers the ability to duplicate an object without actually creating a physical copy. This means no storage costs are assessed for the clone. Furthermore, Snowflake's native functionality allows you to set limits on your credit consumption costs. These Snowflake resource monitors can be set to take actions such as notifying or suspending consumption. Additionally, Snowflake offers a lot of usage data for companies to understand their costs, and this makes customers on Snowflake more cost-effective.

When taking advantage of Snowflake's usage-based cost approach features, consideration of software delivery operations should be made from the outset. Fortunately, Snowflake has several ways to alleviate the unique challenges of database change management and reduce software development costs.

Prep Work

Create a new worksheet titled *Chapter8 Managing Costs*. Refer to "Navigating Snowsight Worksheets" on page 8 if you need help creating a new worksheet. To set the worksheet context, make sure you are using the SYSADMIN role and the COMPUTE_WH virtual warehouse.

Later in this chapter we're going to create some Snowflake resource monitors. Resource monitors help to monitor the usage of Snowflake virtual warehouses. To prepare for the resource monitors section, we'll need to create some Snowflake virtual warehouses. A best practice is to use the SYSADMIN role to create the new virtual warehouses:

```
USE ROLE SYSADMIN;
USE WAREHOUSE COMPUTE_WH;
CREATE OR REPLACE WAREHOUSE VW2_WH WITH WAREHOUSE_SIZE = MEDIUM
    AUTO_SUSPEND = 300 AUTO_RESUME = true, INITIALLY_SUSPENDED=true;
CREATE OR REPLACE WAREHOUSE VW3_WH WITH WAREHOUSE_SIZE = SMALL
    AUTO_SUSPEND = 300 AUTO_RESUME = true, INITIALLY_SUSPENDED=true;
CREATE OR REPLACE WAREHOUSE VW4_WH WITH WAREHOUSE_SIZE = MEDIUM
    AUTO_SUSPEND = 300 AUTO_RESUME = true, INITIALLY_SUSPENDED=true;
CREATE OR REPLACE WAREHOUSE VW5_WH WITH WAREHOUSE_SIZE = SMALL
    AUTO_SUSPEND = 300 AUTO_RESUME = true, INITIALLY_SUSPENDED=true;
CREATE OR REPLACE WAREHOUSE VW6_WH WITH WAREHOUSE_SIZE = MEDIUM
    AUTO_SUSPEND = 300 AUTO_RESUME = true, INITIALLY_SUSPENDED=true;
```

Snowflake Monthly Bill

Organizations can create and manage multiple Snowflake accounts. Each Snowflake account incurs fees that are summarized in the organization's monthly bill. Your total Snowflake monthly bill includes three distinct charges per account: storage fees, data transfer costs, and credits consumed. We'll review each type of charge; you can also follow along by looking in your Snowflake org to see your current charges.

Use the Home icon to navigate to the Main menu. Make sure your role is set to ACCOUNTADMIN. Click Admin → Usage, as shown in Figure 8-1.

Figure 8-1. The Snowflake Account → Usage menu

In the Usage section, you'll have the option to select All Usage Types, Compute, Storage, or Data Transfer (as shown in Figure 8-2).

Figure 8-2. Account usage information

In this section, we'll be focusing on billing at the account level. For account-level billing, we're going to start getting an understanding of storage fees and then review transfer costs. Finally, we'll take an in-depth look at Snowflake credits. The most current Snowflake service consumption table pricing is available on the Snowflake website (*https://oreil.ly/8l8N7*).

Storage Fees

Snowflake monthly storage fees are calculated based on the average terabytes used per month, based on periodic snapshots of all data stored in an account. You'll notice that capacity pricing offers steep discounts for upfront payments.

Note that while storage pricing is a consideration of which region to select for your Snowflake account, you'll also want to consider which region could minimize latency and give you access to any features you may require. It's important to note that if you decide later to move your data to a different region, data transfer costs will be incurred.

> Try to make more use of transient tables as they are not maintained in the history tables, which in turn reduces the data storage costs for history tables. More information about transient tables can be found in Chapter 3.

Data Transfer Costs

Data transfer costs are assessed when data stored in Snowflake is transferred from one region to another, within the same cloud platform, or when data is transferred out of the cloud.

> Snowflake does not charge *data ingress* fees. The *data egress* fees you pay are a reimbursement to Snowflake coming from the three cloud data providers applying data egress charges when data is transferred.

Data egress charges apply only when unloading data from Snowflake, when external functions are used, or when replicating data to a Snowflake account in a region or cloud platform that is different from where your primary Snowflake account is hosted.

Compute Credits Consumed

The consumption of resources on Snowflake is paid for with Snowflake credits, which are a unit of measure. That measure is the equivalent of one hour of usage by a single compute node.

While one credit is equivalent to one hour, the actual billing for virtual warehouses is on a per-second basis with a one-minute minimum.

You can purchase credits as you go, on demand. The price of on-demand credits is dependent on which cloud provider, region, and service edition is selected. Alternatively, you can prepurchase credits at a negotiated discounted rate.

A Snowflake credit is consumed only when you use resources. Snowflake resources are used, or consumed, in one of three ways: running virtual warehouses, when the cloud services layer is performing work, or using serverless features such as automatic clustering or maintaining materialized views.

The credits consumed for Snowflake running virtual warehouses are based on the size of the warehouse. For example, the credit consumption for an X-Small virtual warehouse is billed at one Snowflake credit per hour of usage.

Optimally managing the operational status of your compute clusters with features such as auto-suspension and auto-resume can help manage the Snowflake consumption credits that are billed. More information about creating and managing virtual warehouses can be found in Chapter 2.

The credits consumed for the cloud services layer are free for up to 10% of the consumed daily virtual warehouse compute. Anything above the 10% daily threshold for cloud services layer consumption is billed and appears in your Snowflake account as a charge to the CLOUD_SERVICES_ONLY virtual warehouse.

The credits consumed for using serverless features are billed at a distinctly different rate, depending on the serverless feature.

Snowflake's many native features, such as micro-partitions and automatic compute clustering, lessen the need for credit consumption, which in turn decreases overall costs. Snowflake's highly elastic compute and per-second billing model also helps keep credit consumption charges low. These features come to you from Snowflake out of the box; however, there are also things you can do to take a more proactive role in understanding and managing your Snowflake consumption credit usage.

Creating Resource Monitors to Manage Virtual Warehouse Usage and Reduce Costs

Snowflake's usage-based pricing is easy to understand. It's straightforward, and you only pay for what you use. One goal, then, would be to monitor the amount you use.

A Snowflake virtual warehouse consumes credits when it's in use. The number of Snowflake credits consumed by a virtual warehouse depends on two factors: the size of the virtual warehouse and how long it runs.

We learned in Chapter 2 that virtual warehouse sizes increase by a factor of two up to the 4X-Large size. As such, an X-Small virtual warehouse consumes one Snowflake credit per hour whereas a 4X-Large virtual warehouse consumes 128 credits for each hour the virtual warehouse runs.

Virtual warehouse consumption is billed on a per-second basis, with a 60-second minimum.

Monitoring credit consumption will help prevent unexpected credit usage, and as such, provides a means with which to control compute costs. Snowflake provides the necessary tools, known as resource monitors, to help automate the task of monitoring credit consumption and to trigger actions based on preset thresholds.

A resource monitor is a first-class Snowflake object that can be applied to both user-managed virtual warehouses and virtual warehouses used by cloud services.

A Snowflake resource monitor has the following properties:

- Credit Quota (Number of Snowflake credits)
- Credit Usage (Total Snowflake credits consumed during each billing period)
  - Monitor Level: account or specific virtual warehouse(s)
  - Schedule
    - Frequency: daily, weekly, monthly, yearly, never
    - Start and End, although it is uncommon to have an end value

- Triggers (Actions)
  — Notify
  — Notify and Suspend
  — Notify and Suspend Immediately

Conceptually, resource monitor planning looks like what is shown in Figure 8-3.

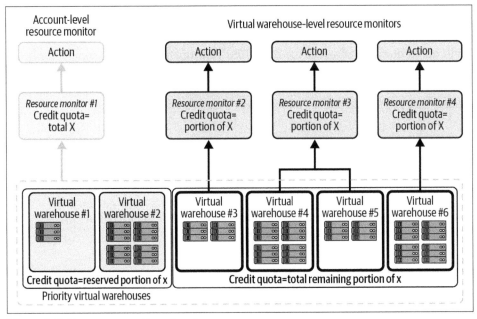

Figure 8-3. Resource monitor planning

The recommended steps for resource monitor planning are as follows:

1. Determine the overall account level credit budget that will be used to establish an account-level resource monitor. In Figure 8-3, this is the Total X value.

2. Define priority virtual warehouses and assign a portion of the credit budget, referred to as the Reserved Portion of X in Figure 8-3, for all priority virtual warehouses. Priority virtual warehouses are those virtual warehouses that you would not want to be suspended.

3. Assign the remaining portion of the budget to all other nonpriority virtual warehouses by way of creating virtual warehouse–level resource monitor(s). Doing so will limit their individual credit usage to ensure there is enough budget reserved for the priority virtual warehouses. Note that there isn't a limit to the number of resource monitors you can create. If you want, you can assign a resource monitor to each individual virtual warehouse.

4. Determine the schedule, if you are not going to use default settings.

5. Decide on the actions for each resource monitor. Most likely, you'll want to establish the account-level resource monitor with a "Notify-only" action so that the priority virtual warehouses do not get suspended.

Resource Monitor Credit Quota

An account-level resource monitor credit quota, stated in terms of Snowflake credits, is based on the entire amount of cloud service usage. However, the warehouse-level credit quota does not consider the daily 10% adjustment for cloud services. Only an account-level resource monitor can monitor credit usage for virtual warehouses that provide cloud services. Resource monitors, at the virtual warehouse level, can only be created for user-created and user-managed virtual warehouses.

 When a credit quota threshold is reached for a virtual warehouse whose resource monitor action is set to Suspend Immediately, additional Snowflake credits might still be consumed. Thus, you might want to consider utilizing buffers in quota thresholds for trigger actions if you want to strictly enforce your quotas. For example, set your threshold for 95% instead of 100% to ensure that your credit usage won't exceed your actual quota.

Resource Monitor Credit Usage

As stated, resource monitors can be created at the account level or the virtual warehouse level.

 Account-level resource monitors only control the credit usage of virtual warehouses created in your account; not Snowflake-provided virtual warehouses for serverless features such as those used for Snowpipe, automatic clustering, or materialized views.

Snowflake resource monitors can be created to impose limits on the number of Snowflake credits that are consumed, either for a specified interval or for a date range.

For a default schedule, a resource monitor starts tracking the assigned virtual warehouse as soon as it is created, and the credit usage tracking resets to 0 at the beginning of each calendar month.

Customizing the schedule so that the resource monitor resets at a specific interval, such as daily or weekly, requires that you select *both* a frequency and a start time. Selecting an end time is optional.

Resource Monitor Notifications and Other Actions

Resource monitors can be created to trigger specific actions, such as sending alert notifications and/or suspending a virtual warehouse.

 There is a limit of five Notify actions, one Suspend action, and one Suspend Immediately action for each resource monitor.

By default, resource monitor notifications are not enabled. ACCOUNTADMIN role users can receive notifications only if they provide a *verified* valid email address and enable notifications.

To enable notifications via the web interface, make sure your role is set to ACCOUNTADMIN. You can select Preferences and then Notifications. You'll need to choose your notification preference as Web, Email, or All. If you select Email or All, you'll be prompted to enter a valid email address.

The difference between the Suspend action and the Suspend Immediately action has to do with whether statements being executed by the virtual warehouse(s) will be allowed to complete or not.

When a trigger causes a virtual warehouse to suspend, the suspended virtual warehouse cannot be resumed until one of the following conditions occurs:

- The resource monitor is no longer assigned to the virtual warehouse or is dropped.
- Either the credit quota for the monitor or the credit threshold for the trigger is increased.
- A new monthly billing cycle starts.

Resource Monitor Rules for Assignments

Resource monitor rules for assignments can be summarized as follows:

- An account-level resource monitor can be set at the account level to control credit usage for all virtual warehouses in an account; however, there can be only one account-level resource monitor.
- There is a one-to-many relationship between virtual warehouses and virtual warehouse–level resource monitors. Each virtual warehouse can be assigned to only one virtual warehouse–level resource monitor; one resource monitor can be assigned to one or more virtual warehouses.

- The credit quota and credit usage properties are both required to create a resource monitor. If a schedule is not explicitly stated, the default schedule applies. By default, the credit quota resets at the beginning of each calendar month. Setting triggers is optional.
- Before it can perform monitoring actions, a resource monitor must be assigned to a virtual warehouse or account after it is created.

Let's use what we've learned thus far about resource monitors to create a resource monitor plan (as shown in Figure 8-4) for a large enterprise with about 10,000 employees. We'll implement the resource monitor plan in the next section.

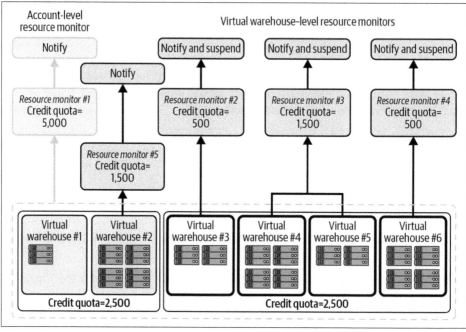

Figure 8-4. Example of an implementation plan for resource monitoring

Assume we want to limit our credit consumption to 5,000 credits. We'll need to create an account-level resource monitor in which the credit quota equals 5,000, and we'll want to be notified when that credit quota has been reached. We'll elect to use the default schedule.

Out of the six virtual warehouses in our account, we've identified two priority virtual warehouses for which we want to allocate half our credit budget. This means 2,500 credits are being reserved from the 5,000 total credits. The other four virtual warehouses will need to split the remaining 2,500 credits, and we'll create virtual warehouse–level resource monitors to notify and suspend whenever the credit quota has been reached. Additionally, we've decided to be notified when the second of our priority virtual warehouses reaches a credit quota of 1,500.

If applicable, a virtual warehouse will be suspended if either the account-level resource monitor or the virtual warehouse–level resource monitor reaches its threshold and there are suspend actions associated with the resource monitors. In our example, though, we have established a "Notify-only" action for the account-level resource monitor. We've also created a resource monitor associated with virtual warehouse #2, one of the priority virtual warehouses, that has a "Notify-only" action. Therefore, the first two virtual warehouses will never suspend as a result of either of the resource monitors reaching its threshold. The remaining virtual warehouses will suspend if/when their associated resource monitor reaches its threshold.

> Virtual warehouses that share the same resource monitor also share the same thresholds. An example would be virtual warehouses #3 and #4 in Figure 8-4. This could result in the credit usage for one virtual warehouse impacting the other assigned virtual warehouse(s).

DDL Commands for Creating and Managing Resource Monitors

By default, Snowflake resource monitors can only be created, viewed, and maintained by the ACCOUNTADMIN role. Although the creation of Snowflake resource monitors is exclusive to the ACCOUNTADMIN role, a Snowflake account administrator can enable other roles to view and modify resource monitors.

If you're using a role other than the ACCOUNTADMIN role, that role will need to have two privileges in order for you to view and edit resource monitors:

- MODIFY
- MONITOR

Snowflake resource monitors can be created in the web interface or by using SQL in a worksheet. For our examples in this chapter, we'll be using the SQL option to create and manage resource monitors.

Snowflake Data Definition Language (DDL) commands for creating and managing resource monitors include the following:

CREATE RESOURCE MONITOR
    Assigns virtual warehouse(s) to a resource monitor

ALTER RESOURCE MONITOR
    Modifies an existing resource monitor

```
SHOW RESOURCE MONITOR
```
Views an existing resource monitor

```
DROP RESOURCE MONITOR
```
Deletes an existing resource monitor

To create a resource monitor, you need to assign at least one virtual warehouse to the resource monitor, unless you are setting the monitor at the account level. You are required to assign the virtual warehouse at the time of creation if you create the resource monitor in the web interface. If you use SQL to create the resource monitor, you'll have to create the resource monitor first and then use the ALTER WAREHOUSE command to assign one or more virtual warehouses to the resource monitor.

Let's first create an account-level resource monitor. Navigate back to the *Chapter8 Managing Costs* worksheet and execute these statements:

```
USE ROLE ACCOUNTADMIN;
CREATE OR REPLACE RESOURCE MONITOR MONITOR1_RM WITH CREDIT_QUOTA = 5000
     TRIGGERS on 50 percent do notify
             on 75 percent do notify
             on 100 percent do notify
             on 110 percent do notify
             on 125 percent do notify;
```

You'll notice that we created five different notify actions and no suspend actions, following the plan we created earlier. After we create the resource monitor, we'll need to assign it to our Snowflake account:

```
USE ROLE ACCOUNTADMIN;
ALTER ACCOUNT SET RESOURCE_MONITOR = MONITOR1_RM;
```

Next, we'll create a virtual warehouse–level monitor. We want to create the resource monitor for one of our priority virtual warehouses, and we'll use the same notify actions for the priority virtual warehouse as we did for the account-level resource monitor. After we create the resource monitor, we'll assign it to our priority virtual warehouse:

```
USE ROLE ACCOUNTADMIN;
CREATE OR REPLACE RESOURCE MONITOR MONITOR5_RM WITH CREDIT_QUOTA = 1500
     TRIGGERS on 50 percent do notify
             on 75 percent do notify
             on 100 percent do notify
             on 110 percent do notify
             on 125 percent do notify;
ALTER WAREHOUSE VW2_WH SET RESOURCE_MONITOR = MONITOR5_RM;
```

Now let's use the SHOW RESOURCE MONITORS command to see the resource monitors we've created thus far:

```
USE ROLE ACCOUNTADMIN;
SHOW RESOURCE MONITORS;
```

In Figure 8-5, you'll notice that we have one account-level and one virtual ware-house–level resource monitor. Both of them have a monthly frequency stated, as expected, since we didn't explicitly state a different schedule.

	name	credit_quota	used_credits	...	remaining_credits	level	frequency	start_time	end_time	notify_at
1	MONITOR1_RM	5000.00	0.00		5000.00	ACCOUNT	MONTHLY	2022-05-31 17:00:00.000 -0700		100%,110%,125%,50%,75%
2	MONITOR5_RM	1500.00	0.00		1500.00	WAREHOUSE	MONTHLY	2022-05-31 17:00:00.000 -0700		100%,110%,125%,50%,75%

Figure 8-5. Results after creating two resource monitors

We're ready to create another virtual warehouse–level resource monitor:

```
USE ROLE ACCOUNTADMIN;
CREATE OR REPLACE RESOURCE MONITOR MONITOR2_RM WITH CREDIT_QUOTA = 500
    TRIGGERS on 50 percent do notify
            on 75 percent do notify
            on 100 percent do notify
            on 100 percent do suspend
            on 110 percent do notify
            on 110 percent do suspend_immediate;
ALTER WAREHOUSE VW3_WH SET RESOURCE_MONITOR = MONITOR2_RM;
```

Everything is good thus far. Now let's purposely make a mistake to see what happens. We'll create a resource monitor and assign it to a virtual warehouse, and then we'll create another resource monitor and assign it to the same virtual warehouse. We know that a virtual warehouse can only be assigned to one resource monitor, so we expect that our second attempt at assigning a resource monitor to the same virtual warehouse will result in either a failed command or the second resource monitor assignment overriding the first assignment. Let's see what happens:

```
USE ROLE ACCOUNTADMIN;
CREATE OR REPLACE RESOURCE MONITOR MONITOR6_RM WITH CREDIT_QUOTA = 500
    TRIGGERS on 50 percent do notify
            on 75 percent do notify
            on 100 percent do notify
            on 100 percent do suspend
            on 110 percent do notify
            on 110 percent do suspend_immediate;
ALTER WAREHOUSE VW6_WH SET RESOURCE_MONITOR = MONITOR6_RM;
```

You'll notice from our planning diagram that we don't have a sixth resource monitor planned, so it was a mistake to create the sixth resource monitor. No worries, though. We'll delete the unneeded resource monitor in a little while. For now, let's create the correct resource monitor that should be assigned to the virtual warehouse:

```
USE ROLE ACCOUNTADMIN;
CREATE OR REPLACE RESOURCE MONITOR MONITOR4_RM WITH CREDIT_QUOTA = 500
    TRIGGERS on 50 percent do notify
            on 75 percent do notify
            on 100 percent do notify
            on 100 percent do suspend
```

```
        on 110 percent do notify
        on 110 percent do suspend_immediate;
ALTER WAREHOUSE VW6_WH SET RESOURCE_MONITOR = MONITOR4_RM;
```

The statement was executed successfully. So, let's run a SHOW RESOURCE MONITORS command and see the results, as shown in Figure 8-6:

```
USE ROLE ACCOUNTADMIN;
SHOW RESOURCE MONITORS;
```

	name	...	credit_quota	used_credits	remaining_credits	level	frequency
1	MONITOR1_RM		5000.00	0.00	5000.00	ACCOUNT	MONTHLY
2	MONITOR2_RM		500.00	0.00	500.00	WAREHOUSE	MONTHLY
3	MONITOR4_RM		500.00	0.00	500.00	WAREHOUSE	MONTHLY
4	MONITOR5_RM		1500.00	0.00	1500.00	WAREHOUSE	MONTHLY
5	MONITOR6_RM		500.00	0.00	500.00		MONTHLY

Figure 8-6. Results of the SHOW RESOURCE MONITORS command

We can see that the sixth resource monitor appears to have nullified when we assigned the fourth resource monitor to the virtual warehouse. We can confirm that by using the SHOW WAREHOUSES command:

```
USE ROLE ACCOUNTADMIN;
SHOW WAREHOUSES;
```

Figure 8-7 shows the results of our statement. Just as we suspected, assigning the resource monitor to the virtual warehouse overrode the previous assignment.

	name	resource_monitor
1	COMPUTE_WH	null
2	VW2_WH	MONITOR5_RM
3	VW3_WH	MONITOR2_RM
4	VW4_WH	null
5	VW5_WH	null
6	VW6_WH	MONITOR4_RM

Figure 8-7. Results of the SHOW WAREHOUSES command

We can now get rid of the resource monitor we created in error:

```
DROP RESOURCE MONITOR MONITOR6_RM;
```

Let's create the last resource monitor from our planning diagram. We'll assign the resource monitor to two virtual warehouses:

```
USE ROLE ACCOUNTADMIN;
CREATE OR REPLACE RESOURCE MONITOR MONITOR3_RM WITH CREDIT_QUOTA = 1500
    TRIGGERS on 50 percent do notify
            on 75 percent do notify
            on 100 percent do notify
            on 100 percent do suspend
            on 110 percent do notify
            on 110 percent do suspend_immediate;
ALTER WAREHOUSE VW4_WH SET RESOURCE_MONITOR = MONITOR3_RM;
ALTER WAREHOUSE VW5_WH SET RESOURCE_MONITOR = MONITOR3_RM;
```

You can once again take a look at all the resource monitors in your Snowflake account:

```
USE ROLE ACCOUNTADMIN;
SHOW RESOURCE MONITORS;
```

You'll notice that the dropped resource monitor does not appear in the list of resource monitors. At this point, we can run another SHOW WAREHOUSES statement. We can also take it a step further to get a list of any of our virtual warehouses that have not been assigned to a virtual warehouse–level resource monitor. Note, however, that in order for the following statement to work, you'll need to have just run the SHOW WAREHOUSES statement most recently:

```
SELECT "name", "size"
FROM TABLE (RESULT_SCAN(LAST_QUERY_ID()))
WHERE "resource_monitor" = 'null';
```

We can see that COMPUTE_WH, the virtual warehouse that came with our Snow-flake account and what we are referring to as virtual warehouse #1, has not been assigned to a resource monitor (as shown in Figure 8-8). If we review our planning diagram, we see that is as we would expect.

	name	...	size
1	COMPUTE_WH		X-Small

Figure 8-8. Result showing that the virtual warehouse was not assigned to a resource monitor

We've created and managed our resource monitors using SQL in a worksheet. Alternatively, we could have created and managed our resources in the web UI. We'd need to make sure we are using the ACCOUNTADMIN role. Then we would be able to view the resource monitors we just finished creating, and we'd be able to create any new resources from the web UI, as shown in Figure 8-9.

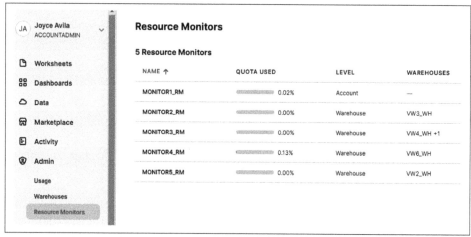

Figure 8-9. The Snowflake web UI showing resource monitors for the ACCOUNTADMIN role

One final note about resource monitors is that for Snowflake provider accounts that have created reader accounts, there exists a RESOURCE_MONITORS view which can be used to query resource monitor usage of the reader account. You can find more information about Snowflake provider and reader accounts in Chapter 10.

Using Object Tagging for Cost Centers

Object tagging was introduced in Chapter 7 when we created tags for data governance purposes. In the examples from that chapter, we learned that Snowflake object tags can be assigned to tables, views, or columns to help keep track of the type of data being stored and whether that data included sensitive information.

In addition to using object tags for security reasons, Snowflake tags can be created for objects to help track resource usage. For example, cost center tags could have values such as accounting, finance, marketing, and engineering. In that case, cost center object tagging would allow for more granular insight, at a department level. Additionally, tags can be used for tracking and analyzing resource usage by specific short-term or long-term projects.

Querying the ACCOUNT_USAGE View

To get more granular detail about virtual warehouse costs, we can leverage queries on the Snowflake ACCOUNT_USAGE view.

Access to the ACCOUNT_USAGE view is given only to the ACCOUNTADMIN role by default. Thus, we will use that role in our examples for querying the view.

This query provides the individual details of cost, based on virtual warehouse start times and assuming $3.00 as the credit price:

```
USE ROLE ACCOUNTADMIN;
SET CREDIT_PRICE = 3.00;
USE DATABASE SNOWFLAKE;
USE SCHEMA ACCOUNT_USAGE;
SELECT  WAREHOUSE_NAME, START_TIME, END_TIME, CREDITS_USED,
    ($CREDIT_PRICE*CREDITS_USED) AS DOLLARS_USED
FROM SNOWFLAKE.ACCOUNT_USAGE.WAREHOUSE_METERING_HISTORY
ORDER BY START_TIME DESC;
```

This query summarizes the costs of each virtual warehouse for the past 30 days, assuming $3.00 as the credit price as set in the previous query:

```
SELECT WAREHOUSE_NAME,SUM(CREDITS_USED_COMPUTE)
    AS CREDITS_USED_COMPUTE_30DAYS,
    ($CREDIT_PRICE*CREDITS_USED_COMPUTE_30DAYS) AS DOLLARS_USED_30DAYS
FROM ACCOUNT_USAGE.WAREHOUSE_METERING_HISTORY
WHERE START_TIME >= DATEADD(DAY, -30, CURRENT_TIMESTAMP())
GROUP BY 1
ORDER BY 2 DESC;
```

The previous code samples provided an example of how you can query the ACCOUNT_USAGE view to monitor virtual warehouse metering for compute warehouse credits consumed. Similar queries can be created to monitor compute credits consumed from Snowpipe, clustering, materialized views, search optimization, and replication. There are also some good code examples in the "Snowflake Resource Optimization: Billing Metrics Quickstart" in the Snowflake tutorials (*https://oreil.ly/YVSty*).

Using BI Partner Dashboards to Monitor Snowflake Usage and Costs

If you have access to the Snowflake business intelligence (BI) and analytics partners tools, you'll be able to access one or more plug-and-play dashboards to help you monitor your Snowflake usage. Here is a list of some of the prebuilt dashboards that are currently available:

Tableau Dashboards
    Compute cost overview

Sigma
    Compute cost, storage cost, and Snowflake cost (reader accounts)

Looker
    Snowflake cost and usage analysis

Microsoft Power BI
    Snowflake usage report

Qlik
    Snowflake usage dashboard

Snowflake Agile Software Delivery

Managing Snowflake costs is not just limited to reviewing the Snowflake monthly bill. Current Snowflake charges are the result of past decisions, including architecture choices, what data to store, and how to construct certain queries to access the data. But organizations and their needs are always changing. Thus, it is expected that an organization's Snowflake environment will change as well.

There are costs associated with changing any software, including making changes to your Snowflake software as a service (SaaS) account environment. It takes employees time to architect and build new software and/or enhance existing software. Any disruptions to the business also have a cost associated with them. Minimizing software development costs and disruption to the business while working as quickly as possible to make improvements requires an established set of practices and an agile software delivery mindset.

DevOps is a term used to describe the set of practices that are established with the goals of high software quality and helping software developers and IT operations shorten the systems development lifecycle and provide continuous delivery. Database change management (DCM) is a subset of DevOps that specifically focuses on the changes made to databases. DCM has unique challenges, but the good news is that Snowflake features, such as zero-copy cloning and Time Travel, make it considerably easier for teams to use an agile approach for DevOps.

Why Do We Need DevOps?

It is crucial that an audit trail of software and application changes be maintained, because of regulatory and compliance requirements applicable to an organization's software systems and data. For many reasons, it is also important that any bug fixes be resolved quickly. New features and requested enhancements should also be released frequently to give organizations a competitive advantage in today's fast-paced environment, especially given the vast number of powerful software application development tools available. Achieving these things requires careful consideration. And most importantly, it requires automation.

Automation of software development, testing, and release is the most likely way to innovate more quickly, deliver improved applications in greater numbers, adhere to regulatory requirements, and obtain greater return on investment. It is the objective of DevOps to minimize the manual aspects of software development, testing, and deployment.

Continuous Data Integration, Continuous Delivery, and Continuous Deployment

Achieving continuous integration and continuous delivery (CI/CD) through the ongoing automation of development, testing, and deployment occurs in a connected way through a CI/CD pipeline (as illustrated in Figure 8-10).

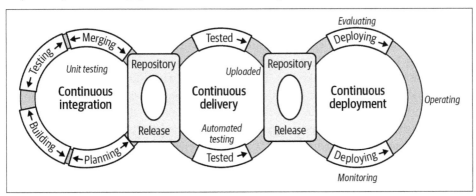

Figure 8-10. The CI/CD pipeline

In general terms, continuous integration is a DevOps software development practice whereby developers merge their code regularly into a central repository. Continuous delivery occurs when application changes are automatically tested and uploaded to a source control repository, such as GitHub, where the operations team can then deploy them to production. Continuous deployment automates the next stage in the pipeline by automatically releasing changes from the repository to production.

What the terms *continuous integration, continuous delivery,* and *continuous deployment* mean for each specific organization is dependent upon how much automation has been built into the organization's CI/CD pipeline.

What Is Database Change Management?

Database DevOps is often referred to as database change management (DCM). Database DevOps, especially for virtual warehouses, have some unique challenges as compared to the difficulties of DevOps for software applications. Snowflake's unique architecture solves for many of these problems. Specific DCM tools are also available which work easily with Snowflake.

Overcoming the unique challenges of database changes

Making changes to databases presents its own unique set of challenges, especially for traditional on-premises databases, which have to deal with the problems of downtime for hardware upgrades and with explicitly having to back up databases beforehand so that they will be available for restoration, if needed. In the event a rollback is needed, an operations freeze with no work happening during the restoration process is required. In addition, there is the problem of drift whereby developers could be working on a different version of the database than the version in production, and there is also the problem of load balancing.

With Snowflake, these top challenges no longer exist for users. Hardware fixes and upgrades are handled by the Snowflake team, with no impact on users. For rollback and version control, Snowflake has Time Travel and fail-safe, which eliminate the need to make traditional data backups. Time Travel and fail-safe are part of Snowflake's continuous data protection lifecycle. To alleviate the problem of drift, Snowflake users can utilize zero-copy cloning, described in the previous section, to simplify the loading and seeding of databases in different environments.

Given all this, and because most everything in Snowflake can be automated via SQL, the DCM process could be handled quite simply in Snowflake by creating a lightweight DevOps framework for small deployments. For a more heavyweight Snowflake DevOps framework, however, there are DCM tools available.

DCM tools for a heavyweight Snowflake DevOps framework

DCM refers to a set of processes and tools used to manage objects within a database. The most important tool to consider for Snowflake DCM is a source control repository and pipeline tool. Examples of hosted options for DCM include AWS CodeCommit and CodePipeline, Azure DevOps, GitHub Actions, and Bitbucket.

In addition to a source control repository and pipeline tool, you'll need database migration tools to deploy the changes to the database. Several DCM tools can be used with Snowflake. Some are primarily SaaS tools or data transformation tools, and many of them are community developed. Examples of tools that can be used as a database migration tool include Sqitch, Flyway, snowchange, schemachange, SqlDBM, Jenkins, and dbt.

Lastly, a testing framework such as JUnit, pytest, or DbFit is needed.

Using DCM tools that automate the data integration and delivery pipeline can provide all the DevOps benefits previously mentioned and enable you to achieve continuous delivery and deployment.

How Zero-Copy Cloning Can Be Used to Support Dev/Test Environments

Zero-copy cloning was introduced in Chapter 2. Because zero-copy cloning is a metadata-only operation, there is no additional storage charge for Snowflake cloned objects unless and until changes are made.

Zero-copy clones are frequently used to support working in-development and test environments as part of the development lifecycle. I am going to demonstrate concepts in this section that show how zero-copy cloning can be used in Snowflake agile development. Changes to a Snowflake production environment can take the form of new development. Creating a new table is one example. Changes could also be in the form of enhancements to an existing object in production. We'll look in depth at how zero-copy cloning can be used for new development.

In our example, we'll use some role-based access control (RBAC) best practices that we learned about in Chapter 5. However, in a real-world setting, you'd likely need to have different roles and privileges to set up to properly manage the CI/CD process. The purpose in this chapter, as it relates to role-based access, is to give you a little more hands-on practice.

In our example, let's assume that Table A already exists in our production environment, and we want to add an additional table in production. What we'll do first is create a clone of the production database in which we can develop. That is where we'll create the new table. We'll also want to create a clone of the development database in which we can perform our testing, or quality assurance activities. Figure 8-11 illustrates our first steps.

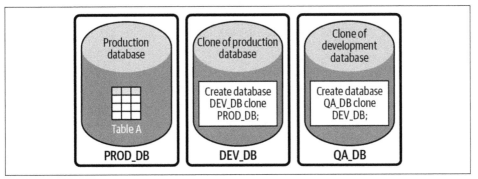

Figure 8-11. Agile development using zero-copy cloning

Let's first create some specific roles for our production, development, and QA environments. As a best practice, we'll assign the new custom roles back to the SYSADMIN role:

```
USE ROLE SECURITYADMIN;
CREATE OR REPLACE ROLE PROD_ADMIN;
CREATE OR REPLACE ROLE DEV_ADMIN;
CREATE OR REPLACE ROLE QA_ADMIN;
GRANT ROLE PROD_ADMIN TO ROLE SYSADMIN;
GRANT ROLE DEV_ADMIN TO ROLE SYSADMIN;
GRANT ROLE QA_ADMIN TO ROLE SYSADMIN;
```

Next, we'll want to give some privileges to the new roles so that they can create databases on the account:

```
USE ROLE SYSADMIN;
GRANT CREATE DATABASE ON ACCOUNT TO ROLE PROD_ADMIN;
GRANT CREATE DATABASE ON ACCOUNT TO ROLE DEV_ADMIN;
GRANT CREATE DATABASE ON ACCOUNT TO ROLE QA_ADMIN;
```

Let's assume that we want to assign a separate virtual warehouse to each administrator. We can rename three of the virtual warehouses that we created earlier:

```
USE ROLE SYSADMIN;
ALTER WAREHOUSE IF EXISTS VW2_WH RENAME TO WH_PROD;
ALTER WAREHOUSE IF EXISTS VW3_WH RENAME TO WH_DEV;
ALTER WAREHOUSE IF EXISTS VW4_WH RENAME TO WH_QA;
SHOW WAREHOUSES;
```

You can see from the SHOW command that the virtual warehouses have now been renamed. Let's grant usage for these virtual warehouses to each associated role:

```
USE ROLE ACCOUNTADMIN;
USE WAREHOUSE COMPUTE_WH;
GRANT USAGE ON WAREHOUSE WH_PROD TO ROLE PROD_ADMIN;
GRANT USAGE ON WAREHOUSE WH_DEV TO ROLE DEV_ADMIN;
GRANT USAGE ON WAREHOUSE WH_QA TO ROLE QA_ADMIN;
```

We need to create a production environment database, schema, and table. We'll also grant usage on the database to the development administrator:

```
USE ROLE PROD_ADMIN; USE WAREHOUSE WH_PROD;
CREATE OR REPLACE DATABASE PROD_DB;
CREATE OR REPLACE SCHEMA CH8_SCHEMA;
CREATE OR REPLACE TABLE TABLE_A
    (Customer_Account int, Amount int, transaction_ts timestamp);
GRANT USAGE ON DATABASE PROD_DB TO ROLE DEV_ADMIN;
```

Now the development administrator can create a clone of the production database and grant usage of the cloned database to the QA administrator role:

```
USE ROLE DEV_ADMIN;
USE WAREHOUSE WH_DEV;
```

```
CREATE OR REPLACE DATABASE DEV_DB CLONE PROD_DB;
GRANT USAGE ON DATABASE DEV_DB TO ROLE QA_ADMIN;
```

The QA administrator now creates a clone of the development database and grants usage to the production administrator role:

```
USE ROLE QA_ADMIN;
USE WAREHOUSE WH_QA;
CREATE OR REPLACE DATABASE QA_DB CLONE DEV_DB;
GRANT USAGE ON DATABASE QA_DB TO ROLE PROD_ADMIN;
```

Now we're ready for the development work. Back in the development database, we use the DEV_ADMIN role to create a new development schema and a new table:

```
USE ROLE DEV_ADMIN; USE WAREHOUSE WH_DEV; USE DATABASE DEV_DB;
CREATE OR REPLACE SCHEMA DEVELOPMENT;
CREATE OR REPLACE TABLE TABLE_B
    (Vendor_Account int, Amount int, transaction_ts timestamp);
GRANT USAGE ON SCHEMA DEVELOPMENT TO ROLE QA_ADMIN;
GRANT ALL PRIVILEGES ON ALL TABLES IN SCHEMA DEVELOPMENT TO ROLE QA_ADMIN;
```

Once development is done, the QA team can do their testing by creating a new table in the testing environment from the newly created table in the development environment:

```
USE ROLE QA_ADMIN; USE WAREHOUSE WH_QA; USE DATABASE QA_DB;
CREATE OR REPLACE SCHEMA TEST;
CREATE OR REPLACE TABLE QA_DB.TEST.TABLE_B
    AS SELECT * FROM DEV_DB.DEVELOPMENT.TABLE_B;
GRANT USAGE ON SCHEMA TEST TO ROLE PROD_ADMIN;
GRANT ALL PRIVILEGES ON ALL TABLES IN SCHEMA TEST TO ROLE PROD_ADMIN;
```

> The new table in the QA environment could be created using either the CREATE TABLE AS SELECT (also known as CTAS) command, or the CREATE TABLE LIKE command. The difference between the two is that the latter creates an empty copy of the existing table whereas the former creates a populated table:

When the QA team has completed their testing, the production administrator can then copy the table into production:

```
USE ROLE PROD_ADMIN;
USE WAREHOUSE WH_PROD;
USE DATABASE PROD_DB;
USE SCHEMA CH8_SCHEMA;
CREATE OR REPLACE TABLE TABLE_B AS SELECT * FROM QA_DB.TEST.TABLE_B;
```

If you'd like to get a complete idea of what was created, you can use the SYSADMIN or the ACCOUNTADMIN role. With that role, you can see what was created in the development, production, and testing environments (as shown in Figure 8-12).

Figure 8-12. Results of creating the databases, schemas, and tables in this section

For development that involves enhancing an existing object, you'll most likely want to use a combination of zero-copy cloning and Time Travel. You can clone the production database as it was a certain number of days prior, make the enhancements to the tables using scripts, and then rerun the data loads for the prior number of days. When you compare the results, the only difference between the two should be the enhancements.

If you'd like to see how much compute you used for the exercises in this example, you can rerun the code we saw earlier in the chapter which summarized the cost of each virtual warehouse for the past 30 days.

Code Cleanup

We can clean up our Snowflake environment in just a few quick steps. We can drop our databases and the new custom roles we created:

```
USE ROLE ACCOUNTADMIN;
DROP DATABASE DEV_DB; DROP DATABASE PROD_DB; DROP DATABASE QA_DB;
DROP ROLE PROD_ADMIN; DROP ROLE DEV_ADMIN; DROP ROLE QA_ADMIN;
```

Let's drop our resource monitors next:

```
DROP RESOURCE MONITOR MONITOR1_RM; DROP RESOURCE MONITOR MONITOR2_RM;
DROP RESOURCE MONITOR MONITOR3_RM; DROP RESOURCE MONITOR MONITOR4_RM;
DROP RESOURCE MONITOR MONITOR5_RM;
```

And finally, let's drop our virtual warehouses. Note that we will drop the virtual warehouses we created but will not attempt to drop the COMPUTE_WH warehouse:

```
DROP WAREHOUSE WH_PROD; DROP WAREHOUSE WH_DEV; DROP WAREHOUSE WH_QA;
DROP WAREHOUSE VW5_WH; DROP WAREHOUSE VW6_WH;
```

Summary

Throughout this chapter, we focused on Snowflake costs and how to manage them. Managing costs can be achieved by understanding Snowflake's usage-based pricing, by using Snowflake resource monitors and object tagging for cost centers, by querying the ACCOUNT_USAGE view, and by using BI partner dashboards. Usage-based pricing is shifting how teams budget and plan. With on prem, they couldn't scale past their original plan without another planning cycle. On Snowflake, there is a lot more elasticity and, thus, it is simple to scale without the friction of adding more hardware.

We've also considered the cost of making changes in a Snowflake environment. Managing costs is important. Just as important as managing costs is having a solution that works well. Effective and efficient Snowflake performance is critical for success. In the next chapter, we'll learn about Snowflake's unique micro-partitions, how to take advantage of clustering, and how to improve query performance.

Knowledge Check

The following questions are based on the information contained in this chapter:

1. What are the three major categories of a Snowflake monthly bill?

2. The region selected is an important factor in determining storage costs. Other than storage cost considerations, what other things are important to think about when selecting a region?

3. The price of on-demand Snowflake credits is dependent on what three things?

4. What are the three properties of a Snowflake resource monitor? Which property is required to be included in the SQL statement in order to create a resource monitor?

5. Is there a limit to the number of Snowflake resource monitors that can be created?

6. Is there a limit to the number of Snowflake resource monitor actions?

7. What are some of the unique challenges associated with database changes?

8. What are some unique characteristics of Snowflake's zero-copy cloning?

9. What is the difference between the CREATE TABLE AS SELECT (also known as CTAS) command and the CREATE TABLE LIKE command?

10. What happens if you assign a virtual warehouse resource monitor to a virtual warehouse that is already assigned to a resource monitor?

Answers to these questions are available in Appendix A.

Analyzing and Improving Snowflake Query Performance

Snowflake was built for the cloud from the ground. Further, it was built to abstract away much of the complexity users typically face when managing their data in the cloud. Features such as micro-partitions, a search optimization service, and materialized views are examples of unique ways Snowflake works in the background to improve performance. In this chapter, we'll learn about these unique features.

Snowflake also makes it possible to easily analyze query performance through a variety of different methods. We'll learn about some of the more common approaches to analyzing Snowflake query performance, such as query history profiling, the hash function, and the Query Profile tool.

Prep Work

Create a new worksheet titled *Chapter9 Improving Queries*. Refer to "Navigating Snowsight Worksheets" on page 8 if you need help creating a new folder and worksheet. To set the worksheet context, make sure you are using the SYSADMIN role and the COMPUTE_WH virtual warehouse. We'll be using the SNOWFLAKE sample database; therefore, no additional preparation work or cleanup is needed in this chapter.

Analyzing Query Performance

Query performance analysis helps identify poorly performing queries that may be consuming excess credits. There are many different ways to analyze Snowflake query performance. In this section, we'll look at three of them: QUERY_HISTORY profiling, the HASH() function, and using the web UI's history.

QUERY_HISTORY Profiling

We first learned about the INFORMATION_SCHEMA in Chapter 3. As a reminder, the SNOWFLAKE INFORMATION_SCHEMA, often referred to as the data dictionary for table data, is automatically created for each Snowflake database. The QUERY_HISTORY table function used on the INFORMATION_SCHEMA provides very useful information about the queries executed against a particular database.

You can execute the following query to obtain details about all queries run by the current user in the past day, with the records returned in descending order of the total elapsed time:

```
USE ROLE ACCOUNTADMIN;
USE DATABASE <database name>;
SELECT *
FROM TABLE(INFORMATION_SCHEMA.QUERY_HISTORY(
            dateadd('days', -1, current_timestamp()),
            current_timestamp()))
ORDER BY TOTAL_ELAPSED_TIME DESC;
```

The results of this query give you what you need in order to discover long-running queries that are run frequently. In this way, you can analyze those queries first for possible performance improvement to make the most difference for your users.

It is possible to narrow the focus of the query history by selecting a particular user, session, or virtual warehouse you wish to know more about. Those functions are as follows:

- QUERY_HISTORY_BY_USER
- QUERY_HISTORY_BY_SESSION
- QUERY_HISTORY_BY_WAREHOUSE

HASH() Function

Snowflake's hash function is a utility function that returns information, such as descriptions of queries. It is not a cryptographic hash function.

The following query was written to return the queries executed for a particular database, in order of frequency and average compilation time. In addition to average compilation time, the average execution time is also included to compare the two times:

```
USE ROLE ACCOUNTADMIN;
USE DATABASE <database name>;
SELECT HASH(query_text), QUERY_TEXT, COUNT(*),
    AVG(compilation_time), AVG(execution_time)
FROM TABLE(INFORMATION_SCHEMA.QUERY_HISTORY(dateadd('days', -1,
    current_timestamp()),current_timestamp() ) )
```

```
GROUP BY HASH(query_text), QUERY_TEXT
ORDER BY COUNT(*) DESC, AVG(compilation_time) DESC ;
```

Web UI History

We can easily review individual queries using the Snowflake web interface. The graphical representation Snowflake provides allows us to view the main components of the query's processing plan and the statistics for each component. We can also see the overall statistics of the query.

To review queries using the Snowflake web interface, click Activity in the Main menu, followed by Query History, as shown in Figure 9-1.

Figure 9-1. The Snowflake menu

You should see a list of all the queries that were executed, with the most recent query listed at the top (as shown in Figure 9-2).

Query History							
SQL TEXT	QUERY ID	STATUS	USER	WAREHOUSE	DURATION	STARTED	
with active_contracts as (select contract..	01a4d28b-0000-07fd-00..	Success	JKAVILA	COMPUTE_WH	1.0s	8/8/2022, 9:19 PM	
with active_contracts as (select contract..	01a4d28a-0000-07f7-00..	Success	JKAVILA	COMPUTE_WH	1.6s	8/8/2022, 9:18 PM	
with active_contracts as (select contract..	01a4d289-0000-07f7-00..	Success	JKAVILA	COMPUTE_WH	1.7s	8/8/2022, 9:17 PM	
with active_contracts as (select contract..	01a4d288-0000-07f7-00..	Success	JKAVILA	COMPUTE_WH	2.6s	8/8/2022, 9:18 PM	
CREATE OR REPLACE TABLE TABLE_B AS SELECT ..	01a4d285-0000-07f7-00..	Success	JKAVILA	WH_PROD	423ms	8/8/2022, 9:13 PM	

Figure 9-2. A history of all the queries, in descending order

Using Snowflake's Query Profile tool

Snowflake's Query Profile tool provides the execution details of a query to assist you in spotting common mistakes in SQL query expressions. You can use Query Profile to learn more about the performance or behavior of the query, which will help you locate potential performance bottlenecks and identify opportunities for improvement.

From the list of queries shown in Figure 9-2, we can click a specific query from the SQL text or from the Query ID column to view a graphical representation of the query details. The default tab is Query Details, so be sure to click the Query Profile tab (as shown in Figure 9-3).

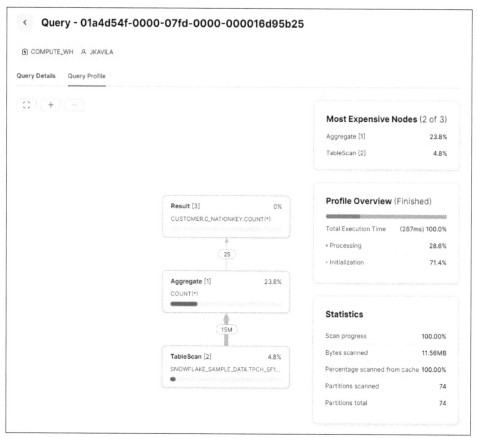

Figure 9-3. Query Profile details

One of the things you'll notice is that statements such as USE and DESCRIBE do not have a query profile (as shown in Figure 9-4).

Figure 9-4. USE and DESCRIBE statements have no Query Profile

Query Profile provides a wealth of information about an individual query. For complete details on how to analyze queries using Query Profile, visit the Snowflake online documentation (*https://oreil.ly/SVKKR*).

Understanding Snowflake Micro-Partitions and Data Clustering

Data stored in Snowflake tables is divided into micro-partitions dynamically. There is no need to manually define or maintain partitions, as is the case in traditional partitioning. Snowflake automatically takes care of that for you. At the time that the data is loaded into a Snowflake table, the metadata about each micro-partition is stored so that it can be leveraged to avoid unnecessary scanning of micro-partitions when querying the data.

To better understand and appreciate how innovative Snowflake micro-partitions are, we'll first take a deep dive into the topic of partitions so that we can better understand how traditional partitioning works. Once we compare that to Snowflake partitions, the benefits of Snowflake micro-partitions will become much more apparent.

Partitions Explained

Partitioning a relational database will result in large tables divided into many smaller parts, or partitions. Databases are most often partitioned to improve scalability, assist in backup and recovery, improve security, and improve query performance. For a partitioned database, the query only has to scan relevant partitions, not all the data. This reduces the response time needed to read and load data for SQL operations.

There are two traditional methods by which relational databases can be partitioned: horizontal and vertical. We'll demonstrate both methods with some examples. Let's start with a horizontal partitioning example. We'll begin with an original table consisting of eight columns and eight rows representing customers' purchases from our United States website, retail store, and direct channel (as shown in Figure 9-5).

CID	Fname	Lname	Reward	Zip	Channel	Amount	Date
1	Arnold	Johnson	Gold	94015	Web	$2,500	8/7/2022
2	Janice	Switzer	Bronze	76012	Retail	$450	8/7/2022
3	Amy	Majors	Gold	76015	Web	$1,220	8/7/2022
6	Marty	Anders	Silver	45032	Direct	$3,315	8/7/2022
3	Amy	Majors	Gold	76012	Web	$795	8/7/2022
7	Harold	Webb	Silver	94011	Web	$490	8/8/2022
5	Nathan	Harris	Silver	76010	Retail	$1,115	8/8/2022
4	Cathy	Amos	Silver	45615	Web	$635	8/8/2022

Figure 9-5. The original customer transaction table

Horizontal partitioning, also known as sharding, stores table rows in different database clusters. Each partition has the same schema and columns but contains different rows of data (as shown in Figure 9-6). The most important benefit of sharding is that it allows an otherwise too-large database the ability to scale out horizontally.

Horizontal partition #1 (Last name A–J)

CID	Fname	Lname	Reward	Zip	Channel	Amount	Date
1	Arnold	Johnson	Gold	94015	Web	$2,500	8/7/2022
6	Marty	Anders	Silver	45032	Direct	$3,315	8/7/2022
5	Nathan	Harris	Silver	76010	Retail	$1,115	8/8/2022
4	Cathy	Amos	Silver	45615	Web	$635	8/8/2022

Horizontal partition #2 (Last name K–Z)

CID	Fname	Lname	Reward	Zip	Channel	Amount	Date
2	Janice	Switzer	Bronze	76012	Retail	$450	8/7/2022
3	Amy	Majors	Gold	76015	Web	$1,220	8/7/2022
3	Amy	Majors	Gold	76012	Web	$795	8/7/2022
7	Harold	Webb	Silver	94011	Web	$490	8/8/2022

Figure 9-6. Horizontal partitions in the customer transaction table

It is important to note that Snowflake users don't need to worry about how to solve the problem of scaling out. Snowflake is column based and horizontally partitioned, and the Snowflake multicluster virtual warehouse feature means that sharding isn't needed to scale out a database. Chapter 2 describes the Snowflake multicluster virtual warehouse feature in more detail. In the next section, I'll explain what column based and horizontally partitioned mean in regard to Snowflake.

The second type of partitioning is vertical partitioning, also known as column-based partitioning. Vertical partitioning is undertaken by creating tables with fewer columns and storing the remaining columns in additional tables; a practice commonly known as row splitting.

Vertical partitioning is a physical optimization technique, but it can be combined with a conceptual optimization technique known as normalization. Normalization removes redundant columns from a table and puts them into another table while linking them with a foreign key relationship. In our examples, the foreign keys will be the customer ID (CID) and product ID (PID) fields.

Continuing with the same example, we'll create two vertical partitions: one for customer data and one for transaction data (as shown in Figure 9-7).

Vertical partition #1 (customer information)						Vertical partition #2 (transaction information)			
CID	Fname	Lname	Reward	Zip		CID	Channel	Amount	Date
1	Arnold	Johnson	Gold	94015		1	Web	$2,500	8/7/2022
2	Janice	Switzer	Bronze	76012		2	Retail	$450	8/7/2022
3	Amy	Majors	Gold	76015		3	Web	$1,220	8/7/2022
6	Marty	Anders	Silver	45032		6	Direct	$3,315	8/7/2022
7	Harold	Webb	Silver	94011		3	Web	$795	8/7/2022
5	Nathan	Harris	Silver	76010		7	Web	$490	8/8/2022
4	Cathy	Amos	Silver	45615		5	Retail	$1,115	8/8/2022
						4	Web	$635	8/8/2022

Figure 9-7. Vertical partitions in the customer transaction table

There are many benefits of data normalization, including being able to update data more easily and eliminate duplicates. Data normalization is also an important part of building machine learning models as it can be done to change the distribution shape of the data when needed. While normalizing data does incur costs, one of the benefits of using Snowflake is that you can store large amounts of data and then only normalize the data as you need it.

Probably the most common vertical partitioning method is to split static data from dynamic data. The intent is to reduce performance costs based on how frequently the data is accessed and how often the table changes. A related example using a product inventory table (as shown in Figure 9-8) will be used for demonstration purposes.

PID	Product	Price	Location	Qty
1001	Laptop	$2,500	L2	296
1002	Printer	$450	R3	1468
1010	Desk	$1,220	A3	32
1007	Desktop	$3,315	L2	1047
1013	Monitor	$795	A4	997
1012	Scanner	$490	R3	354

Figure 9-8. The original product inventory table

One way the data can be modeled is to store the static or slowly changing information in one table and the dynamic or frequently changing information in a different table (as shown in Figure 9-9). Modeling data in this way is especially beneficial when using Snowflake because you'll be able to take advantage of Snowflake features, such as caching, to help improve performance and lower costs.

Vertical partition #1 (static product information)

PID	Product	Price
1001	Laptop	$2,500
1002	Printer	$450
1010	Desk	$1,220
1007	Desktop	$3,315
1013	Monitor	$795
1012	Scanner	$490

Vertical partition #2 (dynamic product information)

PID	Location	Qty
1001	L2	296
1002	R3	1,468
1010	A3	32
1007	L2	1,047
1013	A4	997
1012	R3	354

Figure 9-9. Vertical partitions in the product inventory table

To summarize, horizontal partitioning decomposes tables row-wise. Horizontal partitions include all fields and hold a specific subset of the data. In contrast, vertical partitioning decomposes tables column-wise. Vertical partitions hold all the relevant data relating to a subset of fields. Vertical partitions that include a foreign key, linking them to another partition, are taking advantage of normalization.

Snowflake Micro-Partitions Explained

All Snowflake data is stored in database tables. Logically, tables are structured as collections of rows and columns. This logical structure of rows and columns is mapped to the Snowflake physical table structures known as micro-partitions. Snowflake's unique micro-partitioning approach is transparent to users, unlike traditional data warehouse partitioning approaches in which the user has to independently manipulate partitions by using Data Definition Language (DDL) commands.

 Snowflake users cannot partition their own tables. Instead, all Snowflake tables are automatically divided into micro-partitions using the ordering of the data as it is inserted or loaded.

A Snowflake micro-partition is a small physical cloud storage block that stores between 50 MB and 500 MB of uncompressed data. However, the actual storage block size is even smaller because Snowflake data is always stored compressed, and Snowflake automatically determines the most efficient compression algorithm for columns in each micro-partition. As a result, a Snowflake micro-partition holds about 16 MB of compressed data.

There are many benefits of having a small micro-partition size in which each block represents a set of rows from the table. Snowflake's micro-partitions allow for efficient scanning of columns, effective finer-grain query pruning of large tables, and prevention of skews. In addition, Snowflake stores the metadata about all the rows stored in micro-partitions. Among other things, this metadata includes the range of values and the number of distinct values for each column.

Snowflake is well designed for bulk inserts and updates. As previously stated, all data in Snowflake is stored in tables and is transparently partitioned as data is inserted or loaded. Data Manipulation Language (DML) operation changes intended for these micro-partition blocks cannot result in updates within each micro-partition file. Instead, DML operations will add a new partition block and/or remove an existing partition block. These micro-partition additions and deletions are tracked in the Snowflake metadata.

Now let's turn to an example. The customer and transaction tables from the previous section will be used to demonstrate how micro-partitions work. In our example, we'll assume the micro-partitions each hold six records. Note that this is an arbitrary number I selected to make our example easy to demonstrate. In practice, Snowflake automatically determines the number of records per micro-partition.

Assuming six records per micro-partition, Figure 9-10 demonstrates how the data from our transaction table would be physically stored. You can see that the eight records initially loaded ended up in two micro-partitions, with the second micro-partition having only two records. You'll also notice that the data is physically grouped together by column in the micro-partitions.

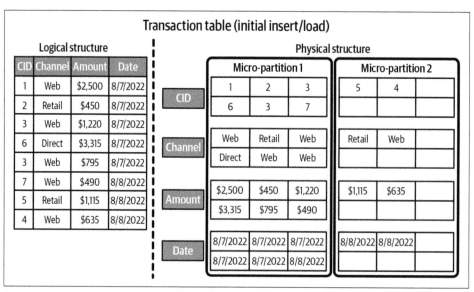

Figure 9-10. Logical versus Snowflake physical structures in the transaction table from Figure 9-7

If three new records are added the following day, they will not be added to the second micro-partition; instead, a third micro-partition will be created (as shown in Figure 9-11).

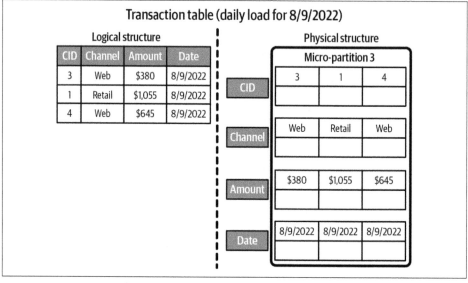

Figure 9-11. New records create an additional Snowflake micro-partition

Now let's take a look at the customer table and how the initial data load would be stored. You'll notice that while we have eight transactions, we have seven customers, so seven customer records will be loaded. The seven customers will be stored in two micro-partitions (as shown in Figure 9-12).

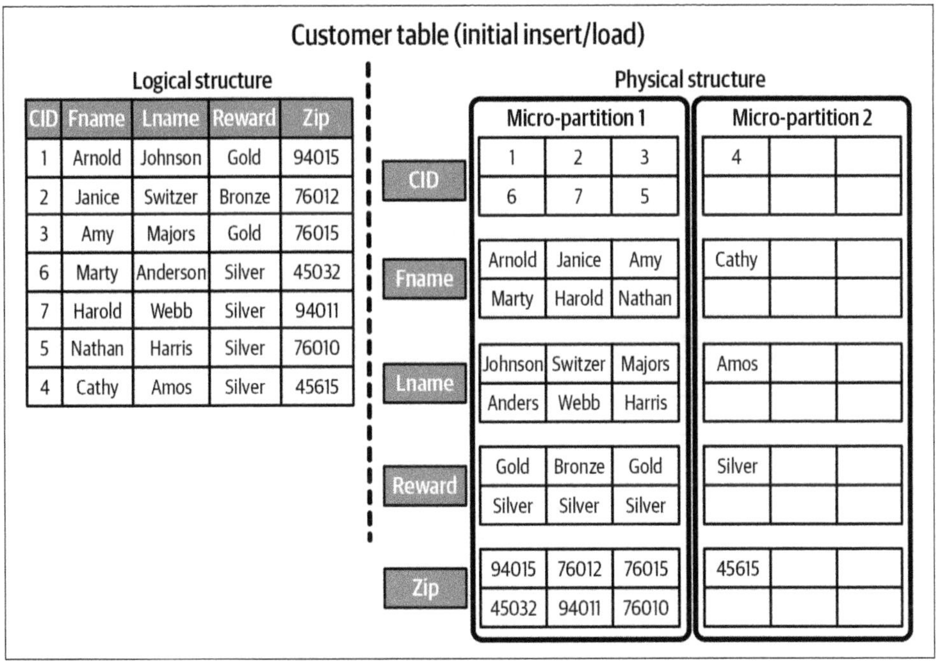

Customer table (initial insert/load)

Logical structure

CID	Fname	Lname	Reward	Zip
1	Arnold	Johnson	Gold	94015
2	Janice	Switzer	Bronze	76012
3	Amy	Majors	Gold	76015
6	Marty	Anderson	Silver	45032
7	Harold	Webb	Silver	94011
5	Nathan	Harris	Silver	76010
4	Cathy	Amos	Silver	45615

Physical structure

Micro-partition 1

CID:
| 1 | 2 | 3 |
| 6 | 7 | 5 |

Fname:
| Arnold | Janice | Amy |
| Marty | Harold | Nathan |

Lname:
| Johnson | Switzer | Majors |
| Anders | Webb | Harris |

Reward:
| Gold | Bronze | Gold |
| Silver | Silver | Silver |

Zip:
| 94015 | 76012 | 76015 |
| 45032 | 94011 | 76010 |

Micro-partition 2

CID:
| 4 | | |

Fname:
| Cathy | | |

Lname:
| Amos | | |

Reward:
| Silver | | |

Zip:
| 45615 | | |

Figure 9-12. Logical versus Snowflake physical structures of the customer table from Figure 9-7

For our customer table, we'd expect there to be new additions but probably no deletions. We'd also expect there could be updates to the table because we're storing the customer's zip code, which would need to be updated if the customer moved.

What happens to the stored data when there is an update to the record?

As depicted in Figure 9-13, Snowflake deletes the existing partition file and replaces it with a new file when an update or delete operation is performed.

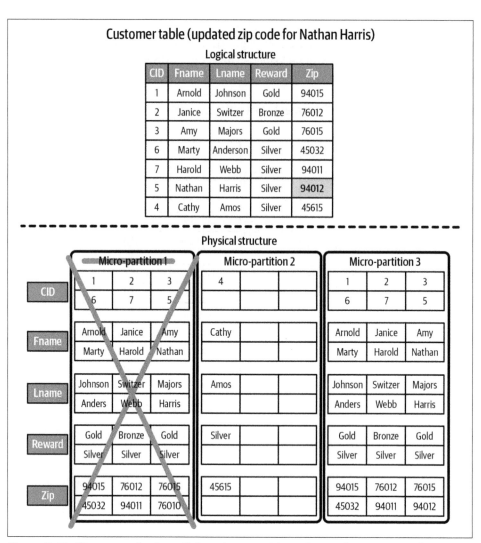

Customer table (updated zip code for Nathan Harris)

Logical structure

CID	Fname	Lname	Reward	Zip
1	Arnold	Johnson	Gold	94015
2	Janice	Switzer	Bronze	76012
3	Amy	Majors	Gold	76015
6	Marty	Anderson	Silver	45032
7	Harold	Webb	Silver	94011
5	Nathan	Harris	Silver	94012
4	Cathy	Amos	Silver	45615

Physical structure

	Micro-partition 1			Micro-partition 2			Micro-partition 3		
CID	1	2	3	4			1	2	3
	6	7	5				6	7	5
Fname	Arnold	Janice	Amy	Cathy			Arnold	Janice	Amy
	Marty	Harold	Nathan				Marty	Harold	Nathan
Lname	Johnson	Switzer	Majors	Amos			Johnson	Switzer	Majors
	Anders	Webb	Harris				Anders	Webb	Harris
Reward	Gold	Bronze	Gold	Silver			Gold	Bronze	Gold
	Silver	Silver	Silver				Silver	Silver	Silver
Zip	94015	76012	76015	45615			94015	76012	76015
	45032	94011	76010				45032	94011	94012

Figure 9-13. Changes to the Snowflake micro-partition when updating a record

Indeed, micro-partitions are inherently small in size and are stored as columnarized sets of rows. Storing the data in this way, where columns are stored independently within the micro-partitions, allows for efficient column scanning and filtering. This is especially beneficial for very large tables that could have many millions of micro-partitions. Using micro-partitions allows for granular pruning on large tables. Effective and efficient pruning is important because scanning entire tables is not optimal for most queries.

Snowflake's unique micro-partitions and the use of metadata about the rows in each micro-partition, including the range and distinct values for each column, lays the foundation for optimized queries and highly efficient query processing. Additionally, the data in Snowflake tables is stored in its natural ingestion order, which works well for data such as transaction data, which is rarely updated or deleted and is often queried by date. For other situations, natural ingestion may not be the optimal physical order, especially if there are frequent updates to the table's data. For those use cases, we can use clustering.

Snowflake Data Clustering Explained

In the previous section, we learned how Snowflake micro-partitions are created. When data is loaded into Snowflake, Snowflake creates micro-partitions automatically based on the order in which the data is loaded. This works well, for the most part, as Snowflake generally produces well-clustered data in tables using the micro-partitioning approach. However, sometimes Snowflake tables are not optimally clustered, especially if DML actions occur frequently on very large tables containing multiple terabytes of data. When this happens, we should consider defining our own clustering key(s).

A clustering key is a subset of columns in a table or expressions on a table. The purpose of creating a clustering key is to co-locate data in the same micro-partitions in the table.

 Clustering keys are not meant to be created for all tables. Before deciding whether to cluster a table, it is recommended that you test a representative set of queries on the table to establish a query performance baseline. The query performance of the table, along with the size of the table, should determine whether to define a clustering key. In general, it may be time to create a clustering key when queries run slower than expected and/or have noticeably degraded over time. A large clustering depth is another indication that the table needs to be clustered, but the clustering depth is not a precise measure. The best indicator of a well-clustered table is its query performance.

Clustering Width and Depth

Snowflake can determine how well clustered a table is by considering how many partitions overlap. Micro-partitions can overlap with one another in a partition; the number of overlaps is known as the clustering width. Micro-partitions can overlap at a specific point in the partition; the number of overlaps at that specific point determines the clustering depth. Let's take a look at a few examples.

In the first example, we have six partitions in the micro-partition, all of which are overlapping on the one specific value and with one another (as shown in Figure 9-14). This is an example of a least well-clustered micro-partitioned column.

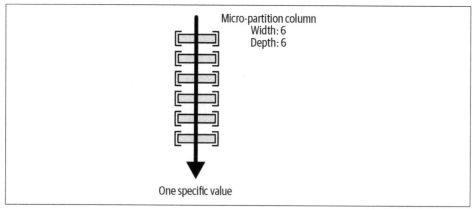

Figure 9-14. A least well-clustered micro-partitioned column

The next example is of a perfectly clustered micro-partition. One partition overlaps the specific value, and no partitions overlap one another (as shown in Figure 9-15).

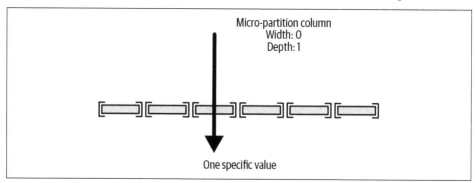

Figure 9-15. A perfectly clustered micro-partitioned column

In the third example, three partitions overlap the specific value and four partitions overlap one another (as shown in Figure 9-16).

 The smaller the depth, the better the table is clustered. A table with no micro-partitions has a clustering depth of zero, which indicates that the table has not yet been populated with data.

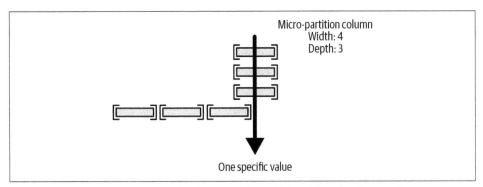

Figure 9-16. A micro-partitioned column with a width of 4 and a depth of 3

Changing the specific value for which we are querying could change the clustering depth, whereas the clustering width would not change (as shown in Figure 9-17).

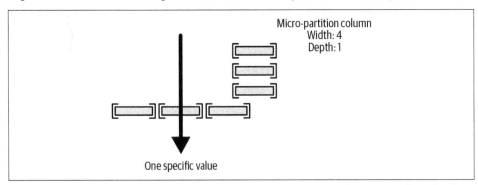

Figure 9-17. The depth of a micro-partitioned column changes when a specific value has changed

If we were to look at all three micro-partitions, assuming they were the only three micro-partitions in the table, we'd be able to see the full range of values within the table (as shown in Figure 9-18).

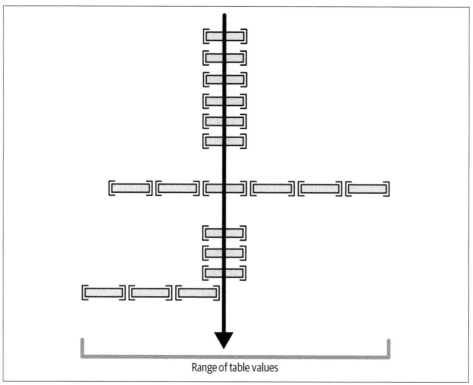

Range of table values

Figure 9-18. The micro-partitions' total width equates to the range of values in the table

We can see from the examples that the width of the table gives us the range of values. If the range of table values spanned 40 values, for example, we could get the average clustering depth by calculating the average of all 40 depths.

On tables within Snowflake, you are able to see the clustering depth, among other details, by using the SYSTEM$CLUSTERING_INFORMATION function. If a table has been clustered, you don't need to specify the column. If a table has not been clustered, you'll need to include the column(s) in your statement. Here is an example of a column whose details you can view. Navigate back to the worksheet and execute the following statements:

```
USE ROLE ACCOUNTADMIN;
USE DATABASE SNOWFLAKE_SAMPLE_DATA;
USE SCHEMA TPCH_SF100;
SELECT SYSTEM$CLUSTERING_INFORMATION( 'CUSTOMER' , '(C_NATIONKEY )' );
```

From our examples in this section, we see that loading data into a Snowflake table creates micro-partitions based on the order in which the records are loaded. When we use SQL to query the data, the WHERE clause is used to prune the search space of the partitions that need to be scanned. If the way the data is currently loaded into a table is not efficient for searching, we can create a clustering key that allows us to reorder the records so that the data is co-located with the same micro-partition. Doing so often results in significant performance improvements, especially if the queries make use of the clustering key as a filter in the WHERE clause.

Choosing a Clustering Key

When deciding whether or not to cluster a table, it is important to remember that the main goal in clustering a table is to help the query optimizer achieve better pruning efficiency. As such, it is recommended that, by default, clustering keys be defined on tables larger than 1 TB.

A clustering key can include one or more columns or expressions from a table. When deciding which column(s) to use for the clustering key, the data characteristics of the table should be evaluated first. It's important to remember that the degree to which pruning efficiency can be achieved depends, in part, on the particular queries in users' workloads.

Table data characteristics and workload considerations

When deciding on a clustering key, a good rule of thumb is to select a key that has enough distinct values for effective pruning, yet not so many values that Snowflake is unable to effectively group rows in the same micro-partitions. The number of distinct values in a table is its *cardinality*. A table's cardinality is part of the formula used to calculate *selectivity*; the measure of how much variety there is in the values of the table column. Selectivity is a value between 0 and 1. A value closer to 0 indicates less variety in a column's values. A value of 1 indicates that every value in the table column is unique.

We'll use a Snowflake sample data table to demonstrate cardinality and selectivity. Let's first run a few queries to get the distinct count of NATIONKEY values as well as the total count of records:

```
USE ROLE ACCOUNTADMIN;
USE DATABASE SNOWFLAKE_SAMPLE_DATA;
USE SCHEMA TPCH_SF100;
SELECT COUNT(DISTINCT C_NATIONKEY) FROM CUSTOMER;
SELECT COUNT(C_NATIONKEY) FROM CUSTOMER;
```

The results indicate that there are 25 distinct values for the C_NATIONKEY column in the CUSTOMER table, which has 15 million records. The cardinality is 25. To calculate the selectivity, we can use the following statement, which gives us a value of 0.000002; a very low selectivity value:

```
USE ROLE ACCOUNTADMIN;
USE DATABASE SNOWFLAKE_SAMPLE_DATA;
USE SCHEMA TPCH_SF100;
SELECT COUNT(DISTINCT C_NATIONKEY) / Count(C_NATIONKEY) FROM CUSTOMER;
```

If we consider that this column could be a good candidate for a clustering key, we'd want to take a closer look at the data distribution before deciding:

```
SELECT C_NATIONKEY, count(*) FROM CUSTOMER group by C_NATIONKEY;
```

The results of the query, shown in Figure 9-19, indicate that the records are pretty evenly distributed between the NATIONKEYs.

...	C_NATIONKEY	COUNT(*)
1	10	600,195
2	23	599,045
3	1	600,231
4	5	600,226
5	19	600,502
6	7	599,804
7	14	599,406
8	9	601,133
9	4	601,008
10	15	599,480
11	20	600,300
12	13	600,006
13	16	599,835
14	0	599,274
15	21	600,098
16	17	600,098
17	8	599,202
18	12	599,713
19	22	598,913
20	6	600,335
21	2	600,381
22	3	601,469
23	11	600,007
24	18	599,613
25	24	599,726

Figure 9-19. Distribution of the C_NATIONKEY column in the CUSTOMER table sample data

For comparison, let's look at the selectivity value of the C_NAME column in the customer table:

```
USE ROLE ACCOUNTADMIN;
USE DATABASE SNOWFLAKE_SAMPLE_DATA;
USE SCHEMA TPCH_SF100;
SELECT COUNT(DISTINCT C_NAME) / Count(C_NAME) FROM CUSTOMER;
```

The result is exactly 1, which means that every one of the 15 million records has a unique name.

A column with very high cardinality, such as one containing customer name or nanosecond timestamp values, has such a high selectivity value that it would probably yield poor pruning results. At the other extreme, a field with very low cardinality, such as gender or a binary column with Yes/No values, would likely not be a good candidate to use as a clustering key.

 A column with very high cardinality can be used as a clustering key more effectively if it is defined as an expression on the column rather than on the column directly. In this way, an expression can preserve the original ordering of the column. An example would be using a timestamp column as a clustering key by casting the values to dates instead of timestamps. If the column name were TIMESTAMP_NTZ, the statement would be similar to the following:

```
CREATE OR REPLACE TABLE <table name>
    CLUSTER BY (to_date(TIMESTAMP_NTZ));
```

The effect would be to reduce the number of distinct values to the number of days instead of the number of timestamps. This would likely yield better pruning results.

Creating a Clustering Key

A clustering key can be defined at the time of table creation by adding the command CLUSTER BY (column name(s)) to the CREATE statement:

```
ALTER TABLE <table name> CLUSTER BY (column name(s));
```

A clustering key can be added or changed after table creation and can be dropped at any time.

 When creating the clustering key, it is recommended that you choose no more than three or four columns or expressions. While the number of columns is an important consideration, it is most important to focus on selecting the right columns or expressions for the clustering key and putting them in the best order.

If more than one column or expression is used to cluster a table, it is recommended that the columns most actively used in selective filters be prioritized. For tables in which date-based queries are used, it makes sense to choose the date column for the cluster key.

> If you select a string data type column in which the leading characters are the same, you can use the substr expression to truncate the common leading characters.

It could be a good idea to include columns that are frequently used in join predicates, if there is room for additional cluster keys after considering other, higher-priority columns. The balance between query workload and DML workload should be carefully considered when choosing the columns for a clustering key.

That said, as a general rule, Snowflake recommends ordering selected columns from lowest to highest cardinality assuming evenly distributed data. Doing so will allow columns with fewer distinct values to come earlier in the clustering key order. Of course, there could be exceptions to this general rule, so don't let it override what would otherwise be a better selection order.

Reclustering

Over time, data in a table might become less clustered as DML operations are performed on the table. To maintain optimal performance, it might be necessary to recluster a table periodically. No manual intervention or maintenance is needed for reclustering; Snowflake automatically reclusters tables as needed.

> Reclustering consumes credits and also results in storage costs. The amount of data and the size of the table determine the number of credits that will be consumed to perform the recluster. The additional storage costs are the result of the deleted data from reclustering that remains available for the Time Travel retention period and the subsequent fail-safe period.

Clustering is just one tool we can use to improve query performance. Another option is to create materialized views.

Performance Benefits of Materialized Views

Materialized views were first introduced in Chapter 3. Materialized views contain an up-to-date copy of a subset of data in a table. As such, materialized views can be used to improve query performance.

It's important to remember that similar to other Snowflake securable objects, materialized views are owned by a role. When materialized views are created, however, they do not automatically inherit the privileges of the base table.

 Altering the base table does not change a materialized view; instead, a new materialized view will need to be created. More specifically, adding a new column to the base table will not cause a new column to be added to the materialized view. If changes are made to an existing column in the base table, such as changing the label or dropping the column, all materialized views on that base table will be suspended.

As we saw in Chapter 3, materialized views realize security benefits. They also realize performance benefits in several different use cases:

- Snowflake materialized views can improve the performance of queries that use the same subquery results repeatedly.
- Querying materialized views is typically slower than using cached results but faster than querying tables.
- Materialized views are especially useful when a query is meant for external table data, in which data sets are stored in files in an external stage. The reason is because query performance is generally faster when querying internal tables as compared to querying external tables.

A materialized view supports clustering. Importantly, you can cluster a materialized view on different columns than the columns used to cluster the base table upon which the materialized view is defined.

 As a general rule of thumb, a materialized view is recommended over a regular view when the query results are used often and the results change infrequently, especially if the query consumes a lot of resources.

The performance benefits of creating materialized views need to be weighed against cost considerations. Unlike regular views that do not cache data, materialized views do use storage. Thus, there are storage fees associated with materialized views. Materialized views also consume credits for maintenance.

While materialized views have many benefits, there are a few constraints. A materialized view doesn't support DML operations, can query but one table alone, and cannot query another view or a user-defined function. Additionally, a materialized view does not support joins and cannot include any of the following clauses: HAVING, ORDER BY, LIMIT, or GROUP BY.

Exploring Other Query Optimization Techniques

In addition to clustering a table and creating materialized views, Snowflake's search optimization service is another way to optimize query performance. There is an important distinction between Snowflake's search optimization service and the other two query optimization techniques. Materialized views and clustered tables can speed up both range searches and equality searches; the search optimization service can only speed up equality searches.

Equality searches use equality predicates such as *<column name>* = *<constant value>* whereas range searches query ranges in time.

In addition to equality searches, the search optimization service supports predicate searches within lists using the IN conditional expression for the following data types:

- Fixed-point numbers such as INTEGER and NUMERIC
- DATE, TIME, and TIMESTAMP
- VARCHAR
- BINARY

Search Optimization Service

The goal of Snowflake's search optimization service is to improve the performance of selective point lookup queries, which are queries that return only one or a small number of distinct rows. In Snowflake, we'll most likely run more aggregation queries than queries that return only a few rows out of a large volume of rows in a table. Thus, there likely won't be many use cases in which the search optimization service will be the optimal choice. However, for the very specific use cases that could benefit from Snowflake's search optimization service, the query performance improvement could be significant.

The Snowflake search optimization service is available in Snowflake Enterprise and higher editions.

To take advantage of the search optimization service, you'll need to register the table with the service. When search optimization is added to a Snowflake table, a maintenance service runs in the background. We know that the search optimization service is meant for finding one or a small number of records based on using = in the WHERE clause but, fortunately, we don't have to decide when it makes sense to use the service. When a query is executed, the Snowflake optimizer automatically decides when to use the search optimization service.

Before deciding whether to register a table with the service, you may want to consider estimating the cost of adding search optimization to a table. You can do so by using the function SYSTEM$ESTIMATE_SEARCH_OPTIMIZATION_COSTS.

Once you've determined that it makes sense to add search optimization to a table, you can use the ALTER TABLE command to do so:

```
ALTER TABLE [IF EXISTS] <table name> ADD SEARCH OPTIMIZATION;
```

The search optimization service is a serverless feature that incurs compute costs. Because the search optimization service maintains search access paths, there are also storage costs associated with the service. The costs are directly proportional to the number of tables on which the feature is enabled, the number of distinct values in those tables, and the amount of data that changes in the tables.

Query Optimization Techniques Compared

Thus far, we've taken an in-depth look at three of the most used Snowflake query optimization techniques. Table 9-1 summarizes some of the differences between the different optimization techniques.

Table 9-1. Snowflake query optimization techniques compared

	Table clustering	Materialized view	Search optimization service
Storage costs		X	X
Compute costs	X	X	X
Serverless feature		X	X
Use case	For use on large tables; generally good for all workloads except full table reads	Most beneficial when using the same subquery repeatedly, or for external table queries	When you need to access specific row(s) based on selective point lookup queries in a large table

In most cases, it would be redundant to use Snowflake's search optimization service on a clustered table unless the query is on columns other than the primary cluster key.

Summary

In this chapter, we learned several different ways to analyze Snowflake query performance. We discovered that QUERY_HISTORY profiling lets us evaluate queries by user, session, or virtual warehouse. We created a statement using a hash function that returned a list of database queries executed in order of frequency and average compilation time. We viewed how to access the Snowflake Query Profile tool from the Snowflake web UI.

We learned about three Snowflake optimization techniques: clustering, materialized views, and the search optimization service. We also took a deep dive into partitioning to better understand why Snowflake's unique micro-partitions are so innovative and beneficial.

Until now, we've focused on gaining an understanding of all the various parts of the Snowflake architecture and functionality. We've carefully laid the foundational understanding of Snowflake and what makes it so unique. Going forward, we'll be able to leverage our deepening knowledge of Snowflake for some really interesting topics with important implications.

The next chapter is a deep dive into Snowflake's data sharing capabilities and offerings. Snowflake created its secure data sharing feature to be incredibly powerful yet simple to set up and maintain.

Code Cleanup

No code cleanup is needed.

Knowledge Check

The following questions are based on the information contained in this chapter:

1. What is the difference between the QUERY_HISTORY function and the QUERY_HISTORY_BY_USER function?

2. For what purpose would you use the HASH() function in Snowflake?

3. What are the two traditional methods by which relational databases can be partitioned?

4. What is a Snowflake micro-partition and why is it so important?

5. What happens to the physical data stored in a Snowflake table when there is an update to a record?

6. How does Snowflake determine how well clustered a table is?

7. Which Snowflake function can you use to see the clustering depth in a table?

8. What is a good rule of thumb when deciding on a clustering key?

9. What is the maximum number of columns or expressions you should choose for a clustering key?

10. Which of the following query optimization techniques is/are serverless?

- Table clustering
- Materialized view
- Search optimization service

Answers to these questions are available in Appendix A.

Configuring and Managing Secure Data Sharing

Data sharing supports collaboration among business partners, provides opportunities to inform customers, and gives you a way to obtain real-time information from vendors and suppliers. Data sharing also provides opportunities for you to monetize your data. However, there are impediments to effective and efficient data sharing when using traditional data sharing options. For one thing, traditional data sharing options, such as FTP transfers, API calls, sending and receiving CSV files, and ETL tools and processes, often require building complex infrastructure.

Similarly, traditional data sharing approaches, which involve transferring data copies and reconstructing and storing duplicate data, are expensive. There is often no single source of truth with traditional data sharing options, and fewer actionable insights result from having delayed access to stale and sometimes incomplete data. Overcoming many of these sharing challenges, however, can be accomplished by using Snowflake's Secure Data Sharing technology.

Secure Data Sharing makes it possible for data to be accessible via a live connection so that updated data is automatically available to data consumers in real time. The business logic, along with the data, can also be shared. In addition to being secure, efficient, and a great way to monetize data, Snowflake Secure Data Sharing comes with the peace of mind of knowing you can revoke access at any time.

These powerful capabilities are made possible because of Snowflake's unique architecture.

Snowflake Architecture Data Sharing Support

In Chapter 2, we learned how traditional data platform architectures have a fixed ratio of compute and storage. This is in contrast to how Snowflake's multicluster shared data architecture has storage capability that can expand and contract automatically, and has independent compute clusters that can read and write at the same time as well as instantly resize.

When you separate compute from storage and you share data access control, as Snowflake does, you can have multiple virtual warehouses working on the same data at the same time. As such, Snowflake's architecture supports the ability to have one single source of truth.

If you share data within the same cloud provider and region, there is no need to copy the data to share it. If you share data to a different region or different cloud provider, Snowflake replicates the data. However, it does so via auto-fulfillment, so you don't need to do any manual work. *Snowgrid* is the term to describe data replication for the purpose of facilitating data sharing.

The Power of Snowgrid

Snowgrid is global, seamlessly connecting Snowflake users who may be separated by region or cloud. Snowgrid achieves this through replication via auto-fulfillment. Even when sharing data across clouds and regions, the shares are *transactionally consistent*, meaning the source of truth is still maintained. Within Snowgrid are all the native cross-cloud governance controls that serve as the foundational building blocks for enabling federated governance. For more details about the specifics of database replication, refer to Chapter 7.

With the power of Secure Data Sharing and Snowgrid, Snowflake providers can create and share any number of data shares with data consumers worldwide. Each share encapsulates the necessary access control, so it is secure. Once a provider's outbound share appears as an inbound share in the data consumer's account, the consumer is then able to create a database from that share. The metadata points back to the original data source, so the data continues to exist only in the provider account.

Data Sharing Use Cases

Many industries have begun adopting features from Snowflake's data sharing capabilities. For example, financial services and insurance companies leverage Snowflake's secure storage and data sharing capabilities to efficiently ingest Internet of Things (IoT) data as well as transactional and clickstream data. Enriching that data with third-party Snowflake data, such as Equifax data, provides a more complete view of customers. Having a complete 360-degree view of customers provides organizations with the opportunity to identify high-value customers and ensure that they have a good experience at every touchpoint.

Healthcare and life sciences organizations can take advantage of Snowflake data sharing capabilities to replace decades-old methods of data sharing such as FTP, DVDs, and other physical media. In fact, payers storing petabytes of protected health information (PHI) and personally identifiable information (PII) that needs to be shared with insurance brokers, providers, and other vendors are turning to Snowflake as a solution because data sharing in the healthcare industry is mandated and regulated. Healthcare providers that own massive amounts of data often collaborate with healthcare consortiums or are affiliated with universities; thus, sharing data in real time, rather than in batches, is absolutely essential.

Trucking companies that can optimize fleet routing by using IoT data and retailers that are able to improve the supply chain by sharing data with logistics partners are two more examples of industries that incorporate Snowflake's live data sharing capabilities. Also, some enterprise companies use different Snowflake accounts for development, testing, and production purposes. Data sharing provides the ability to incorporate strong audit controls and move data in a controlled manner, rather than having to prepare flat files and reload them into a different environment.

Publishers, advertising agencies, and brands need to develop a new data sharing paradigm quickly as we are fast approaching a world without the existence of third-party cookies. As third-party cookies are being deprecated, marketers will need to find new ways to identify people online so that they can optimize marketing campaigns and continue to personalize messages.

Snowflake Support for Unified ID 2.0

Cookies, developed in 1994 as a tiny piece of software code installed on your web browser when you visit a website to facilitate revisiting and tracking, are an outdated technology. Today, internet usage occurs more frequently in mobile apps and on connected TV devices where cookies are mostly irrelevant. Cookies often contain a wealth of personal data that could potentially identify you without your consent; thus, they are subject to the European Union's General Data Protection Regulation (GDPR) and the ePrivacy Directive (EPD). The EPD will eventually be replaced by the ePrivacy Regulation (EPR). Major platforms such as Apple, Firefox, and Google have begun limiting the use of third-party cookies. In the near future, changes to internet platforms' privacy policies could even render cookies, the internet's first universal identifier, obsolete. You can visit *https://cms.law/en/deu/insight/e-privacy* if you are interested in learning more about ePrivacy.

Concerns over user privacy and more regulation have necessitated the consideration of new approaches. Unified ID 2.0, developed by The Trade Desk, is an open source, industry-governed identity solution to provide anonymization, greater transparency, and better control for users. A person's UID 2.0 is a random string of numbers and letters generated from an email address that cannot be reverse engineered to an email address or any other form of identification. Currently, Unified 2.0 is accepted by *The Washington Post*, Oracle, Nielsen, and Tubi TV, among others.

Snowflake supports Unified ID 2.0 for use with Secure Data Sharing, most notably with data clean rooms, which are discussed in more detail later in this chapter. As such, Snowflake customers can join first-party and third-party data directly in the Snowflake platform in a more privacy-conscious way. The power of the Snowflake Data Cloud and Unified ID 2.0 provides for a single view of the customer.

Snowflake Secure Data Sharing Approaches

There are four different ways to approach Snowflake's Secure Data Sharing. The simplest way is to engage in account-to-account data sharing, whereby you can share data directly with another account and have your data appear in their Snowflake account without having to move or copy it. The other account could belong to a different internal business unit, for example, or to a different organization altogether.

You can use Snowflake's Marketplace, a public Secure Data Sharing approach that connects global providers of data with consumers around the world.

You can even create your own Snowflake Private Data Exchange to collaborate with others; you'll get to control who can join the data exchange and which members can provide data, consume data, or both.

Alternatively, you can use a data clean room, a framework for sharing data between two or more parties; the data is brought together under specific guidelines so that PII is anonymized and processed, and can be stored in a way that allows compliance with privacy regulations. Figure 10-1 summarizes the four main Snowflake Secure Data Sharing approaches.

Figure 10-1. Four Snowflake Secure Data Sharing approaches

We'll now take care of some preparation work, and then we'll explore each Snowflake Secure Data Sharing approach.

Prep Work

We're ready to create a new worksheet, titled *Chapter10 Data Sharing*. Refer to "Navigating Snowsight Worksheets" on page 8 if you need help creating a new worksheet.

If you are working in a Snowflake free trial account, you'll notice that when you first log in, you'll see that you've been assigned the SYSADMIN role. Working with data shares requires certain privileges to be assigned to your role, unless you are using the ACCOUNTADMIN role. For the lessons in this chapter, we'll be using the ACCOUNTADMIN role, so make sure you set your role appropriately. As a reminder, you can change your role using either the drop-down menu or a SQL statement in the worksheet.

Next, we'll want to create a new database and table for the hands-on examples in this chapter. In your new *Data Sharing* worksheet, execute the following commands:

```
USE ROLE ACCOUNTADMIN;
USE WAREHOUSE COMPUTE_WH;
CREATE OR REPLACE DATABASE DEMO10_DB;
USE SCHEMA DEMO10_DB.PUBLIC;
CREATE OR REPLACE TABLE SHARINGDATA (i integer);
```

Let's go ahead and take a look to see what data has been shared with us. Navigate back to the Main menu by clicking the Home icon, and then click the Data → Private Sharing option in the menu. You can see in Figure 10-2 that I currently have access to data from two direct data shares.

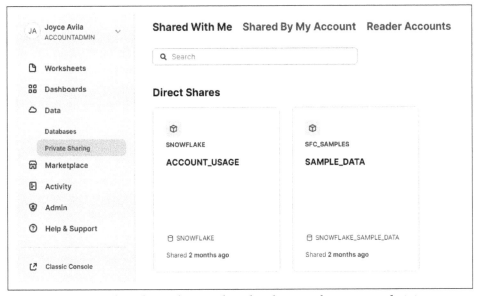

Figure 10-2. Direct data shares that are shared with me as the account administrator

Throughout the chapters in the book, we have used the SAMPLE_DATA share for examples. We've also discussed the Snowflake ACCOUNT_USAGE share. We'll review details about this special ACCOUNT_USAGE share in a later section.

The default for the Shared Data menu option is Shared With Me, which you can see at the top middle of the screen. To see any of your outbound data shares, you can click Shared By My Account, as shown in Figure 10-3.

Figure 10-3. Data I've shared with others

Snowflake's Direct Secure Data Sharing Approach

Direct sharing, Snowflake's simplest form of data sharing, results when a Snowflake provider creates an outbound data share which then becomes an inbound share in a consumer's Snowflake account. A provider can share a Snowflake database table, a secure view, or a secure user-defined function (UDF) via a share object. It is important to realize that the share is not created *from* objects, but rather is granted privileges to the database, schema, table, view, or UDF.

Creating Outbound Shares

When you are creating outbound shares your account is the Snowflake *provider* account, whereas the account to which you are sharing your data is the Snowflake *consumer* account. It's important to know that a share can contain only a single database.

To include multiple databases in a share, you can create a secure view which can be shared. This is possible provided the objects referenced in the share reside in the same Snowflake account.

To create a share object, click the Share Data button in the upper-right corner of the screen, and then click the Select Data button. Be sure to select the DEMO10_DB database, PUBLIC schema, and SHARINGDATA table. It is important to check the box next to the table in order to select it to be included in the share (as shown in Figure 10-4). When you're finished, click Done.

Figure 10-4. Selecting data when creating a share object

You'll see that the Secure Share Identifier field is now filled (as shown in Figure 10-5), but you can change the identifier. It's important to note that the secure share identifier must be unique for the account in which the share is created, and that the identifier is case sensitive. Also notice that you could share the object with a specific consumer by entering the accounts in your region by name.

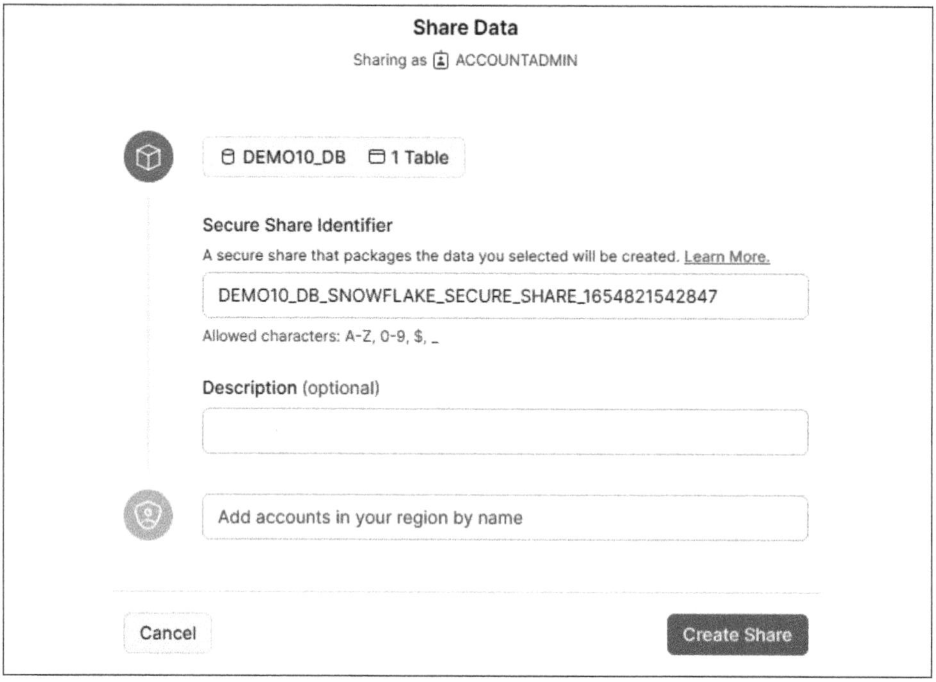

Figure 10-5. Naming the secure share and adding consumers to a share object

Let's change the identifier that was automatically generated, and let's skip adding new consumers at this time. In the Secure Share Identifier field, enter **DEMO10_SHARE** and then click the Create Share button. You'll receive confirmation that the share was created (as shown in Figure 10-6).

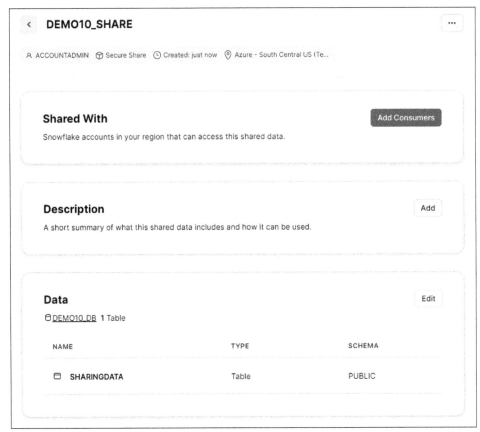

Figure 10-6. The share object has been created successfully

Another way to create an outbound share is to use SQL commands within a worksheet. Navigate back to the *Data Sharing* worksheet and execute the following statement:

```
USE ROLE ACCOUNTADMIN;
CREATE OR REPLACE SHARE DEMO10_SHARE2;
GRANT USAGE ON DATABASE DEMO10_DB TO SHARE DEMO10_SHARE2;
GRANT USAGE ON SCHEMA DEMO10_DB.PUBLIC TO SHARE DEMO10_SHARE2;
GRANT SELECT ON TABLE DEMO10_DB.PUBLIC.SHARINGDATA TO SHARE DEMO10_SHARE2;
```

One of the things you'll notice is that you are assigning access privileges to the shares that will be used by the data consumers. This should look familiar. The way in which you grant access to objects for data shares is part of the same role-based access control examples we went through together in Chapter 5.

Now, if you go back to the menu option for Data → Private Sharing → Shared By My Account, you'll see both shares we just created (as shown in Figure 10-7). If both shares don't show up immediately, try refreshing the page.

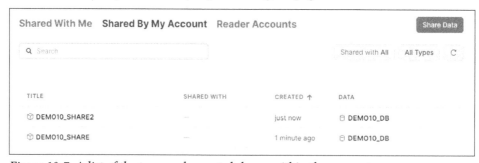

Figure 10-7. A list of the two newly created shares within the account

Data providers' role in creating and managing shares

Snowflake data providers create an outbound share object and assign privileges on one or more database tables, secure views, or secure UDFs using data stored in their account. As such, the data provider is responsible for bearing the cost of data storage. The consumer is not billed for any data storage costs because the data share, and objects accessed via the share, are not copied or moved to the consumer's account.

 A Snowflake provider can share an outbound share with a virtually unlimited number of accounts, and there is never a cost for the act of sharing data across accounts within the same cloud provider region. The Snowflake data provider can also set terms, through a contract, to limit the resharing of data.

If you are ready to give consumers access to the DEMO10_SHARE, you can click the share listing and then the Add Consumers button on the right (as shown in Figure 10-8).

Figure 10-8. Adding data consumers to an existing share

We won't be adding any consumers here in the UI, so go ahead and hit the Cancel button. In addition to using the UI, a Snowflake provider can use a SQL command in the worksheet to add one or more consumers who have their own Snowflake accounts. That command would look like this:

```
ALTER SHARE <name_of_share> ADD ACCOUNTS = <name_of_consumer_account>;
```

 You can add multiple consumer accounts by separating names with a comma.

Remember, of course, that you can restrict certain data from being accessible either by excluding the data altogether or by masking the data that can be seen. Some examples are dynamic data masking and row-level security, which we discussed in Chapter 7.

What if you want to share specific records within a data share with different consumers? One way to achieve that goal is to separate the storage of those records and then create many different data shares, but that is time-consuming and prone to errors. Fortunately, there is an easier and better way. A provider can maintain one data share and, using Snowflake's Current Account capability, provide access to custom slices of the data to the current account. It's also possible to provide specific slices of the data to each consumer account external to the current account.

Let's see this in action. For this example, we'll have different countries with data, and we'll associate the countries to a specific region. We want this regional data to be accessible to different accounts. We need to create the table and insert the values for that base table in our Snowflake instance. We'll designate the ID as the region. Navigate back to the *Data Sharing* worksheet and execute the following statements:

```
USE ROLE ACCOUNTADMIN;
USE DATABASE DEMO10_DB;
CREATE OR REPLACE SCHEMA PRIVATE;

CREATE OR REPLACE TABLE DEMO10_DB.PRIVATE.SENSITIVE_DATA
    (nation string,
    price float,
    size int,
    id string);

INSERT INTO DEMO10_DB.PRIVATE.SENSITIVE_DATA
    values('USA', 123.5, 10,'REGION1'),
          ('USA', 89.2, 14, 'REGION1'),
          ('CAN', 99.0, 35, 'REGION2'),
          ('CAN', 58.0, 22, 'REGION2'),
          ('MEX', 112.6,18, 'REGION2'),
          ('MEX', 144.2,15, 'REGION2'),
          ('IRE', 96.8, 22, 'REGION3'),
          ('IRE', 107.4,19, 'REGION3');
```

Next, we'll create a table that will hold the mapping to individual accounts:

```
CREATE OR REPLACE TABLE DEMO10_DB.PRIVATE.SHARING_ACCESS
    (id string,snowflake_account string);
```

Let's give our current account access to the data in REGION1, which includes the USA data, by inserting those details into the SHARING_ACCESS mapping table:

```
INSERT INTO SHARING_ACCESS values('REGION1', current_account());
```

Now we'll assign REGION2 and REGION3 the values associated with their respective accounts, and then take a look at the contents of the SHARING_ACCESS table:

```
INSERT INTO SHARING_ACCESS values('REGION2', 'ACCT2');
INSERT INTO SHARING_ACCESS values('REGION3', 'ACCT3');
SELECT * FROM SHARING_ACCESS;
```

You'll notice in Figure 10-9 that we have each region associated with a Snowflake account. You can see in the results that my Snowflake trial account identifier is VL35342; your Snowflake account is different and will be unique to your organization.

	ID	SNOWFLAKE_ACCOUNT
1	REGION1	VL35342
2	REGION2	ACCT2
3	REGION3	ACCT3

*Figure 10-9. Results of SELECT * on the SHARING_ACCESS table*

In our example, we used ACCT2 and ACCT3, but if you were to create this SHARING_ACCESS table in your production Snowflake org, you'd want to substitute actual Snowflake account identifiers for ACCT2 and ACCT3.

Our next action is to create a secure view where we'll join all the data in the SENSITIVE_DATA base table with the SHARING_ACCESS mapping table:

```
CREATE OR REPLACE SECURE VIEW DEMO10_DB.PUBLIC.PAID_SENSITIVE_DATA as
    SELECT nation, price, size
    FROM DEMO10_DB.PRIVATE.SENSITIVE_DATA sd
    JOIN DEMO10_DB.PRIVATE.SHARING_ACCESS sa on sd.id = sa.id
    AND sa.snowflake_account = current_account();
```

We'll want to grant the SELECT privilege to the secure view for all roles, which we can do by granting this privilege to the PUBLIC role:

```
GRANT SELECT ON DEMO10_DB.PUBLIC.PAID_SENSITIVE_DATA to PUBLIC;
```

Let's take a look at the SENSITIVE_DATA base table. Remember that this table holds all eight records:

```
SELECT * FROM DEMO10_DB.PRIVATE.SENSITIVE_DATA;
```

As expected, Figure 10-10 shows that we're able to view all eight records.

	NATION	PRICE	SIZE	ID	...
1	USA	123.5	10	REGION1	
2	USA	89.2	14	REGION1	
3	CAN	99	35	REGION2	
4	CAN	58	22	REGION2	
5	MEX	112.6	18	REGION2	
6	MEX	144.2	15	REGION2	
7	IRE	96.8	22	REGION3	
8	IRE	107.4	19	REGION3	

Figure 10-10. All records in the SENSITIVE_DATA table

Now let's find out what records we are able to see in the secure view:

```
SELECT * FROM DEMO10_DB.PUBLIC.PAID_SENSITIVE_DATA;
```

Our current Snowflake account is mapped to REGION1, which includes the nation USA. As expected, we see both of the USA records (as shown in Figure 10-11).

	NATION	PRICE	...	SIZE
1	USA	123.5		10
2	USA	89.2		14

Figure 10-11. Records in the PAID_SENSITIVE_DATA secure view accessible to our account

Let's use a session variable to simulate our Snowflake account being ACCT2, and take a look at what we'll be able to see in the secure view:

```
ALTER SESSION SET simulated_data_sharing_consumer='ACCT2';
SELECT * FROM DEMO10_DB.PUBLIC.PAID_SENSITIVE_DATA;
```

As ACCT2, we can see all REGION2 data, which includes the nations of Canada and Mexico (as shown in Figure 10-12).

	NATION	PRICE	...	SIZE
1	CAN	99		35
2	CAN	58		22
3	MEX	112.6		18
4	MEX	144.2		15

Figure 10-12. Records in the PAID_SENSITIVE_DATA secure view accessible to ACCT2

And, finally, let's see what is shown to us if we set our Snowflake account to ACCT3:

```
ALTER SESSION SET simulated_data_sharing_consumer='ACCT3';
SELECT * FROM DEMO10_DB.PUBLIC.PAID_SENSITIVE_DATA;
```

As Figure 10-13 shows, we can see the nation of Ireland, which is part of REGION3.

	NATION	...	PRICE	SIZE
1	IRE		96.8	22
2	IRE		107.4	19

Figure 10-13. Records in the PAID_SENSITIVE_DATA secure view accessible to ACCT3

We want to return our Snowflake account to our original account:

```
ALTER SESSION UNSET simulated_data_sharing_consumer;
```

Now that we have successfully tested how our data will be shared with different accounts, we are ready to create a new share:

```
USE ROLE ACCOUNTADMIN;
USE DATABASE DEMO10_DB;
USE SCHEMA DEMO10_DB.PUBLIC;
CREATE OR REPLACE SHARE NATIONS_SHARED;
SHOW SHARES;
```

You'll notice that this new share will be included in the list of outbound shares. But we are not done yet. We need to grant privileges to the new share:

```
GRANT USAGE ON DATABASE DEMO10_DB TO SHARE NATIONS_SHARED;
GRANT USAGE ON SCHEMA DEMO10_DB.PUBLIC TO SHARE NATIONS_SHARED;
GRANT SELECT ON DEMO10_DB.PUBLIC.PAID_SENSITIVE_DATA TO SHARE NATIONS_SHARED;
```

You can use the SHOW GRANTS statement to confirm the contents of the share:

```
SHOW GRANTS TO SHARE NATIONS_SHARED;
```

Again, you'll notice that the grantee name has your current account information (as shown in Figure 10-14).

privilege	granted_on	name	granted_to	grantee_name	grant_option	⋯	granted_by
USAGE	DATABASE	DEMO10_DB	SHARE	VL35342.NATIONS_SHARED	false		ACCOUNTADMIN
USAGE	SCHEMA	DEMO10_DB.PUBLIC	SHARE	VL35342.NATIONS_SHARED	false		ACCOUNTADMIN
SELECT	VIEW	DEMO10_DB.PUBLIC.PAID_SENSITIVE_DATA	SHARE	VL35342.NATIONS_SHARED	false		ACCOUNTADMIN

Figure 10-14. Privileges granted to the NATIONS_SHARED share

Now all that is left to do from the provider perspective is to add accounts to the share:

```
//This is pseudocode; you need to replace with actual Snowflake accounts
ALTER SHARE NATIONS_SHARED ADD ACCOUNTS = ACCT2, ACCT3;
```

If you'd like to retrieve a list of all the Snowflake consumer accounts that have a database created from a share, you can use the following command:

```
SHOW GRANTS OF SHARE NATIONS_SHARED;
```

It is important to remember that provider accounts pay for the data storage costs of the shared data and consumer accounts pay for the virtual warehouse cost of compute for querying the data. This assumes that both the data provider and data consumer each has their own Snowflake account.

A situation could arise in which a data provider would like to share data with a consumer who does not currently have a Snowflake account. In that case, the provider can establish and manage a Snowflake reader account. When a provider establishes a reader account for the consumer, the reader account will offer read-only capability for the consumer.

Setting up a reader account

In the previous section, we navigated to the Private Sharing section of the Data main menu and clicked Shared By My Account. We then clicked the specific share for which we wanted to add a consumer. If, instead, we wanted to create a reader account, we would click the Reader Accounts section at the top of the screen, and then click the + New button. We would then be given a dialog page where we can create a reader account (as shown in Figure 10-15).

The dialog page asks you to provide the reader account name, and the user name and password for the person who will be given admin privileges.

 The reader account created will be the same edition, region, and cloud as your own Snowflake account, and the admin login information is what you will use to manage the reader account.

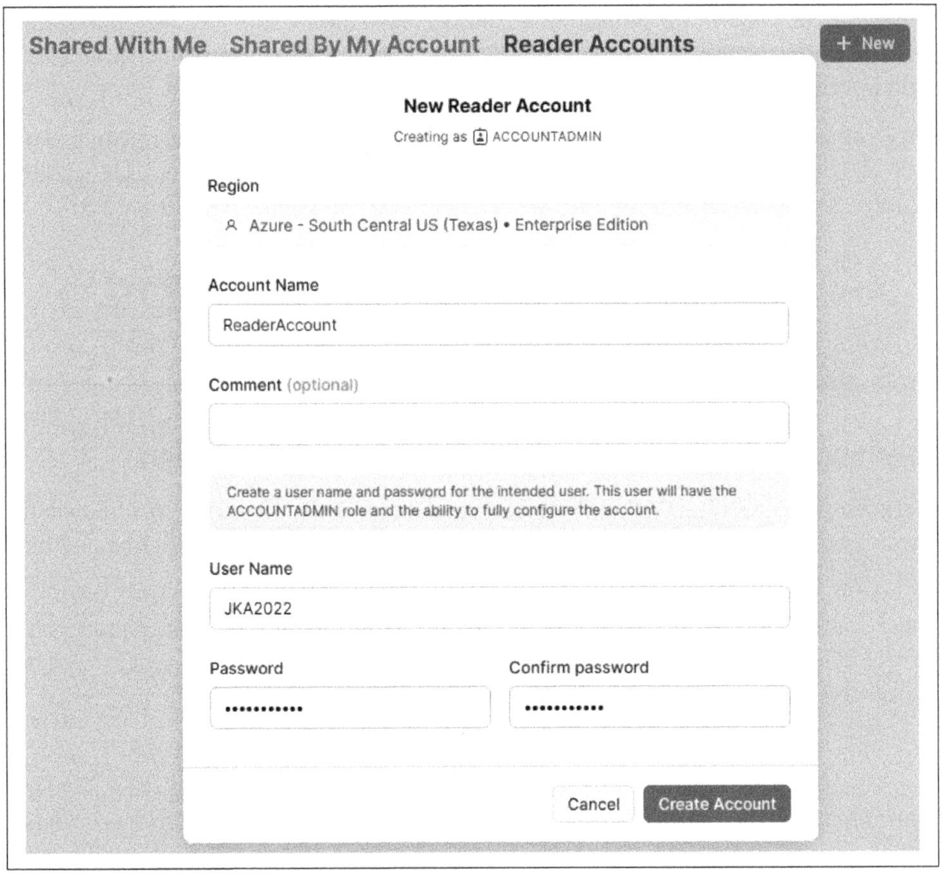

Figure 10-15. Creating a new reader account

After you create the reader account, click the ellipsis on the right side of the page and the option to Drop the reader account will appear (as shown in Figure 10-16).

Shared With Me	Shared By My Account	**Reader Accounts**				+ New

Q Search   C

1 Reader Account ⓘ

NAME ↑		CLOUD	REGION	LOCATOR	LOCATOR URL	CREATED	
READERACCOUNT Pending		Azure	South Central US (Texas)	OP31893	🔗	just now	...
							Drop

Figure 10-16. Dropping a reader account

Once you click the Drop button, you'll notice that the locator URL for the reader account will copy the URL to your clipboard. You can then use that URL and the login information you created to log in to the reader account.

Once you are logged in to the reader account as the data provider admin, you'll want to create a database from an inbound share and set up a data consumer user account to assign to the person you want to have access to the Snowflake reader account.

 As the data provider, you are responsible for the compute charges incurred when the data is queried, so you may want to consider setting up a resource monitor to limit the total costs or to be notified when a specified number of credits have been consumed.

How Inbound Shares Are Used by Snowflake Data Consumers

Using the ACCOUNTADMIN role, a data consumer who is the owner of a Snowflake account can create a database from the provider's outbound share, which is now the consumer's inbound share.

In the Snowflake worksheet, here is the statement that a consumer would use to create the shared database. Notice that for this statement to execute you'll need to include the database name and inbound share name:

```
CREATE DATABASE <name_of_new_database> FROM SHARE <name_of_inbound_share>;
```

As previously discussed, it is not possible to edit shared data. Shared databases are read-only; thus, the data cannot be updated and no new objects within the database can be created by the data consumer. There are some additional limitations for this newly created database. One unique property of the shared database is that the comments cannot be edited.

The data consumer is unable to clone a shared database or the objects within it. However, it is possible to copy the shared data into a new table. While it is technically possible to make a copy of the shared database, it might be a violation of the terms of the contract if both parties entered into such an agreement. For data consumers who are the owners of a Snowflake account where the database resides, there is no limit on the number of times the data can be queried. It is important to keep in mind, though, that data consumers bear the compute cost of querying the data.

Understanding consumer accounts: reader accounts versus full accounts

Both reader accounts and full accounts are types of consumer accounts used in Snowflake data sharing. Reader accounts pay none of the compute costs for querying the data. Those costs are paid by the provider account that created the reader account. As such, providers may choose to limit the queries of the reader accounts by using resource monitors. Reader accounts can be useful as an intermediate step for partners who are not yet ready to transition from their current data processes. Setting up and maintaining reader accounts for their partners' use does require additional effort by providers.

 Full consumer accounts also have the ability to join their data with the shared data directly in Snowflake, while a reader account can only view the data shared with them in Snowflake.

How the ACCOUNT_USAGE share is different from all other inbound shares

The ACCOUNT_USAGE share, a type of inbound share, was introduced in Chapter 3 when we compared the ACCOUNT_USAGE share from the SNOWFLAKE database to the INFORMATION_SCHEMA, a schema that is provided for each database. The SNOWFLAKE database, viewable only by the ACCOUNTADMIN by default, is similar to the INFORMATION_SCHEMA in that they both provide information about an account's object metadata and usage metrics. However, there are three major differences between the two:

- The ACCOUNT_USAGE share, with multiple views, includes records for dropped objects.
- The ACCOUNT_USAGE share also a longer retention time than the INFORMATION_SCHEMA.
- The ACCOUNT_USAGE share has an average latency of about two hours, whereas there is no latency when querying the INFORMATION_SCHEMA.

Share privileges are imported, and most inbound shares allow you to create and rename a database as well as drop the database from which you created the inbound share. However, the ACCOUNT_USAGE share is different. You cannot create, rename, or drop the database associated with the ACCOUNT_USAGE share. You also cannot add a comment. The ACCOUNT_USAGE share is managed differently because it is a way in which Snowflake communicates with you about your account.

Throughout this chapter, when we refer to *inbound* shares we are referring to all inbound shares other than the ACCOUNT_USAGE share, which is unique. Unlike the ACCOUNT_USAGE share, inbound shares can be removed, or a new database can be created with a different name than the inbound share name.

Comparison between databases on inbound shares and regular databases

As we've seen, share privileges are imported and shared data is read-only. As shown in Table 10-1, inbound shares allow you to create and drop a database for the inbound share, but not to change the structure of the database.

Table 10-1. Differences between an inbound share and a regular database

	CREATE, RENAME, or DROP database	CREATE, ALTER, or DROP schema, table, stage, and/or view in the existing database	GRANT/REVOKE ALL, MONITOR, or CREATE schema in the existing database
Inbound share	Yes[a]	No	No
Regular database	Yes	Yes	Yes

[a] Except for the ACCOUNT_USAGE share

One important note is that, unlike most traditional databases, Snowflake supports cross-database joins, including joins with databases built from inbound shares (see Figure 10-17). Consumers, other than those with reader accounts, can also create views in their own database which can combine their own data with data from the shared database. This is highly beneficial, because the consumer can enrich their own data to make it even more valuable.

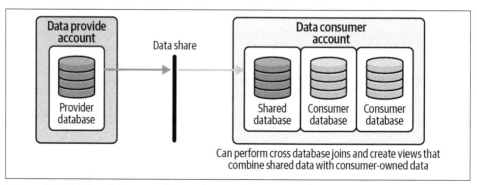

Figure 10-17. Shared data can be used in combination with consumer-owned data

When new records are created within the provider's Snowflake account as part of the shared database, the records are almost instantly available in a data consumer's inbound shared database. However, when the provider creates new objects within the shared database, those objects are not automatically shared with the data consumer. The provider has to grant authorization to the data share before the records in those objects are viewable by the consumer.

How to List and Shop on the Public Snowflake Marketplace

Data providers can be publicly connected with data consumers globally via the Snowflake Marketplace. As a potential consumer of third-party data, you can access the Marketplace directly from the Snowflake user interface.

First, make sure you have your role set to ACCOUNTADMIN, and then click the Marketplace option, as shown in Figure 10-18. If your role is not currently set to ACCOUNTADMIN, be sure to click the drop-down arrow next to your name and change your role.

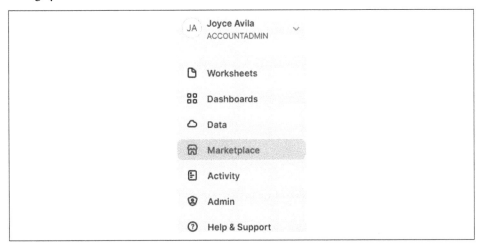

Figure 10-18. Accessing the Marketplace directly from the user interface

From your Snowflake UI, you can now search the Marketplace (see Figure 10-19). When you search the Marketplace, you'll find standard listings, which are available for you to access immediately, and personalized listings for which you can send a request to access.

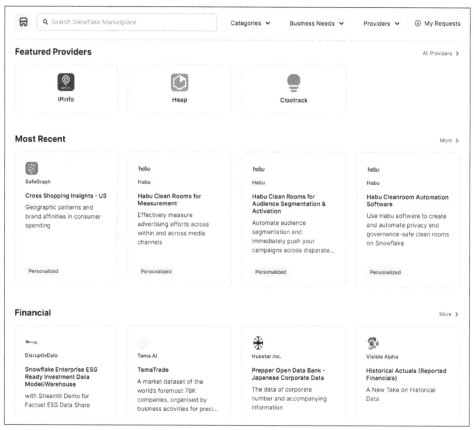

Figure 10-19. The Snowflake Marketplace

Some third-party data providers offer data access for free or sometimes charge you a fee to access their data. They may also require a contract to ensure that you won't reshare their data. Whether the access to the data is free or the provider charges you a fee, that arrangement between you and the data provider is separate from your arrangement with Snowflake. You'll be billed by Snowflake only for the compute you use to query the shared data. The data storage charges are the responsibility of the data provider.

Snowflake Marketplace for Providers

For data providers, the Snowflake Marketplace provides an opportunity to monetize data in ways never before possible. You can provide secure, personalized data views using your own customized business model. Snowflake isn't a party to the transaction between a data provider and data consumer, and there is no cost for the act of sharing data on the Data Cloud. Instead, Snowflake enables data sharing on its platform and earns revenue when data consumers use virtual warehouses to query the data.

To become an approved Snowflake data provider, you'll need to submit a request, sign the Snowflake provider agreement, and agree to operate within the Snowflake provider policies. Importantly, your data will have to meet certain requirements.

One requirement is that your data must be fresh and nonstatic, meaning that the historical data you'll provide must be relatively recent and that you have a plan to continue updating the data going forward.

Another requirement is that the data cannot be sample, mocked-up data. To be clear, sample data can be provided to help consumers determine whether they want to use the full data set or not. The full data set itself, though, cannot be only sample or mocked-up data.

Finally, you must possess the right to make the data available and ensure that the data doesn't include sensitive private information. For each of your listings, object identifiers for tables, columns, and share names must be written in all *uppercase* letters and must use only *alphanumeric* characters. You'll also need to provide at least one usage example for each listing. The ZoomInfo usage example is shown in Figure 10-20.

ZoomInfo SQL Query

Select all companies and their core firmographics + advanced attributes including employee range, revenue range, primary industry

```
SELECT "ZoomInfo Company ID",
"Company Name",
"Website",
"Company HQ Phone",
"Fax",
"Ticker"
"Revenue (in 000s)",
"Revenue Range",
"Employees",
"Employee Range",
"SIC Code 1",
"SIC Code 2",
"SIC Codes",
"NAICS Code 1",
"NAICS Code 2",
"NAICS Codes",
"Primary Industry",
"Primary Sub-Industry",
"All Industries",
"All Sub-Industries",
"Industry Hierarchical Category",
"Secondary Industry Hierarchical Category",
"ZoomInfo Company Profile URL",
"Ownership Type",
"Business Model",
"Certified Active Company",
"Company Street Address",
"Company City",
"Company State",
"Company Zip Code",
"Company Country",
"Company Is Acquired",
"Company ID (Ultimate Parent)",
"Entity Name (Ultimate Parent)",
"Company ID (Immediate Parent)",
"Entity Name (Immediate Parent)",
"Relationship (Immediate Parent)"
FROM "PROD_MASTER_DB"."COMPANY"."COMPANY_DATABRICK_TABLE"
```

Show less ^

Figure 10-20. ZoomInfo usage example for the Snowflake Marketplace

Provider Studio

Provider Studio offers the ability to perform required actions to get listings approved and to review data requests from consumers. Additionally, Provider Studio makes it possible for Snowflake providers to view key analytics relating to Marketplace listings by selecting the Analytics tab. Access to Provider Studio is available only to Snowflake data providers.

Standard Versus Personalized Data Listings

All Snowflake Marketplace listings include details about the shared data as well as sample queries and usage examples. Listings also include information about the data provider. The difference between the two types of listings, standard and personalized, is whether the shared data is instantly accessible or not.

A Snowflake Marketplace standard listing, which provides instant access to a published data set, is best used for generic, aggregated, or non-customer–specific data. A personalized data listing is one in which a request to access data sets must be made. Once the request is made, the data provider is notified and then contacts the consumer.

An example of a standard listing is shown in Figure 10-21.

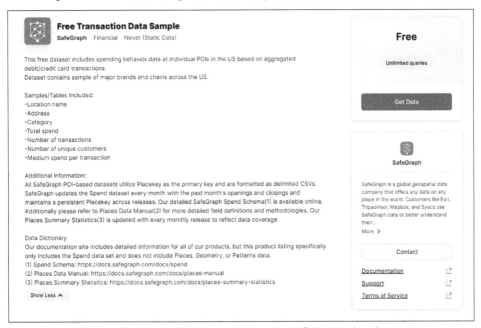

Figure 10-21. Example of a standing listing in the Snowflake Marketplace

You can tell that the listing in Figure 10-21 is a standard listing in a few ways. First, the word *Personalized* wasn't included on the listing's main page. Also, when you click the listing, you'll see the Get Data button which, when clicked, will show the details about the listing as well as one final button you'll need to click, the Get Data button (as shown in Figure 10-22). Notice that you can add more roles, in addition to the ACCOUNTADMIN role, to give more roles access to the shared database.

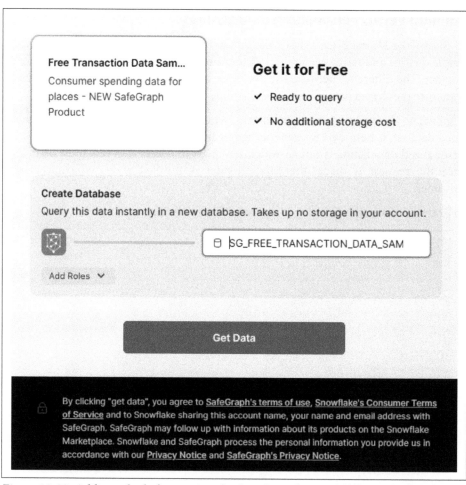

Figure 10-22. Adding roles before getting the data from the Marketplace standard listing

When you click the Get Data button, you'll see that the data is now ready to query (as shown in Figure 10-23).

Figure 10-23. Confirmation that the data from the Marketplace standard listing is ready to query

Figure 10-24 shows Knoema's example of a personalized listing in the Snowflake Marketplace. You would click the Request Data button to request access from Knoema.

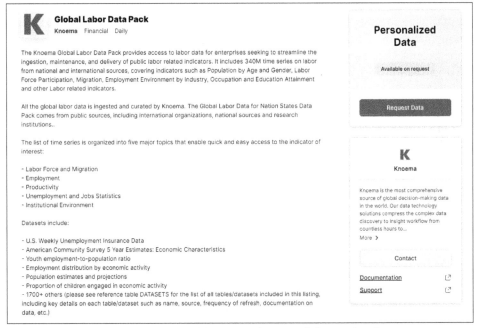

Figure 10-24. Knoema's personalized listing in the Snowflake Marketplace

Today there are hundreds of providers who participate in the Snowflake Marketplace and hundreds of listings that include many well-known data providers. The latest counts and details of all Snowflake Marketplace data sets can be found in the UI. The Snowflake Marketplace is also described on Snowflake's website (*https://oreil.ly/oJms9*).

Harnessing the Power of a Snowflake Private Data Exchange

A Snowflake Private Data Exchange enables organizations to privately share data sets with a select group of participants. In this way, organizations can create their own private version of the Snowflake Marketplace but with control over what data can be listed and who can access the listings. A Snowflake Private Data Exchange is a great option for a company with different divisions, each of which has its own Snowflake account and wants to have control over which data is shared throughout the organization. A Snowflake Private Data Exchange could also be used by a retailer that wants to share data with its suppliers.

Getting a Snowflake Private Data Exchange set up is a fairly easy process and generally only takes one or two business days. You will want to navigate to the Snowflake support page and submit a case. You'll need to provide a business case justification, a unique name for the new data exchange, and the data exchange display name and your account URL. You'll also need to provide the organization ID if you are using the organization Snowflake feature.

Once you have set up your Private Data Exchange, you can access it by selecting Data → Shared Data → Manage Exchanges. You'll then see the Private Data Exchange. In this example, I've created a Private Data Exchange with the name *SpringML* (as shown in Figure 10-25).

Figure 10-25. Managing a Private Data Exchange

Once you click the name of the Private Data Exchange, you'll see its details and be able to add a member to it (as shown in Figure 10-26).

Figure 10-26. Details of a Private Data Exchange

If you click the Add Member button, you'll have the option to add a new account and allow that account to participate in the Private Data Exchange as a consumer, provider, or both (as shown in Figure 10-27).

Figure 10-27. Adding members to a Private Data Exchange

Snowflake data exchanges are a great way to scale your business by inviting partners, customers, vendors, and others to participate.

Snowflake Data Clean Rooms

A data clean room on Snowflake is a design pattern for sharing data between two or more parties in a privacy-protected way. A popular use case of data clean rooms is to link anonymized marketing and advertising data from multiple participants. This gives participants a way to adhere to privacy laws, such as the GDPR and the California Consumer Privacy Act (CCPA), because data clean rooms don't allow data points that can be tied back to a specific user to leave the environment.

Traditional data clean rooms require all data to be stored in one physical location. In contrast, a data clean room on Snowflake does not require participants to move their data from its existing location in order to list their data in the Snowflake Data Exchange. Instead, participants use Secure Data Sharing in which PII included in the clean room is secured and encrypted.

Using Snowflake to create distributed data clean room functionality is unique in that Snowflake provides the ability for each data clean room participant to control their own data without having to trust a single party with all the data. In addition to limiting who can access the data, Private Data Exchange participants can use secure functions and access controls to protect their data while still allowing join data analysis to occur.

A data clean room on Snowflake starts with setting up a Private Data Exchange and uses current Snowflake features to allow the parties involved to join data in a single query that produces aggregate results, without allowing access to the underlying low-level data. Secure functions, as well as joins, can be used to establish individual links to people, devices, or cookies without needing to exchange or make visible any PII.

In addition to the Snowflake Secure Data Sharing technology, which automatically and securely shares tables among multiple Snowflake accounts, there are other technology features that are used for data clean rooms. Row access policies match customer data without exposing PII, and stored procedures validate query requests. Snowflake streams and tasks monitor for data clean room requests and respond automatically. Guidelines are established to determine what data is allowed in and what data, if any, can leave from a distributed data clean room on Snowflake.

Important Design, Security, and Performance Considerations

Snowflake shares are relatively quick and easy for providers to set up and make available for consumers. Before creating a new share, however, it is a good idea to think about the design, security, and performance implications for shares.

Share Design Considerations

As records get added to a provider's object that is shared with a consumer, they are immediately available to the consumer. However, if an object such as a new table gets added to the database, the new table is not automatically shared with the consumer. The producer must take action to share that new object.

From a technical perspective, different shares can use the same schema, but then it will appear as if all the objects are part of a share even when they aren't. This makes it particularly difficult to add new objects to existing shares that are part of the same schema.

 Separate schemas for each listing are not required. However, from a design perspective, planning to create a separate schema for each listing could reduce the possibility of confusion and of accidentally sharing an object.

An inbound share can only contain one database, but it is possible for a producer to share data from multiple databases by using a secure view. A Snowflake provider can create a secure view which references schemas, tables, and other views from several databases as long as those databases belong to the same account.

Share Security Considerations

Sharing a secure object works the same way as sharing a table. Rather than sharing the table, you could easily devise a way to share the object securely. One option is to create an internally available schema in which the base table resides and then create an externally available schema for the secure object. That way, you can share the external schema and secure object without exposing the base table.

 The following Snowflake objects can be shared: tables, external tables, secure views, secure materialized views, and secure UDFs. However, to ensure that sensitive data in a shared database is not exposed to users in consumer accounts, it is strongly recommended that you share secure views or secure UDFs, rather than directly sharing tables.

By using dynamic data masking or row access policies, it is possible to share a portion of the data in a base table with different consumer accounts without having to create separate views for each consumer.

 It is also possible to share only specific rows of data by using the CURRENT_ACCOUNT() function. Note that it is only possible to use CURRENT_ACCOUNT() for Secure Data Sharing when using secure views and secure materialized views.

Share Performance Considerations

When sharing data from massively large tables, it is recommended that you, as the provider, define clustering keys on the tables. This will prevent your consumers from being negatively impacted with degraded performance when they query the database share.

Difference Between Database Sharing and Database Cloning

Oftentimes, people ask what the difference is between cloning a database and using the Snowflake Secure Data Sharing feature. The answer is that database cloning effectively takes a snapshot of the database, and while the original database continues to change, the cloned database does not. It is important to note that instead of actually making a physical copy of the data, the metadata is used to display a view of the original database as it existed at that point in time. The original database and the cloned database both exist within the same account. In contrast, data sharing occurs across different accounts, and the shared data is a live view of the data which changes whenever changes are made in the original database.

Data Shares and Time Travel Considerations

Snowflake Time Travel makes it possible to access historical data at a specified point in time. For security reasons, Time Travel is not enabled for data shares. Otherwise, the consumer might travel back to a time when they could access a view they now shouldn't be allowed to access.

Sharing of Data Shares

A consumer cannot reshare a shared object to another account. A shared object also cannot be cloned by a consumer. However, a consumer could copy the data into a table to create a copy of the data that technically could be shared. This risk isn't just limited to data shares, though. Any data shared with others via traditional methods such as an API or FTP, for example, is at risk of being shared further. Really, anyone who owns a mobile phone and has access to your data can copy and share it. As such, any restrictions, such as not allowing shared data to be shared with anyone outside the organization, is best taken care of using contractual agreements.

Summary

In this chapter, we were reminded how Snowflake's architecture supports Secure Data Sharing and we considered specific use cases to highlight the importance of data sharing. We took a deep dive into the four Snowflake Secure Data Sharing approaches: direct Secure Data Sharing, the Private Data Exchange, the public Snowflake Data Exchange, and data clean rooms. Differentiating between the provider and consumer roles for Secure Data Sharing became more evident as we focused our attention on learning how to create outbound shares and understanding how inbound shares are used by Snowflake data consumers.

Having enough data, going both deep and wide, as well as having the right kind of data often means we need to incorporate external, or third-party, data. Snowflake's Secure Data Sharing capabilities allow us to do just that. Keeping our own data secure and having access to the shared data we need is a necessary first step for being able to extract valuable data insights. One important way we can obtain better insights is by visualizing data. In the next chapter, we'll get some hands-on experience to understand the visualization capabilities of Snowsight, and we'll learn about Snowflake partners who offer powerful data visualization tools native to Snowflake.

As a reminder, we used the ACCOUNTADMIN role throughout this chapter for simplicity, but it is a best practice to use the SYSADMIN role to create new Snowflake objects and to grant privileges as needed to custom roles.

Code Cleanup

All that is necessary for code cleanup for this chapter is to drop the database we created. However, let's see what happens when we attempt to do that:

```
USE ROLE ACCOUNTADMIN;
DROP DATABASE DEMO10_DB;
```

We receive an error because we cannot drop a database when there are active shares associated with it (as shown in Figure 10-28). So, we need to revoke share access to the database if we want to drop it.

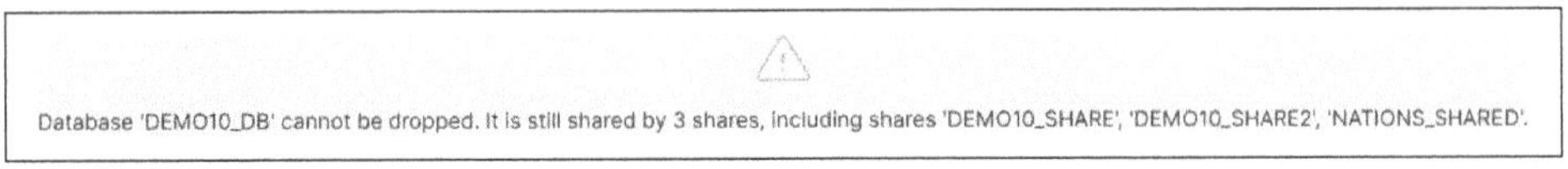

Database 'DEMO10_DB' cannot be dropped. It is still shared by 3 shares, including shares 'DEMO10_SHARE', 'DEMO10_SHARE2', 'NATIONS_SHARED'.

Figure 10-28. Error message received when attempting to drop a database that has active shares

Let's revoke privileges and then see if we are able to drop the database:

```
REVOKE USAGE ON DATABASE DEMO10_DB FROM SHARE NATIONS_SHARED;
REVOKE USAGE ON DATABASE DEMO10_DB FROM SHARE DEMO10_SHARE;
REVOKE USAGE ON DATABASE DEMO10_DB FROM SHARE DEMO10_SHARE2;
DROP DATABASE DEMO10_DB;
```

You'll notice that we only needed to revoke access at the database level, because once that database access was removed, there was no longer access at the schema or table level. Also, we only needed to drop the database, which will then result in any schemas, tables, and views within the database being dropped.

Knowledge Check

The following questions are based on the data sharing information contained in this chapter:

1. What are the four different Snowflake Secure Data Sharing approaches?
2. Does Snowflake support cross database joins? Explain the relevance as it relates to Secure Data Sharing.
3. Can a data share include more than one database?
4. What is the difference between the Snowflake Marketplace and the Snowflake Data Exchange?

5. Which role(s) can be used to create and maintain data shares?

6. Which Snowflake account is assessed data storage charges, in relation to data shares?

7. Who pays the virtual warehouse compute charges incurred when querying a data share?

8. Explain the term *Snowgrid*.

9. What Snowflake objects can be used to create data shares? Are there any best practices related to selecting the objects to create data shares?

10. What are the requirements for receiving approval to list on the Snowflake Marketplace?

Answers to these questions are available in Appendix A.

Visualizing Data in Snowsight

Data visualization makes it much easier to identify trends, patterns, and outliers and to discover insights within complex data. Information displayed in a visual context, such as a graph or a map, is a more natural way for the human mind to comprehend large amounts of data. Business intelligence (BI) tools such as Domo, Power BI, Sisense, Sigma, Tableau, and ThoughtSpot are used in this way for corporate reporting and for building complex dashboards in which many users are consumers of a particular dashboard.

Sometimes individuals or small groups of users in an organization simply need to undertake ad hoc data analysis, perform data validation while loading data, or quickly create minor charts and dashboards that can be shared and explored together as a team. For those use cases, Snowflake's Snowsight visualization tools are great choices. Snowsight visualization tools include automatic statistics with interactive results and dashboards with chart tiles.

Before we dive into Snowsight's visualization tools, we need to discuss sampling. This is a consideration because we often deal with data sets that are too large for Snowsight statistics and visualizations to manage. Snowsight is especially useful in helping to identify outliers and quality issues with initial data loads, but its capabilities are intended for use on only a small number of rows. We can reduce a large data set into a smaller subset through the LIMIT clause or the SAMPLE clause so that we can use the Snowsight visualization tools. In this chapter, we'll compare the LIMIT and SAMPLE clauses.

Prep Work

To prepare for our first exercise, let's create a new folder. In the upper-right corner, click the ellipses and then click New Folder (as shown in Figure 11-1).

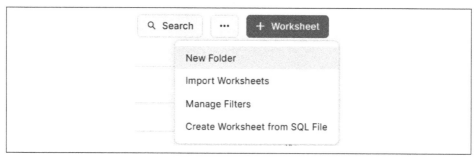

Figure 11-1. Creating a new folder

Name the new folder *Chapter11* and then click the + Worksheet button to create a new worksheet. Name the worksheet *Visualization* (as shown in Figure 11-2).

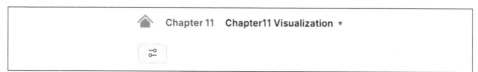

Figure 11-2. Environment setup with the Chapter11 folder and the Visualization worksheet

We'll be using Snowflake's sample database; therefore, no additional prep work is needed in this chapter.

Data Sampling in Snowsight

Sampling data is an important topic for both productivity and visualization purposes. After loading large data sets, ETL developers or software engineers who are responsible for loading data can scan a sample of the data to ensure that nothing unusual stands out. Likewise, business analysts can view a sample of unfamiliar data as a first step in exploring the data, and auditors can obtain a sample of the data on which to perform analysis.

There are limits to the number of records that can be used for Snowsight visualizations. For automatic statistics visualizations, and for charts and dashboards, there must be fewer than one million rows. Thus, it is often impossible to visualize a full data set in Snowsight. In these situations, it is important to obtain a sample of the data to visualize.

Sampling allows you to create a dashboard with a limited subset of the data that closely resembles the full data set. Sampling returns a subset of rows from a specified table. The number of rows returned from sampling a Snowflake table depends on which one of two different approaches you choose. You can choose to return rows based on an exact number you specify, or you can have Snowflake return a certain percentage of the table rows.

Fixed-Size Sampling Based on a Specific Number of Rows

It is possible to sample a fixed number of rows specified in the query. If you want a data sample rather than all the data rows returned, be sure to specify the number of rows for sampling to be less than the total number of rows in the table. The number of rows can be any integer between 0 and 1,000,000. Note that the Bernoulli sampling method is used when you sample by number of rows, and the System/Block and Seed methods are not supported in this case. Bernoulli sampling is a sampling process in which each row would have an equal chance of being selected.

Fraction-Based Sampling Based on Probability

You can sample a portion of the table, with the exact number of rows returned depending on the size of the table. One way to accomplish this is to specify a seed and then state the specified probability for a particular row being included in the sample.

In Snowsight, either the Bernoulli or System sampling method can be used. System sampling is often faster than Bernoulli sampling, but the sample could be biased, especially for small tables. If not specified, Bernoulli is the default sampling method.

 Bernoulli sampling is an equal-probability, without-replacement sampling design. Each row has an equal chance of being selected and, thus, Bernoulli sampling can be referred to as row sampling. When using System sampling, the probability is that a particular block of rows will be selected. System sampling is sometimes referred to as block sampling. For large tables, the difference between these two sampling methods is negligible.

Previewing Fields and Data

For these examples, we'll need to set the role to SYSADMIN and use one of the schemas in the SNOWFLAKE_SAMPLE_DATA database:

```
USE ROLE SYSADMIN;
USE DATABASE SNOWFLAKE_SAMPLE_DATA;
USE SCHEMA TPCDS_SF100TCL;
```

On the left-hand side of the screen, expand the tables underneath the TPCDS_SF100TCL schema (as shown in Figure 11-3).

Figure 11-3. The list of tables in the TPCDS_SF100TCL schema

Next, hover your cursor over the STORE_SALES table, or look in the dedicated section at the bottom, and you'll see a preview that shows there are more than 288 billion rows in the table. In addition to seeing the approximate number of data table rows in the STORE_SALES table, you can examine a list of fields. Numeric fields are prefaced with *123* and text fields are prefaced with *Aa* (as shown in Figure 11-4).

Figure 11-4. The list of fields in the STORE_SALES table

Just to the right of the number of table rows is a Magnifying Glass icon; click the icon and Snowflake will return the first 100 rows for you to view (as shown in Figure 11-5). You can scroll using the horizontal and vertical scroll bars to scan through the rows to get a sense of the data that exists.

SS_SOLD_DATE_SK	SS_SOLD_TIME_SK	SS_ITEM_SK	⋯	SS_CUSTOMER_SK	SS_CDEMO_SK	SS_HDEMO_SK	SS_ADDR_SK	SS_STOI
1	2,451,228	44,837	222,547		7,674,212	108,170	3,281	18,686,039
2	2,451,228	44,837	222,547		7,674,212	108,170	3,281	18,686,039
3	2,451,228	44,837	222,547		7,674,212	108,170	3,281	18,686,039
4	2,451,228	44,837	222,547		7,674,212	108,170	3,281	18,686,039
5	2,451,228	44,837	222,547		7,674,212	108,170	3,281	18,686,039
6	2,451,228	44,837	222,547		7,674,212	108,170	3,281	18,686,039
7	2,451,228	44,837	222,547		7,674,212	108,170	3,281	18,686,039
8	2,451,228	44,837	222,547		7,674,212	108,170	3,281	18,686,039
9	2,451,228	44,837	222,547		7,674,212	108,170	3,281	18,686,039
10	2,451,228	44,837	222,547		7,674,212	108,170	3,281	18,686,039
11	2,451,228	44,837	222,547		7,674,212	108,170	3,281	18,686,039
12	2,451,228	44,837	222,547		7,674,212	108,170	3,281	18,686,039

Figure 11-5. The first 100 rows in the table, which can be seen after you click the Magnifying Glass icon

An active virtual warehouse is required to preview data.

When we preview the data, we see the first 100 rows, but those rows may not give us an accurate representation of the data. We're able to get a more accurate picture of the data if we obtain a sample of the data, especially when we have large data sets.

Sampling Examples

Once you have entered your SQL statement to obtain 100 records by limiting the number of rows returned, position your cursor either above or within the query text in the text editor and execute this statement:

```
SELECT * FROM STORE_SALES LIMIT 100;
```

Next, click the Run button, which is a blue arrow within a circle located at the upper right of the screen. Alternatively, press Cmd + Return on macOS or Ctrl + Enter on Windows.

When you scroll down through the results, you'll see that exactly 100 rows were returned. They are different from the 100 rows that you previewed. This is probably what you expected. The LIMIT clause is nondeterministic, randomly picking rows to be returned, so it makes sense that it would be different from the preview which shows the first 100 rows.

Run the query again and you'll notice that the same 100 records are returned. Is this what you expected? Given that the LIMIT clause is nondeterministic, you might have expected to see a different set of 100 records. The reason the same 100 rows were returned is because of Snowflake caching, described in Chapter 2. The query results cache holds the results of every query executed in the past 24 hours. As such, the same 100 records returned using the LIMIT clause will be returned when you rerun the same query.

Will the same thing happen when we use sampling? Let's see. Query the same table to have 100 rows returned, but this time use SAMPLE instead of LIMIT:

```
SELECT * FROM STORE_SALES SAMPLE (100 ROWS);
```

The results are an example of the fixed-size sampling method. If you run the SAMPLE query again, you will not receive the same results. That may not be what you expected. What do you think will happen when we look at a fraction-based sampling example?

For our fraction-based sampling example, we'll use TABLESAMPLE instead of SAMPLE. They are interchangeable. We'll also specify the sampling as System sampling and put the percentage at 0.015%. We selected a very low percentage because we have in excess of 288 billion rows:

```
SELECT * FROM STORE_SALES TABLESAMPLE SYSTEM (0.015);
```

You'll notice that the results returned more than 30 million records for the sample. That is OK for the sample size, if we need and want a sample size that large, but because the sample size exceeds 999,999 rows, Snowsight isn't able to generate statistics. We'll be looking at statistics a little later in this chapter.

 Sample query results are unique in that they are not cached. You saw this when you ran the fixed-size sampling query a second time. Now try executing the fraction-based sampling query again and see what happens. Just like before, you'll receive a different subset of records if you run the same sampling query again and again.

Using Automatic Statistics and Interactive Results

One way we can visualize data in Snowsight is by using automatic statistics with interactive results. Snowsight uses metadata proactively to quickly provide interactive results no matter how many rows are returned. As you load and query the data, Snowflake puts all the rich metadata that is stored behind the scenes into a GUI so that you can start to understand some of the trends in your data and/or catch any errors early on. For example, you can tell right away whether there are a lot of null values in a field. This is especially advantageous to ETL engineers who will then be able to detect loading errors or gaps in the data being received.

In addition to Snowsight automatic contextual statistics which tell you how many rows are filled, you'll also see histograms for all date, time, and numeric columns, as well as frequency distributions for categorical columns. Additionally, Snowflake provides email domain distributions for email columns and key distributions for JSON objects.

Let's take a look at some of Snowsight's automatic statistics and interactive results. Run a SELECT * statement on the CATALOG_RETURNS table and limit the results to five million. You'll see the query details, but no statistics, to the right of the results (as shown in Figure 11-6):

```
SELECT * FROM CATALOG_RETURNS LIMIT 5000000;
```

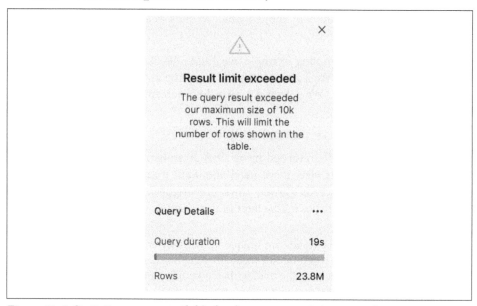

Figure 11-6. Statistics are not available for data sets containing more than 9,999 rows

Remember that the reason we can't see the statistics is because the number of rows in the result set was greater than the number allowed. To view statistics, the number of rows returned must be less than ten thousand (as shown in Figure 11-7). Let's try it again with a smaller number:

```
SELECT * FROM CATALOG_RETURNS LIMIT 9999;
```

 If you don't see the statistics for a little while, try refreshing the screen.

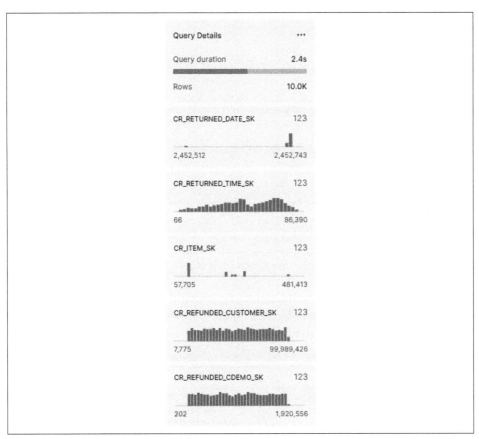

Figure 11-7. The query details and statistics

The statistics results are interactive. If you click the statistics for the CR_CATA-LOG_PAGE_SK column, the 13th chart down, you'll see that 98% of the records have a PAGE_SK value (as shown in Figure 11-8).

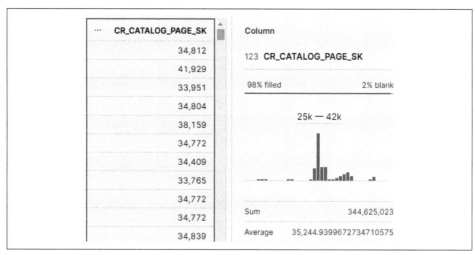

Figure 11-8. The query results statistics for an individual column

We may be interested in knowing something about the records that don't have a PAGE_SK value. To see those records, click on the "2% invalid" text. What you'll notice is that the column has been sorted so that now all the rows with null values are listed first (as shown in Figure 11-9).

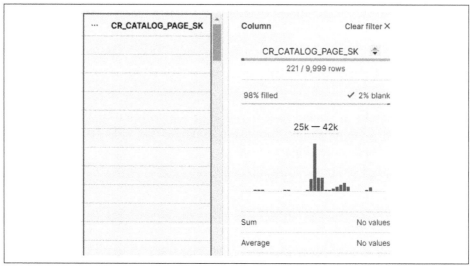

Figure 11-9. Clicking "2% invalid" shows rows with a null value

If you clear the filter, complete statistics information will appear. You can use the scroll bar to scroll down and see information about each column. We'll take a look at one more interactive chart together. Click the CR_RETURN_QUANTITY chart (as shown in Figure 11-10).

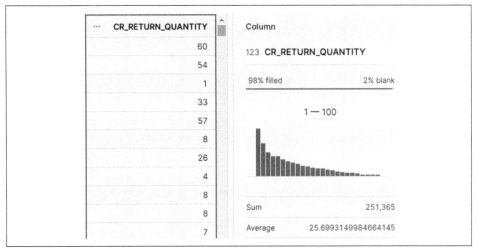

Figure 11-10. CR_RETURN_QUANTITY details and statistics

Now hover your cursor over the chart and click one of the bars in the bar chart. I selected the number 21 (as shown in Figure 11-11). Once you select a bar in the chart, you'll be able to see the records associated with that value in the column to the left.

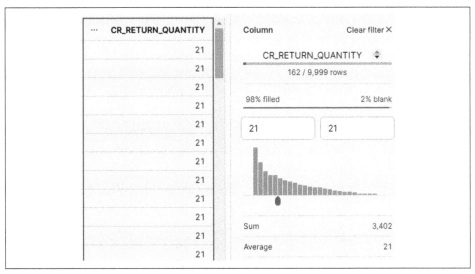

Figure 11-11. A single bar selected in the Statistics section

You can even select a range of values in the chart (as shown in Figure 11-12).

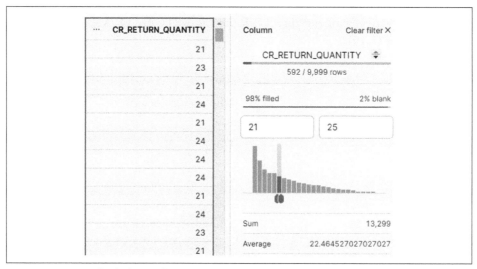

Figure 11-12. Multiple bars selected in the Statistics section

Rather than having to write individual queries or change over to a data science or visualization tool to find out how complete the data is and what are the distinct values or date ranges for each column, the user can now use Snowsight's automatic statistics and interactive results.

Snowsight Dashboard Visualization

It is incredibly helpful to have the ability to preview 100 rows of data, and especially to be able to use automatic statistics and interactive results to quickly learn a lot about the data. However, viewing the metadata often isn't enough. We'll want to use the new Snowsight visualization tools to get a more complete story about the data.

Creating a Dashboard and Tiles

Navigate back to the Visualizations folder and click the Dashboards menu option (as shown in Figure 11-13).

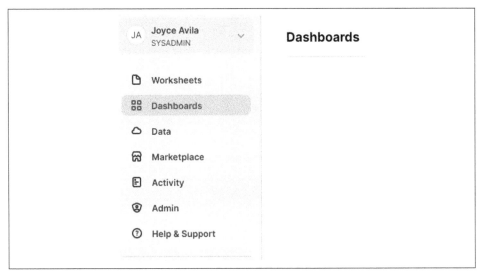

Figure 11-13. The Dashboards menu option

To the right, click the + Dashboard button to create a new dashboard (as shown in Figure 11-14).

Figure 11-14. Creating a new dashboard in Snowsight

Give the dashboard the name *Chapter11*, and click the Create Dashboard button (as shown in Figure 11-15).

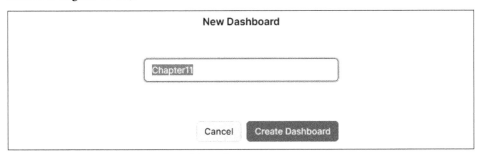

Figure 11-15. Naming the new dashboard

Next, click the + New Tile button to add a new dashboard tile (as shown in Figure 11-16).

Figure 11-16. Adding a new dashboard tile

Once you click the + New Tile button, a worksheet-style screen opens up. Using the drop-down menu in the middle of the screen, select the database and schema as shown in Figure 11-17.

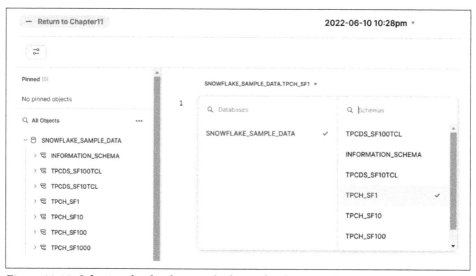

Figure 11-17. Selecting the database and schema for the new Chapter11 dashboard

We previously spent time reviewing the interactive statistics in Snowsight, which are very helpful for looking at data on the fly. Now let's explore some chart visualizations that we can use to build a dashboard.

Working with Chart Visualizations

We'll start with a basic query that returns 10,000 rows:

```
SELECT * FROM TPCH_SF1.LINEITEM LIMIT 10000;
```

Click the Chart button at the bottom to see the chart. You'll notice that it defaults to a line chart (as shown in Figure 11-18).

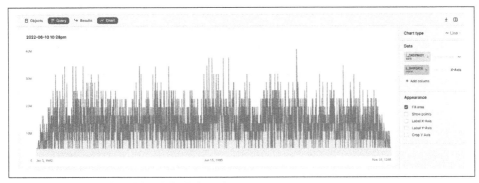

Figure 11-18. Results of the default line chart

On the right, there is a chart drop-down menu (as shown in Figure 11-19). Select Bar and see what happens.

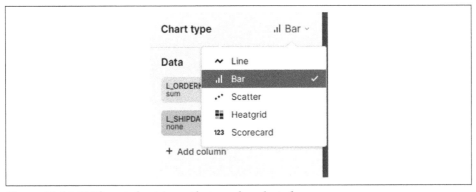

Figure 11-19. Different chart types that can be selected

After you select the bar chart, change the orientation. Notice that the orientation is right below the Appearance section label. Make sure Descending is selected as the order direction (as shown in Figure 11-20).

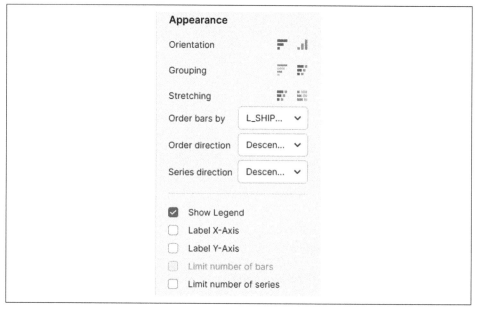

Figure 11-20. Appearance orientation and order direction selections for the chart

Once you have made the selections, your chart should look like Figure 11-21.

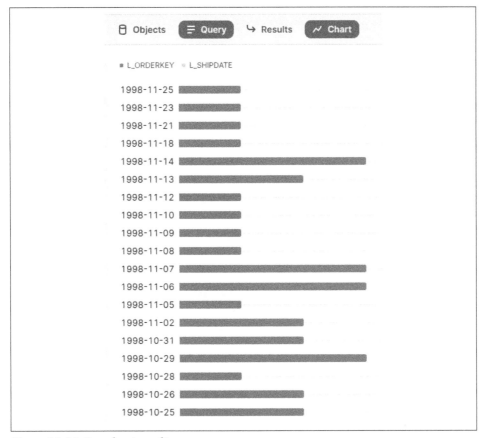

Figure 11-21. Bar chart results

Aggregating and Bucketing Data

Having the chart results at the daily level and in descending order doesn't provide the visual picture that we think would be helpful. Let's see if we can make some improvements.

Click the SHIPDATE button to the right. You can change the Bucketing from None to another value you think would be best. Try selecting Month and changing the direction to Ascending so that the time goes from left to right. Additionally, select the Label X-Axis and Label Y-Axis options and return the orientation to its original selection (see Figure 11-22).

Figure 11-22. Bucketing the SHIPDATE column

The changes I made give me a more appealing visualization from which I can gain some insights (as shown in Figure 11-23).

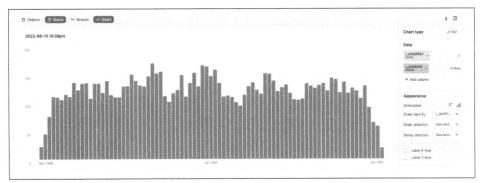

Figure 11-23. Visualization of the data after bucketing the SHIPDATE column

Note that if you hover your cursor over the top of any of the bars, you'll see the month and year as well as the number of orders for that particular month.

In the upper-left corner, you'll see a Return to Chapter11 option, with Chapter11 being the name of your dashboard (as shown in Figure 11-24).

Figure 11-24. The ability to return to the dashboard is provided in the upper-left corner of the screen

Go ahead and click the Return to Chapter11 option. You'll see the tile on your dashboard. You'll also have the option to create another tile by clicking the plus sign (+) just below the Chapter11 dashboard label (as shown in Figure 11-25).

Figure 11-25. Adding another tile in the dashboard

Create a new worksheet by clicking the + symbol in the upper-left corner. Now click the New Tile from Worksheet button to create a new tile in a new worksheet (as shown in Figure 11-26).

Figure 11-26. Creating a new tile in a new worksheet

Take some time to build additional tiles for your dashboard if you want.

Editing and Deleting Tiles

Even when placed on the dashboard, individual tiles can be edited. In the upper-right corner of the chart (as shown in Figure 11-27), click the ellipsis and select from the options. Of course, you can edit the chart by editing the underlying query, and one handy feature is that you can duplicate a tile. Duplicating a tile duplicates the underlying worksheet and queries.

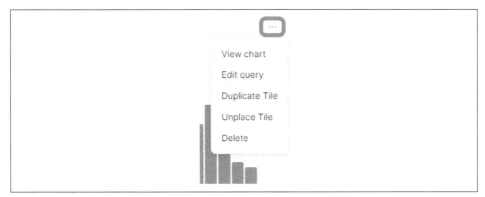

Figure 11-27. Tile options accessible after clicking the ellipsis

Deleting a tile from a dashboard also permanently deletes the underlying worksheet. You won't be able to retrieve the tile or worksheet after you perform a delete action.

Deleting a tile is not recommended unless you are certain that you will not need the worksheet upon which the chart is built.

One alternative to deleting a tile is to simply select Unplace Tile so that it still exists but is not viewable on the dashboard.

Collaboration

The goal of sharing work product and collaborating is to allow the group to benefit from the work of individuals without each person or business unit having to re-create the work. It also provides the opportunity for more innovation and improvements since everyone can contribute to the knowledge base and move it forward more quickly.

Sharing Your Query Results

To share the results of any query, first make sure you navigate back to the worksheet. Then simply click the down arrow to download a CSV file of the query results. The results can then be shared with others (as shown in Figure 11-28).

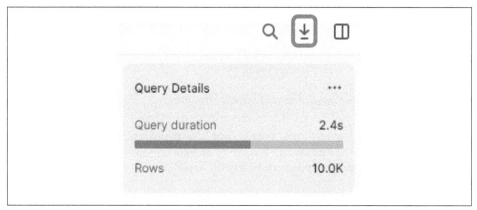

Figure 11-28. Use the down arrow to begin the process of sharing query results with others

Using a Private Link to Collaborate on Dashboards

One of the most important features of Snowsight is the ability for individuals to collaborate on a dashboard. It's easy to do. Navigate back to the Chapter11 dashboard. In the upper-right corner there is a Share button (as shown in Figure 11-29).

Figure 11-29. The Share button allows for sharing with others for dashboard collaboration

Click the Share button and you'll see an option to invite users or to let everyone with a link have access to the dashboard. You can authorize a few different privileges for people with the dashboard link, including the ability to only view the results, or to run the dashboard, which gives them the ability to refresh the dashboard for the latest results (as shown in Figure 11-30).

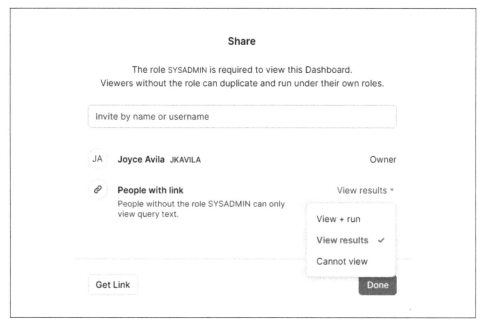

Figure 11-30. Assigning privileges for people with a link to the dashboard

A user can filter the results and chart the data to create a dashboard. Within a few minutes, they can then share the dashboard with a colleague—without ever having to leave Snowflake and using only SQL.

Summary

As demonstrated in this chapter, Snowsight supports data analyst activities in a variety of ways. Additionally, it's possible to share queries and dashboards, making it easy to collaborate with others.

One important thing to remember is that Snowsight visualizations are not a substitute for power BI tools meant to handle very large data sets. In the next chapter, one of the topics we'll cover is the analytics workload.

Code Cleanup

Because we used Snowflake's sample database, no code cleanup is needed for this chapter.

Knowledge Check

The following questions are based on the information covered in this chapter:

1. What are the different ways you can instruct Snowflake to return a subset of rows via the sampling technique? Why might we need to use sampling when creating Snowsight visualizations?

2. To use the preview option, do you write a SQL query? How many rows are returned when you use the preview option?

3. When you rerun a sampling query, are the same rows returned the second time as were returned the first time?

4. Is an active virtual warehouse required to run a sampling query? Is an active virtual warehouse required to preview the data?

5. What are the different ways you can bucket the data in Snowsight?

6. What happens when you delete a tile from a dashboard?

7. What are some of the use cases for using Snowsight visualizations?

8. What is an alternative to deleting a tile from the dashboard?

9. How many charts can you create from one worksheet?

10. Does Snowflake allow for visualization from internal data sources, external data sources, or both?

Answers to these questions are available in Appendix A.

Workloads for the Snowflake Data Cloud

A data workload is a capability, service, or process that can assist with data acquisition and data access, and that helps to extract value from the data or serves as a foundation upon which to develop something others can use. Throughout the previous chapters, we saw many examples of Snowflake's built-from-the-ground-up approach to data workloads while we spent time mastering the Snowflake building blocks and learning how to harness Snowflake's power.

In this chapter, we'll focus on how to apply the many Snowflake workloads to deliver business value from the Snowflake data platform. We'll summarize all of the Snowflake workloads, including the data engineering, data warehousing, data lake, data analytics, and data science workloads (as shown in Figure 12-1).

Further, we'll cover the data collaboration workload to discuss ways to leverage Snowflake's Secure Data Sharing capabilities for data monetization. We'll also be introduced to several examples of Snowflake's data application workload, which is used to develop large-scale data-intensive applications. We'll also learn about a new Snowflake workload, cybersecurity, and using Snowflake as a security data lake. Finally, we'll learn about Snowflake's newest workload, Unistore, which can be used to unify analytical and transactional data.

Figure 12-1. The Snowflake workloads

Prep Work

Create a new folder titled *Chapter12 Workloads*. Refer to "Navigating Snowsight Worksheets" on page 8 if you need help creating a new folder and worksheet. To set the worksheet context, make sure you are using the SYSADMIN role and the COMPUTE_WH virtual warehouse.

You'll notice in the following code that we are altering our session so that we don't use cached results. The reason for this is because we'll want to see how long it takes for some queries to run and we don't want the cached results to affect the performance time if we run the query a second time:

```
USE ROLE SYSADMIN;
USE WAREHOUSE COMPUTE_WH;
CREATE OR REPLACE DATABASE DEMO12_DB;
CREATE OR REPLACE SCHEMA CYBERSECURITY;
ALTER SESSION SET USE_CACHED_RESULT = FALSE;
```

Data Engineering

The goals of data engineering are to extract, transform, load, aggregate, store, and validate data. To achieve these goals, data engineers need to build efficient data pipelines. Data pipelines are the lifeblood of the modern enterprise, and efficient data pipelines can be the difference between architecture that delivers real value to the business and architecture that becomes a burden.

Data engineering pipelines also need to be built in such a way that the data will adhere to data governance rules and regulations. Although data engineers are not responsible for creating these governance rules and regulations, they are tasked with implementing them. Many examples of data governance controls were presented in Chapter 7. Some hands-on examples we completed in that chapter were for object tagging, classification, data masking, and row access policies.

As detailed in Chapter 6, Snowflake supports a wide range of data integration and processing tools, which provides Snowflake data engineers more architecture choices. For example, an ELT-style data engineering approach is made possible due to Snowflake's many different integration tools and its ability to deploy and scale virtual warehouses almost instantly.

Snowflake's data ingestion process is streamlined. It's easy to ingest JSON, XML, Avro, Parquet, and other data without transformations. There is no need to adjust the pipeline when the schema changes. In Snowflake, it's also easy to use SQL to query structured and semi-structured data. And, as we saw in Chapter 4, Snowflake also supports unstructured data.

In Chapter 6, we learned about Snowflake's data loading tools as well as how to unload data. We discovered how to load data using SQL in Snowflake worksheets and how to use the web UI data load feature. We explored the SnowSQL command-line interface (CLI), where we became familiar with the SQL COPY INTO and PUT commands. We also learned about data pipelines for continuous loading and streaming and were introduced to third-party ELT tools. In Chapter 8, we learned about agile software delivery, including continuous data integration, continuous delivery, and continuous deployment.

Throughout the previous chapters, we learned that with Snowflake's unique Data Cloud platform, organizations can collect more data than ever before. Additionally, data engineers can build simple, reliable data pipelines in the language of their choice using the Snowflake data platform, allowing them to deliver the performance and scalability that modern enterprises need to support thousands of concurrent users without resource contention.

In addition to its ability to ingest, transform, and query data in near-real time, Snowflake is an incredibly low-maintenance platform. As we saw in Chapter 9, Snowflake takes care of defining and maintaining partitions for you. Its automatic clustering capability seamlessly and continuously manages all reclustering; a table is reclustered only when needed. Snowflake also takes care of query optimization, metadata and statistics management, index management, and compute scaling. For that matter, administration of the Snowflake platform is simple; it's easy for you to set up users, create objects, and implement cost monitoring solutions.

Data Warehousing

Organizations build data warehouses to store and centralize data generated across the organization with the goal of performing fast data analytics and reporting. Of course, organizations want to accomplish these goals with a data warehouse that is low maintenance and low cost. Snowflake's data warehousing workload can easily meet these requirements.

As we've seen, Snowflake automatically handles performance tuning at scale with automatic caching and query optimization. Snowflake also handles remedial database administrator activities such as storage allocation, capacity planning, resource scaling, encryption, and seamless backups and upgrades. Snowflake's near-unlimited storage, scale, and speed means analysts can run any query at any time and quickly receive answers.

Snowflake's Data Cloud platform architecture makes it possible to fulfill an organization's data warehousing needs. Yet, more is required to ensure the successful fulfillment of data management initiatives. It is also important to develop a data model that will best organize the information in a data warehouse. In addition, it's important to consider the data modeling approach that is best suited for an organization's requirements, because an effective and sustainable data modeling approach provides a solid foundation for a data warehouse.

Snowflake supports all the standard data models, including the Inmon third normal form approach, the Kimball dimensional model, the new Data Vault model, and more. If you remember from previous chapters, with the exception of NOT NULL, referential integrity constraints are informational in Snowflake, which allows for more flexibility in approaches.

You're probably familiar with database schema design approaches, including the third normal form for relational databases which was defined in 1971. The third normal form uses normalizing principles to reduce the duplication of data, avoid data anomalies, ensure referential integrity, and simplify data management. The Inmon data modeling approach is built on the third normal form and identifies key subject areas and key business entities. The Kimball model, which allows users to construct several star schemas to fulfill various reporting needs, was introduced in 1996. The Inmon and Kimball data warehouse designs are two of the most widely discussed approaches; however, the Data Vault data model approach has become quite popular.

Data Vault 2.0 Modeling

The Data Vault system of business intelligence (BI) modeling organizes data in a way that separates structural information, such as a table's unique identifier or foreign key relationship, from its attributes. Architected to specifically meet the needs of modern

---

data warehouses, the Data Vault method is a hybrid approach that incorporates the best of the third normal form and the star schema modeling methods.

Data Vault was invented by Dan Linstedt while working for Lockheed Martin. It was introduced to the public in early 2000. Originally, Data Vault focused on modeling techniques and data loading processes for data warehouses. Later, the scope of Data Vault expanded to include a reference architecture, agile project delivery, automation, and continuous improvement, and Data Vault was labeled Data Vault 2.0.

Snowflake supports Data Vault 2.0, and you can likely obtain better results on Snowflake using the Data Vault modeling approach. This is because Data Vault 2.0 can take advantage of Snowflake's massively parallel processing compute clusters and optimized columnar storage format. Additionally, with Snowflake, you don't need to preplan partitioning or distribution keys. You also don't need to build indexes to get great performance.

The Data Vault model is composed of the following basic table types (as shown in Figure 12-2):

Hub tables

Hub tables hold all unique business keys of a subject. A hub also includes metadata describing the origin of the business key, known as the *record source*, which is used to track where and when the data originated. For example, HUB_EMPLOYEE may use an employee number to identify a unique employee.

Link tables

Link tables track all relationships between hubs, essentially describing a many-to-many relationship. Links can link to other links. Links are frequently used to deal with changes in data granularity, which reduces the impact of adding a new business key to a linked hub. For example, LINK_EMPLOYEE_STORE would track the relationship between an employee and the location of the store where they work.

Satellite tables

Satellite tables hold any attributes related to a link or hub and update them as they change. This is similar to a Kimball Type II slowly changing dimension. Whereas hubs and links form the structure of the data model, satellites contain temporal and descriptive attributes. These metadata attributes contain the date the record became valid and the date it expired. As such, satellites provide powerful historical capabilities. For example, SAT_EMPLOYEE may include attributes such as an employee's first and last names, title, or hire date.

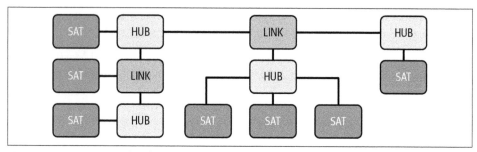

Figure 12-2. An example of a Data Vault relationship for hubs, links, and satellites

The Data Vault model is particularly useful in certain scenarios. Data Vault makes adding attributes simple; thus, it provides the most benefit when many data source systems exist or when there are constantly changing relationships. The Data Vault approach also enables faster data loading because tables can be loaded in parallel at the same time, which means you can load data quickly from multiple systems. Data Vault can accomplish this because there are fewer dependencies between tables during the load process. Also, the ingestion process is simplified due to having only inserts, which load quicker than merges or upserts. Data Vault is also a good choice when you need to easily track and audit your data, because Data Vault inherently enables auditing. Record sources are entered for every row, and load times are included as part of the primary key in satellites.

As described, Data Vault is most useful if you need to load data quickly from multiple source systems, your data relationships change frequently, or you need to easily track and audit your data. These scenarios are where the Data Vault method shines. If, however, your data is more straightforward, the Kimball dimensional model may be a better choice because implementing Data Vault would require an increased amount of business logic where it isn't needed.

Another consideration is that Data Vault requires more storage than other modeling approaches. Dividing a subject area into three different tables will increase the number of tables. Thus, if you only have a single source system, or the data is relatively static, it probably doesn't make sense to use Data Vault.

To summarize the differences in terms of complexity and implementation time, the Data Vault approach and the Kimball approach are relatively simple and require less time to implement as compared to the Inmon methodology. The Kimball approach is based on a four-step normalization process whereas Data Vault uses an agile methodology. In general, the cost to implement the Data Vault modeling approach is the lowest among the three, but Data Vault does require more storage, and is not the best choice when the data is straightforward and data auditing is not needed.

Transforming Data within Snowflake

An often-overlooked topic is how to transform data within Snowflake. Raw data ingested into Snowflake frequently comes from different sources that are often disparate. As such, you'll likely need to align these data types or assign default values to empty columns. There may exist a need to convert numbers to strings or strings to numbers. And you might need to flatten semi-structured data or rename columns. There are excellent third-party tools, like dbt, that can help you transform your data. Other data transformation tools, like the data build tool (dbt) from dbt Labs, can be used when streamlining and cleaning, in addition to transforming data, and might be needed by data scientists. There are also some native approaches you can employ for data transformation.

One straightforward way to transform data in Snowflake on an ongoing basis is by using tasks to automate an `INSERT OVERWRITE` statement. Tasks, first introduced in Chapter 3, have the ability to combine data from multiple source tables. There are also other advantages to using tasks for data transformation: they can be used to perform more complex transformations in a performant way, and the compute costs associated with using tasks can be tracked using resource monitors.

Materialized views are another native data transformation approach that is frequently used for real-time simple transformations. The advantage of using materialized views is that they are simple to create and provide transformed data in real-time.

Data Lake

Organizations build data lakes to harness the massive amounts of data coming from a variety of data sources for the purpose of eventually consolidating all the data and providing a single source of truth. Ultimately, the goal is to make all data available to the intended users and for the appropriate use cases.

Moving to the cloud has simplified data infrastructure and data management in many ways so that users can take advantage of the data lake workload to achieve many of their goals. However, until recently, it was not feasible to build data applications off a data lake environment. The data analytics workload was also a missing piece in the data lake workload. Snowflake's architecture, however, eliminates the need to maintain separate data storage and enterprise data warehouse environments. The distinction between the data lake and warehouse was removed with Snowflake's extensible data architecture.

Using Snowflake, you can mix and match components of data lake patterns to unleash the full potential of your data. Analysts can query data directly over the data lake with unlimited elastic scalability and no resource contention or concurrency issues. Data engineers can work with a streamlined architecture to run reliable and performant data pipelines. With built-in governance and security, all users can access all data in the data lake with granular-level access and privacy control. Snowflake can be used as a full data lake for all data and all users.

In "Data Warehousing" on page 374, we learned about data modeling techniques. Specifically, we were introduced to the Data Vault 2.0 approach. It is important to understand that Data Vaults and data lakes are complementary, addressing different parts of the analytics requirements for organizations. Data lakes provide a persistent staging area, meant to capture a superset of the data that arrives in too great a volume, too quickly, or with too much structural variation for traditional relational systems to handle. Data lakes are a great choice for data science activities. For integrating the most useful data for business users, a subset of the data from the data lake can be fed to the Data Vault.

We mentioned that a data lake architecture is useful for a data science workload. In the coming sections, we'll also learn other ways users can benefit from Snowflake's data lake workload. In "Data Applications" on page 383, we'll see examples of how large-scale, data-intensive applications can be built on Snowflake. We'll also learn how Snowflake, as a security data lake, supports the new Snowflake cybersecurity workload.

Data Collaboration

Secure Data Sharing enables data collaboration. The importance of the Snowflake Secure Data Sharing workload cannot be overly stressed. Chapter 10 is devoted to explaining the four Snowflake Secure Data Sharing approaches (as shown in Figure 12-3).

Figure 12-3. The four Snowflake Secure Data Sharing approaches

It is important to understand the mechanics of how Snowflake Secure Data Sharing works, how to harness the power of the Snowflake Data Exchange, and how to list and shop on the Snowflake Marketplace. With the rise of the Snowflake Marketplace comes the data network effect whereby the data that resides in the Marketplace becomes more valuable as it is more frequently requested and additional data providers offer their data as well. The Snowflake Marketplace makes it possible for organizations to leverage the copy-less sharing and security features of Snowflake Secure Data Sharing to offer their proprietary data and insights. Monetizing data has never been easier.

Data Monetization

If your organization is open to the possibility of monetizing its data, you'll want to start by creating an inventory of shareable data. Any information, such as trade secrets, that would jeopardize your competitiveness or information that would violate privacy laws should not be considered. Operational data, such as transaction records and sensor logs, are one option. You might also want to consider monetizing aggregated or de-identified marketing data such as customer information, preferences, or web traffic. Alternatively, you may possess open source data-like social network posts or government statistics which are of interest to others.

Once you've identified data that you'd consider monetizing, you'll need to decide whether the raw data is valuable enough or whether you might want to augment the data with additional data sets. For example, a retailer's store-level data would be much more valuable if it were combined with demographics data sets.

The next thing you'd want to consider is how to price your data. Two common pricing strategies are *cost pricing* and *value pricing*. In a cost pricing approach, you'd first need to calculate your costs involved in sourcing, packaging, and sharing the data and then add an amount above that cost which would be your profit margin. For a value pricing approach, you'd want to consider the value of the data from a customer's perspective. The value to a customer will be based on factors such as the uniqueness of the data, the level of difficulty required to obtain the data, and how many competitors already offer the same data. The value of your data is also determined by how frequently the data is updated and the amount of historical data you'll be offering. Additionally, your data could be more valuable if it is global, rather than local, in scope. As part of your pricing strategy, you'll also want to decide whether to sell the data as a set or as a subscription. Or you could decide to charge based on usage of the data.

Consider a freemium pricing structure, which features a limited amount of data for free, a basic charge for standard access, and then a premium charge for additional service features. A freemium pricing structure is a great way to gain new customers.

Regulatory and Compliance Requirements for Data Sharing

In addition to monetizing data, which is more of a *pull* to a data marketplace, it is expected that there will be more *pushes* to a centralized data marketplace because of regulatory and compliance requirements. A recent example is the U.S. National Institutes of Health (NIH), the world's largest funder of biomedical research. In January 2023, the NIH will begin requiring most of its annually funded 2,500 institutions and 300,000 researchers to make their data publicly available.

The NIH's mandate is meant to combat the *reproducibility crisis* in scientific research, an ongoing methodological crisis in which scientific results are increasingly difficult or impossible to reproduce. The reproducibility crisis wastes taxpayers' money and undermines public trust in science. Once NIH research data becomes publicly available next year, it will be interesting to see how the scientific community and others respond. Being able to access raw data upon which analyses can be independently performed will lend credibility to research findings.

The unique Secure Data Sharing capabilities of Snowflake make it possible to fully leverage Snowflake's powerful data analytics and data science workloads. As you'll see in the next section, Secure Data Sharing often plays a major role in data analytics workloads.

Data Analytics

Data analytics helps users make sense of data. Choosing the right data analytics tools is important, especially when trying to create a clear path to data analytics democratization. Data analytics democratization enables everyone in an organization to easily access and work with the organization's data. That way, people are empowered to make data-informed decisions and to leverage data to provide outstanding customer experiences.

A vast number of different kinds of native business intelligence (BI) tools are available from Snowflake partners to help with data democratization. Snowflake-native BI tools include familiar names such as Domo, Power BI, Sisense, Sigma, Tableau, and ThoughtSpot. A complete list of Snowflake BI partners can be found in the Snowflake online documentation (*https://oreil.ly/Zo9Su*).

Let's focus our attention on learning more about how these analytics tools are used in various industries. As you explore the following examples, observe how frequently you see data sharing capabilities as part of the overall analytics solutions.

A few years ago, it would have been unthinkable for most organizations to be in a position to leverage advanced analytics such as sentiment analysis, cluster analysis, predictive modeling, machine learning, and artificial intelligence. The adoption of advanced analytics has been growing, though, especially with the proliferation of cloud platforms. A portfolio of advanced analytics solutions specific to industries has been evolving and is especially evident across certain industries such as finance, healthcare, manufacturing, retail, and communication. Let's explore some specialized advanced analytics solutions for those industries.

Advanced Analytics for the Finance Industry

Financial institutions include commercial and investment banks, credit unions, credit card companies, stock brokerages, foreign exchange services, and insurance companies. Financial services firms operate in an environment where they are under intense competitive pressures from emerging firms, and where they are required to fulfill ever-changing regulatory requirements.

To succeed in this challenging environment, financial institutions must also find ways to reduce risks associated with fraudulent transactions and credit defaults. It is in the area of risk reduction that financial institutions have made the most progress by using data science techniques. Financial services firms are able to detect fraudulent activity in real time by using advanced, machine learning–based early-warning systems capable of mining data as transactions occur. It is also possible to vet potential borrowers more quickly *and* thoroughly, by deploying analytics-powered digital credit assessments and credit collection analyses.

Many of the world's leading financial services firms have realized the value of sharing information seamlessly to help manage and lower risk. As such, there is a growing amount of financially relevant data that is natively available on the Snowflake data platform. That data can now be shared much more easily with regulatory bodies, for example, by using the Snowflake Secure Data Sharing functionality. It can also be utilized as third-party data to enhance organizations' advanced analytics models. Equifax, First American Data & Analytics, and S&P Global Market Intelligence make their data available in the Snowflake Marketplace so that their clients can access the data simply and quickly, in real time, without having to store a copy of the data.

Advanced Analytics for the Healthcare Industry

Healthcare analytics includes 360-degree patient views, clinical trials data management, and connected medical devices and applications. Operational efficiency improvements with facility utilization and staffing are also a priority in the healthcare industry where significant cost savings are possible.

Additionally, the need to share patient information has dramatically increased because of the financial incentives of outcome-based treatment, a relatively new concept in the United States. This value-based care model, rather than the traditional fee-for-service model, has resulted in a fundamental shift toward data sharing in the healthcare industry, especially in the United States.

Centralized electronic health record (EHR) systems are quickly replacing the traditional handwritten notes filed in patient charts. Securely sharing patient information, without the need to transfer this sensitive information, is made easier through Snowflake's Secure Data Sharing capabilities. And data from the Internet of Medical Things (IoMT), including consumer health wearables, sensor-enabled hospital beds, and medication-tracking systems, can easily be ingested, integrated, and analyzed using today's sophisticated data science tools.

Access to more complete data from EHR and IoMT data provides limitless opportunities. With advanced analytics and more complete data, healthcare providers could diagnose patients more quickly and more accurately, uncover trends that could lead to groundbreaking cures, and innovate with new business use cases that could result in new revenue streams.

Advanced Analytics for the Manufacturing Industry and Logistics Services

Manufacturers use advanced analytics techniques to improve product quality and increase manufacturing operations productivity. Real-time feeds from manufacturing operations' sensors can be used to identify quality control issues before they become excessive. Fluctuations in labor needs can be better anticipated and managed by predicting the ups and downs in production demands.

By implementing Secure Data Sharing with partners, manufacturers can break down data silos that often occur across traditional supply change management systems, enterprise resource planning platforms, order fulfillment systems, and Internet of Things (IoT) devices. Combining Secure Data Sharing and advanced analytics can help to make supply chains more efficient by tracking shipments and inventory in real time to reduce bottlenecks and interruptions.

Marketing Analytics for Retail Verticals and the Communications and Media Industry

Creating and maintaining a positive reputation for your brand, your products, and your business is important. A potential customer's initial reaction to your products or services is often shaped by the reviews or responses they encounter on social media. That is why it's important to tap into the emotions about your brand online to calculate a score which indicates whether a social media post or a product review is negative, neutral, or positive. It's also relevant to apply the scoring to emails and phone conversations through the use of text-to-speech. In doing so, you can determine the specific products and services, or social media marketing efforts, that elicit the positive reactions you want. It also allows you to identify any breakdowns in customer service. Sentiment analysis is the method you can use to automate the process of assigning scores to words and determining whether your reputation is positive overall, or not.

Not only are the words your customers use to describe you or your products important, so are the words you use to market to them. Content strategy can employ serial testing, with an unsupervised learning algorithm, to discover which word choice or color is the most effective in your digital advertising campaigns. Content strategy can also be influenced by third-party data such as weather or COVID-19 data; data that is available on the Snowflake Marketplace. Content strategy can be combined with channel optimization, which uses tools such as affinity analysis and market basket analysis. As one example, channel optimization helps to highlight missed opportunities on specific social media platforms such as Instagram, Pinterest, and YouTube. Additionally, some channels make it possible to use recommendation engines to suggest similar products or upsell items.

Data science and machine learning models can also help identify things that might improve customer loyalty because it is easier and cheaper to market to an existing customer than to a new lead. To assist, third-party loyalty data can be obtained from technology company Ibotta on the Snowflake Marketplace. When marketing to a new lead, the likelihood of success can be significantly improved with lead scoring. Leads are most accurately scored when using augmented third-party data along with your own marketing data. In addition to being used for lead scoring, predictive analytics can be used to help identify customers with a higher potential lifetime value. In summary, marketing analytics and data science is intended to provide valuable insight into customers' preferences and behaviors, for the purpose of marketing budget optimization and profit maximization.

One of the things you might have noticed in these marketing analytics examples is that marketing analytics often takes a more tactical approach to analytics at the individual level. The same can be said of many of the healthcare industry's advanced analytics solutions, which can be used at the most granular levels.

Whatever industry or vertical space you are operating in and whatever BI tool you choose, you need access to the data necessary for analysis. One of the most important data sources for many organizations is customer data captured by the customer's own internal data application. As we'll see next, the Snowflake data application workload is one of the most desirable choices for custom-built data-intensive applications.

Data Applications

A data application developer's goal is to build applications that deliver value to the company while meeting the practical and qualitative needs of end users. Achieving this goal, while at the same time consistently providing high-quality user experiences, is a difficult task, especially when developing large-scale data-intensive applications.

Data-intensive applications process terabytes of fast-changing data in billions of rows and leverage that data to deliver value to users. Applications include sales and retail tracking systems, IoT, health, and Customer 360 apps, with the latter used for targeted email campaigns and for generating personalized offers. Embedded analytics and machine learning apps are further examples of data-intensive use cases.

To build applications that deliver high value quickly, many developers build their applications on platform foundations with the required infrastructure elements, such as data storage, processing, management, and security, built in. Using this strategy, these developers look for cloud platforms that are easy to use; are secure; support scalability, concurrency, and the use of semi-structured data; and include intelligent query execution. Snowflake is a cloud-based platform containing all these foundational elements, and with its near-zero management capability, developers can focus on application development rather than on data platform management and data platform security.

Examples of popular public-facing data-intensive applications in which the Snowflake cloud platform is used include the bike sharing app Lime, the grocery delivery app Instacart, the online travel app Hotel Tonight, and the digital learning app Blackboard. Another highly performant application built on Snowflake is Twilio SendGrid, a marketing campaign app that sends billions of emails per month on behalf of thousands of customers.

A key feature of the Snowflake data platform is that it is developer friendly. It allows app developers to choose among several programming languages, including Node.js, .NET, Go, Java, Python, and SQL. For example, the Snowflake SQL REST API can be used to build applications and integrate custom plug-ins. Using Snowflake's SQL API playground, you can gain hands-on experience developing data applications and integrations using the SQL REST API. In the playground, you can explore predefined queries and responses, or use it to experiment with and execute real queries in your Snowflake environment. You can also download the API's Postman Collection or explore the OpenAPI specification file. The Snowflake SQL API playground can be accessed at *https://api.developers.snowflake.com*.

In 2021, Snowflake introduced the connected application deployment model known as Powered by Snowflake, a program to help companies build, operate, and grow applications in the Data Cloud. A number of Powered by Snowflake partners, such as AuditBoard, Hunters, MessageGears, Securonix, and Supergrain, have adopted the connected app model for their apps.

To accelerate your Snowflake application journey, it is possible to take advantage of the Powered By Snowflake program to join workshops and request access to experts to help you design the right data architecture for your customer-facing applications. To see examples of Powered By Snowflake applications, visit the Snowflake website (*https://oreil.ly/oOuFg*).

Moreover, it is possible to use the Snowflake Snowpark developer framework to build data-intensive applications for consumption by internal business users. Snowpark is frequently used to build complex pipelines for creating machine learning applications. The Snowpark framework can be used by application developers to collaborate on data projects in coding languages and constructs familiar to them. Most importantly, developers can build apps that process data within Snowflake without having to move data to a different system where the application code exists.

Whether you need a data application workload to build an application for your customers, employees, or internal business users, the Snowflake platform allows you to build large-scale data applications with no operational burden.

The new Snowflake Native Application Framework takes connected applications to the next level by allowing providers to easily build, sell, and deploy applications within the Data Cloud via Snowflake Marketplace. The framework includes telemetry tools to make it easy for providers to monitor and support their applications. The native application deployment model complements both connected and managed application deployment models.

Data Science

The many benefits of Snowflake data engineering, data warehousing, and data lake workloads have been detailed throughout the previous chapters and also summarized in earlier sections of this chapter. These particular Snowflake workloads provide the foundation for a robust data science workload on the Snowflake platform, and the many unique capabilities of the Snowflake Secure Data Sharing workload enhance the data science workload. As such, Snowflake's Data Cloud can be used to accelerate the collection and processing of internal and third-party data for data science workloads.

Powerful tools are available from several Snowflake data science partners, including Alteryx, Amazon (SageMaker), Anaconda, Dataiku, DataRobot, H20.ai, and Microsoft (Azure ML). Snowflake's website includes a complete listing (*https://oreil.ly/ CJcEQ*) of all Snowflake technology partners, including data science partners. In addition to the wide range of data science tools and platforms available through the Snowflake partner network, there are also Snowpark and Streamlit, two new Snowflake features.

In addition to the wide range of data science tools and platforms available through the Snowflake partner network, there is also a new Snowflake feature called Snowpark.

Snowpark

Snowpark is a developer framework that brings new data programmability to the Data Cloud by extending Snowflake's capabilities. The Snowflake API makes it possible for developers, data scientists, and data engineers to use their language of choice to deploy code in a serverless manner. Snowpark currently supports Java, Scala, and Python. Future enhancements to Snowpark include Python Worksheets, which will allow you to write and run Python code within the Snowflake UI—much like a notebook environment. Snowflake Worksheets for Python are currently in private preview.

Snowpark, first released to customers about a year ago, represents a major foray into new programmability options within Snowflake. As the Snowflake platform has grown into the Data Cloud, there was a natural progression to expand ways developers could interact with the platform, because not every developer wants to write their code in SQL and not every data problem is well suited to a SQL solution.

Snowpark makes it easy for data engineers and data scientists to create complex data pipelines which negate the need to move data to the system where the application code exists. Instead, processing of the application code is brought directly to where the data resides. Snowpark provides a single layer to access the data and opens up the use of a DataFrame API, which provides for more efficient coding capabilities, especially with large data sets.

Snowpark taps into Snowflake's readily available virtual warehouses, so there is no time lag for accessing resources, which means statistics and computations from machine learning models or web session analysis can be provided in near real time. In fact, no cluster outside of Snowflake is required, because all computations are done within Snowflake. Because Snowpark is native to Snowflake, there is no need to manage partitions, which is a common and difficult problem that frequently occurs with file-based data lakes.

One of the best features of Snowpark is that you can create user-defined functions (UDFs) in your code, which Snowpark can then push to the server where the code will directly operate on the data. Snowflake allows you to build complex logic into your UDFs and to take advantage of powerful external functions. Currently, there is Snowflake support for Java, JavaScript, and Python UDFs as well as external functions.

The Snowpark library is distributed as a JAR file through Maven and can be used to develop applications in many different environments including Jupyter notebooks, as well as in application development tools such as IntelliJ IDEA and Visual Studio. Once you've set up your development environment for Snowpark, you'll need to create a session with the Snowflake database to use the Snowpark library. Be sure to close the session when you are done.

Specifically, how does Snowpark work once you've created a session? In your development environment, you'll orchestrate transformations and trigger actions to occur within the Snowflake compute environment. Common Snowpark transformation operations include SELECT, JOIN, FILTER, and PIVOT, and common actions include WRITE, FIRST, and COUNT.

 Calling certain actions, such as COLLECT and TAKE, will download data into the memory of your running client or driver application and could result in an Out of Memory error.

Using the Snowpark library, you read each Snowflake table as a DataFrame which creates a memory reference to the table. It is possible to perform transformations on the memory reference, but all the transformations will only be processed once you perform an action. In other words, Snowpark DataFrames are lazily evaluated. At the time an action is performed, the Snowpark library summarizes all the submitted transformations as it generates an equivalent SQL query statement. This SQL statement is then passed to the Snowflake compute resources where it is executed (as shown in Figure 12-4).

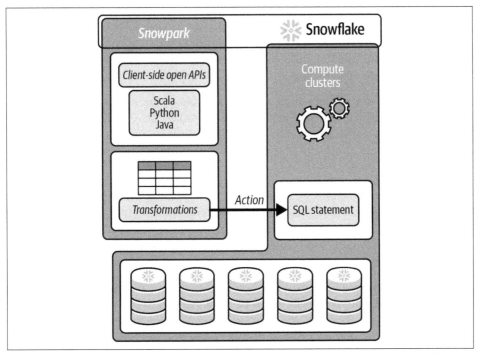

Figure 12-4. A SQL statement is executed in Snowflake once an action is triggered from Snowpark to aggregate transformations into a SQL query

 It is possible to test or debug the SQL query manually in the Snowflake UI. You can find the SQL statement in your client or driver application log.

It was mentioned previously that you take advantage of Snowflake's UDFs if your transformation code is too complex to be represented as a DataFrame operation. A UDF will process one record at a time and return a new column value that can be appended to the DataFrame.

With Snowpark, you can create UDFs with no parameters. Up to 10 parameters can be passed as DataFrame columns.

One limitation of the UDF parameters available for Snowpark is that there are some data types, most notably arrays, that are not natively supported via the Snowpark API. There are some workarounds available by using the Snowflake variant data type, but they are not optimal solutions. However, if you find that there is a need for complex coding that cannot be handled easily with Snowflake's UDFs, there is another option. Just as you can take advantage of Snowflake's UDFs, it is also possible to incorporate external functions into your Snowpark solution. External functions are UDFs stored outside of Snowflake.

If you'd like to get some hands-on experience with Snowpark or some of the data science partners' tools, you can take part in the Snowflake Data Cloud Academy's complimentary Data Scientist School (*https://oreil.ly/4RGuB*).

Streamlit

Snowflake acquired Streamlit in March 2022. Streamlit has many machine learning and data science use cases that can be used to build complex and dynamic applications. For example, within the Streamlit framework, users can create rich interactive visualizations with Python code. Some other great benefits of Streamlit are that it is structured and simple.

Another exciting feature of Streamlit, when used in conjunction with Python Worksheets, is that Streamlit applications can be rendered directly in the Snowflake user interface. Once those Streamlit apps are deployed on Snowflake as Native Applications, users will be able to make those apps available to other Snowflake users through role-based authentication in much the same way as is done today with data.

Cybersecurity Using Snowflake as a Security Data Lake

The high costs of security breaches make cybersecurity a top priority for company executives. Some of these costs include loss of revenue, customer trust, and intellectual property. Maintaining a strong security posture is critical and challenging. For one thing, with the exponential growth of data, it takes great effort and time to identify and contain a breach. Traditional approaches to solving this problem relied heavily on legacy security information and event management (SIEM) tools not designed for today's needs.

There are many challenges associated with a SIEM-only architecture. First, SIEMs charge by volume, which makes it cost prohibitive to ingest and process all logs. Not only are they expensive, but SIEMs are time-consuming solutions to run; thus, events identified as noncritical are often excluded from SIEM processing.

Second, data silos leave investigators with invisibility gaps, an incomplete picture of events, and failed audits (as shown in Figure 12-5). It is not unusual for teams to use 10 or more different security products at a time. A lot of the tools used to collect security logs and security data are separated and siloed. Without a unified way to manage these tools, security analysts often find themselves hopping from tool to tool, in a *swivel chair* approach. This also requires manual work, such as downloading data and creating a combined report, as well as spending time unnecessarily investigating too many false positives. This approach results in a loss of visibility, speed, and efficiency.

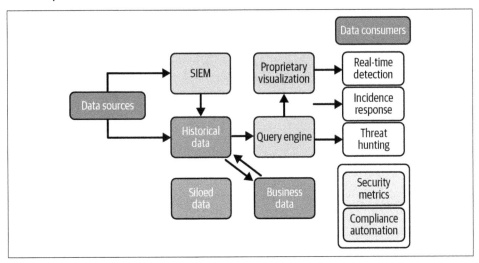

Figure 12-5. Legacy cybersecurity architecture

Finally, SIEMs only support proprietary languages; thus, users cannot join data across different sources or use commonly known languages to investigate logs. As a result, there's a high demand for cybersecurity analysts but there doesn't exist a large pool of talent who possess the specific skills security teams need.

Overcoming the Challenges of a SIEM-Only Architecture

To overcome these challenges, security teams augmented the traditional SIEM-only approach with security orchestration, automation, and response (SOAR) and extended detection and response (XDR) products. SOAR tools, sometimes built into SIEM tools, simplify manual remediation efforts. Still, these SOAR tools are often add-ons and plug-ins that require configuring and tuning, and the combination of SIEM and SOAR tools doesn't address the problem of siloed data.

The latest generation of SIEM tools may offer XDR capabilities that attempt to improve threat detection and response times by centralizing and normalizing data from across multiple security layers. The goal of XDR solutions is to better validate alerts, thereby reducing false positives and increasing reliability. SIEMs are more proactive whereas XDR is a reactive system. While SIEM solutions collect shallow data from many sources, XDR collects deeper data from targeted sources. XDR can also provide better context for events and eliminate the need for manual tuning or integration of data.

XDR has resulted in improvements in cybersecurity, but the need for a solution that can frequently accept, store, and process large amounts of unstructured as well as structured data still exists. One solution to those challenges is a data lake approach which can be employed to manage, share, and use different types of data from different sources. An XDR–data lake process collects data from all layers, feeds the data into a data lake, sterilizes it, and then correlates the data to any penetrated attack surface (as shown in Figure 12-6). In doing so, the XDR–data lake process is able to mine for patterns or insights that arise when attackers exploit gaps in security silos, which allow them to slip between siloed products and then move laterally over time as they learn more about a network's defenses and prepare for future attacks.

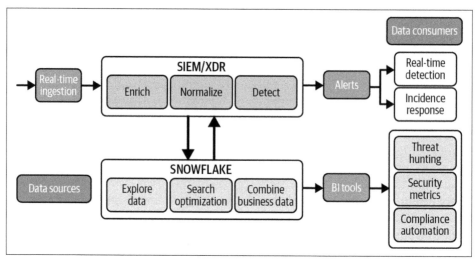

Figure 12-6. Modern cybersecurity architecture

Today, many organizations are adopting a security data lake as a foundation of their cybersecurity strategy. A security data lake allows companies to capture and efficiently store data from all log sources, access all log sources to respond to incidents, and hunt for threats. With a security data lake, it is possible to cost-effectively store years of data in a single place, run analytics across security logs with other enterprise data sources, and provide partners with seamless, governed access to your data. Snowflake is a natural choice as a security data lake.

Snowflake's unique architecture provides many value propositions. With separation of compute from storage, security analysts can more quickly perform query searches and historical analysis than they can with SIEMs, which frequently take 30 minutes or more to return results. Using Snowflake as a security data lake to store unlimited data allows you to break down those data silos, and it is a much more scalable approach than using SIEMs. Additionally, there is no limit to how long you can store data inexpensively in Snowflake. It is possible to store an infinite number of logs, with unlimited retention, in a single hot tier at $23 per terabyte.

With regard to the languages available to users, Snowflake supports many languages including universal languages such as SQL and Python. This support allows organizations that use Snowflake as a security data lake to leverage the people they already have who possess those skills to help with security tasks.

Another value proposition is that by using Snowflake as a security data lake, it is possible to combine different types of data sets for analytics that traditional SIEMs or legacy systems cannot combine. Traditional SIEMs are only able to ingest certain types of security logs whereas Snowflake can support structured, semi-structured, and unstructured data types. Additionally, Snowflake's ecosystem includes enterprise BI tool options, which makes it easy to build dynamic dashboards. In contrast, traditional SIEMs are very limited in the way results can be presented in only a few different templates.

To be clear, using Snowflake as a security data lake has value beyond just inexpensive cloud storage and instant compute scalability. With Snowflake, there is a rich ecosystem of partners who provide Snowflake-connected applications to deliver next-level security capabilities. For example, detection services or workflows out of the box, event timelines, and more can be delivered via Snowflake partners such as Hunters, Lacework, and Panthers Lab. In essence, these partners provide intuitive front-end user interfaces which leverage Snowflake as the backbone of their cybersecurity strategy.

Using Snowflake as a security data lake, companies can get full visibility into all their log data sources in a single system, they can reduce risk, and they can improve their overall security posture. Snowflake removes data silos and enables automated analytics to help teams make better-informed decisions using relevant metrics and dynamic dashboards. In addition, Snowflake continues to innovate and find ways to support the cybersecurity workload with such features as its search optimization service.

Search Optimization Service Versus Clustering

Snowflake's search optimization service improves the performance of point lookup queries. A point lookup query returns one or a few distinct rows. Point lookup queries are frequently used by business users who need fast response times for critical dashboards with highly selective filters and by data scientists who need a specific subset of a large data set.

Snowflake's search optimization service runs in the background to collect metadata information about columns that are used to populate search access paths. Search optimization may appear similar to clustering, but there are some key differences. For one thing, search optimization is enabled for all columns whereas clustering is done on one key or a set of keys. Another difference is that search optimization speeds up equality searches only whereas clustering speeds up both range and equality searches. An equality search uses a filter to identify records that contain a specific value for a given attribute whereas a range query retrieves all records in which some value is between an upper and lower boundary. One other important difference is that clustering adds only compute costs to run a background process for reclustering whereas the search optimization service incurs both compute and storage costs. Storage costs are incurred to store the search access path.

Here is an example to help demonstrate the differences between clustering and search optimization. We'll use Snowflake sample data to create a table. Because we can't clone the Snowflake sample data, we'll need to create a base table using the Snowflake sample data so that we can clone the table a few times. The table has 600 million rows, so it will take a few minutes to create a clone:

```
CREATE OR REPLACE TABLE BASETABLE AS
    SELECT * FROM SNOWFLAKE_SAMPLE_DATA.TPCH_SF100.LINEITEM;
```

First, clone the table to use for the clustering example and enable clustering:

```
CREATE OR REPLACE TABLE CLUSTEREXAMPLE CLONE BASETABLE;
ALTER TABLE CLUSTEREXAMPLE CLUSTER BY (L_SHIPDATE);
```

Verify that the clustering is complete by first looking at the clustered table:

```
SELECT SYSTEM$CLUSTERING_INFORMATION('CLUSTEREXAMPLE','(L_SHIPDATE)');
```

Figure 12-7 shows the clustering information for the CLUSTEREXAMPLE table.

```
Aa SYSTEM$CLUSTERING_INFORMATION('CLUSTEREXAMPLE','(L_SHIPDATE)')

{
  "cluster_by_keys" : "LINEAR(L_SHIPDATE)",
  "total_partition_count" : 919,
  "total_constant_partition_count" : 5,
  "average_overlaps" : 8.2002,
  "average_depth" : 5.4875,
  "partition_depth_histogram" : {
    "00000" : 0,
    "00001" : 3,
    "00002" : 14,
    "00003" : 122,
    "00004" : 166,
    "00005" : 158,
    "00006" : 170,
    "00007" : 147,
    "00008" : 108,
    "00009" : 31,
    "00010" : 0,
    "00011" : 0,
    "00012" : 0,
    "00013" : 0,
    "00014" : 0,
    "00015" : 0,
    "00016" : 0
  }
}
```

Figure 12-7. Clustering information for the CLUSTEREXAMPLE table

Now let's compare those results to the unclustered base table:

```
SELECT SYSTEM$CLUSTERING_INFORMATION('BASETABLE','(L_SHIPDATE)');
```

Figure 12-8 shows the results.

```
Aa SYSTEM$CLUSTERING_INFORMATION('BASETABLE','(L_SHIPDATE)')

{
  "cluster_by_keys" : "LINEAR(L_SHIPDATE)",
  "total_partition_count" : 906,
  "total_constant_partition_count" : 2,
  "average_overlaps" : 263.4746,
  "average_depth" : 159.9106,
  "partition_depth_histogram" : {
    "00000" : 0,
    "00001" : 1,
    "00002" : 0,
    "00003" : 0,
    "00004" : 0,
    "00005" : 0,
    "00006" : 0,
    "00007" : 0,
    "00008" : 0,
    "00009" : 0,
    "00010" : 0,
    "00011" : 0,
    "00012" : 0,
    "00013" : 0,
    "00014" : 0,
    "00015" : 0,
    "00016" : 0,
    "00032" : 5,
    "00064" : 41,
    "00128" : 234,
    "00256" : 625
  }
}
```

Figure 12-8. Clustering information for the BASETABLE table

You'll notice that the number of partitions is just slightly higher for the clustered table, but other than that, there is not much difference at this point between the clustered and unclustered tables. The reason is because clustering, which runs in the background, takes some time to complete, especially on a large table such as the one we're using. We'll come back and review the clustered table again later. For now, let's go ahead and clone the table to use for a search optimization example:

```
CREATE OR REPLACE TABLE OPTIMIZEEXAMPLE CLONE BASETABLE;
ALTER TABLE OPTIMIZEEXAMPLE ADD SEARCH OPTIMIZATION;
```

Verify that the search optimization is complete by using the SHOW TABLES command:

```
SHOW TABLES LIKE '%EXAMPLE%';
```

You should see that the value for the SEARCH_OPTIMIZATION_PROGRESS column for the OPTIMIZEEXAMPLE table is now at 100, which indicates that the search optimization is complete. You'll also notice that the AUTOMATIC_CLUSTERING column value is ON for the CLUSTEREXAMPLE table.

Next, we'll want to run a point lookup query on the original table, which has neither clustering nor optimization enabled. Let's use the following command to get an example of a record we can use later for the point lookup query:

```
SELECT * FROM BASETABLE
LIMIT 1;
```

Make note of the L_ORDERKEY value for the record that is returned and use it in the next query:

```
SELECT * FROM BASETABLE WHERE L_ORDERKEY ='363617027';
```

Figure 12-9 shows the results.

	L_ORDERKEY	⋯	L_PARTKEY	L_SUPPKEY	L_LINENUMBER	L_QUANTITY	L_EXTENDEDPRICE
1	363,617,027		5,916,396	416,407	5	40	56,484
2	363,617,027		13,148,870	148,871	2	7	13,427.54
3	363,617,027		3,846,799	96,803	1	46	80,297.6
4	363,617,027		13,046,496	46,497	3	31	44,697.04
5	363,617,027		12,441,597	941,622	4	27	41,525.19

Figure 12-9. Results of the point lookup query on the BASETABLE table

You'll notice that, as shown in Figure 12-10, the query profiler took 4.0 seconds to complete.

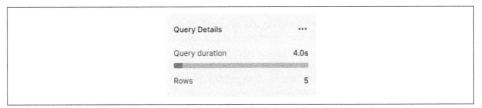

Figure 12-10. The Query Details view for the point lookup query on the BASETABLE table

Click the Home icon to navigate back to the Main menu, and then click Activity → Query History. Click the query you just ran. You can see that the query had to scan all 906 micro-partitions to obtain the results (as shown in Figure 12-11).

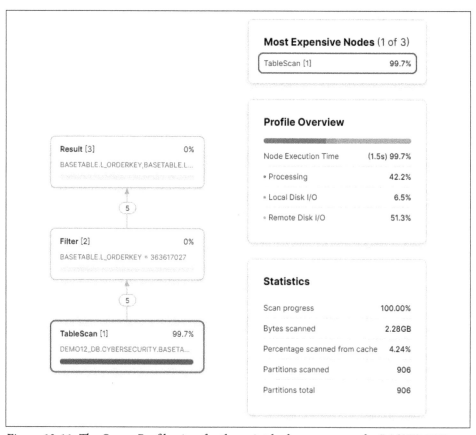

Figure 12-11. The Query Profile view for the point lookup query on the BASETABLE table

Attempting the same query on the clustered table, we notice that it took even longer to return the results (as shown in Figure 12-12):

```
SELECT * FROM CLUSTEREXAMPLE WHERE L_ORDERKEY ='363617027';
```

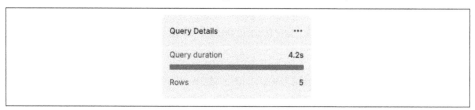

Figure 12-12. The Query Details view for the point lookup query on the CLUSTEREXAMPLE table

And there were even more partitions scanned this time, too (as shown in Figure 12-13).

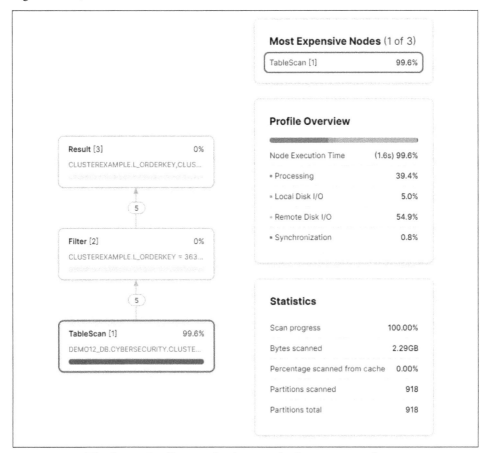

Figure 12-13. The Query Profile view for the point lookup query on the CLUSTEREXAMPLE table

We should be able to rewrite the query in such a way that we can demonstrate how it is possible to take advantage of clustering. Let's see if we can reduce the runtime by scanning on the specific micro-partitions where the clustering key exists (as shown in Figure 12-14). If you look at the results you received earlier, you'll notice that there is an L_SHIPDATE column. Be sure to use the range of dates from the records returned in your search:

```
SELECT * FROM CLUSTEREXAMPLE
    WHERE L_SHIPDATE >= '1992-12-05'and L_SHIPDATE <='1993-02-20'
    AND L_ORDERKEY = '363617027';
```

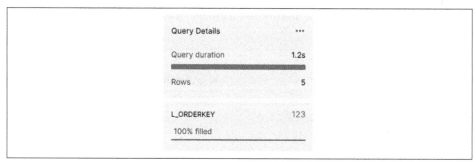

Figure 12-14. The Query Details view for the point lookup query on the CLUSTEREXAMPLE table using a specific range on the clustering key

When we look at the query profile, we notice that it was only necessary to scan 34 partitions to return the results (as shown in Figure 12-15).

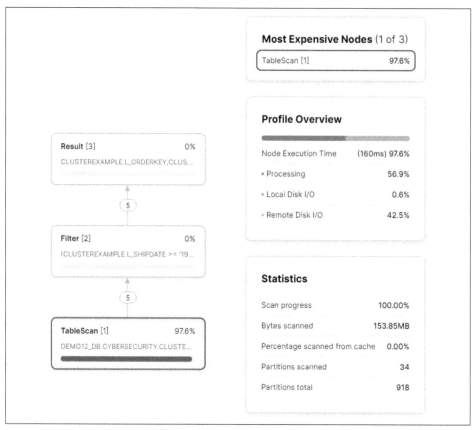

Figure 12-15. The Query Profile view for the point lookup query on the CLUSTEREXAMPLE table using a specific range on the clustering key

What have we learned thus far? We saw that clustering didn't improve performance on point lookup queries. The exception was when we knew, in advance, the range of values for the clustering key that would allow us to narrow down the number of partitions scanned. Realistically, we're rarely likely to see the exception in practice. Therefore, we can say that clustering doesn't improve performance on point lookup queries as a general rule. What about optimization?

When we attempt our SELECT * query on the table where we enabled search optimization, we'll see that with search optimization enabled, the results will be returned much more quickly as the profiler is able to use search optimization (as shown in Figure 12-16):

```
SELECT * FROM OPTIMIZEEXAMPLE WHERE L_ORDERKEY ='363617027';
```

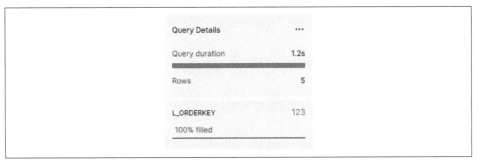

Figure 12-16. The Query Details view for the point lookup query on the OPTIMIZEEXAMPLE table

Interestingly, it was only necessary to scan six micro-partitions to return the results (as shown in Figure 12-17).

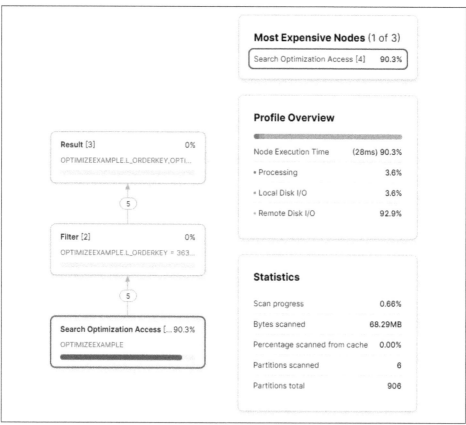

Search Optimization Access [4]   90.3%

Profile Overview

Node Execution Time	(28ms) 90.3%
• Processing	3.6%
• Local Disk I/O	3.6%
• Remote Disk I/O	92.9%

Result [3]   0%
OPTIMIZEEXAMPLE.L_ORDERKEY,OPTI...

5

Filter [2]   0%
OPTIMIZEEXAMPLE.L_ORDERKEY = 363...

5

Search Optimization Access [... 90.3%
OPTIMIZEEXAMPLE

Statistics

Scan progress	0.66%
Bytes scanned	68.29MB
Percentage scanned from cache	0.00%
Partitions scanned	6
Partitions total	906

Figure 12-17. The Query Profile view for the point lookup query on the CLUSTEREXAMPLE table

When used for point lookup queries in a security data lake, Snowflake's search optimization service can have a big impact by speeding up workloads. In addition, using the search optimization service can reduce overall costs by enabling you to use smaller virtual warehouses on existing workloads.

Remember earlier when we looked at the CLUSTERINGEXAMPLE table? Refer back to Figure 12-7 for the results. Now that some time has passed, let's look at the table again (as shown in Figure 12-18):

```
SELECT SYSTEM$CLUSTERING_INFORMATION('CLUSTEREXAMPLE','(L_SHIPDATE)');
```

```
Aa SYSTEM$CLUSTERING_INFORMATION('CLUSTEREXAMPLE';'(L_SHIPDATE)')

{
  "cluster_by_keys" : "LINEAR(L_SHIPDATE)",
  "total_partition_count" : 918,
  "total_constant_partition_count" : 6,
  "average_overlaps" : 5.7211,
  "average_depth" : 4.1383,
  "partition_depth_histogram" : {
    "00000" : 0,
    "00001" : 3,
    "00002" : 32,
    "00003" : 290,
    "00004" : 277,
    "00005" : 180,
    "00006" : 106,
    "00007" : 22,
    "00008" : 8,
    "00009" : 0,
    "00010" : 0,
    "00011" : 0,
    "00012" : 0,
    "00013" : 0,
    "00014" : 0,
    "00015" : 0,
    "00016" : 0
  }
}
```

Figure 12-18. Clustering information for the CLUSTEREXAMPLE table (compare to Figure 12-7)

You should see a big difference now in how the table is clustered.

Unistore

Unistore, Snowflake's newest workload, expands Snowflake's capabilities to enable a modern approach to working with transactional and analytical data together in a single platform. Transactional and analytical data have traditionally been siloed, but with Unistore, Snowflake users can now include transactional use cases such as application state and data serving. The Unistore workload is made possible by Snowflake hybrid tables. To better understand the new Unistore workload, let's first describe the problem.

Transactional Workload Versus Analytical Workload

There are several differences between transactional and analytical workloads, as summarized in Table 12-1.

Table 12-1. Differences between transactional and analytical workloads

	Transactional	Analytical
Purpose	Operational	Analytical
Number of concurrent users	High	Low to medium
Response time	Subsecond	Seconds to hours
Scales	Linearly	Nonlinearly (complex queries)
Data model	Normalized	Columnar store
Freshness	Real time	Historical
Query form	INSERT, DELETE, UPDATE	SELECT

There is an increasing need to close the gap between transactional and analytical workloads. For example, a retailer could use analytical results to identify cross-sell and up-sell opportunities, but only if the results could be obtained quickly enough to take action. One frequently implemented solution to the problem is an operational data store (ODS), which is a type of database often used as an interim local storage area for a data warehouse. While an ODS does partially address the latency issue, it also adds more complexity and increases costs.

We learned in previous chapters how Snowflake was built from the ground up to deliver a scalable solution to analytical workloads, but now, with the new Unistore workload, the solution is extended to transactional workloads. The Unistore workload enforces primary key constraints, and referential integrity is enforced with foreign key constraints. Row level locking, low latency lookups, and unique and nonunique indexes are also features built on the existing Snowflake framework to support the Unistore workload. Snowflake achieves this new functionality with the use of its new hybrid tables.

Hybrid Tables

Hybrid tables enable customers to perform quick analytics on transactional data for immediate context. Snowflake hybrid tables are very similar to other types of Snowflake tables. It is possible to join hybrid tables with existing Snowflake tables for a holistic view across all data, and many common Snowflake features, such as streams, cloning, and UDFs, are available for use with hybrid tables. Because hybrid tables are just another table type in Snowflake, you also experience the same robust syntax and consistent governance and security as other Snowflake table types.

What makes hybrid tables different is that they're designed to support fast, single-row operations and provide you with great analytical query performance. When creating a Snowflake hybrid table, you'll need to make sure you identify the primary key, as the primary key is required. As a result of having a required primary key, Snowflake is able to prevent duplicate records. Duplicate record prevention was a feature not previously supported.

For transactional workloads, it is common to use the Order ID field as the primary key and to also create an index on the order date column so that it is faster to access the most recent orders.

Leveraging Snowflake's hybrid tables, you can get transactional and analytical data together in a single, unified platform without the need to use multiple different products. This simplifies and streamlines enterprise application development and eliminates the need to move your data between systems.

Summary

This chapter described Snowflake's workloads, including data engineering, data warehousing, data lake, data collaboration, data analytics, data applications, data science, cybersecurity using Snowflake as a security data lake, and Unistore. As we went through each of them, we were reminded how easy it is to manage the workloads and how the Snowflake platform is a good choice for many of today's data-intensive applications.

We learned how Snowflake's unique approach to Secure Data Sharing brought us both private and public data exchanges. We discussed how, with the Snowflake Marketplace, you can easily monetize your data and meet ever-increasing compliance and regulatory requirements for maintaining public access to data.

For the data analytics workload, we were introduced to Snowflake's BI technology partners, and we considered some industry-specific solutions using advanced analytics. For the data science workload, we took a deep dive into the new Snowpark developer framework.

And we learned about Snowflake's new cybersecurity workload, which also included some hands-on examples to learn more about Snowflake's search optimization service and how it differs from clustering.

Throughout the book, we took this Snowflake journey together. Along the way, we performed many hands-on exercises, and I provided many instructional tips and warnings to help guide you further in your understanding of Snowflake. My hope is that you'll go beyond the lessons learned in this book to build amazing things as your Snowflake journey continues.

Code Cleanup

All that is necessary for code cleanup for this chapter is the following command:

```
DROP DATABASE DEMO12_DB;
ALTER SESSION SET USE_CACHED_RESULT = TRUE;
```

We only need to drop the database, which will result in any schemas and tables within the database to be dropped.

 Be sure to set USE_CACHED_RESULT back to TRUE or you won't be taking advantage of the cache during your session.

Knowledge Check

The following questions are based on the information covered in this chapter:

1. How frequently does Snowflake issue new releases?
2. What client-side open API languages does Snowpark support?
3. A key feature of the Snowflake data platform is that it is developer friendly. Explain.
4. What is the reason for setting USE_CACHED_RESULT to FALSE?
5. When is it appropriate to use clustering versus search optimization?
6. How does the search optimization service support the Snowflake cybersecurity workload?
7. Why is Data Vault a popular modeling technique to use on the Snowflake platform?
8. How does Data Vault compare to other data modeling methods?
9. Are data engineers responsible for data governance? Explain.
10. What are the two common pricing strategies for data monetization?

Answers to these questions are available in Appendix A.

Answers to the Knowledge Check Questions

Chapter 1

1. The feature to create a support case from within Snowflake is not available for trial or reader accounts. However, there are still plenty of ways to get help (see the following answer).

2. If you are unable to create a support case within Snowflake, you have several options:

   - Consult the Snowflake documentation (*https://oreil.ly/NFW9e*).
   - Consult the Snowflake Knowledge Base (*https://oreil.ly/H3dlg*).
   - Solicit support from the Snowflake Community (*https://oreil.ly/9VdWq*).
   - Review the Stack Overflow Q&A (*https://oreil.ly/etOvg*).
   - Obtain direct support (for activation, password, billing, and cancellation requests only) from within the Snowflake Community:
     1. Log in to the Snowflake Data Heroes Community (*https://oreil.ly/hhrXf*).
     2. Click the "Submit a Case" Quicklink.
     3. Select the account type "I am a 30-day trial user".

3. Setting the context for a Snowflake worksheet means that you'll need to let Snowflake know which role, virtual warehouse, and database you want to use in the worksheet. You can set the context through drop-down menus or with the USE statements in the worksheet (i.e., USE ROLE, USE WAREHOUSE, USE DATABASE).

4. The "Format query" option, available in the drop-down menu, gives you the ability to neatly format your SQL code. It does not correct spelling errors.

5. A Snowflake certification is valid for two years, after which time a recertification exam must be passed. Note that passing any advanced Snowflake certification resets the clock on the SnowPro core certification, so you will have two more years before you'll need to recertify.

6. You can execute a SQL query in a Snowflake worksheet in two ways:
   - Put your cursor at the beginning of the query and click the blue arrow (the Run button).
   - Highlight all statements and press the Ctrl + Enter keys rather than clicking the Run button.

7. The House icon in the upper-left corner of the screen will return you to the Main menu.

8. We'll be using all uppercase letters for naming our Snowflake objects because Snowflake will convert these names to uppercase anyway, even if they are initially given in lowercase or mixed case. The exception is if you enclose your object name in quotes, in which case the object name will not automatically be converted to uppercase. Instead, it will be saved exactly as you entered it in between the quotes. Note that if you elect to enclose an object name in quotes when you create the object, you'll also need to refer to the object name using quotes in future SQL statements.

9. In the book, we use the `CREATE OR REPLACE` syntax so that you can always go back to any point in the chapter and start at that point without having to drop the objects first. Note, however, that this is a practice you won't want to use in a production environment, because using that statement will cause you to end up overwriting the object. If you mistakenly use the `OR REPLACE` syntax in production, there are Time Travel capabilities you can use to restore the object.

10. When you first create a worksheet, the name defaults to the current date and time.

Chapter 2

1. The three Snowflake architecture layers are the cloud services layer, the query processing (virtual warehouse) compute layer, and the centralized (hybrid-columnar) database storage layer.

2. The cloud services layer and the centralized (hybrid columnar) database storage layer are multitenant. The query processing (virtual warehouse) compute layer is not multitenant. Note that Snowflake is a multitenant service and the cloud object store is a multitenant service. As such, data is not truly isolated at the public cloud level. It is encryption that creates the isolation. Snowflake's hybrid

tenancy policy, at the public cloud level, uses a multitenant table to consolidate storage but allocates dedicated compute resources to each tenant.

3. The virtual warehouse cache is located in the compute layer. The result cache is located in the cloud services layer. The metadata storage cache layer is located in the cloud services layer.

4. You might want to investigate the following if you are experiencing higher than expected costs for Snowflake cloud services:

   - Simple queries accessing session information or using session variables

   - Large, complex queries with many joins

   - Single-row inserts, as compared to bulk or batch loading

   - Frequent use of INFORMATION_SCHEMA commands

   - Frequent use of metadata-only commands such as the SHOW command

5. Scaling up is a manual resizing of a virtual warehouse to a larger or smaller size and is most often undertaken to improve query performance and handle large workloads. Scaling out is an automatic process of increasing and decreasing the number of compute clusters and is more often used to maximize concurrency. Scaling out is achieved using multicluster virtual warehouses, which can automatically scale if the number of users and/or queries tends to fluctuate.

6. Compute can be scaled up, down, in, or out. In all cases, there is no effect on storage used.

7. The scalability problem is the main challenge that has been difficult for architectures to solve. Platform architectures need to be scalable to support sharing of the same data at the same time with data-driven teams, large and small, near or far from the data.

8. When Auto-scale mode is selected, the choice of scaling policy is either Standard or Economy:

   - With the Standard scaling policy, the first virtual warehouse immediately starts when a query is queued, or the Snowflake system detects that there is more than one query than the currently running clusters can execute.

   - With the Economy scaling policy, a virtual warehouse starts only if the Snowflake system estimates the query load can keep the virtual warehouse busy for at least six minutes. The goal of the Economy scaling policy is to conserve credits by keeping virtual warehouses fully loaded.

9. You need to configure the following components for multicluster virtual warehouses:

- Mode
  - Auto-scale; can be set to Standard or Economy
  - Maximized; maximized when the Min Clusters value is greater than 1 and both the Min Clusters and Max Clusters values are equal
- Min Clusters
- Max Clusters

10. You can change the virtual warehouse via the drop-down menu. You can use the USE WAREHOUSE SQL command in the worksheet.

Chapter 3

1. We can create two main types of databases: permanent (persistent) databases (default) and transient databases. We can create two main types of schemas: permanent (persistent) schemas (default if within a permanent database) and transient schemas (default if within a transient database). And we can create four main types of tables: permanent (persistent) tables (default if within a permanent schema), transient tables (default if within a transient schema), temporary tables, and external tables.

2. A scalar UDF returns a single value whereas a tabular UDF returns multiple values.

3. Unlike user-defined functions (UDFs), a stored procedure can be used to perform database operations such as SELECT, DELETE, and CREATE.

4. If we use the CREATE DATABASE command and the database we want to create already exists, we'll receive an error message. If a database already exists and we use the optional keywords OR REPLACE, an error will not be returned. Instead, the existing database will be completely overwritten. If you don't want to have an error but also don't want to overwrite an existing database, you can use the IF NOT EXISTS optional statement.

5. The default data retention time for a database is one day. We can change the retention time up to 90 days for a permanent database, assuming we have an Enterprise or higher Snowflake edition. However, we cannot change the default retention time; the default retention time will always be one day.

6. The TRUNCATE TABLE command removes data from a table whereas the DROP TABLE command removes the actual table itself. Note that both the TRUNCATE and DELETE commands remove data from a table but do not remove the table object itself. The TRUNCATE command clears the table load history metadata whereas the DELETE command retains the metadata. Therefore, using the TRUNCATE command allows an external file or a file in a stage to be loaded into the table again.

7. Regular views incur compute costs but not storage costs. Materialized views incur both compute costs and storage costs. A materialized view is a precomputed data set derived from a query specification and stored for later use, thus incurring storage costs. Materialized views are a serverless feature, utilizing Snowflake-managed compute services.

8. A fully qualified object name includes all objects needed to fully identify the object, all separated by a period. An example in which we would want to use the fully qualified name for a table would be *<database_name>.<schema_name>.<table_name>*. A partially qualified object name, without all the qualifiers identified, is allowed but you should understand how partially qualified objects will be resolved. When the database name is omitted, the object is augmented with the current database. When single identifiers are used, how the unqualified objects are resolved depends on whether the object appears in a Data Definition Language (DDL) or Data Manipulation Language (DML) statement, or in a query. More details can be found in the Snowflake documentation (*https://oreil.ly/JGS6q*).

9. The default file format for stages is CSV. However, you can create file formats for other formats, such as JSON, Avro, ORC, Parquet, and XML.

10. The SNOWFLAKE database is owned by Snowflake Inc. and is a system-defined, read-only shared database which provides object metadata and usage metrics about your account. Unlike the SNOWFLAKE_SAMPLE_DATA database imported into your account at the time of setup, the SNOWFLAKE database cannot be deleted from your account.

11. There are two ways to trigger a Snowflake task: tasks can run on a schedule defined at the time the task is created, or task dependencies can be established whereby a task can be triggered by a predecessor task. Note that there is no event source that can trigger a task. A task that is not triggered by a predecessor task must be run on a schedule.

12. METADATA$ACTION specifies the `INSERT` or `DELETE` action. METADATA$ISUPDATE specifies whether the `INSERT` or `DELETE` action is part of an `UPDATE` applied to the rows in the source table or view. METADATA$ROW_ID specifies the unique and immutable ID for the row, which can be used to track changes to specific rows over time.

13. Snowflake streams are a powerful way to handle changing data sets. In Snowflake, one of the most important reasons for using table streams is to keep the staging table and production table in sync. Using a staging table, along with streams, helps to protect undesired changes from being made to the production table. Snowflake table streams are also often used in conjunction with other features, such as Snowflake pipelines and Snowflake tasks.

Chapter 4

1. The following can be used to make a line of text be a comment instead of being treated as code:

   - The COMMENT command
   - /* <commended out code> */
   - // <commented out code>

     Note that you can comment or uncomment multiple lines by highlighting the lines and then pressing Cmd + / (macOS) or Ctrl + / (Windows). The highlighted lines are commented out.

2. Snowflake's string data types are supported by string constants which are always enclosed between delimiters, either single quotes or dollar signs. Using dollar signs as delimiters is especially useful when the string contains many quote characters.

3. External functions make it possible to use existing machine learning services to extract text from images, or to process PDF files to extract key-value pairs. In an external function, you can use any of the AWS, Azure, or GCP functionalities, such as AWS Rekognition, or Azure Cognitive Services. External functions executed on unstructured data, whether stored within internal or external stages, can be used to eliminate the need to export and reimport data.

4. The default duration for long-running queries is two days. You can use the STATEMENT_TIMEOUT_IN_SECONDS duration value at an account, session, object, or virtual warehouse level.

5. Because of the inexact nature of floating-point data types, floating-point operations could have small rounding errors and those errors can accumulate, especially when using aggregate functions to process a large number of rows.

6. Snowflake window functions are a special type of aggregate function that can operate on a subset of rows. This subset of related rows is called a window. Unlike aggregate functions, which return a single value for a group of rows, a window function will return an output row for each input row. The output depends not only on the individual row passed to the function but also on the values of the other rows in the window passed to the function. Window functions are commonly used for finding a year-over-year percentage change, a moving average, a running or cumulative total, and rank rows by groupings or custom criteria.

7. Yes, Snowflake supports unstructured data types.

8. Snowflake supports the following semi-structured data types:

- `VARIANT`
- `OBJECT`
- `ARRAY`

9. Snowflake's `TIMESTAMP` data type supports local time zones. TIMESTAMP_LTZ is an internal UTC time with a specified precision; it is a `TIMESTAMP` with local time zone. Daylight saving time is not supported. TIMESTAMP_TZ values are compared based on their times in UTC, which does not account for daylight saving time. This is important because, at the moment of creation, TIMESTAMP_TZ stores the offset of a given time zone, not the actual time zone.

10. Derived columns, sometimes called computed column values or virtual column values, are not physically stored in a table but are instead recalculated each time they are referenced in a query. Derived columns can be used to calculate another derived column, can be consumed by the outer `SELECT` query, or can be used as part of the `WITH` clause.

11. Following are the three ways you can gain access to unstructured data files in Snowflake:

- Stage file URLs
- Scoped URLs
- Presigned URLs

12. Examples of unstructured data types include video, audio or image files, logfiles, sensor data, and social media posts. Unstructured data, which can be human generated or machine generated, has an internal structure but not one storable in a structured database format.

13. A Snowflake directory table is a built-in read-only table.

Chapter 5

1. Inherent privileges are those privileges granted to every user who has been assigned a role. More specifically, certain system-defined roles come with inherent privileges. For example, the privileges for resource monitors are inherent to the ACCOUNTADMIN role. Note that privileges can also be assigned and inherited, in addition to being inherent to a role.

2. Following are the Snowflake system-defined account roles:

- ORGADMIN
- ACCOUNTADMIN
- SYSADMIN

- SECURITYADMIN
- USERADMIN
- PUBLIC

Most custom roles should be assigned to the SYSADMIN role.

3. Adding defaults for the user makes it easier for the user but adding a default doesn't verify that the privilege has actually been granted to the user.

4. Only an ACCOUNTADMIN can create a new resource monitor.

5. For the ability to view data in a table, a role needs privileges to use the database and schema in which the table resides as well as the ability to use the SELECT command on the table.

6. By default, only the ACCOUNTADMIN role has access to the SNOWFLAKE database.

7. The maximum number of accounts in a Snowflake organization cannot exceed 25 by default; however, you can contact Snowflake support to have the limit raised.

8. Privileges with grant options can be granted to other system-defined or custom roles.

9. The SHOW command returns results based on the role of the user executing the command, so users with different roles could get different results if they have access to different virtual warehouses or different databases, for example.

10. Snowflake has no concept of a super user or a super role. All access to securable objects, even by the account administrator, requires access privileges to be granted explicitly or implicitly by being in a higher hierarchy role.

Chapter 6

1. Following are the three Snowflake data types used for semi-structured data:
   - VARIANT
   - OBJECT
   - ARRAY

   VARIANT is the universal data type.

2. The types of Snowflake stages are as follows:
   - Internal stages: user stages, table stages, and internal named stages
   - External stages

Internal named stages and external stages are database objects. A user stage and table stages cannot be altered or dropped and, thus, are not separate database objects.

3. The INSERT ALL command can be used for either unconditional or conditional multitable inserts.

4. Whenever the key-value pair includes a null value, the key-value pair is not inserted.

5. Following are the error handling options when using the Load Data wizard:
   - Do not load any data in the file.
   - Stop loading, roll back, and return the error (default).
   - Do not load any data in the file if the error count exceeds *<threshold>*.
   - Continue loading valid data from the file.

6. While using the COPY INTO command, it is possible to perform basic transformations such as reordering columns or performing casts using a SELECT command.

7. Snowflake supports the following semi-structured data types:
   - Loading data types: JSON, Parquet, XML, Avro, ORC (semi-structured) and CSV/TSV (structured)
   - Unloading data types: JSON and Parquet (semi-structured) and CSV/TSV (structured)

8. Following are details regarding Snowpipe REST:
   - Available for use with both internal and external stages
   - Manually calls the Snowpipe REST API endpoint, with the name of a pipe and a list of filenames
   - Passes a list of files in the stage location
   - Best option for use cases in which data arrives randomly and/or if preprocessing needs require using an ETL or ELT tool, or in situations when an external stage is unavailable

   Following are details regarding Snowpipe AUTO_INGEST (the more scalable approach):
   - Available for use with external stages only
   - A notification is received from a cloud provider when a new file arrives
   - Processes new files when awakened
   - Best option for uses cases in which files arrive continuously

9. To prevent resource contention, be sure to isolate data load jobs from queries by dedicating separate virtual warehouses for each. Rather than assuming a large

virtual warehouse will necessarily load massive data files any faster than a small virtual warehouse (it likely won't), make sure to instead try splitting large files into small files of about 100 to 250 MB in size. Remember that the number of files being loaded and the size of each file influence performance more than the size of the virtual warehouse.

10. The PUT command loads data into a stage (then the COPY INTO command loads data from a stage to a table). The GET command unloads data from a stage (after the COPY INTO command unloads data from a table to a stage).

Chapter 7

1. Multifactor authentication (MFA) is intended to be used in addition to strong passwords. Snowflake offers self-service MFA to all account levels so that users can enroll themselves.

2. There is no limit to the number of account network policies that can exist, but there can only be one account-level network policy activated at a time. There is also no limit to the number of user network policies that can exist, but there can only be one user-level network policy, per user, activated at a time.

3. Snowflake's root key is in a hardware security module and is the only key stored in clear text.

4. Data masking policies include dynamic masking, conditional masking, and static masking. Data masking is column based whereas row access policies provide dynamic row-level security. Note that a column cannot have both a masking policy and a row access policy at the same time.

5. The Time Travel retention period is automatically enabled for all Snowflake accounts, and the default is 24 hours but can be set to zero at the account and object levels. For Snowflake Enterprise Edition and higher orgs, the retention period can be set up to 90 days for permanent databases, schemas, and tables.

   By setting the retention time as 90 days for a database, all the database objects will also have a 90-day retention time period.

   Changing the data retention time at the schema level will result in all tables in the schema inheriting the schema's retention period unless the table is explicitly given a different retention period. Another thing you should keep in mind is that the order in which you drop objects does affect the retention period if there are differences. When you drop a schema, all the existing tables will be available for the same time period as the schema. If you want to make sure the data retention period for child objects is honored, you'll need to drop them prior to dropping the parent object.

6. A tag does not need to be enclosed in quotes. If you do enclose a tag identifier in double quotes, it is case sensitive and can include blank spaces. If an identifier is unquoted, it cannot be case sensitive, cannot contain blank spaces, and must begin with a letter or underscore.

Snowflake's automatic data tagging can be of two different types:

- Semantic
- Privacy

7. We need to flatten query output whenever there is a nested data layer object. This will allow us to convert a nested data layer object into a new object with only one layer of key-value pairs.

In this chapter, we used the FLATTEN function to flatten the DIRECT_OBJECTS_ACCESSED and BASE_OBJECTS_ACCESSED columns in the Snowflake ACCESS_HISTORY view.

8. Cloned Snowflake objects are replicated physically, rather than logically, to secondary databases. This means that there will be additional data storage costs for any cloned objects that are replicated.

9. The specific ways we can use Time Travel to access historical data are SELECT AT/BEFORE, CLONE AT/BEFORE, and UNDROP.

10. Time Travel and fail-safe, along with active storage, are part of the total calculated storage that incurs storage costs. Replication and failover/failback charges include data transfer costs and the cost of compute resources. For replications of cloned objects, there will also be additional data storage costs.

Chapter 8

1. The three major categories of a Snowflake monthly bill are storage fees, data transfer costs, and credits consumed.

2. While storage pricing is a consideration of which region to select for your Snowflake account, you'll also want to consider which region could minimize latency and could give you access to any required features you may need. It's important to note that if you decide later to move your data to a different region, data transfer costs will be incurred.

3. The price of on-demand Snowflake credits is dependent on the cloud provider, region, and service edition. Alternatively, you can prepurchase credits at a negotiated discounted rate.

4. The three properties of a Snowflake resource monitor are the credit quota, credit usage, and triggers. The credit quota and credit usage properties are both required to create a resource monitor. If a schedule is not explicitly stated, the default schedule applies. By default, the credit quota resets at the beginning of each calendar moth. Setting triggers is optional.

5. There is no limit to the number of virtual warehouse–level resource monitors that can be created, but there can be only one account-level resource monitor.

6. There is a limit of five Notify actions, one Suspend action, and one Suspend Immediately action for each resource monitor.

7. Making changes to databases presents a unique set of challenges, especially for traditional on-premises databases which have to deal with the problem of down time for hardware and explicitly having to back up databases beforehand so that they will be available for restoration, if needed. In the event a rollback is needed, an operations freeze with no work happening during the restoration process is required. In addition, there is the problem of drift whereby developers could be working on a different version of the database than the version in production, and there is also the problem of load balancing. With Snowflake, these top challenges no longer exist for users. Database change management processes can be handled quite simply in Snowflake by creating a lightweight DevOps framework for small deployments. For a more heavyweight Snowflake DevOps framework, there are database change management tools that can be used.

8. Zero-copy cloning is a metadata-only operation; thus, zero-copy cloning offers the ability to duplicate an object without actually creating a physical copy. As such, there is no additional storage charge for Snowflake cloned objects unless and until changes are made.

   Zero-copy clones are frequently used to support working in development and test environments as part of the development lifecycle.

9. An empty table is created using the `CREATE TABLE LIKE` command whereas the `CREATE TABLE AS SELECT` command creates a populated table.

10. Assigning a virtual warehouse resource monitor to a virtual warehouse that is already assigned to a resource monitor will override the previous assignment.

Chapter 9

1. The `QUERY_HISTORY_BY_USER` function narrows the focus of the query history. `QUERY_HISTORY_BY_SESSION` and `QUERY_HISTORY_BY_WAREHOUSE` are also available for use.

2. The Snowflake `HASH()` function is not a cryptographic hash function. Instead, it is a utility function that returns information such as the descriptions of queries.

3. The two traditional methods by which relational databases can be partitioned are horizontal and vertical.

4. All Snowflake data is stored in database tables. Logically, tables are structured as collections of rows and columns. This logical structure of rows and columns is mapped to the Snowflake physical table structures known as micro-partitions. Snowflake's unique micro-partitioning approach is transparent to users, unlike traditional data warehouse partitioning approaches whereby the user has to independently manipulate partitions by using DDL commands.

   A Snowflake micro-partition is inherently small in size and is stored as a columnarized set of rows that holds about 16 MB of compressed data. Storing the data in this way, where columns are stored independently within the micro-partitions, allows for efficient column scanning and filtering. This is especially beneficial for very large tables. Using micro-partitions allows for granular pruning on large tables. Effective and efficient pruning is important because scanning entire tables is not optimal for most queries.

5. DML operations, like an update, will add a new partition block and remove an existing partition block. Micro-partition additions and deletions are tracked in the Snowflake metadata.

6. Snowflake can determine how well clustered a table is by considering how many partitions overlap. Micro-partitions can overlap with each other in a partition; the number of overlaps is known as the clustering width. Micro-partitions can overlap at a specific point in the partition; the number of overlaps at that specific point determines the clustering depth.

   Ultimately, the best indicator of a well-clustered table is its query performance.

7. To see the clustering depth in a table, use the SYSTEM$CLUSTERING_INFORMATION function. If a table has been clustered, you don't need to specify the column. If it has not been clustered, you'll need to be sure to include the column(s) in your statement.

8. When deciding on a clustering key, a good rule of thumb is to select a key that has enough distinct values for effective pruning, yet not too many values that Snowflake is still able to effectively group rows in the same micro-partitions.

9. When creating the clustering key, it is recommended that you choose no more than three or four columns or expressions. While the number of columns is an important consideration, it is most important to focus on selecting the right columns or expressions for the clustering key and putting them in the best order.

10. Materialized view and the search optimization service are serverless. Table clustering incurs compute costs and is not a serverless feature.

Chapter 10

1. Direct Share, Data Exchange, Global Marketplace, and Data Clean Room

2. Unlike most traditional databases, Snowflake supports cross-database joins, including joins with databases built from inbound shares. This means that consumers, other than those with reader accounts, can also create views in their own database which can combine their own data with data from the shared database. This provides great benefit because the consumer can enrich their own data to make it even more valuable.

3. An inbound share can only contain one database, but it is possible for a producer to share data from multiple databases by using a secure view. A Snowflake provider can create a secure view that references schemas, tables, and other views from several databases as long as those databases belong to the same account.

4. The Snowflake Marketplace and Data Exchange both utilize Snowflake secure data sharing to connect providers of data with consumers. The Marketplace is a public global marketplace that facilitates sharing among third parties. The Data Exchange is your own private hub for securely collaborating around data, with a selected group of members that you invite.

5. By default, the ACCOUNTADMIN has the inherent privileges to create and maintain data shares.

6. Only the data provider is assessed data storage charges in relation to a data share.

7. The data consumer pays for charges incurred to query a data share. Whenever a reader account is used to query a data share, the charges are paid for by the data provider.

8. *Snowgrid* is the term to describe data replication for the purpose of facilitating data sharing. With the power of secure data sharing and Snowgrid, Snowflake providers can create and share any number of data shares with data consumers worldwide. Snowgrid spans globally, seamlessly connecting Snowflake users who may be separated by region or cloud. Snowgrid achieves this through replication via auto-fulfillment. Even when data is shared across the cloud and regions, the shares are transactionally consistent, meaning the source of truth is still maintained.

9. Snowflake allows you to share the following objects:

   - Databases
   - Tables
   - External tables

- Secure views
- Secure materialized views
- Secure UDFs

Best practices include the following:

- Creating a separate schema for each listing is recommended, but not required. The reason for creating separate schemas is because this could reduce the possibility of confusion and accidentally sharing an object.
- To ensure that sensitive data in a shared database is not exposed to users in consumer accounts, it is strongly recommended that you share secure views or secure UDFs rather than directly sharing tables.
- When sharing data from massively large tables, it is recommended that you, as the provider, define clustering keys on the tables.

10. The following requirements must be met in order to receive approval to list on the Snowflake Marketplace:

- Data must be fresh and nonstatic.
- Data cannot consist of only sample, mocked-up data.
- Data cannot contain private data.
- You must possess the right to make the data available.

Chapter 11

1. You can instruct Snowflake to return a subset of rows via sampling technique in the following ways:

- Fixed-size sampling based on a specific number of rows (Bernoulli sampling)
- Fraction-based sampling based on a percentage of table rows:
  — Bernoulli sampling (default)
  — System sampling

There are limits to the number of records that can be used for Snowsight visualizations. The number of rows for automatic statistics visualizations, as well as for charts and dashboards, must be less than one million. Thus, it is often impossible to visualize a full data set in Snowsight. In these situations, it is important to obtain a sample of the data to visualize.

2. A SQL query is not needed to preview the data. You just need to click the Magnifying Glass icon to preview the data. When we preview the data, we see the first 100 rows. We do not need an active virtual warehouse to preview the data.

3. When you rerun a query that uses the `LIMIT` clause, you will get the same rows returned the second time. However, when you rerun a sampling query, you will *not* get the same rows returned the second time as were returned the first time. Sample query results are unique in that the results are not cached.

4. An active virtual warehouse is required to run a sampling query but is not required to preview the data using the Magnifying Glass.

5. You can bucket the data in Snowsight in the following ways:
   - None
   - Date
   - Second
   - Minute
   - Hour
   - Week
   - Month
   - Quarter
   - Year
   - Via filter

6. Deleting a tile from a dashboard permanently deletes the underlying worksheet. You will not be able to retrieve the tile or worksheet after you perform a delete action.

7. Some of the use cases for using Snowsight visualizations include the following:
   - When individuals or small groups of users need to undertake ad hoc data analysis
   - Performing data validation while loading data
   - Quickly creating minor charts and dashboards that can be shared as a team

8. One alternative to deleting a tile is to simply unplace the tile so that it still exists but is not viewable on the dashboard.

9. You can create an unlimited number of charts from one worksheet.

10. Snowflake allows for visualization from internal data sources and external data sources.

Chapter 12

1. Every week, Snowflake deploys two planned/scheduled releases which may include the following:
   - Full release (deployed any day of the week except Friday)
     — New features
     — Feature enhancements or updates
     — Fixes
   - Patch release

   Every month, Snowflake deploys one behavior change release.

2. Snowpark supports the following client-side open API languages:
   - Node.js
   - .NET
   - Go
   - Java
   - Python
   - SQL

3. The Snowflake data platform is said to be developer friendly because it allows app developers to choose among several programming languages.

4. We set USE_CACHED_RESULT to FALSE because we don't want to take advantage of the cache results for our examples since we are testing the query performance for clustering and the search optimization service. If we didn't change the value to false, we would get accurate performance testing results if we reran the query two or more times.

5. It is more appropriate to use search optimization, rather than clustering, for point lookup queries. Regarding clustering, Snowflake produces well-clustered data in tables, in general. However, over time, particularly as DML occurs on very large tables, the data in some table rows might no longer cluster optimally on desired dimensions. Also, for very large tables in which the ordering is not ideal, there could be a better way to co-locate the data in the same micro-partitions. In both cases, that is where Snowflake's clustering can help.

6. The cybersecurity workload often involves teams who need fast response times for critical dashboards with highly selective filters which often necessitate point lookup queries. As such, the search optimization service, which is useful for point lookup queries, can be used to support the Snowflake cybersecurity workload.

7. The Data Vault modeling approach can take advantage of Snowflake's massively parallel processing compute clusters and optimized columnar storage format.

8. The Data Vault approach and the Kimball approach are relatively simple and require less time to implement as compared to the Inmon methodology. The Kimball approach is based on a four-step normalization process whereas Data Vault uses an agile methodology. In general, the cost to implement the Data Vault modeling approach is the lowest, but Data Vault does require more storage, and is not the best choice when the data is straightforward and auditing of the data is not needed.

9. Data engineers are not responsible for creating governance rules and regulations, but they are tasked with implementing them.

10. The two common pricing strategies for data monetization are cost pricing and value pricing.

Snowflake Object Naming Best Practices

General (Character Related)

- Create names that are brief and meaningful. Use abbreviations when possible, especially if the length exceeds eight characters. Although a name can contain up to 128 characters, it's best not to exceed 24 characters. Rather than use more characters in the name, consider using comments or tags as descriptors.

- Avoid mixed-case letters. If you elect to use something other than all uppercase or all lowercase letters, you'll need to include quotes around the name because, without quotes, Snowflake will convert the name to all uppercase.

- Avoid whitespace. Use an underscore (_) instead. Otherwise, this could cause problems with some third-party applications.

- Use singular terms for both tables and fields. For example, a Customer table could have a CustomerID field.

- Avoid special characters such as #, - , @, and !. Even though some are allowable in Snowflake, they can cause problems with some third-party applications, so it's best to avoid them.

General (Not Character Related)

- Use the recommended Snowflake system-defined role to create objects. For example, use the SYSDAMIN role to create databases and virtual warehouses. For more details, refer to Figure 5-12 in Chapter 5.[1]

---

1 For simplicity, sometimes we won't use the recommended Snowflake system-defined role to create objects. In those examples, I'll mention that we're using a different role than the recommended role.

- Use the syntax IF NOT EXISTS when creating new objects.[2]

- Standardize on language, choosing a region or dialect such as American English. For example, use COLOR instead of COLOUR.

- Avoid prepositions. For example, use ERROR_CODE rather than CODE_FOR_ERROR.

- Avoid postpositive adjectives. For example, use APPROVED_ARTICLES instead of ARTICLES_APPROVED.

- Avoid generic phrases such as OTHER and MISC.

- Avoid prefixes for tables and columns. Use underscores sparingly.

- Avoid the same name as is in use by a different object type. For example, do not give the same names to both a temporary and permanent table in the same schema. Temporary tables are session based; thus, they are not bound by uniqueness requirements. Even though you can create a temporary table with the same name as another table, it is not a good practice to do so as it could result in unintended consequences.

- Avoid reserved words. A list of reserved keywords is available in the Snowflake documentation (*https://oreil.ly/IrCGj*).

Standard Label Abbreviations

DEV
Development environment (prefix) used for databases and roles

EXT
External (prefix) used for stages and tables

FB
Feature branch environment (prefix) used for databases and roles

FF
File format (prefix)

POC
Proof of concept environment (prefix) used for databases and roles

---

2 For chapter exercises, we use the syntax CREATE OR REPLACE instead of CREATE IF NOT EXISTS. We use the OR REPLACE syntax so that you can always go back to the beginning of the chapter exercises to start over without having to drop objects first. In practice, though, be sure to use the IF NOT EXISTS syntax, especially in a production environment. If you mistakenly use the OR REPLACE syntax in production, you have the option to use Snowflake Time Travel capabilities to return the object to its original state.

PROD
Production environment (prefix) used for databases and roles

QA
Test/quality assurance environment (prefix) used for databases and roles

SP
Stored procedure (prefix)

TSK
Task (prefix)

DB
Database

INT
Integration

MVW
Materialized view

RM
Resource monitor

STG
Stage

SVC
Service accounts

TBL
Table (optional)

VW
View

WH
Warehouse

Setting Up a Snowflake Trial Account

Most public cloud provider solutions require you to be logged in to the administrative portal to provision an instance of a data warehouse or database service. Snowflake's approach is different. With Snowflake, there is a single and consistent entry point for users, which reduces complexity and administrative overhead.

Once you sign up for a Snowflake account, you'll be provided with a unique URL ending in *Snowflakecomputing.com*, and once the instance has been created, you really don't need to know about the underlying cloud platform. The mapping is managed by Snowflake. Also, Snowflake delivers a single data experience across multiple clouds and regions.

Visit the Snowflake sign-up page (*https://oreil.ly/vZKq8*) to begin the process of setting up a new Snowflake trial account (as shown in Figure C-1).

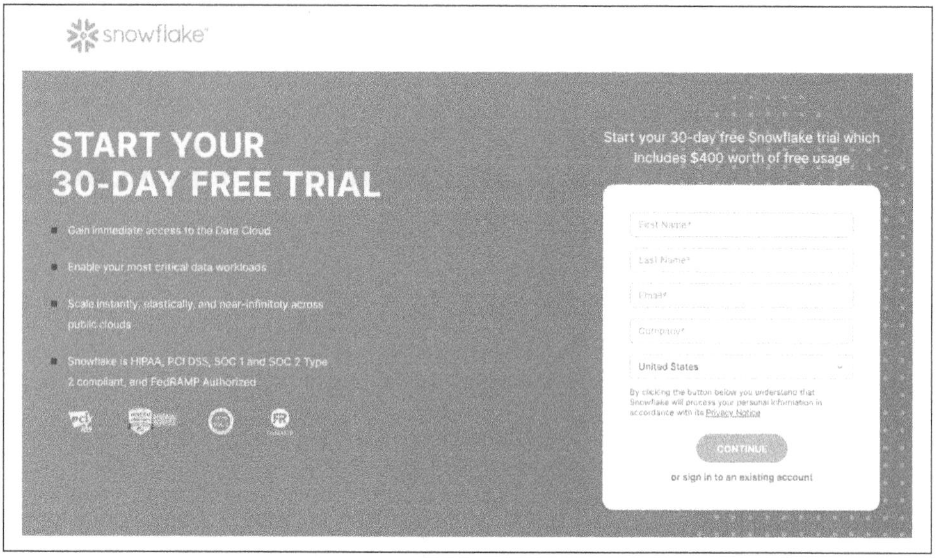

Figure C-1. Snowflake offers a 30-day trial

Once you fill out the information on the first screen, you'll need to make choices about the type of Snowflake edition, the cloud provider, and the region. There are factors to consider when making these choices. You'll probably want to choose the same public cloud and region where most of your data applications reside since that will make it easier and less costly to manage data transfers should you need to do so.

Table C-1 summarizes the major differences in the Snowflake editions. If you are signing up for a Snowflake trial account to complete the exercises in the book, the Enterprise Edition is probably your best choice. The Snowflake Enterprise Edition will give you access to all the features you need to complete all the exercises in the book.

Table C-1. Comparison of the Snowflake editions

	Standard	Enterprise	Business Critical	Virtual Private Snowflake (VPS)
Complete SQL data warehouse	X	X	X	X
Secure data sharing across regions/clouds	X	X	X	X
Encryption in transit and at rest	X	X	X	X
One day of Time Travel (default)	X	X	X	X
Customer-dedicated virtual warehouses	X	X	X	X
Federated authentication	X	X	X	X
Database replication	X	X	X	X
External functions	X	X	X	X
Snowsight	X	X	X	X

	Standard	Enterprise	Business Critical	Virtual Private Snowflake (VPS)
Create your own Data Exchange	X	X	X	X
Marketplace access	X	X	X	X
Multicluster warehouse		X	X	X
Up to 90 days of Time Travel		X	X	X
Annual rekeying of encrypted data		X	X	X
Materialized views		X	X	X
Search optimization service		X	X	X
Dynamic data masking		X	X	X
External data tokenization		X	X	X
HIPAA support			X	X
PCI compliance			X	X
Data encryption everywhere			X	X
Tri-Secret Secure using customer-managed keys			X	X
AWS and Azure private link support			X	X
Database failover/failback for business continuity			X	X
External functionals—AWS API Gateway private endpoint support			X	X
Customer-dedicated metadata store				X
Customer-dedicated virtual servers wherever the encryption key is in memory				X

Index

About the Author

Joyce Kay Avila has more than 25 years as a business and technology leader. She is a Texas Certified Public Accountant and currently holds certifications in Snowflake and Amazon Web Services. She also holds 12 Salesforce certifications, including the Tableau CRM and Einstein Discovery certification as well as several Salesforce Architect-level certifications.

Joyce earned bachelor's degrees in computer science and accounting business administration, obtained a master's degree of business administration, and completed her PhD coursework in accounting information systems.

In support of the Salesforce and Snowflake communities, Joyce produces a running series of how-to videos on her YouTube channel. In 2022, she was selected by Snowflake as one of 48 Snowflake Data Superheroes worldwide.

Colophon

The animal on the cover of *Snowflake: The Definitive Guide* is a junco (*Junco*), a type of New World sparrow. There are multiple species within the genus, but the exact number is debated.

The dark-eyed junco is one of the most common in North America. They prefer the ground for many of their activities, such as foraging for insects and seeds, and building their nests. They tend to lay three to five eggs in a clutch with an incubation period of eleven to thirteen days. Juncos usually live in dry and forested areas, and those that live up north migrate south for the winter.

Many of the animals on O'Reilly covers are endangered; all of them are important to the world.

The cover illustration is by Karen Montgomery. The cover fonts are Gilroy Semibold and Guardian Sans. The text font is Adobe Minion Pro; the heading font is Adobe Myriad Condensed; and the code font is Dalton Maag's Ubuntu Mono.